MEDIATION

PRINCIPLES AND PRACTICE

Second Edition

By

Kimberlee K. Kovach

WEST
GROUP

ST. PAUL, MINN., 2000

TEXT IS PRINTED ON 10% POST
CONSUMER RECYCLED PAPER

1st Reprint — 2001

For Katie & Kaela

*

Preface to the Second Edition

It has been over five years since the first edition of this text was published, and over twenty since I was first trained as a mediator. At both of those prior times, if someone would have predicted where the filed of ADR and in particular mediation would be at turn of the millennium, I would have never believed it. But, as some of us had hoped, mediation practice has moved through a time of experimentation to widespread implementation. Many developments occurred during that time; yet many issues remain undetermined. And although the wisdom of doing so is often debated, it appears that mediation is now in a time of regulation.

Clearly it can no longer be said that that mediation is in its infancy, but rather is experiencing a turbulent adolescence. Many questions and issues face courts, agencies and mediator organizations. It is my intention that this edition of the text demonstrates the recent changes in the field of mediation as well as illuminate the many unanswered issues that remain.

As was the case with the first edition, this text was written in an effort to combine the theory, law and practice of mediation within one work. It is primarily intended for use in skill based or focused courses. Therefore, the coverage of both theory and law is not exhaustive. It is, however, sufficient to provide the reader an adequate background in the subject matter. Those wishing further detail are encouraged to go to the sources included and cited in this work.

My objective was a work that could be used in teaching and training the general principles of the mediation process. It is also intended to serve as a quick reference for both novice and experienced mediators. I attempted to present a variety of views about the mediation process and the issues surrounding its practice, and struggled to not often advocate my personal views. It is my belief that as teachers of mediation, we also have a duty to empower students of mediation to arrive at their own decisions about the myriad of dilemmas facing the 'profession'.

A note on form. The cases and articles which are included have been edited and unnecessary material deleted. The deleted portions of text are indicated by asterisks. In most instances, both citations and footnotes have been omitted without indication. In those instances where the footnotes do appear, the number of the original material has been retained.

*

Acknowledgements

First I would like to thank those individuals who have contributed so much to the field of ADR, and in particular mediation. While the names are far too numerous to mention individually, it is the collective and collaborative work of those in this field that it has evolved to the extent and with the vitality that it has. Several individuals, however, have, over the years, provided me with support and encouragement, in addition to making their own exceptional contributions. These include Professors Lela P. Love, Jacqueline Nolan-Haley, Wendy and Stephen Huber, Richard Reuben, Jim Coben, Carol Izumi, Andrea Schnieder, Alan Rau, Maureen Laflin, Randy Lowry, Peter Robinson, Scott Hughes, Ellen Waldman, Len Riskin, Deans Jim Alfini, Edward Sherman, Jay Folberg, John Feerick, and Ed Dauer; and all of my friends and colleagues of the ABA Section of Dispute Resolution, especially Jack Hanna. I am also particularly grateful to Professor Nancy Rogers, and all of those who are working so diligently and thoughtfully in the effort to draft a Uniform Mediation Act.

I would also like to recognize the insight of Capital University School of Law, who was a leader in the field of dispute resolution over twenty-five years ago and remains so today.

I would also like to thank all of those law students and mediators who have participated in my classes and trainings, and have commented on the first edition of this book. They clearly provide me with an education as well. And all the mediators whom I have met through my travels. It is because of colleagues like you that this field is so very exciting, stimulating and special.

I am also grateful to Susan Alexander, Lannhi Tran, Gregory Litt, and Scott Vdoviak for research and administrative assistance in the preparation of this edition.

And finally, of course, my heartfelt gratitude goes to my husband and beloved conflict resolver, Eric Galton for all that he is, and does.

I also thank the following sources, which have granted permission to reprint excerpts for the noted copyright material.

Professors Frank E.A. Sander and Stephen B.Goldberg, Fitting the Forum to the Fuss: A User-Friendly Guide to Selecting an ADR Procedure, 10 Negotiation J. 49 (1994). By permission of Plenum Publishing Corp.

The South Texas College of Law Review, (Vol. 38 No. 2) Annual Ethics Symposium: The Lawyer's Duties and Responsibilities in Dispute Resolution (1997). In particular, the following articles from that Symposium Issue.

Prof. Lela P. Love, Mediation: The Romantic Days Continue 38 S. Tex. L. Rev. 735

Dean John D. Feerick, Toward Uniform Standards of Conduct for Mediators, 38 S. Tex. L. Rev. 455

Edward F. Sherman, Confidentiality in ADR Proceedings: Policy Issues Arising from the Texas Experience, 38 S. Tex. L. Rev. 541

Jacqueline Nolan-Haley, Court Mediation and the Search for Justice Through Law, 74 Wash. U. L. Q. 47 (1996)

Robert Mnookin, Why Negotiations Fail: An Exploration of Barriers to the Resolution of Conflict, 8 Ohio St. J. on Disp. Resol. 235 (1993)

Deborah L. Levi, The Role of Apology in Mediation, 72 N.Y.U.L. Rev. 1165 (1997)

Charles W. Ehrhardt, Confidentiality Protections: An Open Question in Federal Courts 5 Disp. Resol. Mag. 17 (1999)

Charles Pou, Confidentiality in Federal Agency ADR: A Troubling Decision 5 Disp. Resol. Mag. 9 (1999)

Leonard L. Riskin, Understanding Mediators' Orientations, Strategies, and Techniques: A Grid for the Perplexed, 1 Harv. Negotiation L. Rev. 7 (1996)

Kimberlee K. Kovach & Lela P. Love, Mapping Mediation, The Risks of Riskin's Grid, 3 Harv. Negotiation L. Rev. 71 (1998).

Summary of Contents

*

Table of Contents

MEDIATION

PRINCIPLES AND PRACTICE

Second Edition

*

Chapter One

OVERVIEW OF THE
ADR UNIVERSE

A. INTRODUCTION

People resolve disputes every day. Some people are better at it than others. Yet, conflict resolution is a discipline that is rarely formally taught. In fact, analysis of the origin and nature of disputes and conflict rarely occurs. Admittedly, discussion and debate about the content of conflict are common. But these discussions infrequently turn to the examination of the skills involved in resolving disputes. The *process* of dispute resolution is virtually ignored. Conflict resolution is not an integral part of our education systems. We constantly search for ways to resolve conflict. But unfortunately we rely upon some sort of "automatic pilot" or "knee jerk" approach, instead of a more analytical, process-oriented method. Due to hectic schedules, discomfort, or ignorance, avoidance is often the response to conflict. At the most unfortunate end of the continuum, some opt for violence. Fortunately, many options for conflict resolution exist somewhere between avoidance and fighting.

Many professionals, such as diplomats, police officers, lawyers and judges, deal with conflict resolution on a daily basis. However, most professionals are not educated in skills vital to the constructive resolution of conflict. This text will explore a rather old, yet traditionally under-utilized method of dispute resolution: mediation.

Mediation, as a process of resolving conflict, has been gaining popularity and acceptance in the United States since 1976. This has been primarily as part of the trend to explore, particularly in legal or quasi-legal disputes, alternatives to formal, expensive litigation. Such exploration of alternatives has been a direct result of the often voiced frustration and disappointment associated with the use of our justice system as a means of dispute resolution. This criticism, at least in part, explains the development of the Alternative Dispute Resolution (ADR) movement.

Alternative Dispute Resolution procedures do not ignore the fact that disputes exist; rather, ADR focuses on new and creative methods to resolve disputes. Such an approach often includes an examination of the underlying causes of conflict. This chapter will first briefly explore the

1

nature of conflict and more traditional means of its resolution. An overview of the ADR universe is then provided. This universe is not static; rather, it continues to grow and expand as society continues to investigate the nature and causes of disputes.

B. WHAT ARE DISPUTES?

Many words may be used to describe disputes: arguments, disagreements, challenges, contests, debates, conflicts, quarrels, lawsuits, fights, altercations, controversies, feuds, wrongs, combat, and war. A detailed analysis of the differences in these terms and the specific instances in which one may evolve into another provides some understanding regarding the nature of conflict.[1] Because the work of the mediator necessarily involves intervention in a dispute, consideration of the disputing process is necessary. Since the mediator's job is to assist in the resolution of conflict,[2] it is important that she[3] have an understanding of the many forms and functions of conflict.[4]

The word conflict is derived from the Latin *con* (together) and *fligere* (to strike). Conflict is defined as "an encounter with arms, a fight, a battle, a prolonged struggle."[5] Additional definitions include a mental or spiritual struggle within a person; the clashing or variance of opposed principles, statements, or arguments.[6] It has been suggested that conflict exists when there are incompatible activities.[7] Conflict has also been defined as a set of divergent aims, methods, or behavior.[8] Conflict is also seen to be "an expressed struggle between at least two interdependent parties who perceive incompatible goals, scarce rewards, and interference from the other party in achieving their goals."[9] Some even go so far as to declare that conflict has its own life cycle.[10] We have all observed that conflict varies in intensity and duration. It is crucial that the mediator, as an intervenor in another's conflict, be aware of the variety of factors affecting conflict.

When we initially think of conflict or disputing, what usually comes to mind is manifest conflict, that conflict which we can observe. Yet in many situations, even where there is such overt conduct, underlying conflict also exists. This is the implicit, often hidden or denied, conflict. And, it is these hidden aspects which may truly fuel the conflict. In order

---

1. For analysis of disputes, see William L. F. Felstiner, et al., *The Emergence and Transformation of Disputes: Naming, Blaming, Claiming*, 15 L. & Soc'y. Rev. 63 (1980–81).

2. This is but one of the many descriptions of the work of a mediator. The role is examined in greater detail in Chapter 2, Sec. D.

3. Gender will be systematically alternated throughout the book.

4. For an in-depth study of conflict, see Joyce L. Hocker & William W. Wilmot, Interpersonal Conflict (4th ed. 1995).

5. The Oxford English Dictionary 713 (2nd ed. 1989).

6. *Id.*

7. Morton Deutsch, The Resolution of Conflict 10 (1973).

8. Jay Folberg & Alison Taylor, Mediation: A Comprehensive Guide to Resolving Conflicts Without Litigation 24 (1984).

9. Hocker and Wilmot, *supra* note 4, at 21.

10. Folberg & Taylor, *supra* note 8, at 22.

to achieve a complete or final resolution of a dispute, the underlying conflict must be identified and resolved. These underlying issues are often referred to as the "hidden agenda." One goal of the mediation process is to uncover the underlying motivations of the parties.

Another significant aspect of conflict is that it often exists internally. This is termed "intrapersonal conflict," i.e., conflict existing within one's self. These intrapersonal conflicts range from difficulty in choosing between a health-conscious meal and a favorite but high calorie dinner, to choices between career and family. While some of the dispute resolution principles set forth in this text may apply to intrapersonal conflict, such conflicts are better treated by those within the psychology or social work fields.[11] Therefore, this work will deal primarily with the disputes or conflicts between individuals or groups, i.e., interpersonal conflict. The mediator should nonetheless be aware of intrapersonal conflict, and appreciate that it may impact the interpersonal dispute, or vice versa.

Conflict consists of a number of variables. We know that overt conflict takes many forms, ranging from a slight look of exasperation to a pistol shot. Further, the intensity of conflict varies. In some instances, conflict, if left unresolved, will escalate. In other situations, time and space may act to minimize the dispute. There is also variation in what conflict affects. It can range from a slight influence on only two parties in dispute, to the complete destruction of a community or nation.

The communication process is an integral part of conflict. The exchange of both verbal and nonverbal messages is the most significant part of disputing. How conflict is viewed can depend on the participants' method of communication. The manner in which individuals dispute can also depend upon factors such as the culture, history, and relationship of the parties. In fact, it has been observed that disputing can, in fact, define the relationship.[12] A mediator must be cognizant of the disputing process and its attendant characteristics.

Conflict appears constantly in the United States as well as other societies. The response has been more police, more courts, and even more violence. With this approach has come a view of conflict that is primarily negative. When asked to respond to the term conflict, pejorative terms such as *frustrating*, *anxiety*, and *struggle* are generally used. Historically disputes were battles to be won, usually by force. Consequently, the resolution of disputes is often seen as a win-lose proposition, with conflict perceived as necessarily carrying negative consequences. Yet conflict can be positive. As many point out, the Chinese sign for conflict translates to both "danger and opportunity."[13] In some instances conflict can be an exciting and inspiring experience. Conflict may lead to a closer examination of issues and an assessment of situations.[14] Conflict

11. See for example, Deutsch, *supra* note 7, Chapter 3.

12. Jerold S. Auerbach, Justice Without Law 16 (1983).

13. Hocker and Wilmot, *supra* note 4, at 20.

14. Stephen Worchel & Sharon Lundgren, The Nature of Conflict and Conflict

can result in creative and new resolutions. Relationships can be established or strengthened. And in fact, conflict is at the root of personal and social change.[15] While mediation has as its philosophical basis the creative and constructive means of dispute resolution, this has not been a traditional approach to conflict.

C. TRADITIONAL MEANS OF RESOLVING DISPUTES

If conflict is viewed as a struggle, then it is not surprising that traditional means of resolution include fight, force, or coercion. These responses have resulted in the win-lose perspective of conflict resolution. An often-used alternative to force is the flight or avoidance mechanism. But, to ignore the conflict in most instances is to not resolve it. Other traditional responses to conflict include accommodation, compromise or splitting down the middle, decision making by an individual outside of the dispute, a gamble or chance method of determining the outcome, and counseling.[16] Each of these more traditional means of resolving disputes has merit as well as drawbacks.

When conflict is encountered, the initial means of dispute resolution usually considered is the win-lose approach. This is essentially the violence or fight response which has been used throughout history, as well as on the street today. In many instances, an individual's survival instinct probably leads to the use of this alternative. The response becomes automatic for many people. The media, sports, and even the courts assist in perpetuating this method. The underlying theory is that in order to effect a resolution, one side must win and the other must lose. Seen in the best light, the loser then goes away. The worst case scenario results in injury or elimination of the loser, that is, his death.

Avoidance is also a common response to conflict. Even when faced with it directly, many people continue to ignore conflict. In some cases, this can be an appropriate response. Where the dispute is not of great significance to one or all of the parties, or the dispute is of low priority, it may fade away. This is more likely to occur where the disputing parties will have no future relationship. Psychologists and personal experience teach us, however, that unresolved and internalized conflicts usually linger. The manifest conflict may no longer be apparent, but the underlying conflict remains intact. Ordinarily it intensifies. This is particularly true where there is an ongoing relationship between the parties in conflict. In order to resolve the conflict, it must be disclosed. If the matters in dispute are not out on the table and resolved, it is very likely that the dispute will recur, or simply manifest itself in another manner.

Those who accommodate when faced with conflict are seen as quite cooperative, since they merely cede to the other person's wishes or

Resolution in Community Mediation 17 (Karen Grover Duffy, et al. eds., 1991).

15. Deutsch, *supra* note 7, at 9.

16. This list is not exhaustive, but rather only suggestive as to traditional methods of response to conflict.

demands.[17] Though the individual seeks, and on the surface attains, harmony, other needs are not met. This may lead to later frustration. In using compromise as a means of resolution, all parties move from their initial positions in nearly equivalent increments until the middle ground is reached. Seen initially as a cooperative style of negotiation, compromise has disadvantages. The movements toward the middle may not be of equal magnitude. Resentment is then felt by one of the parties, and it lingers. Moreover, important underlying interests or needs are often not identified, let alone met.

Another method of dispute resolution is to voluntarily relinquish responsibility for the conflict. This is accomplished by turning it over to chance. Chance may consist of a third party who has no interest in the conflict, or it may be an object (such as dice or a lottery drawing). Chance intervenes and makes the decisions for the parties. Today in the United States this method can be observed in the court system. The third party, either the judge or the jury, determines the outcome of the dispute for the parties. Individuals can avoid responsibility for their disputes by relying on these outside entities. If the result is unsatisfactory to a party, the system can be blamed. This partly accounts for what has been termed the "litigation explosion." Admittedly, in some instances it is important that a neutral party make the decision. Litigation and arbitration are viable options for dispute resolution. However, in many instances the parties have more information and understanding about the dispute. Therefore, decisions made by the parties on their own would likely be better than those made by outsiders. While each of the previous methods of dispute resolution are used every day, more creative methods of resolving conflict are needed. Each of the preceding processes is appropriate in some instances.

Another way to characterize dispute resolution emphasizes the outcomes sought by the disputing parties. These outcomes are 1) to reconcile underlying interests, 2) to determine who is right, and 3) to conclude who is more powerful.[18] Each is appropriate in different circumstances. The choice may depend upon how the parties relate to one another and the nature of the dispute. Previous experience is also a key ingredient in selection of these alternatives. Determining rights and making power plays are currently the most commonly known methods of resolving disputes. Interest-based dispute resolution is also seen as collaboration, the most integrative method of dispute resolution. It is also recognized as the most productive conflict-handling behavior. This method, which increases the reconciliation of interests, is also identified as the most effective system of dispute resolution. If the primary goal of reconciling interests is not successful, then a rights determination should be next, leaving a power resolution as the last resort.[19]

17. Deborah Borisoff and David A. Victor, Conflict Management: A Communication Skills Approach 10 (1998).

18. William L. Ury, et al., Getting Disputes Resolved: Designing Systems to Cut the Costs of Conflict 4 (1993).

19. *Id.* at 18.

As we, as individuals and as a society, grow and evolve, so should our means of dispute resolution. We have observed a shift in the methods used to resolve conflict. A number of alternatives have developed which employ neutral third parties to resolve disputes. The degree of influence which the third party has over the final result varies with each process. But this is only the beginning. The ADR Universe is clearly in its infancy.

D. THE VARIETY OF ADR DEVICES

In general, Alternative Dispute Resolution (ADR) is the term which identifies a group of processes through which disputes, conflicts, and cases are resolved outside of formal litigation procedures. ADR has developed in the United States primarily as an adjunct to our legal system. ADR procedures include negotiation, mediation, arbitration, case evaluation techniques, and private judging. These processes have been designed and developed to assist those involved in a dispute to arrive expeditiously at a mutually satisfactory resolution of a matter.

At the basis of alternative dispute resolution is the negotiation process. But, for a number of reasons, direct negotiations do not always result in satisfactory settlements.[20] Often, when direct negotiations fail to produce a resolution, a neutral third party can provide assistance. ADR processes, as developed, involve a third party neutral[21] who assists parties in reaching a resolution to a dispute. When selecting an ADR method, an examination of the factors which will most likely move the case toward a resolution is necessary.

The type of assistance provided for resolving the dispute depends largely on the neutral's role. That role determines the effect the neutral has on the negotiation. In fact, what the third party neutral does to assist in settlement defines the ADR process. The following provides a closer examination of the more common ADR processes. They can be categorized into three primary types: adjudicative, evaluative, and facilitative.

1. ADJUDICATIVE

In adjudicatory dispute resolution processes, the neutral adjudicates, or makes a decision. Adjudication is the basis of the legal system. When a case is submitted to the court or to a jury, someone other than the parties makes the decision. Many times this is necessary because the parties clearly want or need an outside decision maker. Arbitration and private adjudication, or private judging, are the ADR procedures most similar to formal court proceedings. While traditional adjudication (such

---

20. An in-depth look at the negotiation process, including an examination of negotiation difficulties, is provided in Chapter 9. See also, Robert Mnookin, *Why Negotiations Fail: An Exploration of Barriers to the Resolution of Conflict*, 8 Ohio St. J. On Disp. Resol. 235 (1993).

21. Although the term is used here in the singular, in many dispute resolution processes the *neutral party* may be two or more individuals.

as jury verdicts, court judgements and administrative hearings) always results in binding decisions, arbitration and neutral fact finding can vary; binding, non-binding, or advisory decisions are possible.

a. Arbitration

Arbitrations are generally conducted by a sole arbitrator or a panel of three.[22] In the arbitration process, arbitrators listen to a typically adversarial presentation of all sides of the case, and thereafter render a decision, usually termed an award. Arbitration procedures are generally more formal than the other dispute resolution techniques. Although strict adherence to rules, such as those governing court procedure and evidence rarely occurs in arbitration, some rules may control the process. Often attorneys are involved. The parties, either through the attorneys or pro se, make the presentations to the arbitrators. Often live witnesses testify, and actual evidence may be submitted. Experts may be involved, and, in some cases, the arbitrators may visit the actual site of the dispute, e.g., a construction area. Post-hearing briefs may be submitted. Thereafter, the arbitrators take a period of time, usually no more than thirty days, to deliberate and render their decision. Arbitration awards are generally binding, where the parties have previously contracted for arbitration.

The process for appeal from a binding arbitration differs significantly from the normal court appellate process. In most instances there are very limited, statutorily defined rights of appeal. Of course, where the arbitration award is non-binding or advisory the parties may disregard it. Mandatory court arbitration programs are of an advisory nature. If, however, parties in a lawsuit voluntarily agree to participate in arbitration either by contract or stipulation, the award may be binding. A great deal of case law has developed in the arbitration arena, and there are many treatises on the subject.[23]

There are a number of other variables which should be considered when employing the arbitration process. These include determination of the rules of procedure, if any, which will be followed; the appropriate time during the life of the dispute for the use of arbitration; the amount of discovery to be completed prior to the arbitration; should the arbitrators explain their award or simply issue a naked award; whether the parties wish for the arbitrators to make findings of fact and conclusions of law; whether the parties wish to contract to expand the scope of appealability; and the background of the arbitrators. Arbitration may be used before suit is filed, during discovery, and as a substitute for trial or appeal. Most of these decisions may be made by the participants, except for those cases involved in a court-annexed program.

In the cases where the arbitration is conducted by a three person panel, a common practice is for each side to choose an arbitrator, each

---

22. For simplicity, the plural form will be used in this discussion.

23. See Ian Macneil, Richard Speidel and Thomas J. Stipanowich, Federal Arbitration Law: Agreements, Awards & Remedies Under the Federal Arbitration Act (1994).

designated a "party" arbitrator. The two "party" arbitrators then select the third, usually the chair. This individual is essentially the real "neutral." While the better practice requires that a consensus among all three arbitrators be reached to support an award, some procedures allow for the award to be issued upon a majority decision.

Over the long history of arbitration use, a number of modifications of the process have occurred. Two of the more common variants are high-low arbitration and final offer arbitration. In high-low arbitration, the parties in a monetary dispute minimize risk by choosing the parameters of the arbitration award. In advance of the arbitration, two figures are determined, a high number which is automatically awarded if plaintiff prevails, and a low number, the award if there is a finding for the defendant. In final offer arbitration, each party submits, usually in confidence, a final offer to the arbitrators. The final award must be one of the submitted offers. Consequently, parties tend to submit reasonable offers.

Arbitration is most effective in cases where the parties cannot agree on the facts or where the dispute is purely monetary. Arbitration is also appropriate where the matter is highly complex or technical, and an expert decision is needed. In many instances, arbitrators, who are not necessarily attorneys, have expertise in the subject matter of the dispute.[24]

b. *Private Judging*

Another distinct ADR tool falling within the adjudicatory sphere is known as private or special judging. With this option, which originated in California, the parties hire a retired or former judge to hear the case and render a decision. In several states, courts can order a referral of a civil or family case to this procedure, also known as "rent-a-judge," or the parties themselves can agree to take the matter to the private judge. The judge, also termed a referee, can either decide all issues or just a portion of the case. Thus while private judging resembles traditional litigation, important differences such as the expertise of the judge, speed of decision making and flexibility in rules and procedure exist. Essentially, private judging consists of a formal presentation of the case by counsel, utilizing witnesses and documents, and generally following the rules of procedure and evidence.[25] The private judge presiding over the process has essentially the same powers as a trial judge. A record of the trial is made by a private court reporter, and the decision is entered by the referring court as a judgment of the court.[26] Thus the rights of appeal are the same as if the judgment had been rendered by the referring court.[27]

---

24. For further detail on the arbitration process, see John S. Murray, Alan Scott Rau & Edward F. Sherman, Processes of Dispute Resolution, (Chapter Five) (2d Ed. 1996).

25. Amy L. Litkovitz, Note, The Advantages of Using a Rent-a-Judge System, 10 Ohio St. J. on Disp. Resol. 491, 494 (1998).

26. For example, see Tex. Civ. Prac. & Rem. Code Ann. § 151.011 (West 1997).

27. Litkovitz, *supra* note 25, at 495.

Because private judging is essentially the retention of a special judge for a fee, this type of procedure has been criticized as private justice, only available to the wealthy.[28] However, with time, cost and other savings resulting from the use of this procedure, in the long run, private judging may be more economical than traditional litigation. A California study indicates that while these criticisms were valid, because of the infrequent use of the process, no actual abuses were found. Close monitoring of the process by court rules was recommended.[29]

Several states have statutes outlining the specific procedures to be followed in the use of this process.[30] In some cases, it is mandated that the private judge be a former or retired judge,[31] although other statutes do not require judicial experience.[32] As a practical matter, however, at least in California and Texas, retired judges are used. And while most states have enacted statutes allowing such a process, as a practical matter it is rarely used.[33] Use of a private judge is probably most useful in cases where a dispute of both law and fact is the impediment to settlement. The parties see a need for the decision maker to possess judicial expertise, and therefore select a former judge.

c. Fact–Finding

Neutral Fact–Finding is another adjudicatory process. In this procedure, the neutral third party, after gathering information from all parties, makes a determination of the facts. This determination may be binding or merely advisory. Recommendations for final resolution of the matter may be included in the fact-finder's report. Neutral fact-finding may be used on a portion of the matter or to determine the final resolution. For example, neutral fact-finding used primarily in the resolution of public sector labor relations disputes, is seen as only quasi-adjudicatory in that the recommendations of the neutral are not final.[34] Courts have also defined the duties of a neutral fact to include providing sufficient information to a final decision maker, if that decision maker is bound by the result of neutral fact finding.[35] Yet opinions differ as to whether courts are subsequently bound by the fact-finder's decisions. A variation of this process is termed expert fact-finding. In this process, the parties employ neutrals to render expert opinions on technical, scientific or legal questions. If advisory, however, a court or subsequent adjudicator is free to make a new determination.

28. For example, see David S. Shapiro, *Private Judging in the State of New York: A Critical Introduction*, 23 Colum. J.L. & Soc. Probs. 275, 293 (1990).

29. 4 World Arb. & Med. R. 108 (1993).

30. See, for example, West's Ann. Cal. Civ. Proc. Code §§ 638–645.1, N.Y.–C.P. L. & R. §§ 4301–4321 (McKinney 1992). Tex., Civ. Prac. & Rem. Code Ann. § 151.001 et seq. (1997).

31. Tex. Civ. Prac. & Rem. Code Ch. 151.001, et seq. (1997).

32. West's Ann. Cal. Civ. Proc. Code §§ 638–645.1, N.Y. C.P. L. & R. §§ 4301–4321 (McKinney 1992).

33. Litkovitz, *supra* note 25 at 505, 506.

34. Leonard Bierman, *Factfinding: Finding the Public Interest*, 9 Rutgers–Camden L.J. 667, 668 (1978).

35. See Tim K. Klintworth, Note, *The Enforceability of an Agreement to a Non-Arbitral Form of Dispute Resolution: The Rise of Mediation and Neutral Fact Finding*, 1995 J. Disp. Resol. 181, citing Blair v. Lovett, 196 Colo. 118, 582 P.2d 668 (1978),

2. EVALUATIVE

Case evaluation consists of providing the lawyers and the litigants with feedback as to the merits of the case. Case evaluation may be defined as a process whereby advocates present their version of the case to one or more third party neutrals, who then evaluate the strengths and weaknesses of each. In particular, the primary purpose of neutral case evaluation is to provide an objective, non-binding, confidential, evaluation of the case, which may be used by the lawyers and clients in further settlement negotiations.[36] Often, parties are unable to reach a settlement in a matter due to unrealistic expectations about the final outcome. Ideally, neutral case evaluation will provide an opportunity to reconsider settlement options. Depending on the dispute and type of evaluation sought, feedback can be provided by peers, professionals, experts, or lay persons.

a. *Peer Evaluation*

"Peer evaluation in a confidential setting" has been the phrase used to describe the Moderated Settlement Conference.[37] The Moderated Settlement Conference (MSC), a process designed in Texas, utilizes a panel of three neutral, experienced attorneys who listen to a presentation consisting of both factual and legal argument by counsel for each party. The panel then questions the attorneys as well as the clients who are present throughout the entire process. After deliberation, the panel renders an advisory, confidential evaluation of the strengths and weaknesses of the case and often provides a range for settlement. The evaluation is not binding upon the parties, but the objective is that it will assist with further settlement negotiations.

A very similar process is "Michigan Mediation."[38] In both the MSC and Michigan Mediation, the neutral panel consists of three attorneys, and those coordinating the process are careful to mix the expertise of the panel members. For instance, the panel in a personal injury case will be made up of a plaintiff's attorney, a defense attorney, and a neutral, such as a lawyer whose expertise is commercial or family law.

Peer evaluation may be adapted to better assist the litigants in achieving resolution of the case. Modification of the panel in either the

and Olson v. Lovett, 457 N.W.2d 224 (Minn. Ct.App.1990).

36. Kimberlee K. Kovach, Neutral Case Evaluation, St. Mary's Alternative Dispute Resolution Institute at C–8 (1989).

37. R. Hanson Lawton, The Dynamics and Mechanics of ADR, St. Mary's Alternative Dispute Resolution Institute at C–13 (1988).

38. Although it is termed *mediation*, the process used in Michigan state courts is case evaluation. Proposed changes to the court rules in Michigan would rename this process "case evaluation." New court rules will also authorize the use of "real" mediation. See 5 Disp. Resol. Mag. 2 (Winter 1998). For a detailed report of the use of Michigan mediation, see Kathy L. Shuart, et al., *Settling Cases in Detroit: An Examination of Wayne County's "Mediation" Program*, 8 Just. Sys. J. 307 (1983). Michigan Mediation has two additional components to the process. First the panel makes a specific recommendation for settlement. If a party rejects the recommendation and chooses to go to trial, and the position is not improved by at least ten percent, a penalty is assessed.

MSC or Michigan Mediation may result in peer evaluation for both the attorneys and one or both of the parties, particularly where the dispute involves technical expertise. For example, in a pilot program for medical malpractice cases in El Paso County, Texas, the three-moderator panel consisted of two attorneys and one physician.

One of the most common evaluative processes is termed "neutral evaluation," or "neutral case evaluation."[39] In this process, an attorney serves as the sole evaluator. This method of neutral case evaluation has been used informally, where a magistrate or colleague provides feedback to attorneys about their case. However, there are now court programs which provide a more structured process. The first court to institute the process was the Northern District of California. The process was termed Early Neutral Evaluation (ENE).[40] In the ENE procedure, the attorney evaluator is hand-selected by the court. The process takes place very early in the life of the case, usually upon the filing of the response. The initial goals of the process included the following: to force the parties to confront their case as well as that of the opponent, to identify the actual matters in dispute, to develop an efficient discovery process, and to obtain an assessment of the case.[41] In practice the process often became a settlement conference, and more than one-third of the cases were settled.[42] Settlement was later added as an explicit goal.[43] Many neutral case evaluation procedures in other jurisdictions now have settlement of the case as an explicit and primary goal.

During the ENE process, after the neutral makes his opening explanatory remarks, each side is given an opportunity to present an uninterrupted fifteen minute statement, consisting of the legal theories and evidence of the case.[44] Thereafter the neutral questions the participants in an attempt to clarify issues and arguments as well as to probe for case strengths and weaknesses.[45] A written case evaluation is often provided the parties and if they desire, the neutral will then engage in assisting them in settlement discussions.[46] But even if a settlement is not reached, the parties will have established a time-line for administration of the case including discovery practices, which is an effective method of expediting the resolution of the case.

Modifications of neutral case evaluation are possible, and research has demonstrated that the process differs in focus depending upon the style of the neutral. This variation ranges from a process that resembles non-binding arbitration to one similar to mediation; and thus it is

39. These are the most common generic terms used to describe the process.

40. David I. Levine, *Northern District of California Adopts Early Neutral Evaluation to Expedite Dispute Resolution,* 72 Judicature 235 (1989).

41. For an excellent in-depth examination and analysis of the California ENE program, see Joshua D. Rosenberg and H. Jay Folberg, *Alternative Dispute Resolution:*

An Empirical Analysis, 46 Stan L. Rev. 1487 (1994).

42. Levine, *supra* note 40, at 236.

43. Id., at 235.

44. Rosenberg and Folberg, *supra* note 41, at 1490.

45. *Id.*

46. *Id.*

currently difficult to truly define the process with specificity.[47] In fact, in those cases where participants were dissatisfied with the ENE, they indicated dissatisfaction with the particular neutral.[48] As the use of neutral case evaluation expands and evaluators are more educated and trained in the process, more consistency is anticipated.

b. Lay Evaluation—The Summary Jury Trial

Many litigants want their day in court—they have a right to a trial by a jury of their peers and will not be satisfied with anything less. To provide such a trial in a summary fashion saves time and dollars for the parties and the court. For this reason, the summary jury trial (SJT) procedure was developed.[49]

During the summary jury trial, the attorneys present an abbreviated version of their evidence to an advisory jury usually selected from the regular jury pool. Some courts will inform the jurors in advance that their verdict is only advisory, while others argue that the SJT will be more effective if the jurors return a "true" verdict.[50] After making an opening statement, each attorney summarizes in a narrative manner what the evidence would show if the case went to trial. In about fifty percent of the cases, the court will permit live testimony. However, testimony is often limited to one witness per side, usually the primary party to the dispute. These individuals are able to tell the jury their "story" in their own words. In most cases, each presentation is limited to one half day in duration. The lawyers also present closing arguments. Normally, all details of the SJT are worked out at a pre–trial conference.[51] After the presentation is complete, the jury, usually a panel of six, deliberates and returns a non-binding, advisory verdict. The parties and their attorneys may then poll and question the jurors to gain feedback about the case. The information gained from this process can then be used as a basis for further settlement negotiations.

The summary jury trial is utilized when the parties or the court feel that a preview of what a jury might do would be helpful to better assess the case for purposes of settlement. This procedure is typically more adversarial than peer review since each side is trying to persuade the jurors to return a verdict in their favor.

As with all ADR devices, the summary jury trial can be modified to provide the parties feedback which will assist in settlement. In some cases, the procedure has been conducted with two juries, who simultaneously watch the case presentation, but who deliberate separately. It is

---

47. *Id.* at 1495, 1496.

48. *Id.* at 1489.

49. This procedure was first designed by the Hon. Thomas Lambros of the District Court for the Northern District of Ohio. He found that a trial normally taking six to eight weeks could be condensed to one or two days. See, Thomas Lambros, *The Summary Jury Trial—An Alternative Method of*

Resolving Disputes, 69 Judicature 286 (1986).

50. Richard A. Enslen, *ADR: Another Acronym, or a Viable Alternative to the High Cost of Litigation and Crowded Court Dockets? The Debate Commences*, 18 N.M.L. Rev. 1, 13 (1988).

51. *Id.*

also possible for parties to stipulate in advance that the jury's verdict will be binding. The parties may also submit only part of the case for evaluation; for example, a summary jury trial may be held on the liability issue only.

c. Judicial Evaluation

In some instances, the knowledge, experience and temperament a retired judge can bring to a case can be quite helpful in assisting the parties reach a settlement.[52] In contrast to private judging where the judge actually decides the case, in a case evaluation process the judge will merely point out to the lawyers and litigants the strengths and weaknesses of the case. This assessment is based, in part, upon past judicial experience. As with other types of case evaluation, the parties may engage in more expanded dialogue to gain additional feedback. The litigants are then free to accept or reject the evaluation. In some cases, the judge will assume a role of mediator or assist in the actual negotiation in order to reach a final settlement.

Informal judicial evaluation may also take place in a less structured setting, such as when the judge presides over a pre-trial conference during a pending case. While this practice has been used for years to encourage settlement of cases, it is only with the advent of ADR that its use has become more defined and made available in the private sector.

d. Specialist or Expert Evaluation

Many cases turn on a technical issue which is sometimes beyond the understanding of the court, the lawyers, and the jury. By providing an independent, neutral, expert evaluation of such an issue, a resolution may be achieved in a case which would otherwise take months to try. Examples include matters of construction, computer design, securities, or biomedical technology. As long as all parties agree to the selection of the neutral expert, the results are generally accepted as definitive. The expert evaluation can apply to the entire case or to only a single issue.

Expert evaluation can also be included as part of another process, such as mediation. For example, in those cases where a lawsuit is pending, many times the lawyers, in anticipation of a trial or adjudication, will have hired their experts. Cases are evaluated, at least in part, on the opinions of the experts. In the adjudicative model of dispute resolution, the decision maker finds one expert more credible than the other. However, in other instances, the experts, if taken out of their roles as witnesses, can provide insight and information which increases the parties' understanding of the problem and its genesis.[53] Moreover, it

---

52. This was the theory behind the creation of Judicial Arbitration and Mediation Service (JAMS) which was founded by Retired Judge, Hon. Warren Knight in 1979 in Orange County, California.

53. Eric R. Galton, The Use of Experts at Mediation, unpublished manuscript, on file.

has been found that experts prefer collaboration and can often work together to find a workable solution to the dispute.[54]

3. FACILITATIVE

In facilitative processes, the neutral does not render a decision or an evaluation. Rather, the neutral provides assistance to the parties so that they may reach an acceptable agreement. Three common facilitative processes are mediation, conciliation, and consensus building.

Mediation is the process where the third party neutral, whether one person or more, acts as a facilitator to assist in resolving a dispute between two or more parties.[55] Mediation is the least adversarial approach to conflict resolution and encourages the parties to communicate directly. The role of the mediator includes facilitating communication between the parties, assisting in identifying the real issues of the dispute and the interests of the parties, and generating options for settlement. The goal of facilitative processes is that the parties themselves arrive at a mutually acceptable resolution of the dispute.

As with all types of ADR, the mediation process is flexible. Primary variables affecting the process include the type of dispute, the style of the mediator and the relationship of the parties. While mediators may come from all walks of life, most litigation cases are handled by attorney mediators. An exception is in the family law area, where two mediators, generally an attorney and a therapist, are used.[56]

Mediation is appropriate in all types of cases, and it is effective even at the appellate level. Mediation is of particular value in those instances where the parties want to maintain the relationship, whether personal or professional, or where there are issues and interests underlying the dispute which need to be identified and explored.

Historically the terms mediation and conciliation have been used interchangeably, but there are some differences worth noting. Mediation, while quite an informal process, usually maintains more structure than pure conciliation. For instance, it may be possible to achieve conciliation over the telephone, whereas telephonic mediation is rarely used. Moreover, the term conciliation usually denotes that the disputing parties have been reconciled, and the relationship has been mended. In mediation, although maintenance of the relationship is an important factor, resolution of a case will often occur without an actual reconciliation between the disputants.

Consensus building is another process which is facilitative in nature.[57] Consensus building may be thought of as an extended mediation, involving large groups and a number of conflicts. Unlike traditional

---

54. *Id.*

55. As the remainder of the text is concerned with these processes, only a brief explanation is provided here.

56. See Chapters 16 § B and 17 § A3 discussing the process of co-mediation. See

also Folberg and Taylor, *supra* note 8, which focuses on divorce mediation.

57. See Chapter 17 § A2 which describes consensus building in greater detail.

mediation which is, by design, usually a one time, one day intervention, the consensus building process takes place over a more extended period of time. Additionally, because interested parties may be large groups of people, it is unlikely that everyone attends the process. Each group will have representatives who then must obtain ratification of any decision reached at the consensus building session.

4. COMBINED PROCESSES AND HYBRIDS

It is also possible to design additional ADR procedures by blending processes to create completely new techniques termed *hybrids*. This is how some of the processes previously mentioned were invented.[58] Alternatively, ADR devices may be used in conjunction with one another. This mixture of the primary processes is known as combined processes. For instance, if the parties are unable to reach a settlement after presentation of the evaluation in a neutral case evaluation, it may be appropriate to utilize a mediator for facilitation, or an arbitrator for a rendition of an award. Or, if, after a summary jury trial the parties agree on liability, but cannot reach an agreement on damages, a mediator or arbitrator can assist with these remaining issues. The most common combined process is Med–Arb, which combines the mediation and arbitration processes. In fact, it has been applied in so many instances that modifications have resulted. There are currently at least three different versions of the Med–Arb process.[59]

The Mini–Trial, used primarily in large corporate litigation, is a hybrid of negotiation, mediation, and case evaluation. With a focus on business, the mini-trial has as its pragmatic basis the realization that it may be mutually beneficial for companies to resolve disputes without protracted litigation. Continued business dealings will enhance each company's profitability. Therefore, preservation of the business relationship is a key element in the resolution. It is imperative that a high level corporate decision maker attends the process. The attorneys and corporate executives meet with an expert, third party neutral advisor; and all sides present their "best case." Direct negotiation by the corporate executives, usually without the attorneys or the neutral present, follows. If unsuccessful after a predetermined amount of time, the expert advisor provides a non-binding opinion or evaluation regarding the merits of the case. Thereafter, the executives, armed with this additional information, negotiate again. If a resolution is not reached, the neutral may act as a mediator.

Another recently developed hybrid process is the jury-determined settlement. It is a blend of the summary jury trial and arbitration. In the jury determined settlement (JDS) proceeding, the jury is empaneled, and the trial proceeds similar to a summary jury trial. At the conclusion of the JDS, however, the jury provides a binding settlement rather than a

58. For example, the summary jury trial can be seen as a hybrid of two more traditional processes: the jury trial and a settlement conference.

59. Med–Arb will be examined in greater detail, as will all mediation combinations and derivatives, in Chapter 17.

verdict.[60] Moreover, the parties are more directly active in the process and set limits of the settlement in advance through the use of a high-low agreement.[61]

E.   USE OF ADR

The ADR processes described above are designed to assist disputing parties in reaching a final resolution of a matter. But each process differs in exactly how that is accomplished. How does one determine, then, which process to select from this diverse ADR "menu"—a menu with many entrees? A specific, scientific means for choosing the most appropriate process has not been established. Determining the type of assistance needed to reach resolution of a case is a helpful first step. However, it is often difficult to precisely identify in advance the barriers to settlement. Cases, as well as clients, differ, and the exact nature of both is relevant in selecting which method is most advantageous in a given case. Perhaps it is only with continued use and experimentation that the answers will become clear.

Current informal reports, however, indicate that there are no bad choices; that is, most procedures have been successful in effectuating settlements in a variety of cases. The ADR menu is still expanding and flexible. Therefore, modification of ADR procedures may be appropriate. For example, the litigants might stipulate beforehand that the panel's evaluation in a moderated settlement conference be binding. Likewise, the parties may agree to accept the summary jury's verdict as final. Perhaps only part of a case may receive ADR treatment. Thus, in most situations, after consideration of the client's objectives and an analysis of the available dispute resolution techniques, it is likely that an appropriate procedure can either be found or designed. As ADR programs and procedures develop, they will do so in relation to variations inherent in particular jurisdictions. Although in a few jurisdictions general ADR use has been integrated into the courts, in most locations, ADR processes are still developing and evolving.

FRANK E.A. SANDER AND STEPHEN B. GOLDBERG, FITTING THE FORUM TO THE FUSS: A USER–FRIENDLY GUIDE TO SELECTING AN ADR PROCEDURE

10 Negotiation J. 49, 50, 52-55, 59-60, 66 (1994).

* * *

In this article, we examine the suitability of various dispute resolution processes from the perspective of the parties to the dispute, and then from the public-interest perspective. We use this two-step approach

---

60. Neil Vidmar and Jeffrey Rice, *Jury–Determined Settlements and Summary Jury Trials: Observations About Alternative Dis-* *pute Resolution in an Adversary Culture*, 19 Fla. St. U.L. Rev. 89, 98 (1991).

61. *Id.* at 99.

because we believe that doing so provides a more realistic view of the manner in which decisions regarding the choice of dispute resolution are made.

The initial determination regarding the choice of dispute resolution procedure will be made by each attorney in consultation with his or her client. In these considerations, both court and various types of ADR will, and perhaps must, be considered. Next, the attorneys will discuss with each other the decision each has reached with the client, and will seek to agree upon a procedure. If they do not agree, the complaining party will be free to take the dispute to court. Then, if the court has an ADR program, as is increasingly common, court personnel will decide if the dispute is suitable for some aspect of that program. If the court's ADR program is optional, the parties will be free to reject the court's recommendation; if that program is mandatory, the court will order the parties into some type of ADR.

As counsel for the disputing parties consider which dispute resolution procedure is appropriate for their clients, they face two basic questions: First, what are the client's goals, and what dispute resolution procedure is most likely to achieve those goals? Second, if the client is amenable to settlement, what are the impediments to settlement, and what ADR procedure is most likely to overcome those impediments?

When the decision regarding an appropriate dispute resolution procedure is made from a public perspective, the second question is similar to the kind of analysis an attorney should give to any client; the first question, however, is more complex. Initially, court personnel or public agencies making a recommendation regarding appropriate procedures for resolving a dispute must consider the goal of all parties to the dispute. Furthermore, they must consider the public interest in that dispute. While a private settlement may serve the interests of all parties to the dispute, the public interest may lie in public adjudication (e.g., because of a need for judicial interpretation of a newly enacted statute).

* * *

The value of various procedures in meeting specific client objectives is set forth in Table 1. An important point to note is that the values assigned to each procedure in Table 1 (as well as in Table 2, which follows) are not based on empirical research but rather upon our own experience, combined with the views of other dispute resolution professionals. Moreover, the numerical values assigned to each procedure are not intended to be taken literally, but rather as a shorthand expression of the extent to which each procedure satisfies a particular objective.

If, for example, the client's goals are to maintain the relationship and receive a neutral opinion while also maximizing privacy, adding the numerical scores would lead to the following result: mediation 6; minitrial 8; summary jury trial 7; early neutral evaluation 6; arbitration 7; and court 3. One could not, however, conclude from these scores that the minitrial is the preferred procedure. Our analysis of the capacity of each procedure to meet various goals is not that precise. The most that one could conclude at this point in the analysis would be that some ADR procedure is preferable to court.

The next step in the analysis is to list the client's goals in order of priority. If the client is primarily interested in a prompt and inexpensive resolution of the dispute that also maintains or improves the parties' relationship—which is typical of most clients in most business disputes—mediation is the preferred procedure. Mediation is the only procedure to receive maximum scores on each of these dimensions—cost, speed, and maintain or improve the relationship—as well as on assuring privacy, another interest which is present in many business disputes. It is only when the client's primary interests consist of establishing a precedent, being vindicated, or maximizing (or minimizing) recovery that procedures other than mediation are more likely to be satisfactory.

It should be clear from this discussion that our evaluation is based on assumptions concerning how ADR procedures are typically structured. If the procedures are structured differently, by court order or party design, the extent to which they will satisfy client goals will also differ. For example, mediation will generally cost the parties less and be faster than a summary jury trial or the minitrial, which require prepar-

Table 1

Extent to Which Dispute Resolution Procedures Satisfy Client Objectives

Procedures

	Nonbinding				Binding	
Objectives	Mediation	Minitrial	Summary Jury Trial	Early Neutral Evaluation	Arbitration, Private Judging	Court
Minimize Costs	3	2	2	3	1	0
Speed	3	2	2	3	1	0
Privacy	3	3	2	3	1	0
Maintain/ Improve Relationship	3	2	2	1	1	0
Vindication	0	1	1	1	2	3
Neutral Opinion	0	3	3	3	3	3
Precedent	0	0	0	0	2	3
Maximizing/ Minimizing Recovery	0	1	1	1	2	3

0 = Unlikely to satisfy objective   2 = Satisfies objective substantially
1 = Satisfies objective somewhat   3 = Satisfies objective very substantially

ing to present evidence and arguments in a structured setting, but that is not always the case. Some parties will provide for a comparatively simple minitrial, with a minimum of preparation, while others will participate in a lengthy, somewhat formal mediation that will be expensive and time-consuming. Similarly, we have assumed that mediation is a process distinct from neutral evaluation and have set the point values in Table 1 accordingly.

* * *

In some circumstances, a settlement is not in the client's interest. For example, the client may want a binding precedent or may want to impress other potential litigants with its firmness and the consequent costs of asserting claims against it. Alternatively, the client may be in a situation in which there are no relational concerns; the only issue is whether it must pay out money; there is no pre-judgment interest; and the cost of contesting the claim is less than the interest earned on the money. In these and a small numbers of other situations, settlement will not be in the client's interest.

Table 2
Likelihood that the ADR Procedure Will Overcome
Impediments to Settlement

Procedures

Impediment	Mediation	Minitrial	Summary Jury Trial	Early Neutral Evaluation
Poor Communication	3	1	1	1
Need to Express Emotions	3	1	1	1
Different View of Facts	2	2	2	2
Different View of Law	2	3	3	3
Important Principle	1	0	0	0
Constituent Pressure	3	2	2	2
Linkage	2	1	1	1
Multiple Parties	2	1	1	1
Different Lawyer–Client Interests	2	1	1	1
Jackpot Syndrome	0	1	1	1

0 = Unlikely to overcome impediment
1 = Sometimes useful in overcoming impediment
2 = Often useful in overcoming impediment
3 = Most likely to be useful in overcoming impediment

Still, a satisfactory settlement typically is in the client's interest. It is the inability to obtain such a settlement, in fact, that impels the client to seek the advice of counsel in the first place. The lawyer must consider not only what the client wants but also why the parties have been unable to settle their dispute, and then must find a dispute resolution procedure That is likely to overcome the impediments to settlement. Note, however, that, even though it may initially appear that the parties seek a settlement, sometimes an examination of the impediments to settlement reveals that at least one party wants something that settlement cannot provide (e.g. public vindication or a ruling that establishes an enforceable precedent).

The impediments to settlement, along with the likelihood that various ADR processes will overcome them, are set out in Table 2.

* * *

A Rule of Presumptive Mediation

Mediation will most often be the preferred procedure for overcoming the impediments to settlement. It has the greatest likelihood of overcoming all impediments except different views of facts and law, and the jackpot syndrome. Furthermore, a skilled mediator can often obtain a settlement without the necessity of resolving disputed questions of facts or law. Thus, there is much to be said for a rule of "presumptive mediation"—that mediation, if it is a procedure that satisfies the parties' goals, should, absent compelling indications to the contrary, be the first procedure used.

Under this approach, the mediator would first attempt to resolve the dispute by using customary mediation techniques. In doing so, the mediator would gain a clearer sense of the parties' goals and the obstacles to settlement than could be obtained by counsel prior to mediation. If mediation were not successful, the mediator could then make an informed recommendation for a different procedure. For example, if the parties were so far apart in their views of the facts or law that meaningful settlement negotiations could not take place, the mediator might recommend a referral to one of the evaluative procedures to move the parties closer to a common view of the facts and law. Once that had been accomplished, mediated settlement negotiations would recommence.

One of the strengths of this approach is that the mediator's process recommendation might be more readily accepted by both parties than would the suggestion of either of their attorneys, since attorney suggestions are sometimes suspected of being based on tactical considerations. Thus, the approach of "presumptive mediations" seems promising, particularly when the parties are having difficulty in agreeing upon an ADR procedure.

The presumption in favor of mediation would be overcome when the goals of one or both parties could not be satisfied in mediation, or mediation was clearly incapable of overcoming a major impediment to settlement. The most common situation in which this could occur would be when either party has a strong interest in receiving a neutral opinion, obtaining a precedent, or being vindicated, and is unwilling to consider any procedure that forecloses the possibility of accomplishing that objective.

* * *

In addressing the problem of "fitting the form to the fuss," we have suggested two lines of inquiry: What are the disputants' goals in making a forum choice? And, if the disputants are amenable to settlement, what are the obstacles to settlement, and in what forum might they be overcome?

The fact that these inquiries rarely lead to a clear answer to the question of forum selection does not, we think, indicate that the analysis is faulty. Rather, it indicates that the question of forum selection ultimately turns on the extent to which the interests of the disputing parties (and sometimes of the public) will be met in various forums. Thus, the most that analysis can offer is a framework that clarifies the interests involved and promotes a thoughtful weighing and resolution of those interests.

————

Reservations have been expressed about the use of ADR;[62] yet its growth in less than three decades has been phenomenal. And, although once debated, it is now widely acknowledged that ADR is a permanent part of our system of justice. In fact, many of these American ADR processes have not only been recognized, but are beginning to be implemented in courts and communities around the world. When observing this explosive nature of ADR growth, one may question just what it is about these procedures that accounts for such a trend. The answer most likely lies in a combination of factors. The savings in dollars, time and emotional energy are the most often cited reasons for ADR use. And while these are very important factors, others such as confidentiality and party participation should not be overlooked. Courts are limited in the types of resolutions they can provide. When the actual disputants are involved in the process, they can often be creative and fashion relief particular to the matter. By having a part in the decision-making process, the litigants are able to generate settlements with which they are pleased and with which they will comply. Participation in the *process* of dispute resolution also results in party satisfaction. These benefits of ADR, which are rarely attainable through traditional court processes, certainly account for its ever increasing use.

There has been a continuing debate about whether these processes should be part of the legal system—or separate from it. Much of the initial work in the area was done apart from the courts, so it would be seen as truly alternative. Now, however, rather than viewing these processes as a threat, more lawyers are utilizing them to their benefit. Lawyers are finding that these processes can be "tools of the trade." Moreover, as the business world realizes the benefits of ADR use, corporations are demanding that legal counsel be educated in its use. ADR has begun to enhance, rather than restrict, the lawyer's practice. But as these processes are placed in the lawyer's toolbox, other issues emerge.

62. See, for example, Owen M. Fiss, *Against Settlement*, 93 Yale L.J. 1073 (1984); Eric K. Yamamoto, *ADR: Where Have the Critics Gone?* 36 Santa Clara L. Rev. 1055 (1996). See also Chapter 15 § H, which examines more closely some criticisms of mediation.

One concern is whether these ADR processes have become too "legalized."[63] It may appear that the legal system exerted too great an influence on these alternative processes. As the use of ADR processes within the court system has increased, legal issues surrounding such use have been raised. ADR developed as an "alternative" to litigation. Yet it appears that as this ADR universe has become integrated into our legal system, its use has become legalized. This is demonstrated in the new term liti-mediation, used to describe court-annexed or connected mediation.[64] Most recently the view of ADR as "litigation lite" demonstrates the continued influence and impact of the adversarial system on ADR.[65] Adversarial approaches are more common and legal issues about ADR use continue. Thousands of statutes governing ADR now exist. And trial and appellate courts are confronting issues of ADR use with more frequency.[66] The "law" of ADR is now in its developmental stages.[67] It is indeed ironic that as additional dispute resolution options become part of our system, the evolution produces additional legal considerations.

63. See Carrie Menkel–Meadow, *Pursuing Settlement in an Adversary Culture: A Tale of Innovation Co–Opted or "The Law of ADR"*, 19 Fla. St. U.L. Rev. 1 (1991).

64. John Lande, *How Will Lawyering and Mediation Practices Transform Each Other*, 20 Fla. St. U. L. Rev. 839 (1997).

65. Jack M. Sabatino, *ADR as "Litigation Lite": Procedural and Evidentiary Norms Embedded Within Alternative Dispute Resolution*, 47 Emory L.J. 1289 (1998).

66. As demonstrated by the increase in cases included in this text. See also Duane W. Krohnke, *Mediation's Cases Appearances Are More Frequent in 1998*, 17 Alternatives to High Cost Litig. (1999).

67. Menkel–Meadow, *supra* note 63, at 2.

Chapter Two

THE MEDIATION PROCESS

A. OVERVIEW

Mediation is facilitated negotiation. It is a process by which a neutral third party, the mediator, assists disputing parties in reaching a mutually satisfactory resolution. At first glance, the definition of mediation appears simple. Yet over the last few years, especially within the ADR field, very few items spark more controversy than the definition of mediation.[1] In fact, it has been alleged that the term "mediator" is now used so loosely that no one may safely presume that a speaker intends its original meaning: one who helps people reach their own settlement.[2] Of course debate about the "original" definition of mediation is also possible.

The term mediate is derived from the Latin "mediare" which means "to be in the middle."[3] Certainly the mediator finds himself in the middle of a dispute. But mediation involves much more than placement of the mediator. A variety of definitions for the term "mediation" exist. While these definitions differ, and are subject to debate, most people agree on the purpose of the process: to assist people in reaching a voluntary resolution of a dispute or conflict. Definitional debates primarily surround the specifics of how the assistance is actually provided.

Below are some of the more basic definitions of mediation:

• The broad term describing the intervention of third parties in the dispute resolution process.[4]

• A process in which a third party facilitates and coordinates the negotiation of disputing parties.[5]

---

1. See Kimberlee K. Kovach, *What is Real Mediation, and Who Should Decide?*, 3 Disp. Resol. Magazine (Fall 1996); Carrie Menkel–Meadow, *The Many Ways of Mediation: The Transformation of Traditions, Ideologies, Paradigms, and Practices*, 11 Negotiation J. 217 (1995).

2. Linda Singer, Settling Disputes 21 (1990).

3. Merriam Webster's Collegiate Dictionary 722 (10th ed. 1993).

4. John S. Murray, Alan Scott Rau and Edward F. Sherman, Processes of Dispute Resolution 247 (2d Ed. 1996).

5. Roberta S. Mitchell & Scot E. Dewhirst, The Mediator Handbook 13 The Center For Dispute Resolution, Capital University Law and Graduate Center (1990).

• The intervention into a dispute or the negotiation process by an acceptable impartial and neutral third party who has no authoritative decision-making power. This individual will assist disputing parties in voluntarily reaching their own neutral acceptable settlement of the issues in dispute.[6]

• A process where third parties not involved in the controversy assist disputing parties in their negotiations.[7]

• A private, voluntary, informal process where a party-selected neutral assists disputants to reach a mutually acceptable agreement.[8]

• Mediation is a process by which a third party neutral, whether one or more, acts as a facilitator to assist in the resolving of a dispute between two or more parties. It is a non-adversarial approach to conflict resolution where the parties communicate directly. The role of the mediator is to facilitate communication between the parties, assist them on focusing on real issues of the dispute, and generate options for settlement. The goal of this process is that the parties themselves arrive at a mutually acceptable resolution of the dispute.[9]

• A voluntary process where an impartial mediator actively assists disputants in identifying and clarifying issues of concern and in designing and agreeing to solutions.[10]

• A forum in which an impartial person, the mediator, facilitates communication between parties to promote reconciliation, settlement, or understanding among them.[11]

• A process in which a neutral third party assists the parties in developing and exploring their underlying interests (in addition to their legal positions), promotes the development of options and assists the parties toward settling the case through negotiations.[12]

• A informal process in which a neutral third party with no power to impose a resolution helps the disputing parties try to reach a mutually acceptable settlement.[13]

• In its simplest term, mediation is trying to get two people to do that which they least want to do—talk to each other.[14]

---

6. Christopher W. Moore, The Mediation Process: Practical Strategies for Resolving Conflict 8 (2d Ed. 1996).

7. Nancy H. Rogers & Craig A. McEwen, Mediation: Law, Policy, Practice 1 (1994).

8. Alternative Dispute Resolution: An ADR Primer (Standing Committee on Dispute Resolution 3d ed., 1989).

9. Kimberlee K. Kovach, *ADR—Does It Work?*, South Texas College of Law, Advanced Civil Litigation Institute, (1989).

10. Ill. Rev. Stat. ch. 710 § 20/2(b) (1999).

11. Tex. Civ. Prac. & Rem. Code § 154.023(a) (West 1997).

12. U.S. Dist. Ct. Rules W.D.Mo., Early Assessment Program, VII(B)(1)(a).

13. Robert A. Baruch Bush & Joseph P. Folger, The Promise of Mediation: Responding to Conflict Through Empowerment and Recognition 2 (1994).

14. Kent L. Brown, Comment, *Confidentiality in Mediation: Status and Implications* 1991 J. Disp. Resol. 307, 309 (1991).

The number and variety of definitions demonstrate that the mediation process is a flexible one. Although there is a structure to the mediation process, it is not rigid, but rather fluid in nature. Many other definitions of mediation are subject matter specific and often dictate diverse approaches. Since the mediation process deals with human behavior and motivation, it must also be adaptable to individual differences.

There is little doubt that the use of the mediation process has grown tremendously and will continue to do so. Much of this growth can be attributed to the process itself rather than the mediator.[15] The process which is our focus is not new. In fact, the process is deep rooted, having developed over a long period of time.

B. HISTORICAL PERSPECTIVES

When looking for a historical reference to the initial use of mediation, commentators often quote the Bible. Yet it can be argued that mediation was used long before recorded history, particularly in the broad context where a third party neutral served several functions. This brief historical perspective will primarily focus on the mediator in a role close to the term as we currently know it. It should be remembered, however, that because it is a flexible process, mediation has varied over its long history, influenced in part by the circumstances of its use.

1. INTERNATIONAL SPHERE

Use of mediation, similar to that which we see today, can be traced back several hundreds, even thousands of years.[16] Mediation was used in China and Japan as a primary means of conflict resolution. The mediative approach was not an alternative to fighting or adversarial approaches to problem solving. Rather, mediation was the first choice for dispute settlement. Those cultures placed emphasis on peace-making and peace-keeping. A win or lose approach was not an acceptable means of resolution. For instance, China's principle use of mediation was a direct result of the Confucian view of natural harmony and dispute resolution by morals rather than coercion.[17] Chinese society therefore placed emphasis on a conciliatory approach to conflict. This has continued throughout history within that culture. Chinese mediation boards or committees, made up of several individuals from each local community, resolve more than 80 percent of all civil disputes. Today the mediation boards in China, termed People's Mediation Committees (PMCs) are the dominant institution for mediation and resolve over 7.2 million disputes

15. In fact, mediators often refer to themselves as mere caretakers of the process.

16. Use of mediation has been documented in ancient China over two thousand years ago. See, for example, Jerome Alan Cohen, *Chinese Mediation on the Eve of*

Modernization, 55 Cal. L. Rev. 1201, 1205 (1966).

17. Jay Folberg & Alison Taylor, Mediation: A Comprehensive Guide to Resolving Conflicts Without Litigation 2 (1984).

per year.[18] They assist in maintaining peace and social control throughout both urban and rural communities.

In Japan, conciliation was historically the primary means of resolution with village leaders serving as mediators.[19] Current Japanese negotiation style still places an emphasis on the relationship and is often regarded as a purely conciliatory style.[20] In a negotiation, particularly in the business world, time is spent on building the relationship, without which a final agreement may not occur.

In ancient Greece, the preliminary method of dispute resolution was mandatory public arbitration.[21] However, while termed "arbitration" the arbitrator's initial goal was to assist the parties in settling their disputes. It was only if the parties were unable to reach a settlement that the arbitrator then rendered a verdict.[22]

Informal dispute resolution was used in many other cultures as well. For example, Scandinavian fishermen, African tribes, and Israeli Kibbutzim all valued peace and harmony over conflict, litigation and victory.[23] The use of mediation in a historical perspective can also be seen in attempts at resolution of matters between disputing nations.[24] Some of the principles of informal dispute resolution, or mutual satisfaction in settlement rather than conceding power, made their way to the United States.

2. UNITED STATES

The history of current mediation use in the United States has two distinct roots, neither of which is within the formal legal system. One course by which mediation developed was as a method of providing community justice. Disputes in the labor arena was the other area of historical development. It is only relatively recently that the courts have considered the use of mediation.

Often overlooked is the application of facilitative approaches to conflict by both Native Americans and colonists. In the Native American culture, peacemaking is the primary method of problem solving. Conciliatory in its approach, peacemaking is concerned with sacred justice. Disputes are handled in a way which deals with underlying causes of conflict, and mends relationships.[25] Native Americans continue to use peacemaking today.[26]

18. Donald C. Clark, *Dispute Resolution in China*, 5 J. Chinese L. 245, 270 (1991).

19. Folberg & Taylor, *supra* note 17, at 49.

20. A number of books have been recently published on Japanese negotiation style. See, for example, Edward T. Hall, Hidden Differences: Doing Business with Japanese (1987), Chi Nakan, Japanese Society (1970); and generally, U.S. Department of State, National Negotiating Styles (Hans Binnendijk, ed., 1987).

21. Aristotle, The Athenian Constitution, reprinted in THE ATHENIAN CONSTITUTION 98 (1984).

22. *Id.*

23. Jerold S. Auerbach, Justice Without Law 8 (1983).

24. Jacob Bercovitch, *The Structure and Diversity of Mediation in International Relations*, in Mediation in International Relations 2 (Jacob Bercovitch and Jeffery Z. Rubin eds., 1992).

25. For more detail on Native American Peacemaking, see generally Special Issue, 10 Mediation Q. 327 (1993).

Upon settlement in the United States, various groups within the colonies placed a major emphasis on maintenance of peace. The close proximity of living arrangements, along with the need for joint efforts in survival against the crown, contributed to peacekeeping endeavors.[27] The cultural priority of community consensus over an individual, adversarial approach to conflict served as the basis for the use of mediation and other informal means of dispute settlement.[28] In addition, many colonists had developed a negative view of the legal profession, and consequently the use of litigation as a means of dispute settlement was explicitly discouraged. Accordingly, these settlers went about settling their own disputes.[29]

By the end of the seventeenth century, however, use of these non-legalistic dispute resolution methods was in decline. A number of factors accounted for this. The population increased, and with growth and mobility, the sense of community dissipated. Moreover, the development of commerce and industry resulted in more complex dealings, use of documents, and the need for commercial laws. A large portion of common law, initially avoided, was then seen as practical and acceptable, though not in all respects.[30] Competitiveness replaced a cooperative approach to problem solving, and overt conflict increased. Litigation took a greater role in the resolution of disputes by providing a framework for order and authority.[31]

The other distinct area in which mediation was historically used was in labor relations. In the early industrial United States, when disputes occurred within business, quick resolutions were imperative. This was particularly important where the conflict was between labor and management, and if left unresolved, could lead to strikes and a shut down of industry. As labor became unionized and disputes were common, Congress reacted in 1913 by creating the Department of Labor, and providing that the Secretary of Labor act as mediator.[32] Mediation was used so that disputes could be settled expeditiously and strikes could be avoided. A speedy resolution promoted the ongoing relationship between the disputing factions, which was very important to the continued economic development of the United States. As the area of labor relations developed,[33] and need for mediation increased, Congress, in 1947, created the Federal Mediation and Conciliation Service (FMCS).[34] An independent federal agency, FMCS has jurisdiction over disputes in industries which

---

26. Diane LeResch Editor's Notes, 10 Mediation Q. 321 (1993).

27. Susan L. Donegan, *ADR in Colonial America: A Covenant For Survival*, 48 Arb. J. 14 (1993).

28. Auerbach, *supra* note 23, at 20.

29. *Id.* at 23.

30. Paul S. Reinsch, English Common Law in the Early American Colonies 6 (1898).

31. Auerbach, *supra* note 23, at 71.

32. See William E. Simkin, and Nicholas A. Fidandis, Mediation and the Dynamics of Collective Bargaining 25 (2d ed. 1986).

33. For a complete perspective of mediation in the labor area, see *Id.*

34. *Id.* at 38.

engage in interstate commerce, private non-profit health facilities, and agencies of the federal government.[35] The Federal Mediation and Conciliation Service is still quite active today, primarily focused on mediating in labor disputes.[36]

For the general population, courts became the primary dispute resolvers, replacing communities and churches. Yet dissatisfaction with the courts was expressed. This dissatisfaction primarily centered on issues of expense and time, although there was some concern with the complete legalization of disputes[37] as well as the relinquishment of decision making to outside parties. This dissatisfaction served as the catalyst for the current ADR movement. While the current use of mediation has retained some of its historical flavor and philosophy, its primary focus is serving as an alternative or adjunct to the courts.

3. CURRENT "MOVEMENT"

The current ADR movement is most often regarded as beginning with the Pound Conference in 1976.[38] Prior to that, however, there existed several programs, a few of which originally came about as a response to the conflict surrounding the civil rights movement. Others originated as an alternative method of community justice. For example, the American Arbitration Association (AAA)[39] was active in setting up pilot mediation projects funded by the Ford Foundation in the late sixties. These projects were an attempt to ease social tensions through the use of mediation. In the early seventies, the American Arbitration Association also established Dispute Resolution Centers in Philadelphia and Rochester, New York. Cases were referred to the centers from the local court system.[40]

In 1971, through a grant from the United States Department of Justice, Law Enforcement Assistance Administration (LEAA), the Columbus, Ohio City Prosecutor's Office established a mediation program for citizens' disputes. This was likely the first court-system sponsored dispute resolution program. It utilized law students who served as mediators to help resolve disputes involving minor criminal actions. In 1977 the program was designated by LEAA as exemplary, and its replication throughout the country was encouraged.[41] In 1975 the Institute for Mediation and Conflict Resolution opened in New York City, which pioneered mediation program development on the East coast. While these programs introduced mediation to the legal system and selected communities, there was no systematic development or coordination of these mediation programs until the Pound Conference.

---

35. Deborah M. Kolb, The Mediators 7 (1983).

36. *Id.*

37. Auerbach, *supra* note 23, at 120.

38. See Warren E. Burger, *Isn't There a Better Way*, 68 ABA Journal 268 (1982).

39. The AAA, a not for profit corporation established in 1926 with a primary focus on the arbitration of labor matters, is apparently the oldest private provider of arbitration services in the United States.

40. Paul Wahrhaftig, *Non–Professional Conflict Resolution in Mediation: Contexts and Challenges* 49 (Joseph E. Polenski and Harold M. Launer, eds., 1986).

41. *Id.* at 50.

The Pound Conference was called to commemorate the 70th anniversary of Dean Roscoe Pound's dissertation on the public's dissatisfaction with the American legal system.[42] It was at this Conference that the current "movement" was actually born. Conference attendees included federal judges, court administrators, and legal scholars in the American Bar Association who wanted to take a closer look at exactly why people were so dissatisfied with the way justice was administered in the United States. One focus was on the often criticized, overcrowded, and costly court system. The conference consisted of a series of discussions and debates, and a follow-up task force was established.

One result of the conference was a pilot project, consisting of the creation of three Neighborhood Justice Centers (NJC).[43] These centers were to be located in Kansas City, Los Angeles, and Atlanta, and were designed to determine if the mediation process could assist in resolving minor disputes. Funding for the creation of these pilot centers and their evaluation was obtained from the Law Enforcement Assistance Administration (LEAA) Division of the United States Department of Justice. Each center proved to be successful in bringing about timely and inexpensive resolutions of disputes.[44] Cases were referred to the centers from local courts, and most cases were either misdemeanor criminal cases or small claims civil cases.[45] Trained volunteers from diverse backgrounds and socio-economic status served as mediators,[46] and in most instances the services were offered at no cost to the disputants. Party satisfaction with the process was high.[47] Based partially upon the results from these three centers, additional experimental centers were established. Today there are over 400 centers throughout the country. While the centers were designed to provide a form of community justice, most were related to the legal system, by either court or local bar association sponsorship.[48] Many centers have expanded to handle more than "minor" matters, and are not located in the neighborhoods. Hence, most have been renamed Dispute Resolution Centers. There is at least one in every state, and many states have a system wide network of centers.[49]

In many jurisdictions, the work of these centers led to the development of ADR use in the court system. There are a number of reasons which account for this transition. First, many of the centers were located

---

42. Roscoe Pound, *The Causes of Popular Dissatisfaction with the Administration of Justice*, (1906), reprinted in 20 J. Am. Jud. Soc'y. 178 (1936) and as Appendix B in The Pound Conference: Perspectives on Justice in the Future (A. Leo Levin et al. eds., 1979).

43. Griffen B. Bell, Report of Pound Conference Follow-up Task Force, August 1976.

44. Royer F. Cook, et al., Neighborhood Justice Centers Field Test: Final Evaluation Report (1980).

45. Edith B. Primm, The *Neighborhood Justice Movement*, 81 Ky. L.J. 1067, 1070 (1992–93).

46. *Id.* at 1069.

47. Cook, *supra* note 44.

48. One exception is the San Francisco Community Boards Program which is independent of either a court or bar association.

49. Public Services Division of the American Bar Association, Section of Dispute Resolution, 1993 Dispute Resolution Program Directory (1993).

in or near the courthouse. Second, since the programs were often sponsored by bar associations, many of the individuals who worked as center volunteers were attorneys and judges. These lawyers and judges observed firsthand the benefits of mediation and recognized that ADR processes were successful in resolving many problems. Those involved began to believe that if these processes work well in smaller matters, perhaps they would be helpful in larger ones as well.[50] The applicability of ADR in pending lawsuits became clear.

Simultaneously, the idea of a "multi-door" courthouse began to surface. This concept, which was first articulated by Professor Frank E.A. Sander at the Pound Conference,[51] basically consists of a process by which an individual can locate the most appropriate method of resolving a dispute. There is one building, or courthouse, where individuals can go to obtain a multitude of services. The individual seeking assistance would first see an interviewer, called an intake specialist, who would help assess the problem. Thereafter, the party would be directed to the most appropriate "door" for resolution of the problem. Behind these doors an individual could find a number of processes including mediation, arbitration, litigation and social services.

In the mid-eighties, the ABA Standing Committee on Dispute Resolution sponsored and assisted in the establishment of experimental multi-door centers in three cities: Tulsa, Houston, and Washington, D.C. Additional multi-door courthouses have been created in Burlington, New Jersey and Middlesex County, Massachusetts. The design of this experiment, with the location of these "doors" within the courthouse, led many to realize the applicability of ADR processes to disputes even after a lawsuit was filed. Judges heard about these processes, and noted that while most cases settle, they do so very late in the case. Judges realized that by referring a matter to a dispute resolution process early, a settlement could occur more expeditiously—with generally more satisfied participants. By the late eighties, experimentation with ADR in pending litigation was on-going. Today, in many state and federal courts ADR is an integral part of pre-trial procedure.

C. DISSECTION OF THE MEDIATION PROCESS

Discussions about what mediation is are plentiful. Because of its inherent flexibility and wide application, mediation is an art, not a

---

50. When alternatives to the courthouse were initially developed, only minor cases were to be handled. When the ABA created its first committee on this subject, it was termed the *Special Committee on the Resolution of Minor Disputes*. As the movement grew, so did the status of the committee and its work. Soon there was the *Standing Committee on Dispute Resolution*, and 1993

saw the birth of the ABA Dispute Resolution Section.

51. Professor Sander of Harvard Law School initially outlined the concept in a paper he presented at the Pound Conference: Frank E. A. Sander, *Varieties of Dispute Processing in The Pound Conference: Perspectives on Justice in the Future* (A. Leo Levin et al. eds., 1979).

science. Debate occurs about whether, as an art, it can be learned. While many purport that mediators are born, not made, mediation training occurs every day. And although the mediator may be seen as an artist with attendant creativity, the process itself is subject to some technical analysis.

1. GENERALLY: TRADITIONAL MODELS

Mediation has been given many definitions, the broadest being simply the facilitation of a settlement between individuals. The intermediary or mediator serves essentially as a go-between for individuals or groups with different opinions, outlooks, ideas, and interests. Over the years of mediation's growth, numerous outlines or views of the process have developed. As individuals became familiar with the fundamentals of mediation, a number of modifications occurred. However, it is important to first become familiar with the basics of each stage of the mediation process. Authors and trainers have outlined the stages or segments of mediation. These may range from a four or five-stage model to one with ten or more stages. The majority of models set forth similar basic concepts and recognize the inherent fluidity of the process.

For educational purposes, the process can be separated into nine distinct stages, all of which should be present in nearly every mediation. In addition, four components of the process are considered optional. While these stages are generally considered important to the mediation process, they frequently occur as part of another stage. Resolution may also be reached without all of these steps. The optional stages are listed in parentheses, at the approximate points where they might be used. Employment of these optional stages will depend upon the parties, the nature of the matter, and the mediator's style. The basic model is as follows:

Preliminary Arrangements

Mediator's Introduction

Opening Statements by Parties

(Ventilation)

Information Gathering

Issue & Interest Identification

(Agenda Setting)

(Caucus)

Option Generation

(Reality Testing)

Bargaining and Negotiation

Agreement

Closure

While each of these stages will be examined in detail throughout the remainder of the text, the following provides a brief introductory description of each.

The preliminary arrangement stage encompasses everything that happens prior to beginning the actual mediation session. This includes matters of referral, getting to the mediation table, selection of the mediator, the determination of who should attend, issues of fees, settlement authority issues, timing and court orders. Moreover, from the standpoint of the mediator, this stage also includes items such as gathering or gaining information from the parties or their attorneys, as well as dissemination of information about the mediator and mediation process to the parties. Selection of the location, the room or rooms to be used, and arrangement of furniture are also part of the preliminary arrangements stage of the process. Because it is the first stage, initial decisions about the process[52] are made as part of preliminary arrangements. The impact on the process is considerable, and the importance of preliminary matters should not be overlooked.

The mediator's introduction is just that. The mediator introduces himself, the parties, and their representatives, describes the process, and sets out any ground rules that will be followed. By doing this, the mediator provides time for the parties to become comfortable. Goals and objectives from the mediator's standpoint may be set out here, as well as any housekeeping details. This introduction sets the stage for the remainder of the mediation.

In the opening statements, the parties and/or their representatives are invited to make an uninterrupted presentation of their views of the case or dispute. It is important that each side be given this opportunity and not be interrupted by either the other party or the mediator. The opening statement stage is the time for parties to fully express and explain to the mediator, and, more importantly, to each other, in their own words, how they view the dispute. Ideally there should be little restriction placed on the opening statements. However, in complex, multi-party cases, it may be necessary to establish time limits.

If the parties' opening statements do not provide a clear or complete picture of what the dispute is about, as often they do not, the mediator will engage the parties in an information gathering process. In most instances additional information is necessary, and the mediator should ask open-ended questions. During either the opening statements or during the information gathering process, the disputing parties may need to express their feelings. This is termed venting or ventilation. It is important to afford individuals an opportunity to vent their frustration, anger, and other emotions. If such emotions are not expressed, the dispute often cannot be resolved.

52. As the various views of what mediation really is have developed and evolved, attempts at regulation of type and style are currently underway. One method currently in use is a requirement that the mediator inform the parties of the style of mediation which will be used. See Carl T. Hahn, *Using Evaluative Techniques: The Virginia Approach*, 16 Alternatives to the High Cost of Litigation, 149 (1998).

Once it appears that sufficient information about the case has been exchanged, the mediator will attempt to identify exactly what issues are in dispute. This may or may not be similar to identifying the underlying interests of the parties.[53] Once the mediator has the issues identified, he will move the parties toward generating ideas, options, or alternatives which might resolve the case. It is usually during these two stages (identifying issues and underlying interests and option generation) that the mediator may meet privately with each party. This private meeting is also termed a caucus. It is advisable, however, that some attempt at issue identification take place while the parties are together so that there is an agreement between the disputing parties and the mediator as to the actual issues in dispute. In complex cases, the mediator may also want to set an agenda, that is, determine which issues will be dealt with in a specific order. A variety of strategies are useful in agenda setting.

Once the potential options for settlement have been identified by the parties and the mediator, the negotiation process begins. This is the "give and take" part of the mediation, where the mediator assists the parties in their bargaining. As part of this process, the mediator may also engage in "reality testing" that is, checking out with each side the realistic possibility of attaining what he or she is hoping for. If the parties are in a purely positional bargaining approach,[54] this will also help to move them off unrealistic positions.

If the negotiations result in an agreement, the mediator will restate it and, in many instances, draft either the complete agreement or a memorandum of settlement. If no agreement is reached, the mediator will restate where the parties are, noting any progress made in the process. The final stage of the process is closure, although in some models there is subsequent action on the part of the mediator.

While the process usually consists of these stages, it is designed to be flexible, and often there is variation in the occurrence of one or more of the stages. Some of the stages may overlap, and many times the mediator must revisit one or more of the stages.

A number of mediation trainers see the stages a bit differently. Moore has described the process as including twelve stages, five of which take place prior to the actual mediation session. These pre-session events include collecting background information, designing a plan for mediation, and building trust and cooperation.[55]

One of the oldest ongoing programs, The Columbus, Ohio, Night Prosecutor Program, in conjunction with the Center for Dispute Resolution at Capital University Law and Graduate Center, utilizes a seven-stage model of mediation. The stages are

- Introduction

53. Identifying the interests is at the core of Principled Negotiation, as set forth by Roger Fisher, William Ury, and Bruce Patton, Getting to Yes, 2d Ed. (1991).

54. The various types of negotiation are explored in Chapter 9.

55. Moore, *supra* note 6, at 33–34.

- Problem determination
- Summarizing
- Issue identification
- Generation and evaluation of alternatives
- Selection of appropriate alternatives
- Conclusion[56]

Folberg and Taylor also use a seven stage model, which is as follows:

1. Introduction
2. Fact finding and isolation of issues
3. Creation of options and alternatives
4. Negotiation and decision-making
5. Clarification and writing a plan
6. Legal review and processing
7. Implementation, review, and revision

They acknowledge that not all stages will be completed in every case, and that other authors and practitioners may divide the stages differently or use different labels.[57] Compared with most models, this model is "bottom heavy"; the majority of models do not focus on activity after an agreement is reached.

2. RECENT ADAPTATIONS AND MODIFICATIONS

It is beyond this work to belabor the discussion about the use of the more traditional model, also labeled purist or classic, versus recent adaptations and modifications. Even where the process is traditional, the mediator possesses a great amount of control in how mediation is conducted. The ability to adapt and modify the mediation process is a primary benefit of its use. Yet some argue whether "true" mediation exists, or whether it should be called something else. For instance, one well known critique was that once court systems and lawyers were integrated with mediation, it was the end of "good" mediation.[58] It is true that some of the most dramatic changes have been within the legal field. At this stage of mediation use, there is great diversity in practice. For example, some lawyers have simplified the process and divided it into three primary segments or stages: joint session, caucus and conclusion. From a learning or descriptive standpoint, this is too simple and does not provide any indication about what is going on in terms of the problem-solving process. The focus is on where the parties and mediator meet, rather than on the phases, and how the activity within those stages lead to settlement or resolution.

56. Mitchell and Dewhirst, *supra* note 5, at 15.

57. Folberg and Taylor, *supra* note 17, at 22.

58. Statement of Albie Davis, in James J. Alfini, *Styles of Mediation: Trashing, Bashing and Hashing It Out: Is this the End of "Good Mediation"?* 19 Fla. St. U. L. Rev. 47 (1991).

Other modifications have occurred as well. With the increased use of mediation in a greater variety of cases, it has become clear that the basic one-time intervention model may not work in all cases. As mediation was originally designed, particularly by those outside of the labor field, it was viewed as a single intervention. The mediator sat down with the parties and either an agreement was reached that day or it was not. Only in rare instances where another individual or additional information was needed, would the mediation session be rescheduled. However, in some cases, because of the number of parties involved, and the complexity or the nature of the dispute, modification of the single mediation session approach was appropriate.

Family law disputes were the first and most common cases to utilize the multi-session approach. Mediation in family cases is quite different and will be examined in more detail in Chapter 16. Because of the emotional issues involved and the nature of the disputes between the parties, many of the original divorce mediation practitioners felt that the mediation sessions should be broken down over a period of weeks. The parties need time to adjust to their renegotiated relationship and to think through major life changes. Consequently, divorce mediation sessions are often limited to approximately an hour, and take place once a week until all matters are settled.

Another arena in which mediation takes place over an extended period of time is that of public policy matters.[59] In cases of public policy, there are a number of people and groups with a variety of interests involved. It is often impossible to get everyone together at one time, in one place, with all issues on the table. Therefore, the mediation may take place in stages. Likewise, in some complex commercial disputes, the mediator may choose to resolve only portions of the case at a time. Fortunately, the mediation process is adaptable and has been used successfully in all of these instances.

Yet despite concerns about the evolution of mediation and the ongoing debate and dispute in the field about the process itself, scholars and experts maintain optimism about the potential of mediation.

LELA PORTER LOVE, MEDIATION: THE ROMANTIC DAYS CONTINUE
38 S.Tex. L. Rev. 735, 735–37, 743–44 (1997).

* * *

It must be remembered that there is nothing more difficult to plan, more doubtful of success, nor more dangerous to manage, than the creation of a new system. For the initiator has the enmity of all who would profit by the preservation of the old institutions and merely lukewarm defenders in those who would gain by the new ones.

With these prophetic words of Niccolo Machiavelli, Dean Read of South Texas College of Law welcomed the participants to the Symposi-

---

59. This approach is examined in greater detail in Chapter 16.

um on The Lawyer's Duties and Responsibilities in Dispute Resolution ("Symposium").

Dean Read, and other speakers at the Symposium, stood under a large, striking portrait of Abraham Lincoln studying a book with a young man. The Lincoln portrait seemed to address the particular audience of distinguished dispute resolution practitioners and mediation scholars with Lincoln's often-quoted statement: "Discourage litigation. . . . Persuade your neighbors to compromise whenever you can. Point out to them how the nominal winner is often the real loser—in fees, expenses, and waste of time. As a peacemaker the lawyer has a superior opportunity of becoming a good [person]."

Professor Carrie Menkel–Meadow, the first panelist to speak, opened her presentation with the disquieting observation that "[t]he romantic days of ADR appear to be over." Professor Menkel–Meadow's conclusion was based on several factors: 1) the pressing need for potentially limiting policing, codes of ethics, standards of practice, and rules in a field that initially attracted proponents with its promise of flexibility, adaptability, and creativity; 2) the institutionalization and routinization of ADR by diverse practitioners and institutions who have contradictory goals; and 3) the co-optation of mediation by lawyers operating out of an adversarial paradigm who misuse mediation as one more tool in their arsenal to help "win" their case. The coming-of-age of mediation, with the accompanying appendages and strictures of maturity, was presented as dry and formalistic in contrast to the revolutionary fervor of mediation's early years.

Notwithstanding Carrie Menkel–Meadow's opening remarks, the Symposium was lively and marked by the usual optimism and enthusiasm of ADR proponents. Several intense debates fueled the discussions. Should mediators evaluate? Is mediation the practice of law? Participants on the panels and in the debates could not agree, and so the specific issues were not resolved. However, in reviewing exchanges from the Symposium—whether or not I endorsed particular positions on ethical questions—I was intrigued over the common themes and shared visions among the scholars and practitioners present and pleased by the love and enthusiasm for the subject matter.

To the extent there are shared values and similar visions among scholars and practitioners, this common ground may be fashioned into a system to resolve ethical dilemmas. Put another way, we cannot resolve dilemmas without defining the process and the values which give rise to them in the first place. Just as the discovery of common ground is enormously powerful in the mediation context, as the mediation process becomes increasingly utilized, a bright focus on the formative vision and a clear definition of the essential nature of the process is necessary.

As mediation grows in use and acceptance, it has potential access to power, influence, opportunity, and freedom that is tremendously exciting so long as the idealism which characterized its birth and growth can be retained. I came away from the Symposium feeling that—like good mediators—we should work on clarifying common ground and points of agreement before tackling differences.

* * *

To direct and guide the debate, as well as the necessary research, toward answering the difficult ethical issues involved in mediation practice, we must first find our commonalities and articulate our guiding values and principles.

We are in the process of establishing a new paradigm for resolving disputes sharply different from the adjudicative process and its legacy of untold numbers of published decisions. That new ethical codes and rules must be established, that there are turf wars over credentialing and the right to practice, are to be expected. The romantic days of mediation continue because the paradigm it embodies, its underlying values and vision, are as compelling and laden with potential as ever. The old paradigm is (for some) unappealing and (for all) insufficient if we are truly going to offer alternative dispute resolution. The scholars and practitioners, who disagree with respect to particular ethical issues, seem to have points of agreement on core values which need to be explored and more fully articulated.

* * *

Let us hope that in creating a new system we can navigate the dangers that Machiavelli forecast, we can deliver on Abe Lincoln's advice, and we can continue the excitement despite Professor Menkel–Meadow's warning.

In the midst of the student uprisings to end the Vietnam War, a paper was circulated with the following quote: "It was only a small dream of the Golden World. Now you trot off to bed." I can neither locate the quote nor remember its author, but the quote was unforgettable because it galvanized an intent not to "trot off," like an obedient child who has been restored to the status quo view. Mediation represents a large dream, an exciting paradigm. Let's not trot off to court.

D. THE ROLE OF A MEDIATOR

We have looked at the mediation process, but just what a mediator does with it is often a key to its effectiveness. What, then, is the role of this person? The simplest description of the mediator's role is that of a facilitator. But how one facilitates differs. How does he move the parties through the stages of the mediation process? Compiling a complete list of the different hats that a mediator must wear can be an extensive exercise. A mediator has sometimes been called a traffic cop, particularly in directing the communication. A conductor of the negotiation is another role that the mediator plays. Throughout the process the role of the mediator changes. Sometimes the mediator will have to supervise, even parent, the parties. Other times, the mediator will be a teacher, not only in assisting the parties to learn the subject matter of their dispute, but also in teaching the process. At other times the mediator is a clarifier. The mediator can also serve in the role of an advocate. Not for the parties, but for the process and settlement. Attorney mediators seem to often adopt the role of devil's advocate, particularly in those cases where a lawsuit is pending. Certainly few would argue with the role of the mediator as a catalyst, moving the parties in the direction of resolution. Mediators have also been designated as orchestrators, deal makers,[60] and as translators of comments and proposals.[61]

The foregoing terms are descriptive of the many facets of the mediator's work and usually do not meet with controversy. However, an in-depth examination of how the mediator accomplishes his tasks within this conceptual framework has led to much debate.[62] Specifically, what is it that should be expected of this neutral intervenor?[63] There is concern about the degree of influence the mediator should have on the outcome of the case. For instance, the mediator's role can be viewed as promoting an agreement—at whatever cost, thereby achieving efficiency in settlement.[64] The mediator may thus help the parties meet the goals of saving time and money. Alternatively, the mediator's role may be to protect rights by assuring that the agreements reached in mediation are based upon informed consent.[65] Some mediation analysts even go a step or two further and expect the mediator to assure that the agreements are fair and stable.[66] Others want the mediator not only to ensure that the agreement is fair, but also that it is one which a court would enforce.[67]

Probably the primary area of disagreement about mediation practice concerns the specifics of the role or orientation of the mediator. This is due, at least in part, to modification of the process as utilized in lawsuits. Specifically, the mediator is expected to look at the outcome as measured against the probable court result, and in many instances engages in evaluating or measuring proposed solutions alongside court decisions.[68]

60. Kolb, *supra* note 35, at 23.

61. Joseph B. Stulberg, *Training Interveners for ADR Processes*, 81 Ky. L.J. 977, 987 (1992–93).

62. See, for example, Leonard L. Riskin, *Mediation Oriented Strategies and Techniques*, 12 Alternatives to High Cost Litigation (1994); Kimberlee K. Kovach and Lela P. Love, *Evaluative Mediation is an Oxymoron*, 14 Alternatives to High Cost Litigation 31 (1996); John Bickerman, *An Evaluative Mediator Responds*, 14 Alternatives to High Cost Litigation 70 (1996); John Lande, *Stop Bickering! A Call for Collaboration*, 16 Alternatives to High Cost Litigation 1 (1998). This issue is examined in more detail in Chapters 15 and 16.

63. The role of the mediator in light of fairness, neutrality and ethical considerations is also examined in Chapters 7 and 14.

64. Robert A. Baruch Bush, *Efficiency and Protection, or Empowerment and Recognition?: The Mediator's Role and Ethical Standards in Mediation* 41 Fla. L. Rev. 253, 260 (1989).

65. *Id.* at 261.

66. Lawrence Susskind, *Environmental Mediation and the Accountability Problem* 6 Vt. L. Rev. 1, 18 (1981).

67. Leonard L. Riskin, *Toward New Standards for the Neutral Lawyer in Mediation* 26 Ariz. L. Rev. 329, 354 (1984). Jacqueline M. Nolan–Haley, *Court Mediation and the Search for Justice Through Law*, 74 Wash. U. L. Q. 47 (1996). See also Chapter 7 *infra* which discusses this aspect in greater detail.

68. See Leonard Riskin, *Understanding Mediators' Orientations, Strategies, and Techniques: A Grid for the Perplexed*, 1 Harv. Neg. L. Rev. 7 (1996). Nolan Haley, *supra* note 67.

If the mediator is a neutral before, during and after the mediation, and if he must refrain from making judgments, all of which is dictated by codes of ethics,[69] how can he assume these roles? How can we be sure that the parties want their rights protected or their agreements fair? If self-determination by the parties is an overriding feature of the mediation process,[70] then the mediator's role may be to empower the parties to make their own judgments. As conductor of that process, what should the mediator do to promote self-determination and empowerment? How can the mediator assure that the parties make their own decisions? These are just some of the questions which scholars and practitioners of mediation continue to discuss and debate, and will be explored in more detail in subsequent chapters.

The most important thing to remember about the mediator's role is that the mediator is in control of the process. Mediation works in resolving disputes because of the process, not the person. That, of course, is not to say that a skillful mediator will not be more effective than one possessing less skill. But more often it is the procession through the stages of the process that leads parties to a mutually satisfactory resolution. The role of the mediator then, is to safeguard, maintain, and control the process. In contrast, the parties control the content matter of the dispute. Regardless of the subject matter of the dispute, the process remains the same. **The parties are responsible for the content; the mediator is responsible for the process.**

EXERCISES

2–1. Write down all of the distinct tasks that might encompass the mediator's role. Put the list away. Pull your list out for review upon completion of your tenth mediation.

2–2. When observing a mediation session, either real or simulated, focus on the variety of roles the mediator assumes, noting each role change.

(a) What were the causes of the changes?

(b) Was the mediator more effective in some roles than others?

(c) Were any roles assumed by the mediator inappropriate?

---

69. See Jacqueline M. Nolan–Haley, *Informed Consent in Mediation: A Guiding Principle for Truly Educated Decision–Making*, 74 Notre Dame L. Rev. 775, 789 (1999).

70. Id.; Bush, *supra* note 64, at 270.

Chapter Three

MEDIATOR SKILLS

As the use of mediation increased, and more individuals were educated and trained in the process, a closer examination of just what a mediator did was warranted. As the preceding chapter has suggested, there is little specific agreement about proper mediator conduct. Much depends on when and where mediation is used, as well as the mediator's personal style. There is recognition, however, that a wide variety of skills is necessary. Some individuals come to the mediation table with innate skills. Others must learn them. In most mediation training programs, skill development is a major portion of the educational process. These skills include communication, analytical ability, and patience. Efforts have been underway to determine the specific attributes of an effective mediator.[1] However, no consensus has yet been achieved.

Some mediators have been very detailed in describing what it takes to mediate. For instance, former Federal Mediation and Conciliation Service Director William E. Simkin lists sixteen characteristics which a potential mediator ought to possess:

1. the patience of Job
2. the sincerity and bulldog characteristics of the English
3. the wit of the Irish
4. the physical endurance of the marathon runner
5. the broken field dodging abilities of a halfback
6. the guile of Machiavelli
7. the personality-probing skills of a good psychiatrist
8. the confidence-retaining characteristic of a mute
9. the hide of a rhinoceros
10. the wisdom of Solomon
11. demonstrated integrity and impartiality

1. See, for example, Christopher Honeyman, *On Evaluating Mediators*, 6 Negotiation J. 23 (1990) and Brad Honoroff, et al., *Putting Mediation Skills to the Test*, 6 Negotiation J. 37 (1990). See also Chapter 15.

12. basic knowledge of and belief in the negotiation process

13. firm faith in voluntarism in contrast to dictation

14. fundamental belief in human values and potential, tempered by ability to assess personal weaknesses as well as strengths

15. hard-nosed ability to analyze what is available in contrast to what might be desirable

16. sufficient personal drive and ego, qualified by willingness to be self-effacing.[2]

Another labor mediator has noted that one characteristic may transcend the previous lists; that the mediator must be master of the alternative. The mediator should be capable of eliciting acceptable alternatives to the unobtainable positions of the disputing parties.[3] Just how mediator skills and qualities are assessed have historically presented concerns in the labor field. In fact, it was quickly recognized that all the listed characteristics are not to be found in one person, and are not subject to objective assessment.[4] The main difficulty is that many of these skills are purely subjective and can be demonstrated only by performance. These issues now face the general mediation population.[5]

Mediation is an interdisciplinary field. Mediators come from all walks of life. Each mediator is an individual with a variety of life experiences and a personality that must be used in conjunction with the mediation process. Therefore, after initial training in the process, each trainee is encouraged to develop a personal style, depending on those personal characteristics.[6] Yet uniform skills are necessary. Often questioned is what specific skills are involved in mediating, and whether those skills are innate or can be learned. While many within this field are currently examining issues such as these, no definitive answer has emerged.

Because any dispute resolution or problem solving activity involves communication, certainly one of the most important skills for a mediator is the ability to communicate. Not only does the mediator communicate directly with each of the parties, she also facilitates communication between the parties. Often the conflict or dispute has arisen because of faulty communication or misunderstanding. In fact, communication behavior often creates conflict, and is the vehicle for either productive or destructive management of conflict.[7] Destructive or negative communications patterns then escalate the conflict. It is the mediator's responsibility to assess the communication and facilitate it in a positive, productive manner. In other words, the mediator must try to transform a defensive

2. William E. Simkin & Nicholas A. Fidandis, Mediation and the Dynamics of Collective Bargaining 43 (1986).

3. Walter A. Maggiolo, Techniques of Mediation 73 (1985).

4. Simkin & Fidandis, *supra* note 2, at 44.

5. An in depth examination of these dilemmas is provided in Chapter 15.

6. Some identifiable styles of mediation are reviewed in Chapter 15.

7. Joyce L. Hocker and William W. Wilmot, Interpersonal Conflict 22 (4th Ed. 1995).

communication climate into one that is more supportive.[8] In fact, styles of problem solving have been defined in terms of communication. A cooperative approach to conflict resolution is characterized by an open and honest transmittal of information; whereas, the competitive mode encourages either misleading statements or a lack of communication.[9]

Most of the activity which takes place during a mediation involves sending and receiving information, both verbal and nonverbal. Indeed, it has been observed that mediation is a communication process, and that the solving of legal problems is a mere byproduct.[10] We often take communication, and specifically its listening component, for granted. With practice, however, these skills can be improved.

A. COMMUNICATION

Communication consists of both sending and receiving messages. Some hold that the most important part of the mediator's role is that of a listener or recipient of a message.[11] Although this is certainly a major role of the mediator, it should be recognized that feedback or sending a message is actually part of the listening process as well. While the primary focus of our study is on the communication process during the mediation, it actually begins earlier. Information and messages are conveyed prior to the mediation session. This should not be overlooked, as this initial communication can have great impact upon the rest of the mediation.

Once at the mediation session, the primary focus is on direct interpersonal, or face-to-face communication.[12] The mediator must be cognizant of the constant exchange of messages during the mediation session.

1. VERBAL

Interpersonal communication can take at least four forms, as shown by the following diagrams:

A

Conversation (2 way
communication)

B

Listening (primarily 1 way
communication)

8. Gibb, J. Communication (1961).

9. Morton Deutsch, The Resolution of Conflict 29 (1973).

10. [Panel Discussion Series. Topic 3—1983] *Alternative Dispute Resolution: Mediation and the Law: Will Reason Prevail?* 48 Special Committee on Dispute Resolution, Public Services Division, American Bar Association (Larry Ray, et al. eds., 1983).

11. See Nancy H. Rogers & Richard A. Salem, A Student's Guide to Mediation and the Law 12 (1987).

12. Note, however, that the increased use of the Internet for mediation eliminates many of the communication aspects. This can be positive or problematic with regard to resolution. See for example Joel B. Eisen, *Are We Ready for Mediation in Cyberspace*, 1998 B.Y.U. L. Rev. 1305 (1998). Chapter 17 addresses Internet mediation in greater detail.

```
(1) S  ————————>  R          (2) S  ————————>  R Passive
    R  <————————   S          (3) S  ————————>  R Active
                                      <——————
                               (4) S  ————————>  R Interactive
                                      <——————
```

S=Sender   R=Receiver

Diagram A, which depicts a two-way conversation, illustrates a continuous exchange of information. Both parties in this interpersonal communication take turns sending and receiving information or messages. Diagram B represents the various information exchanges which are more illustrative of the listening process that the mediator will initially engage in. When examining how people listen, it is helpful to think in terms of one person designated as the sender of the message or information, and the other as the receiver. Because listening is a continual process, the various roles may alternate.

In the initial stages of the mediation process, the sender (S) is one of the disputing parties or their representative, attorney, or otherwise. The receiver of the message (R) is the mediator. In example number (2), the pattern is identified as passive listening. Here the sender sends a message and receives no feedback from the listener. Examples of such purely passive listening include receiving information from television and radio. In an interpersonal situation, an example might be a lecture in a large hall, where the speaker fails to receive any response, including direct eye contact.

The third example illustrates the active listening mode. When the sender transmits information, there is feedback provided from the listener. A message is imparted back to the sender that informs the sender that the information has been received. Examples of active listening include the nod of a head or a short acknowledgment that lets the individual know that the message has been heard. Verbal acknowledgements include "oh," "I see," "uh-huh," and "really." Nonverbal messages such as nods, direct eye contact, and various facial expressions can also be very effective in providing feedback to the sender to signify that the message has been received.

In an interactive listening mode, as illustrated by the fourth example, the amount of information in the message from the listener going back to the sender has increased. Interactive listening techniques include brief restatements or parroting of the last few words of the speaker, summations, reflective statements, and paraphrasing. This provides even more feedback to the sender, and allows the listener to check with the speaker about the accuracy of the message as received. Asking follow-up questions is also an extension of the listening process, but this element of the communication process will be covered in a later chapter.[13]

It is very important for the mediator to be a good listener for a number of reasons. First, most individuals with a problem or dispute are

13. See Chapter 6.

very interested in feeling that they have been heard. Often the mediation is the only opportunity that disputing parties will have to voice their concerns or explain to anyone what the conflict is about. The mediation session is, in essence, their "day in court." The mediator then provides them with the opportunity to be heard. Second, in order to competently assist in the problem-solving process, a mediator must have sufficient information about the dispute. It is only with acute listening skills that the mediator will be able to gather the information necessary to identify issues, interests, and alternatives. Third, by demonstrating good listening skills, the mediator not only gathers information, but also simultaneously provides feedback which encourages the speaker to provide additional information.[14] However, some parties have a tendency to ramble during the mediation, and for them the mediator must utilize a technique such as close-ended questioning or restating to terminate the information gathering process. Yet, in most instances, encouragement is appropriate.

As a listener, the mediator should model good listening behavior for the parties. Disputes often exist because people have failed to communicate with each other, or have communicated inaccurately. If one disputing party observes the mediator listening intently when the other is discussing the problem, the first may be encouraged to mirror this behavior. By doing so, the party may more accurately hear another view of the matter. Thus listening can act as a catalyst to move individuals off positions by increasing understanding, which leads to increased opportunities for settlement.

The mediator should also be acutely aware of other aspects of communication which affect the process. For example, the use of fillers such as *um*, *you know*, or pauses can diminish the impact of a statement and distance the individuals, thereby making open communication more difficult.[15] The use of sarcasm, hostile joking or caustic questions also impedes productive communication.

An individual may also attempt to avoid dealing with another's concerns through silencing the opposition. Five basic methods to silence another individual are interrupting, changing the topic, avoiding the topic, blaming internal procedures and definitions side-tracking.[16] The mediator should use her own judgment about intervention when she recognizes the use of these strategies. In some cases, directly addressing the behavior is appropriate while in other instances, a private meeting[17] with the party avoiding the subject is a better approach.

2. NONVERBAL MESSAGES

Most of the discussion thus far has focused on verbal communication. It is also important that the mediator pay attention to the nonver-

---

14. Most individuals, realizing that someone is listening, will continue to talk.

15. Deborah Borisoff & David Victor, Conflict Management: A Communications Skills Approach at 61–63 (1998).

16. *Id.*

17. See Chapter 10 for discussion of private caucusing.

bal communication that occurs. Nonverbal communication takes place through three primary channels of expression: proxemics, kinesics, and paralinguistics.[18] Proxemics includes spatial relationships and their influence on communication. Examples include office design, the type and style of furniture, the seating arrangements, and the physical distance separating all parties. Kinesics is essentially body language. This is what most often is termed nonverbal communication, and includes all physical movement. The paralinguistics portion of nonverbal communication is the vocal portion of the message other than the actual words. These include the pace, pitch, tone, and volume of the message.[19]

All three of these methods of nonverbal communication are important to a mediator analyzing the messages sent by the parties. Proxemics can affect the message in the way it is initially directed. This is the one aspect of communication over which the mediator may have initial control. The mediator can influence proxemics by arranging the time and place of the mediation, as well as the seating arrangement of all the participants.[20]

The paralinguistics portion of speech patterns can also have influence on the message. Voice tone and pitch may accent or contradict the content. The pace and volume of speech also provide a great amount of information about the message. Pauses may be filled or unfilled. Unfilled pauses are different from silence. Filled pauses may also lead listeners to perceive the speaker as anxious.[21] It is imperative that the mediator pay close attention to all of these elements of a message. The skillful mediator will soon learn that it is only by attentiveness to all aspects of a message that the most accurate information will be gathered. And the more accurate the information about the matter is, the better the opportunity for understanding, and hence resolution.

The body language, or kinesics, of the parties can affect the message in a number of ways. In fact, some experts believe nonverbals control the message. Studies have shown that the percentage of communication which is nonverbal varies anywhere from about a 50–50 split, to a 93% nonverbal portion.[22] Often the physical movements of the speaker accent or emphasize part of a message. In other instances, the speaker may substitute a nonverbal communication for the verbal message. Nonverbal communication can also contradict the message conveyed by the spoken words.

Five basic purposes or messages can be transmitted through nonverbal communication. "Emblems" are nonverbal messages such as gestures that are translated directly into words. For example, holding the thumb and forefinger in a circle, with a short jerk and momentary hold

18. Robert M. Bastress & Joseph D. Harbaugh, Interviewing, Counseling and Negotiating 132 (1990).

19. *Id.*

20. See also Chapter 5, § A which will examine this in detail.

21. Borisoff & Victor, *supra* note 15, at 96–97.

22. Roberto Aron, et al., Trial Communication Skills 27 (1986).

signifies "OK" or "good." The receiver of this emblem translates the message directly to the meaning of OK.[23] While the "OK" interpretation is virtually universal in the United States, other cultures attribute other meanings to the same sign.[24]

Another category of nonverbal communication consists of "illustrators," which generally accent or reinforce the verbal message. "Affect displays," demonstrated by the face and body convey an emotional state. These are often performed spontaneously in response to a strong emotion and thus can conflict with the verbal message.[25] "Regulators" are those nonverbal message that accompany speech to control or regulate what the speaker says, for example, a nod of the head. Finally "adaptors", movements that fulfill a personal need, such as scratching oneself or twisting paper clips, are often performed without direct awareness and generally increase with anxiety.[26]

The mediator, in the role of listener, must be certain to listen to the two parts of a message: the content or substantive part of the message as well as the affective or feeling part of the message. Most messages have both cognitive and emotional elements, although it is rare that these are evenly split. In some instances where the parties are in need of venting and expressing their feelings, the content portion is small. In other situations, it is the substantive information which is more important. The primary emphasis of the message will usually be evident from the manner of communication, but the mediator should always be aware of both parts of the message.

A word of caution. While in interactive communication, the mediator, as a listener, should acknowledge the individual's feelings, she must be careful not to focus so much on the emotional part of the message that the mediation becomes, in essence, a therapy session.

Although it is imperative for the mediator to be a good listener and ascertain the entirety of each person's message at the mediation, her role differs from that of other individuals in the problem solving process. The mediator does not make a decision as to the truth or veracity of anything that is stated. Therefore, although it is important to listen and to observe the nonverbal behavior, the mediator must do so without regard to the need to determine the facts or who is telling the truth. Moreover, it is important that when listening, the mediator does so in an objective fashion. Part of the mediator's role is to assist the parties in looking at the dispute in a more neutral fashion. Therefore, the mediator must be nonjudgmental in the listening process.

3. GENDER AND CULTURAL CONSIDERATIONS

The mediator should be aware of both gender and cultural factors that contribute to any difficulties in the communication between the

23. Borisoff & Victor *supra* note 15, at 83.

24. See *infra* Section 3 for a discussion of culture and communication.

25. Borisoff & Victor, *supra* note 15, at 85.

26. *Id.* at 87.

parties or with the mediator. The mediator should also recognize that other factors may affect the quality of the communications, such as differences in communication styles, and the assumptions parties may make. While the mediator cannot change communication patterns for the individuals, her awareness of these differences can assist with facilitating the mediation.

The mediator must also guard against reliance on her own stereotypes. For example, if she believes that women just naturally express emotion more than men, she may fail to consider individual differences. Should a female party refuse to express emotion, the mediator *may* want to privately inquire. On the other hand, an overly emotional male should not be made to feel embarrassed or uncomfortable.

Cultural differences can also contribute to the difficulty in mediation. While cross-cultural mediation is often considered a specialized application,[27] awareness of the cultural influence on both communication patterns and conflict behavior is important for the mediator. And these considerations vary widely. For example, in the United States it is common, even expected, that a listener would make direct eye contact with a speaker. As noted earlier, such direct eye contact is considered a method of active listening. In other cultures, however, it may be considered disrespectful to prolong eye contact with those who are older. And yet in other situations, the intensity of eye contact can be so great that Americans are uncomfortable.[28]

B. NOTE–TAKING AND ORGANIZATION

Even though the mediator is busy paying attention to all parts of the messages conveyed, she will most likely also need to be taking notes. Note-taking during listening varies from individual to individual. In complex cases it is very important that notes be taken. It is often the role of the mediator to keep the information straight and to refocus the parties on the main issues. On the other hand, if the mediator is too intent on writing everything down, there is little time or ability to pick up on any of the nonverbal communication. Moreover, one of the most important elements of nonverbal communication is eye contact or oculesics. The mediator may find it difficult to maintain eye contact with the speaker when taking copious notes. The use of phrases and abbreviations in note-taking can be very helpful in this regard.

There is much debate on the amount of note-taking necessary in mediation, and finding the right balance is critical. In many other interview situations, the use of a tape-recording device is suggested.[29] However, because of the confidential nature of mediation, audio or videotaping is strongly discouraged, and in many instances may be

---

27. See Chapter 16, Section L.

28. Borisoff & Victor, *supra* note 15 at 187–188.

29. David A. Binder, et al., Lawyers as Counselors: A Client–Centered Approach 195 (1990).

prohibited. Furthermore, many individuals are reluctant to open up if a recording device is used.

Individuals react differently to note-taking. Some perceive that if someone is writing down what they are saying, then it is more important or relevant than comments that were not recorded. In response, they will emphasize that portion of the discussion even more. On the other hand, there are those who measure the importance of their remarks by the amount of direct eye contact. These matters are then stressed by the speaker. To prevent the parties' inaccurate placement of emphasis on the mediator's note-taking behavior, the mediator should include in her introductory remarks an explanation of note-taking. She should explain that the purpose of taking notes is only to assist the mediator in maintaining accuracy of the information.

Data organization is also part of the information gathering and note-taking process.[30] The manner in which the mediator arranges the information can help the parties focus on the primary issues of the dispute, particularly in complex cases or in the family arena where the mediation occurs over a period of time. By her organization, the mediator assists the parties in looking at the dispute in a systematic manner, which can produce a fresh view of the case. Many parties are then better able to engage in the problem solving process.

How to proceed in note-taking and organizing the data, like many other elements of the mediation process, will be individual decisions for the mediator. However, as with all mediator skills, one will find that as she progresses in the process, experimentation with different methods will assist in finding the right balance.

C. COUNSELING AND CALMING SKILLS

Just as the role of a mediator is not to be an advocate for a party in a legal dispute, so should she refrain from therapeutic intervention.[31] However, this is not to say that some skill and knowledge in counseling cannot be helpful. General empathetic understanding is essential if the mediator is to establish rapport and trust with the parties. Demonstrating awareness of the feelings of those in dispute can provide a positive environment for the exchange of information and pave the way toward resolution. Providing a safe environment where the parties feel comfortable venting their feelings is also part of the mediator's role. However, the mediator must not allow ventilation to become uncontrollable. Parameters or guidelines for venting can be helpful. Venting emotions is important in and of itself, that is, individuals often feel better after expressing their emotions. Moreover, during the ventilation, additional,

30. Jay Folberg & Alison Taylor, Mediation: A Comprehensive Guide to Resolving Conflicts Without Litigation 125 (1984).

31. While some divergence of opinion exists, most mediators contend that providing *any type* of professional advice by the mediator is generally not advised. See Chapters 14 and 15.

often important, information may be revealed. This is termed constructive ventilation. On the other hand, venting can become destructive when it includes threats, name calling, emphatic blaming or repetition. Destructive ventilation should be stopped by the mediator. And while it is the better practice to allow the parties to vent directly to one another, in some potentially volatile situations, the mediator should meet separately with the party to allow controlled private venting.

In cases of overt conflict, the mediation session itself can be a stressful situation for the participants and the mediator.[32] The subject matter of the mediation may be a highly emotional topic. It is common for disputants to experience emotions such as frustration, anger, sadness, and grief during the process. Basic calming techniques, such as softening of the voice, providing tissue, and a light touch on the arm are all useful when a party demonstrates overt emotions. The mediator must be comfortable dealing with these emotional aspects of mediation. In fact, it has been suggested that an important part of becoming a mediator is sensitization to the feelings of others as well as self.[33] Specific counseling techniques employed by the mediator depend upon the nature of the emotion expressed by the party. It is imperative, however, that the mediator refrain from becoming emotionally involved in the matter. Although a demonstration of empathetic understanding is appropriate, the mediator must remain objective and neutral.

D. HUMAN BEHAVIOR AND MOTIVATION: THE MEDIATOR'S ROLE

A thorough analysis of human behavior and motivation is beyond the scope of this work. Likewise, such analysis is beyond the parameters of the mediator's role. Yet, to achieve resolution of a matter, much of the mediator's work will involve motivating human behavior. While the mediator will not actively attempt to influence the specific resolutions of the parties, she should be aware of human decision making behavior. A variety of psychological theories about motivation exist, none of which is strongly advocated as a basis for the mediator's work. However, in general terms, a mediator should remember that people are motivated by needs. Individuals will likely choose a course of action by which needs can thereby be met. Ascertaining these needs or interests is part of the mediator's role. This is very similar to the identification of interests examined in Chapter 8.

Group dynamics also play a significant role in the behavior of the participants in a mediation. A mediation, particularly when structured in a collaborative, problem-solving format, is a collective enterprise; and, as a consequence, group dynamics must be considered.[34] Even apart from

---

32. Mediator *mental health* is a virtually unexplored aspect of mediation practice.

33. Folberg & Taylor, *supra* note 30, at 87.

34. For an in-depth examination of group dynamics, see Deborah G. Ancona, et al., *The Group and What Happens on the Way to "Yes,"* 7 Negotiation J. 155 (1991).

the mediation process, individuals involved in a dispute, and especially those in a lawsuit, can clearly be identified as a *group*. A group is defined as two or more individuals who have at least one characteristic in common, form a distinguishable identity, are aware of positive interdependence of goals, interact, and pursue goals together.[35] As time passes, the group develops norms which guide interaction along with roles composed of specific activities, obligations, and rights.[36] It is likely that the longer the duration of the dispute, the more firmly established these behavioral patterns become. The mediator must first determine what they are. Thereafter, she may need to decide whether these patterns are constructive or destructive with regard to resolution of the matter. If destructive, the mediator may try to influence the group behavior and effect change in the patterns of conduct.

There may also be subgroups within the larger group. For instance, an ongoing group may exist prior to the mediation where the lawyers for the parties have worked together in the past. Specific behavior may have been previously established as the group norm. There may already be a designated leader of the group. It is important for the mediator to pay attention to these dynamics and to recognize what elements of the group are able to be changed as well as those which are not subject to modification. Most importantly, the mediator must determine the influence these dynamics have upon the conflict.

EXERCISES

3–1. The next time a friend or colleague engages you in conversation, pay special attention to the nonverbal parts of the message. Afterwards ask if you may check the accuracy of your perceptions.

3–2. Experiment with your friends and colleagues in both giving and receiving messages. Vary the nonverbals and the paralinguistics, while keeping the content the same. Note how the message, and subsequent reaction, can change.

3–3. You are mediating a dispute between several neighbors in a subdivision. The dispute involves ambiguous deed restrictions. The parties, about ten different families, have been embroiled in this conflict for nearly two years. The first group, comprised of seven couples, is intent on a strict construction of the restriction providing that residences are only for residential purposes. They contend that any hint of commercial use is a violation of the restrictions. Their goal is to enforce these restrictions against the Tuens, who offer piano, voice, and guitar lessons out of their home. Two other homeowners support the Tuens in the enterprise and maintain that the intent of the drafters of the restrictions was to allow flexibility in their application. They contend that actual full-time businesses and shops should be prohibited, but that activities such as occasional music lessons do not violate the restrictions.

35. Deutsch, *supra* note 9, at 49.   **36.** *Id.*

After about three hours of mediation, it appears clear to you that the first group is led by Patti Smith, one of two individuals in the first group who is not employed outside of the home. You, as the mediator, have concluded that this dispute has become Smith's "career." It appears that she has developed a leadership role with the group. Furthermore, based upon general comments, you feel that if Ms. Smith were more open to alternatives, the entire matter could be settled.

How will you approach this problem? What behavioral dynamics will you need to take into consideration? With whom might you meet privately?

Chapter Four

GETTING TO THE MEDIATION TABLE

Mediation is a creative dispute resolution process which offers many benefits unavailable with other procedures. But how do individuals or groups involved in conflict gain access to the process? What are the ways by which a dispute or conflict finds its way to the mediation process? When a dispute or conflict occurs, how do we know if, and when, mediation is appropriate? Who should attend the mediation? Should a party be forced to go? What cases are inappropriate? Is it ever too early for mediation? Too late? What will it cost? How long will it take? What is required during the process? These are a sampling of the questions which surround the use of the mediation process.

A. GENERAL APPROPRIATENESS

The development of mediation as a viable alternative to litigation was due largely to its overt benefits; that is, mediation saves time and money. Clearly in those cases where it is important to the parties to save time and money, mediation is indicated. But there are other factors which also signal that mediation is appropriate. The specific factors which indicate that a case or matter is appropriate for mediation are numerous. An illustrative listing includes the following:

- there is an ongoing relationship that the parties wish to maintain;
- the parties hope to establish an ongoing relationship through the mediation;
- the parties prefer to avoid a legal precedent;
- the parties have a need for assurance of confidentiality about the nature of the dispute, the agreement or both;
- there exists a need for assistance in communication and information exchange;
- the parties demonstrate an inability to identify common interests;
- the parties and/or their advocates need assistance with the negotiation;

52

- there is a need for creativity in resolution;

- the parties express a desire for self-determination;

- one or both parties (or their counsel) has made an unrealistic assessment of the case; and

- despite differences, there is a mutual superordinate goal of a mutually satisfactory resolution.

Most topical literature as well as anecdotal research supports this list, rendering a detailed analysis of the specific issues unnecessary.[1] The more difficult determination is whether there exist cases where mediation should not be used. Many lawyers, judges, and parties contend that mediation is appropriate in nearly every case, conflict, or dispute,[2] at least as a first step. If mediation assists the parties in resolving a matter short of litigation, should it not be made available to all parties?

Some experts have attempted to determine which instances are inappropriate for mediation. It has been hypothesized that mediation may be inappropriate in the following situations: when the decision maker will not attend the session; when the case involves governmental and political issues; when budgetary constraints may obstruct settlement; and those cases in which a settlement had been previously reached but broken.[3] Even within the preceding categories, however, it was recognized that cases could be successfully mediated.[4]

Others have identified a longer list of cases where mediation is inappropriate. These include matters in which:

- the client cannot effectively represent her best interest and is not represented by counsel;

- the client seeks to establish legal precedent;

- a significant person is unable to be present;

- a party is entitled by statute to attorney's fees;

- there is strong business competition between the parties in concentrated markets;

- there is a threat of criminal action;

- one party wants to delay a resolution;

- there is likelihood of bankruptcy;

- discovery is needed;

---

1. For additional detail, see Nancy H. Rogers & Richard A. Salem, A Student's Guide to Mediation and the Law, (Chapter 3) (1987). Also Nancy H. Rogers & Craig A. McEwen, Mediation: Law, Policy, and Practice, (Chapters 3, 4, and 5) (1994 & Supp. 1998).

2. This has been argued in several instances. See, Robert A. Baruch Bush, *Mediation and Adjudication, Dispute Resolution and Ideology: An Imaginary Conversation*, 3

J. Contemp. Legal Issues 1 (1989); Eric R. Galton, Representing Clients in Mediation, 5 (1994). See Frank E.A. Sander & Stephen B. Goldberg, *Fitting the Forum to the Fuss: A User-Friendly Guide to Selecting an ADR Procedure*, 10 Negotiation J. 49 (1994) discussing a rule of "presumptive mediation", (exception Chapter One).

3. Galton, *supra* note 2, at 5.

4. *Id.*

• enforcement of the outcome will be necessary.[5]

It has also been suggested that perhaps this list is the beginning, rather than the end, of the analysis.[6] However, cases with these types of factors have been successfully mediated.

For example, in cases of threatened or actual criminal action, the mediation process has been successfully used, particularly where the parties know each other. One of the oldest mediation programs, the Columbus, Ohio, Night Prosecutor's Program (NPP),[7] involves cases where there have been allegations of criminal activity, albeit misdemeanors. Many other programs, including those in Dispute Resolution Centers, have been established within, or in conjunction with, prosecutors' and district attorneys' offices. Moreover, some police officers are learning the mediation process, and mediate on the spot in neighborhood disputes. Mediation in the criminal sphere is also used to resolve restitution issues between victims and offenders.[8] In fact, use of mediation between victims and offenders appears to be on the increase as part of the focus on restorative justice.[9] Mediation has also been used successfully to settle disputes within a prison system.[10]

Litigants in cases where attorneys' fees are provided by statute should not be dissuaded from the use of mediation. The attorneys' fees can be a factor in the negotiation. While admittedly problems are presented by a waiver of attorneys' fees which are provided by statute,[11] fee waiver can be a problem in any type of case. Cases involving statutorily provided attorneys' fees are now settled through negotiation and mediation on a regular basis.

As the business world has become educated about the benefits of collaborative problem solving, the number of commercial disputes resolved through mediation has increased. Many companies, large and small alike, now require their attorneys to use ADR processes before proceeding with formal legal action. Therefore, it is not uncommon to see parties who are business competitors use mediation, particularly where a speedy resolution is beneficial to all parties.

It is often hypothesized that one of the major factors in reaching a mediated resolution is the parties' willingness to do so. Nonetheless, it has also been documented that even the most unwilling party, once

---

5. Rogers & Salem, *supra* note 1, at 57–58.

6. *Id.* at 59.

7. For a general description of *NPP*, see Chapter 2.

8. See Susan C. Taylor, *Victim–Offender Reconciliation Program—A New Paradigm Toward Justice*, 26 U. Mem. L. Rev. 1187 (1996); Jennifer Gerarda Brown, *The Use of Mediation to Resolve Criminal Cases: A Procedural Critique*, 43 Emory L. J. 1247 (1994); Mark Umbright, *Mediation of Victim–Offender Conflict*, 1988 J. Disp. Resol. 85.

9. Restorative Justice focuses on the restoration of the parties involved in the crime rather than retribution or punishment. See Daniel W. Van Ness and Pat Nolan, *Legislating for Restorative Justice*, 10 Regent U. L. Rev. 53 (1998). See also Harold Zehr, Changing Lenses: A New Focus for Crime and Justice (1990).

10. For further details of the application of mediation in *criminal matters*, see Chapter 16, § I.

11. This was the argument set forth in Rogers and Salem, *supra* note 1, at 58.

forced to the mediation table, will not only participate, but will also walk away with a settlement feeling satisfied with the process.[12] It appears that initial unwillingness to participate in mediation is not an accurate indicator of inappropriateness.

The entire bankruptcy process is essentially a supervised negotiation.[13] The mediation process is facilitated negotiation. Use of mediation to assist in resolving disputes in the bankruptcy process has long been advocated by a few individuals.[14] Although many bankruptcy courts and practitioners hesitated to join the ADR bandwagon, it now appears that the use of the mediation, along with other ADR processes, has permeated bankruptcy matters.[15]

In some situations, the litigants want to delay the court process or are in need of formal discovery. It is inappropriate to use the mediation process to achieve such goals. However, in the case of discovery needs, one option is to postpone the mediation until after information has been exchanged. Another is to use mediation to structure the discovery process. In cases where a party merely wants to delay the court process, it is nevertheless possible to achieve settlement once the mediation begins. These situations also relate to the matter of proper timing of mediation.

In those cases where the decision makers in the dispute are not present, or are present but unwilling to make a decision, mediation should not be utilized. The lack of settlement authority accounts for some of the most difficult situations presented to mediators.[16] In some cases the lack of authority or the limited authority of the mediation representative is used as a negotiation tactic. In other cases, however, it is a legitimate situation. For example, in organizations such as large corporations or political subdivisions with a hierarchical distribution of authority, it is nearly impossible to have the ultimate decision maker present at mediation. Yet, even here it is possible to reach a final decision. Perhaps the mediation can proceed until a tentative settlement is reached. Subsequent ratification to finalize the agreement would later be obtained. In other cases, the mediator may telephone the final decision maker and convey the options. This particular form of "telephonic" or long distance mediation is discouraged, since a crucial part of the mediation process is the presence of all parties at the table, listening to one another. Nevertheless, in the real world this form of mediation

---

12. See Janice A. Roehl & Royer F. Cook, *Mediation in Interpersonal Disputes: Effectiveness and Limitations* in Mediation Research: The Process and Effectiveness of Third Party Intervention (Kenneth Kressel & Dean G. Pruitt, eds. 1989).

13. For full exploration of this issue, see J. Bradley Johnson, *The Bankruptcy Bargain,* 65 Am. Bankr. L.J. 213 (1990) and Theodore Eisenberg, *Commentary on the Nature of Bankruptcy: Bankruptcy and Bargaining,* 75 Va. L. Rev. 205 (1990).

14. I personally am one of those individuals.

15. See Ralph R. Mabey, Charles J. Tabb & Ira S. Dizengoff, *Expanding the Reach of Alternative Dispute Resolution in Bankruptcy: The Legal and Practical Bases for the Use of Mediation and the Other Forms of ADR,* 46 S. C. L. Rev. 1259 (1995).

16. Based upon numerous comments from practicing mediators.

does take place. Remember—mediation is a flexible process. In essence, mediation is probably appropriate in nearly every case. This claim has been documented, although more by anecdotal data than by controlled studies; nonetheless this premise of the nearly universal applicability of mediation is a good place to start.[17]

B. THE REFERRAL PROCESS

The nature or type of case may directly affect the referral to mediation. And certainly the method of referral impacts the mediation process. There are a number of ways in which cases find their way to the mediation table. Along a continuum, these range from the parties' completely voluntary desire to attend mediation and resolve the case to a mandatory, over both parties' objection, court referral. While in the majority of cases the referral process of non-litigation matters and pending lawsuits are similar, because of the intervention of the court system, the two will be examined separately.

1. NON–LEGALIZED MATTERS

The term *non-legalized* is used to connote those disputes or conflicts which have not accessed the legal system. In these cases, further assume that no lawyers are directly involved in the dispute. If individuals involved in the dispute decide to voluntarily go to mediation, they can simply do so. Parties may also participate in mediation prior to litigation in accordance with a contract provision. In either of these instances, locating mediation services merits consideration.

a. *Voluntary*

Many individuals utilize dispute resolution centers. At these centers, mediation services are provided at little or no charge to the parties; and the focus is primarily on smaller cases, those cases in which the amount in controversy is not great.[18] Although those within the ADR field are continuously educating the general public, the use of mediation has not reached the point where most individuals involved in a dispute immediately think of this alternative. The process by which many individuals dispute often discourages disputants from entering mediation spontaneously or voluntarily.[19] Moreover, the character of conflict, along with the adversary culture and social relationships involved, contributes to the need for someone outside of the dispute to strongly urge mediation use.[20] Therefore, voluntary self-referral is not yet common and it is often necessary to utilize a different avenue to encourage disputing individuals

17. However, compare statements of those who oppose the settlement of any case, and hence have the view that mediation is *inappropriate* in every case. For example, see Owen M. Fiss, *Against Settlement*, 93 Yale L.J. 1073 (1984). (See also, Bush, *supra* note 2.)

18. It is recognized that these cases are just as important, or more important, to

some individuals, than multi-million dollar cases. It is for descriptive purposes only that the word *small* is used.

19. Craig A. McEwen & Thomas W. Milburn, *Explaining a Paradox of Mediation*, 9 Negotiation J. 23, 34 (1993).

20. *Id.* at 26.

to access the mediation process. One such method is referral via a citizen complaint center.[21]

In most of these disputes, the individuals are not represented by counsel. Questions then arise as to whether, by direct referral to mediation, a different form of justice is provided to these parties. For instance, in a pending lawsuit, most jurisdictions have a variety of options, including mediation, available. In a non-litigation matter, where the individuals are not represented by counsel, most agencies such as dispute resolution centers provide only the mediation alternative. These individuals do not have the opportunity to choose other options such as arbitration or a hybrid process. A second issue for consideration is whether the individuals truly understand the mediation process. There is no representation by counsel because the amount in controversy does not warrant it, or the parties' income level prohibits it. In many cases, participation in mediation is the only realistic alternative for these individuals other than self-help or avoidance. So they enter into the mediation process, not knowing exactly what that means.[22] While these concerns are important, as a practical matter, in most instances, those who participate in mediation through a dispute resolution center, though unrepresented, are very satisfied with the process. This is true even if no final agreement is reached.[23]

b. Contractual

In cases where mediation is specified by contract in anticipation of future disputes, the parties are less hesitant about the process and usually are easily able to locate a mediator. In fact, the mediator may be identified in the mediation clause. Moreover, the parties are at least vaguely familiar with the process. It is also likely that since the parties voluntarily agreed to the mediation clause, they will comply with it. It is advisable, though, to include in the clause matters which may be subject to disagreement at the time a dispute arises. These matters include the time, place, and cost of the mediation, the identification of the mediator, and who will attend the mediation. With these items agreed to, chances for voluntary compliance are increased.[24]

If disputes occur and one of the disputing parties refuses to participate in mediation, questions arise about enforceability of a mediation clause. Can reluctant parties be compelled to mediate in accordance with mediation clauses included in contracts or other legal documents such as wills or trusts? While the number of cases is slight, it currently appears that most courts will enforce voluntary mediation clauses.[25]

---

21. These centers are often an adjunct of prosecutors' offices.

22. For an in-depth examination of this and several issues surrounding individuals' participation in mediation without counsel, see Jacqueline M. Nolan–Haley, *Informed Consent in Mediation: A Guiding Principle for Truly Educated Decisionmaking* 74 Notre Dame L. Rev. 775 (1999).

23. See Roehl & Cook, *supra* note 12.

24. Rogers & McEwen, *supra* note 1, § 8:03, and Chapter 8 generally.

25. *Id.* See also Lucy Katz, *Enforcing an ADR Clause—Are Good Intentions All You Have?*, 26 Am. Bus. L.J. 575 (1988).

Although the following case discusses mediation, it involves a particular Policy Board mediation. It is included because it illustrates how a court would likely enforce a contractual clause specifying mediation.

DEVALK LINCOLN MERCURY, INC. v. FORD MOTOR CO.

United States Court of Appeals, Seventh Circuit, 1987.
811 F.2d 326.

Automobile dealer and its owner and manager brought action against manufacturer following termination of dealership.

* * *

Plaintiffs believe they fulfilled the first alleged purpose of the mediation clause by writing four letters to Ford detailing [DeValk Lincoln Mercury or DLM] DLM's grievances. Plaintiffs argue these letters gave Ford all the notice it needed of the claims with which plaintiffs were concerned.

As for the second alleged purpose of the mediation clause, plaintiffs contend they presented Ford with ample opportunity to settle their claims prior to litigation. The negotiations between plaintiffs and Ford's representatives spanned over eight months. Both Ford and plaintiffs effectively articulated their respective positions during these negotiations. Plaintiffs argue this negotiation process fulfilled the purpose of allowing Ford to attempt to settle its claims with DLM.

Although it is true that "Michigan follows the substantial performance rule," and that in Michigan "the extent of nonperformance [is] viewed in relation to the full performance promised," we cannot agree with plaintiffs' contention.

* * *

The mediation clause here states that it is a condition precedent to any litigation. As a result, the clause takes itself outside the sphere of influence of the substantial performance rule. Because the mediation clause demands strict compliance with its requirement of appeal to the Dealer Policy Board before the parties can litigate, plaintiffs' substantial performance arguments must fail.

2. Waiver of Mediation Clause

Undaunted, plaintiffs argue that even if the mediation clause operates as a condition precedent to litigation, Ford waived the requirements of that clause by its conduct following the final date on which an appeal could be taken to the Dealer Policy Board. The mediation clause requires the dissatisfied dealer to appeal its claims to the Dealer Policy Board "within one year after the termination or nonrenewal has become effective." Ford accepted DLM's resignation and DLM ceased operations in October 1979. Therefore, any continuing negotiations between DLM and Ford after October 1980, plaintiffs argue, constitute a waiver by Ford of the requirements of the mediation clause.

* * *

Specifically, the conduct giving rise to an interference of waiver may take the form of continued performance by the breaching party without any attempt by the non-breaching party to call a halt to the performance. "[A] party standing silent while the other party to the contract fails to perform a condition will be estopped from later asserting the condition."

In this regard, plaintiffs point us to the law of arbitration clauses as closely analogous area of contractual agreement by which we should be guided. The Supreme Court of Michigan has held that an insurer "may waive the compulsory arbitration provision of its insurance policy by its conduct." Bielski v. Wolverine Insurance Co., 379 Mich. 280, 150 N.W.2d 788, 790 (1967). That court also explained:

> "A clause in an insurance policy providing for arbitration or appraisal of the loss or damage as a condition precedent to a suit by the policyholder to recover insurance is inserted wholly for the protection of the insurer and may be waived by it. Such waivers need not be expressed in terms, but may be implied by the acts, omissions, or conduct of the insurer or its agents authorized in such respect."

Id. (quoting 29A American Jurisprudence Insurance § 1617 (1960)); Capital Mortgage Corp. v. Coopers & Lybrand, 142 Mich.App. 531, 369 N.W.2d 922, 924 (1985).

Superficially, it appears that Ford's conduct after the time expired for an appeal to the Dealer Policy Board possibly constitutes a waiver. And we might find persuasive plaintiffs' arguments in this regard were it not for Ford's response, with which we agree, that Michigan's courts uphold anti-waiver clauses. Because DLM agreed in paragraph 27 of the Sales Agreements that implied waivers of Sales Agreements' provisions would not be permitted, plaintiffs' waiver argument cannot stand.

3. REPUDIATION FOR MATERIAL BREACHES OF CONTRACT

In a final effort to skirt the requirements of the mediation clause, plaintiffs argue that Ford's alleged material breaches of the Sales Agreements relieved DLM of any duty to appeal its grievances to the Dealer Policy Board.

Ford argues, however, that plaintiffs did not raise this repudiation argument in the district court and they thus waive it on appeal. Our review of the record, and plaintiffs' failure in their reply brief to counter Ford's charge, persuade us that indeed this argument was not raised in the district court. It is thus waived on appeal.

IV. *Conclusion*

Even after drawing all the reasonable inferences in favor of plaintiffs' positions on this appeal from an adverse grant of summary judgment, we cannot find any genuine issues of material fact. Because there are no such issues, the judgment granted to defendants by the district judge as a matter of law is

AFFIRMED.

In other instances, mediation clauses are becoming a part of arbitration clauses. In other words, participation in mediation is a condition precedent to enforcement of arbitration.

WEEKLEY HOMES, INC. v. JENNINGS
Court of Appeals of Texas, San Antonio, 1996.
936 S.W.2d 16.

PER CURIAM.

This is an interlocutory appeal from the trial court's denial of appellant's "Motion to Stay and to Compel Arbitration." We affirm.

Appellant and appellees entered a contract for the construction and sale of a new home. Appellees were dissatisfied with the home and sued appellant. The contract at issue contains the following language:

> Any controversy or claim whether such claim sounds in contract, tort, or otherwise, arising out of or relating to (i) this Agreement, (ii) any breach of this Agreement, (iii) the subject matter of the Agreement, (iv) the commercial or economic relationship of the parties to the Agreement, (v) any representations or warranties, express or implied, relating to the Agreement, (vi) any violations of any statute relating to the Agreement or the subject matter of the Agreement, and/or (vii) any related agreements between the parties to the Agreement ("the Disputes") shall be settled by arbitration in accordance with the Construction Industry Arbitration Rules of the American Arbitration Association ("AAA") and the Federal Arbitration Act (Title 9 of the United States Code), and judgement upon the award rendered by the arbitrator(s) may be confirmed, entered, and enforced in any court having jurisdiction.
>
> The parties shall first mediate the Disputes in accordance with the Construction Industry Mediation Rules of the AAA. Mediation of the Disputes is an express condition precedent to the arbitration of the Disputes. The mediation shall be administered by the Houston Regional Office of the AAA and shall occur in Houston, Texas. Mediators must have at least five (5) years of experience serving as AAA mediators or arbitrators and shall have technical expertise and knowledge appropriate to the subject matter of the Dispute.

The only evidence presented to the trial court was a copy of the contract containing this language and the affidavit of appellant's representative stating that the copy is a true and correct copy of the contract entered by the parties and that all claims asserted in appellees' petition fall within the subject matter of claims that must be submitted to arbitration.

Appellant did not present any evidence that the dispute had first been mediated. Indeed, appellant did not even mention this provision of the contract in its motion to compel arbitration.

* * *

When a party seeks to compel arbitration, he must first establish his right to that remedy under the contract.

* * *

Appellant presented evidence that the contract between the parties included an arbitration agreement and that appellees' claims fell within the scope of that agreement. The evidence also demonstrated, however, that the arbitration agreement was subject to an express condition precedent. "Breach of a condition precedent affects the enforceability of the provision to which the condition is attached." Thus, if appellant did not fulfill the condition precedent, it was not entitled to an order compelling arbitration.

Appellant contends that appellees cannot rely on the condition precedent because they did not raise this issue in the trial court. Appellant did not file a statement of facts reflecting whether the condition precedent was brought to the attention of the trial court. Appellees stated at oral argument that they did bring this matter to the court's attention. Appellant did not controvert this statement, but argued that orally bringing the issue to the court's attention is not sufficient. This argument is based on cases holding that an objection, which in those cases happened to be in writing, is not sufficient if it is not supported by controverting evidence. See e.g., Jack B. Anglin Co. v. Tipps, 842 S.W.2d at 269. In the present case, the necessary controverting evidence was contained within appellant's own proof—the contract. Because the proof was before the trial court and the issue was brought to the court's attention, we decline to hold that fulfillment of the express condition precedent was waived.

2. PENDING CASES: PUBLIC OR PRIVATE SECTOR MEDIATION

Where a lawsuit is pending in a court, there are a number of ways through which the suit may find itself in mediation. Although currently rare, certainly the urging of mediation by the parties is an appropriate avenue to mediation. There may have been a previous contractual provision which either advises or mandates participation in mediation in an attempt to settle a case before a lawsuit may be formally pursued. Although these cases technically fall within the voluntary non-litigation cases, in some instances the mediation will not occur until after suit is filed. In other cases, lawyers may suggest mediation to one another, or the court may prompt mediation use.

Lawsuits are settled on a regular basis; however, this often occurs late in the case. If the parties avail themselves of the assistance of a mediator, they may speed up the settlement process. Many courts have become active in referring pending lawsuits to a variety of ADR processes, including mediation. This activity has raised concerns about a court's authority to make such referrals, along with the parties' right to object and demand a trial. Cost considerations are another issue for examination in this context.

a. Mandatory Referral

When examining issues of mandatory referral, it is very important to first distinguish between public or private sector mediation. Public mediation covers those situations in which the mediation process is provided in a public forum[26] at very little or no charge. In these cases the mediator or mediators are either employed by, or volunteers with, the court system in which the case is pending.[27] In private sector mediation, the mediator provides mediation services for a fee. There is little debate about whether individuals, with or without counsel, may voluntarily avail themselves of the private sector mediator for whatever cost they determine appropriate; in essence, the free market principle. However, in instances in which the court compels or mandates participation in a private mediation, substantial concerns arise.

Before addressing cost concerns, however, the initial issue is whether an individual in a dispute or with a claim can be compelled to go to mediation. That is, does the court have the inherent authority to mandate referral, particularly over the objection of one of the litigants? Among the attributes associated with our public justice system are equal access for all, openness to public scrutiny, and neutrals not handpicked by the disputing parties. Should individuals, against their will, be forced to participate in a system of justice that does not afford these alleged safeguards? Most state courts which routinely refer cases to mediation rely upon statutory authority. The number of statutes which have a mediation referral scheme for courts has continued to increase. Some statutes require the court to determine the appropriateness of the case for mediation, while others give the courts carte blanche to make any referrals they wish. The federal courts, in referring cases to other forms of ADR, often relied upon their inherent authority to manage cases or Rule 16 of the Federal Rules of Civil Procedure, which produced inconsistent results.[28] In response to two Congressional mandates,[29] however,

---

26. *Public*, here meaning, accessible by all, not open in terms of nonconfidential.

27. *Examples* include court based California Mandatory Custody Mediation and the Multi–Door Dispute Resolution Division of the Superior Court of the District of Columbia.

28. See Strandell v. Jackson County, 838 F.2d 884 (7th Cir.1987) and In re NLO, 5 F.3d 154 (6th Cir.1993).

29. The Civil Justice Reform Act of 1990, 28 U.S.C.A. §§ 471–482 (1993); and more recently Alternative Dispute Resolution Act, 28 U.S.C.A. § 651–658 (1998). In

addition to the Civil Justice Reform Act of 1990, Congress passed the Alternative Dispute Resolution Act of 1998. This 1998 Act mandates that all federal district courts create and implement ADR procedures for all civil actions. "Each court is required to designate a knowledgeable employee to implement the ADR program, to require litigants in all civil cases to consider the use of an ADR process, and offer litigants a choice of ADR processes." See also Jay E. Grenig, Alternative Dispute Resolution, Second Edition, 1999 Pocket Part, pp. 1, 53.

federal courts have enacted plans and new local rules that embrace, and even mandate the use of ADR.[30]

KEENE v. GARDNER
Court of Appeals of Texas, Dallas, 1992.
837 S.W.2d 224.

* * *

MEDIATION SANCTIONS

In its seventh and eighth points of error, Keene complains that the trial court erred in ordering mediation and imposing sanctions against Keene for not participating in the mediation proceeding.

* * *

Pertinent Facts

On another defendant's motion, the court ordered all parties to participate in mediation beginning on the morning following the court's order. The order required that an executive officer from each corporate defendant, with authority to negotiate a settlement, attend the mediation. Keene explained to the court that its predetermined settlement policy permitted only the company's president to negotiate a settlement. Keene's president was in New York and could not be in Dallas on twenty-four hours' notice. The court maintained that someone with settlement power would have to attend.

The next morning, Keene requested the statutory ten days to file written objections to the court's referral order. The court overruled Keene's request and oral objection. Keene sent a representative without settlement authority to the mediation proceeding. After the representative restated Keene's position, the mediator excused Keene's representatives from further attendance.

Appellees moved for sanctions for Keene's not participating in the mediation. The court conducted a hearing on appellees' motion and ordered that Keene pay all costs of mediation.

Applicable Law

The Texas Civil Practice and Remedies Code authorizes courts to refer a pending dispute to an alternative dispute resolution procedure at any point in the trial or appellate process. *Downey v. Gregory*, 757 S.W.2d 524, 525 (Tex.App.—Houston [1st Dist.] 1988, no writ); *see* Tex.Civ.Prac. & Rem.Code Ann. § 154.021 (Vernon Supp. 1992). The statute also provides a procedure for notice of an objection to the court's referral:

(a) If a court determines that a pending dispute is appropriate for referral under Section 154.021, the court shall notify the parties of its determination.

---

30. Since each federal court has designed its own individual plan, each plan must be reviewed to determine if mediation has been implemented.

(b) Any party may, within 10 days after receiving the notice under Subsection (a), file a written objection to the referral.

(c) If the court finds that there is a reasonable basis for an objection filed under Subsection (b), the court may not refer the dispute under Section 154.021. Tex.Civ.Prac. & Rem.Code Ann. § 154.022 (Vernon Supp. 1992).

Application of Law

[22] Section 154.022 allows parties ten days to file objections once the trial court determines that alternative dispute resolution is appropriate. The trial court required Keene to participate in mediation on twenty-four hours' notice. Keene specifically requested ten days to file objections as provided in the statute.

The statute's stated intent is "to encourage the peaceable resolution of disputes ... and the early settlement of pending litigation through *voluntary* settlement procedures." Tex.Civ.Prac. & Rem.Code Ann. § 154.002 (Vernon Supp. 1992) (emphasis added). Keene requested, and the court denied, ten days to file written objections under the applicable statutory provision. This mediation proceeding was neither voluntary nor in accord with the required statutory procedures.

Although the trial court has an interest in expediting the resolution of pending litigation, it cannot force the parties to follow an unreasonable timetable. If the trial court can force a resisting party to participate in alternative dispute resolution without regard to the ten-day objection period, it renders a portion of the statute meaningless. While the trial court has discretion in determining whether alternative dispute resolution is appropriate, it has no authority to ignore the statute's intent and wording. We sustain points of error seven and eight.

CARMICHAEL v. WORKERS' COMPENSATION COURT OF THE STATE OF MONTANA

Supreme Court of Montana, 1988.
234 Mont. 410, 763 P.2d 1122.

HARRISON, JUSTICE.

Hoagy Carmichael petitioned this Court for a writ of supervisory control challenging the 1987 amendments to the Workers' Compensation Act concerning dispute resolution and mediation, §§ 39–71–2401 and –2406 through –2411, MCA. We granted the writ for the purpose of determining whether these statutes are constitutional as applied to cases where the injury occurred before the effective date of the amendment....

* * *

Because we determine the non-binding mediation requirements unconstitutionally impair a contractual obligation when applied to the facts of this case, we need not go beyond an analysis of the first issue.

Generally, Carmichael's argument is based on the fact that his injury occurred prior to the time the legislature enacted the nonbinding mediation requirements.

* * *

Carmichael demonstrates a substantial impairment of his contractual rights and there is insufficient evidence to demonstrate the mediation statutes achieve their purpose as applied to claimants injured prior to the effective date of the statute. . . .

WEBER, JUSTICE, dissents as follows:

* * *

In my opinion, there has been no showing that the mediation requirement substantially impairs any contractual right. The requirement does not affect Mr. Carmichael's right to workers' compensation payments; it only presents the possibility of a delay in his receiving compensation, provided that he shows he is entitled to it. . . . I therefore disagree with the theory set forth in the majority opinion that the delay presented by mediation is an "additional delay" not existing on the date Mr. Carmichael was injured. . . .

* * *

Mr. Carmichael argues that the mediation requirement violates his due process rights. He has not cited any authority that a delay in re-establishing a right which has been unchallengedly taken away is a deprivation of due process. Further, under the former statutes, there was no right to a decision by the Workers' Compensation Court within any particular time. . . .

* * *

Cal. Fam. Code Ann. (West 1994)

§ 3170. Mediation proceedings; setting matter for mediation

(a) If it appears on the face of a petition, application, or other pleading to obtain or modify a temporary or permanent custody or visitation order that custody, visitation, or both are contested, the court shall set the contested issues for mediation.

(Added by Stats.1993, c. 219 (A.B.1500), § 116.87.)

Mandatory mediation can be described in a number of ways. Discussions about what specifically is mandated by participation in mediation are numerous. A closer look provides a more detailed manner of approaching the issue. The types of participation which may be required include the following: good faith participation, an exchange of position papers and other information, minimal meaningful participation, attendance with settlement authority, and an obligation to pay a mediator's fee.[31]

IN RE: UNITED STATES OF AMERICA, PETITIONER

United States Court of Appeals, Fifth Circuit, 1998.
149 F.3d 332.

PER CURIAM:

The United States has filed a petition for a writ of mandamus seeking an order from this court directing the district court to vacate the requirement in its order of February 2, 1998, in the action United States v. Gordon B. McLendon, Jr., et al., mandating that the United States be represented at mediation by a person with full settlement authority.[1]

Because we find that the district court has not abused its discretion, we deny the Government's petition for a writ of mandamus. See In re Stone, 986 F.2d 898, 902 (5th Cir.1993). However, we request that the district court consider alternatively ordering the Government to have the person or persons identified as holding full settlement authority consider settlement in advance of the mediation and be fully prepared and available by telephone to discuss settlement at the time of mediation. See *id.* at 905.

Petition for Writ of Mandamus DENIED.

CONCURRING OPINION

DENNIS, CIRCUIT JUDGE, specially concurring:

I am writing to specially concur in the denial of mandamus because I believe that a finding of an abuse of discretion or an issuance of mandamus is not appropriate at this time because it is not clear whether the district court actually failed to consider and to reasonably eliminate all alternatives but the one of "last resort." Furthermore, I write specially to explain to the district court my reasons underlying the request and the denial of mandamus.

In *In re Stone*, 986 F.2d 898 (5th Cir.1993), we outlined, in some detail, the peculiar position of the Attorney General and the special problems the Department of Justice faces in handling the government's ever-increasing volume of litigation. *Id.* at 904–05.

We concluded that the district court abused its discretion in routinely requiring a representative of the government with ultimate settlement authority to be present at all pretrial or settlement conferences. *Id.* at 905. Although we did not suggest that the district court could never

---

31. Edward F. Sherman, *Court–Mandated Alternative Dispute Resolution: What Form of Participation Should be Required?* 46 SMU L. Rev. 2079, 2089 (1993).

1. The district court ordered that each party be represented during the entire mediation process by "an executive officer (other than in-house counsel) with authority to negotiate a settlement (the authority required shall be active, i.e., not merely the authority to observe the mediation proceedings but the authority to negotiate, demand or offer, and bind the party represented)."

issue such an order, we declared that it should consider "less drastic steps" before doing so. *Id.*

We set forth examples of less drastic steps the court should consider, such as requiring the government to declare whether the case could be settled within the authority of the United States Attorney, and if so, ordering the United States Attorney to either attend the conference personally or be available by telephone to discuss settlement at the time of the conference. *Id.* In those cases in which routine litigation can not be settled within the authority of the United States Attorney, "and the failure of the government to extend settlement authority is a serious, persistent problem, substantially hampering the operations of the docket,"

We declared that the court could take additional action, such as "requiring the government to advise it of the identity of the person or persons who hold such authority and directing those persons to consider settlement in advance of the conference and be fully prepared and available by telephone to discuss settlement at the time of the conference." *Id.*

Finally, we declared that if the district court's reasonable efforts to conduct an informed settlement discussion in a particular case are thwarted because a government official with settlement authority will not communicate with government counsel or the court in a timely manner, the court, "as a last resort," can require the appropriate officials with full settlement authority to attend a pretrial conference. *Id.*

This case is substantially different from *Stone* in that (a) it is an exceptional case rather than routine litigation; (b) it involves specifically ordered mediation rather than a standing order or an ordinary pretrial settlement conference; and (3) the government agreed to mediation. However, the special problems of the Attorney General still should be given proper consideration and weight, and, if possible, accommodated. The district court does not indicate that it considered or tried the lesser alternative of requiring the government officer with ultimate settlement authority to be fully prepared and available by telephone to discuss settlement at the mediation, instead of requiring the government official with that authority to personally attend the mediation. I agree that the district court should consider alternatively ordering the Attorney General to have the person or persons identified as holding full settlement authority consider settlement in advance of the mediation and be fully prepared and available by telephone to discuss settlement at the time of mediation. I believe that this alternative is a reasonable compromise that takes into account both the court's need to conduct its business in a reasonably efficient manner without unnecessarily wasting valuable judicial resources, and the Government's need for centralized decision-making and its special problems in handling ever-increasing volumes of litigation.

While I am confident that the district court will consider the alternative and, if feasible, adjust its directives accordingly, and that the government will cooperate and comply with such a reasonable alternative order, I would deny the writ of mandamus without prejudice.

GRAHAM v. BAKER
Supreme Court of Iowa, 1989.
447 N.W.2d 397.

Explanatory note: This case involves a farmer/creditor mediation program. The parties are related as follows: The Henrys purchased land from Grahams. When Henrys were unable to make payments, Grahams hired Flagg as the attorney. It appears Baker is affiliated with the Iowa Farmer/Creditor Mediation Service, Inc.

Debtors appealed from an order of the District Court, Warren County, Richard D. Morr, J., which granted creditors' writ of mandamus to force mediation service to issue release.

* * *

Iowa Code section 654A.6 (1987) requires a creditor to request mediation and obtain a mediation release before undertaking forfeiture proceedings. . . .

At that session, Flagg refused to cooperate with the mediator, denying the Henrys any opportunity to put forward their proposals for resolving the situation, and demanding that he be given a mediation release. It was clear that Flagg was hostile to the Henrys, the mediator, and the mediation process. . . .

* * *

Basing its decision on Flagg's behavior, the mediation service refused to issue the Grahams a release, granting instead an extra thirty days to attempt mediation. . . .

* * *

The core of the Henrys' appeal presents us with the question of whether Flagg's behavior at the mediation proceeding constitutes "participation" as that term is intended by the statute. Iowa Code § 654A.11(3). Our review is de novo.

* * *

The single requirement is that the creditor "participate" in one mediation session. Iowa Code § 654A.11(3) (1987).

The word "participate" means "to take part in something (as an enterprise or activity) usu[ally] in common with others." Webster's Third International Dictionary. Participation "means to take part in, to receive or have a part in an activity."

The word "participating" has no clear and unmistakable meaning. In its primary sense, it means simply a sharing or taking part with others but when it is applied to a particular situation, it takes on secondary implications that render it ambiguous. Under some circumstances it may denote a mere passive sharing while under other circumstances an implication of active engagement may accompany its use.

Fireman's Fund Indem. Co. v. Hudson Associates, Inc., 91 A.2d 454, 455, 97 N.H. 434 (1952). Given Flagg's attitude during the session, the mediator urged his supervisors not to issue a release, basing his recommendation upon standards for gauging participation formulated by the mediation service itself. His supervisors concurred and no release was issued. By so doing, however, the mediation service arrogated to itself a discretionary function not granted by the statute.

* * *

Flagg attended the mediation session as required, and participated to the extent of stating that his position was not negotiable.

The statute does not give the mediation service the power to compel either creditor or debtor to negotiate. It merely attempts to set up conditions in which the parties might find a solution to their problems short of forfeiture or foreclosure.

* * *

We find that Flagg's presence at the mediation meeting satisfied the minimal participation required by the statute.

DECKER v. LINDSAY

Court of Appeals of Texas, Houston, First District, 1992.
824 S.W.2d 247.

OPINION

SAM H. BASS, JUSTICE.

We are faced with two questions today: (1) Can a party be compelled to participate in an alternative dispute resolution (ADR) procedure despite its objections?, and (2) Have relators established their right to mandamus relief?

John and Mary Decker, relators, seek mandamus relief against respondent, Judge Tony Lindsay, who signed an order on October 18, 1991 referring their suit against Jordan Mintz,[1] the real party in interest, to mediation under Tex.Civ.Prac. & Rem.Code Ann. § 154.021(a), 1 (Vernon Supp.1992).

Judge Lindsay's mediation order was made on her own motion, without any hearing. She consulted with neither party before entering her order. See Tex.Civ.Prac. & Rem.Code Ann. § 154.021(b) (Vernon Supp.1992). However, only relators objected to the referral (timely, on

---

1. Decker v. Mintz, No. 90–46678 (Dist. Texas).
Ct. of Harris County, 280th Judicial Dist. of

November 1, 1991), and they submitted their objections for a ruling without oral argument.

The October 18, 1991, order requires the parties to agree on a mediation date "within the next 30 days," or by November 18, 1991. If no agreed date is scheduled, the order provides that the mediator will select a date within the next 60 days, or by December 18, 1991. The order also reads, "TO BE MEDIATED PRIOR TO TRIAL SETTING OF 1–20–92."

We are concerned primarily with the following provisions of Judge Lindsay's order:

> Mediation is a *mandatory but non-binding settlement conference,* conducted with the assistance of the Mediator.... Fees for the mediation are to be divided and borne equally by the parties unless agreed otherwise, shall be paid by the parties directly to the Mediator, and shall be taxed as costs. *Each party and counsel will be bound by the Rules for Mediation printed on the back of this Order....*

> Named parties shall be present during the entire mediation process.... *Counsel and parties shall proceed in a good faith effort to try to resolve this case....*

> Referral to mediation is not a substitute for trial, and the case will be tried if not settled.

(Emphasis added.)

Two of the Rules for Mediation, affixed to the order, are relevant to our discussion:

> 2. Agreement of the Parties. Whenever the parties have agreed to mediation they shall be deemed to have made these rules, as amended and in effect as of the date of the submission of the dispute, a part of their agreement to mediate....

> 6. Commitment to Participate in Good Faith. While no one is asked to commit to settle their dispute in advance of mediation, all parties commit to participate in the proceedings in good faith with the intention to settle, if at all possible.

* * *

Relators assert Judge Lindsay's order is void and constitutes a clear abuse of discretion for the following reasons, which they also stated in their objection to mediation filed with the trial court: (1) the lawsuit arises out of a simple rear-end car collision, where the only issues are negligence, proximate cause, and damages; (2) trial is likely to last for only two days; (3) it is relators' opinion that mediation will not resolve the lawsuit, and they have not agreed to pay fees to the mediator; (4) mediation may cause relators to compromise their potential cause of action under the Stowers[2] doctrine; (5) the law does not favor alternative

2. G. A. Stowers Furniture Co. v. Amer-   ican Indem. Co., 15 S.W.2d 544 (Tex.

dispute resolution where one of the litigants objects to it and when the litigants have been ordered to pay for it; and (6) court-ordered mediation, over the relators' objection and at their cost, violates their right to due process under the fifth and fourteenth amendments to the United States Constitution and article I, section 13 of the Texas Constitution.

The real party in interest disputes relators' contention that the lawsuit and its issues are simple. The real party in interest has raised the defense of unavoidable accident and asserts that the parties have wide-ranging disagreement over Mr. Decker's claimed economic and medical damages.

Relators contend that trial will last for only two days. Consequently, it will take only slightly more time than the mediation ordered. However, the proposed joint pretrial order, signed by counsel for the relators and counsel for the real party in interest, provides an estimated trial time of three to four days.

While relators assert that mediation will not resolve the lawsuit, the real party in interest suggests that in a day invested in mediation, where communication between the parties is facilitated, relators may change their evaluation of the lawsuit.

Under Tex.Civ.Prac. & Rem.Code Ann. § 154.054(a) (Vernon Supp. 1992), the court may set a reasonable fee for the services of an impartial third party appointed to facilitate an ADR procedure. Unless otherwise agreed by the parties, the court must tax the fee as other costs of the suit. Tex.Civ.Prac. & Rem.Code Ann. § 154.054(b) (Vernon Supp.1992). No fee was ever set for the mediation in this case. On December 6, 1991, after this proceeding was filed, the mediator advised the parties that she waived her fee in the case.

We cannot say that Judge Lindsay abused her discretion in impliedly finding the first three reasons advanced by relators were not reasonable objections to court-ordered mediation. Mediation may be beneficial even if relators believe it will not resolve the lawsuit. The statute certainly allows a reasonable fee to be charged, and relators never challenged the reasonableness of the fee, but now the fee issue is moot.

Concerning relators' remaining objections, Texas law recognizes that an insurer has a duty to the insured to settle a lawsuit if a prudent person in the exercise of ordinary care would do so. *G.A. Stowers Furniture Co.*, 15 S.W.2d at 547; *American Centennial Ins. Co. v. Canal Ins. Co.*, 810 S.W.2d 246, 250 (Tex.App.—Houston [1st Dist.] 1991, writ granted). If an ordinarily prudent person would have settled the lawsuit, and the insurer failed or refused to do so, it is liable to the insured for the amount of damages eventually recovered in excess of the policy limits. Relators assert that an insured, for example the real party in interest here, frequently assigns to the plaintiff his *Stowers* rights against his insurer, in return for a covenant that the plaintiff will not execute on the insured's personal assets. Therefore, relators contend

Comm'n App. 1929, holding approved).

that by ordering them to mediation, Judge Lindsay is interfering with their right to preserve a potential cause of action against the liability insurer of the real party in interest.

First, relators have no *Stowers* rights against the liability insurer of the real party in interest. Second, there has been no trial; there has been no judgment; there has been no assignment of the real party in interest's *Stowers* rights to relators; there has been no determination that a reasonably prudent person would have decided, at the time relators made their offer, to settle the litigation for the policy limits. A *Stowers* cause of action does not accrue until the judgment in the underlying case becomes final. We cannot say that Judge Lindsay abused her discretion in impliedly finding that court ordered mediation would not cause relators to compromise a potential cause of action under *Stowers*.

Relators rely on *Simpson v. Canales*, 806 S.W.2d 802 (Tex.1991), for their contention that the law does not favor alternative dispute resolution procedures where one of the parties objects to it and when the parties are compelled to pay for it. Relators' reliance on *Simpson* is misplaced. In *Simpson*, the supreme court found that the trial court abused its discretion in appointing a master to supervise all discovery because the "exceptional cases/good cause" criteria of Tex.R.Civ.P. 171 had not been met and the blanket reference of all discovery was unjustified. Although the supreme court commented that the parties had been ordered to pay for resolution of discovery issues by a master that other litigants obtained from the court without such expense, the matter of expense was not a basis for the court's decision.

Relators also argue that chapter 154 of the Texas Civil Practice and Remedies Code presents a "voluntary" procedure, and that mandatory referral to a paid mediator is not within its scope.

Section 154.002 expresses the general policy that "peaceable resolution of disputes" is to be encouraged through "voluntary settlement procedures." Tex.Civ.Prac. & Rem.Code Ann. § 154.002 (Vernon Supp. 1992). Courts are admonished to carry out this policy. Tex.Civ.Prac. & Rem.Code Ann. § 154.003 (Vernon Supp.1992). A court cannot force the disputants to peaceably resolve their differences, but it can compel them to sit down with each other.

Section 154.021(a) authorizes a trial court *on its motion* to refer a dispute to an ADR procedure. However, if a party objects, *and there is a reasonable basis* for the objection, the court may not refer the dispute to an ADR procedure. Tex.Civ.Prac. & Rem.Code Ann. § 154.022(c). The corollary of this provision is that a court may refer the dispute to an ADR procedure if it finds there is no reasonable basis for the objection. A person appointed to facilitate an ADR procedure may not compel the parties to mediate (negotiate) or coerce parties to enter into a settlement agreement. Tex.Civ.Prac. & Rem.Code Ann. § 154.023(b) (Vernon Supp. 1992). A mediator may not impose his or her own judgment on the issues for that of the parties. Tex.Civ.Prac. & Rem.Code Ann. § 154.023(b) (Vernon Supp. 1992).

Therefore, the policy of section 154.002 is consistent with a scheme where a court refers a dispute to an ADR procedure, requiring the parties to come together in court-ordered ADR procedures, but no one can compel the parties to negotiate or settle a dispute unless they voluntarily and mutually agree to do so. Any inconsistencies in chapter 154 can be resolved to give effect to a dominant legislative intent to compel referral, but not resolution.

However, Judge Lindsay's order does not comport with the scheme set forth in chapter 154. Her order, and the mediation rules that are a part of it, do more than require the parties to come together; they require them to "negotiate" in good faith and attempt to reach a settlement.

Finally, relators object to Judge Lindsay's order on the constitutional grounds of due process and open courts.

Relators' brief does not contain any argument or authorities supporting their contention that their due process rights under the fifth and fourteenth amendments to the United States Constitution and article I, section 13 of the Texas Constitution have been violated. Therefore, they have not demonstrated their entitlement to mandamus relief on this ground. They have not brought forth contentions that chapter 154 is in and of itself unconstitutional.

Relators contend that under the "capable of repetition yet evading review" doctrine, the constitutionality of the mediator's fee under the open courts provision should be addressed. They argue that subsequent litigants attempting to challenge the "mediation for pay" orders being issued by trial courts should not be forced to expend substantial sums in filing petitions for writ of mandamus only to have challenged mediators waive their fees.

* * *

Relators do not claim that assessment of mediators' fees is of such short duration that it evades appellate review, particularly by the route of mandamus. Nor do they assert that they may be subject to court ordered mediation again. The doctrine does not apply.

However, in one very important respect, Judge Lindsay's order violates the open courts provision. It requires relators' attempt to negotiate a settlement of the dispute with the real party in interest in good faith, when they have clearly indicated they do not wish to do so, but prefer to go to trial. As we noted above, the order does more than refer the dispute to an ADR procedure; it requires negotiation. Chapter 154 contemplates mandatory referral only, not mandatory negotiation.

Having reviewed the arguments of relators, which do not attack the statute, but only the order of referral, and those of the real party in interest and the documents submitted to us, we conclude that Judge Lindsay's order is void insofar as it directs relators to negotiate in good faith a resolution of their dispute with the real party in interest through mediation, despite relators' objections.

We conditionally grant the petition for writ of mandamus, and order Judge Lindsay to vacate those portions of her order of October 18, 1991, that require the parties to participate in mediation proceedings in good faith with the intention of settling.

TEXAS DEPARTMENT OF TRANSPORTATION
v. PIRTLE
Court of Appeals of Texas, Fort Worth, 1998.
977 S.W.2d 657.

DAUPHINOT, JUSTICE.

A jury found that Appellant, the Texas Department of Transportation ("the department"), was not liable for damages Appellee Don Pirtle incurred in his one-car accident. The trial court assessed all costs of court, including attorney's fees and mediator's fees Pirtle incurred, to the department, finding that it had failed to mediate in good faith. In a single point, the department complains that the trial court erred in assessing costs against it.

The civil practice and remedies code provides that a trial court may order litigants into alternative dispute resolution ("ADR") and that the proper remedy for a party dissatisfied with this order is to file a written objection within ten days.

Instead of filing a written objection, the department attended the mediation but refused to participate. In arguing that it had no duty to mediate in good faith, the department cites Gleason v. Lawson[3], Hansen v. Sullivan[4], and Decker v. Lindsay.[5]

All are inapposite.

Gleason addresses situations where a judge does not order litigants into ADR. Hansen addresses situations where a litigant does mediate in good faith, but is unable to resolve the dispute. Decker addresses situations where a litigant does file a written objection within ten days, but the judge overrules the objection.

The rules of civil procedure provide that, "The successful party to a suit shall recover of his adversary, all costs incurred therein, except ... [t]he court may, for good cause, to be stated on the record, adjudge the costs otherwise." We may reverse a trial court's imposition of costs only for abuse of discretion. In response to the department's insistence that costs be assessed against Pirtle, the trial court stated, "[T]hey pretty much told me from the beginning they weren't going to mediate because it's the position of the Department of Transportation that part of its responsibility in fulfilling its public trust is not to settle disputed liability cases." Had the department exercised its statutory remedy by filing a

---

3. Gleason v. Lawson, 850 S.W.2d 714 (Tex.App.Corpus Christi, 1993, no writ).

4. Hansen v. Sullivan, 886 S.W.2d 467 (Tex. App. Houston [1st Dist.] 1994, no writ).

5. Decker v. Lindsey, 824 S.W.2d 247 (Tex. App. Houston [1st Dist.] 1992, no writ).

written objection, Pirtle would have been spared the expense of attending mediation.

We find that it is not an abuse of discretion for a trial court to assess costs when a party does not file a written objection to a court's order to mediate, but nevertheless refuses to mediate in good faith. We overrule the department's sole point.

Finding no reversible error, we affirm the trial court's judgment.

TEXAS PARKS AND WILDLIFE DEPARTMENT v. DAVIS
Court of Appeals of Texas, Austin, 1999.
988 S.W.2d 370.

MARILYN ABOUSSIE, CHIEF JUSTICE.

The opinion and judgment filed herein on December 10, 1998, are withdrawn, and the following opinion is issued in lieu of the original one. Appellee, Ernest Ray Davis, Jr., sued appellant, Texas Parks and Wildlife Department (the "Department"), for personal injuries he sustained when a concrete bench collapsed under him at Inks Lake State Park, which is operated by the Department.

After the jury returned a verdict in favor of Davis, the trial court rendered judgment for Davis and sanctioned the Department for its alleged failure to negotiate in good faith during court ordered mediation. The Department appeals the trial court judgment on four grounds. We will affirm the judgment rendered on the jury verdict as to liability and damages as well as that part of the sanction imposing costs of mediation; we will reverse the part of the sanction awarding attorney's fees.

BACKGROUND

On September 6, 1992, Davis and his family went to Inks Lake State Park ("Inks Lake") to celebrate Labor Day. Davis sat on a concrete picnic bench at the family's assigned campsite intermittently throughout the day. At approximately 3:00 p.m. the bench collapsed under Davis without warning, injuring him.

Davis sued the Department, an agency of the State of Texas, pursuant to the Texas Tort Claims Act. See Tex. Civ. Prac. & Rem.Code Ann. §§ 101.001–.109 (West 1997) ("Tort Claims Act," "Act"). The parties proceeded to a jury trial. After Davis presented his case, the Department moved for a directed verdict.

* * *

The trial court overruled the motion and submitted the case to the jury. The jury returned a verdict in favor of Davis, and the trial court rendered judgment for Davis. The trial court also sanctioned the Department for its alleged failure to engage in court ordered mediation in good faith by awarding Davis $250.00 as reimbursement for his mediation fee and $1,200.00 for attorney's fees incurred in connection with the mediation. The Department filed a Motion for Judgment Notwithstanding the Verdict and For New Trial on substantially the same grounds stated above. The Department further alleged that the trial court erred in the jury charge because it failed to submit a question establishing Davis's status as either an invitee or a licensee at the time of the accident.

The Department raises four issues on appeal. It reasserts its right to immunity in the first two issues, and it complains that the trial court erred by denying its requested question on Davis's status in the third issue. In its fourth issue, it urges this Court to reverse the trial court's monetary sanction against the Department.

* * *

In its final issue, the Department contends that the trial court erred in sanctioning the Department for its alleged failure to negotiate in good faith during court ordered mediation. The trial court awarded Davis $250.00 as reimbursement for his mediation fee and $1,200.00 for attorney's fees incurred in connection with the mediation.

Chapter 154 of the Texas Civil Practice and Remedies Code establishes procedures for a trial court, on its own motion, to refer a dispute to an alternative dispute resolution ("ADR") procedure. See Tex. Civ. Prac. & Rem.Code §§ 154.021(a) (West 1997).

While a court may compel parties to participate in mediation, it cannot compel the parties to negotiate in good faith or settle their dispute. See Decker v. Lindsay, 824 S.W.2d 247, 250–51 (Tex.App.— Houston [1st Dist.] 1992, orig. proceeding).

Furthermore, section 154.073 requires that communications and records made in an ADR procedure remain confidential; consequently, the manner in which the participants negotiate should not be disclosed to the trial court. See Tex. Civ. Prac. & Rem.Code §§ 154.073 (West 1997). We decline to follow Texas Department of Transportation v. Pirtle, 977 S.W.2d 657 (Tex.App.—Fort Worth 1998, pet. denied), cited by Davis, because the court of appeals in Pirtle based its opinion on facts not present in this case. In Pirtle, the Texas Department of Transportation did not file a written objection within ten days after the trial court ordered the parties into ADR. *See id.* at 658. Instead, the Department of Transportation attended the mediation but refused to participate. *See id.* The court of appeals determined that it was not an abuse of discretion for a trial court to assess costs against a party when that party "does not file a written objection to a court's order to mediate, but nevertheless refuses to mediate in good faith." *Id.* In this case, the Department did file an objection, which the trial court overruled. Nevertheless, the Department attended the mediation and made an offer, so it cannot be said that it did not participate in the mediation. We sustain the Department's complaint as to the trial court's award of attorney's fees as a sanction for the Department's alleged failure to negotiate in good faith.

Finally, we address the mediation fee. Chapter 154 requires the court to "tax the fee for services of an impartial third party as other costs of the suit." Tex. Civ. Prac. & Rem.Code §§ 154.054(b) (West 1997). In its judgment, the trial court properly awarded Davis all original costs associated with the suit. Because the $250.00 mediation fee is an original cost under section 154.054(b), and because the trial court properly awarded Davis the costs expended for the suit, there is no error in taxing the mediation fee against the Department.

Conclusion

For the reasons stated above, we conclude that the Department is not entitled to governmental immunity in this case, that the trial court did not err in denying the Department's request for a jury question on the issue of entry fee payment, and that the trial court properly awarded Davis the cost of his mediation fee. We hold that the award of attorney's fees incurred in connection with the mediation was improper.

Accordingly, we reverse that part of the trial court judgment sanctioning the Department for its alleged failure to negotiate in good faith and render judgment that Davis take nothing in attorney's fees; we affirm the remainder of the judgment.

It appears, however, that statutes advocate a good faith standard for participation in mediation.

Texas Family Code 6.404 (1999)

A party to a proceeding under this title shall include in the first pleading filed by the party in the proceeding the following statement:

"I AM AWARE THAT IT IS THE POLICY OF THE STATE OF TEXAS TO PROMOTE THE AMICABLE AND NONJUDICIAL SETTLEMENT OF DISPUTES INVOLVING CHILDREN AND FAMILIES. I AM AWARE OF ALTERNATIVE DISPUTE RESOLUTION METHODS, INCLUDING MEDIATION. WHILE I RECOGNIZE THAT ALTERNATIVE DISPUTE RESOLUTION IS AN ALTERNATIVE TO AND NOT A SUBSTITUTE FOR A TRIAL AND THAT THIS CASE MAY BE TRIED IF IT IS NOT SETTLED, I REPRESENT TO THE COURT THAT I WILL ATTEMPT IN GOOD FAITH TO RESOLVE BEFORE FINAL TRIAL CONTESTED ISSUES IN THIS CASE BY ALTERNATIVE DISPUTE RESOLUTION WITHOUT THE NECESSITY OF COURT INTERVENTION."

(b) The statement prescribed by Subsection (a) must be printed in boldfaced type or capital letters and signed by the party.

(c) The statement prescribed by Subsection (a) is not required for:

(1) a pleading in which citation on all respondents entitled to service of citation is requested, issued, and given by publication;

(2) a motion or pleading that seeks a protective order as provided by Chapter 71; or

(3) a special appearance under Rule 120a, Texas Rules of Civil Procedure.

IN ST ADR Rule 2.1

Rule 2.1. Purpose

Mediation under this section involves the confidential process by which a neutral, acting as a mediator, selected by the parties or appointed by the court, assists the litigants in reaching a mutually acceptable agreement. The role of the mediator is to assist in identifying the issues, reducing misunderstanding, clarifying priorities, exploring areas of compromise, and finding points of agreement as well as legitimate points of disagreement. Any agreement reached by the parties is to be based on the autonomous decisions of the parties and not the decisions of the mediator. It is anticipated that an agreement may not resolve all of the disputed issues, but the process can reduce points of contention. Parties and their representatives are required to mediate in good faith, but are not compelled to reach an agreement.

19–A Maine Revised Statutes Annotated (West 1999)

§ 251. Mediation

1. Court authority to order mediation. The court may, in any case under this Title, at any time refer the parties to mediation on any issue.

2. Requested mediation. Except as provided in paragraph B, prior to a contested hearing under chapter 27, chapter 29, chapter 55 or chapter 63 when there are minor children of the parties, the court shall refer the parties to mediation.

A. For good cause shown, the court, prior to referring the parties to mediation, may hear motions for temporary relief, pending final judgment on an issue or combination of issues for which good cause for temporary relief has been shown.

B. Upon motion supported by affidavit, the court may, for extraordinary cause shown, waive the mediation requirement under this subsection.

3. Mediated agreement. An agreement reached by the parties through mediation on issues must be reduced to writing, signed by the parties and presented to the court for approval as a court order.

4. No agreement; good faith effort required. When agreement through mediation is not reached on an issue, the court must determine that the parties made a good faith effort to mediate the issue before proceeding with a hearing. If the court finds that either party failed to make a good faith effort to mediate, the court may order the parties to submit to mediation, may dismiss the action or a part of the action, may render a decision or judgment by default, may assess attorney's fees and cost or may impose any other sanction that is appropriate in the circumstances.

5. Failure to appear. The court may also impose an appropriate sanction upon a party's failure without good cause to appear for mediation after receiving notice of the scheduled time for mediation.

6. Waiver of mediation; questions of law. The court may hear motions to waive mediation in cases in which there are no facts at issue and all unresolved issues are questions of law.

LARRY R. OBERMOLLER v. FEDERAL LAND BANK OF SAINT PAUL

Court of Appeals of Minnesota, 1987.
409 N.W.2d 229.

The trial court denied the application of appellants Larry and Connie Obermoller for a temporary injunction to halt the foreclosure sale of their farm. Appellants argue that the trial court abused its discretion and that they should be allowed to set aside their homestead for a separate sale. Respondent has moved to dismiss the appeal on the grounds of mootness. We address the merits and affirm.

FACTS

Respondent, the Federal Land Bank of Saint Paul, held a mortgage on certain farm land owned by appellants. On February 22, 1986, respondent published notice of a foreclosure sale of this land, to be held April 23, 1986. On March 22, 1986, the Minnesota Farmer–Lender Mediation Act, Minn.Stat. §§ 583.20–.32 (1986), became effective. Appellants attempted to take advantage of this new law by filing a debtor mediation request on April 16, 1986.

Respondent, however, proceeded with the April 23 foreclosure sale on the assumption that the legislation did not apply to proceedings commenced before its enactment. Despite this sale, respondent also participated in mediation in June and July of 1986. In July 1986, this court issued its opinion in Laue v. Production Credit Association, 390 N.W.2d 823 (Minn.Ct.App.1986), holding the farmer-lender mediation act applied even where foreclosure proceedings were already pending on the date the act became effective. Respondent continued to mediate, but also maintained the position that the retroactivity issue was on appeal to the Minnesota Supreme Court and, if Laue was reversed, the April 23 foreclosure sale would be valid.

Appellants and respondent were unsuccessful in mediating a settlement and on September 17, 1986, respondent filed notice of a second mortgage foreclosure sale. This sale was to be held November 25, 1986. On November 12, 1986, appellants served a summons and complaint on respondent, seeking to have both the April foreclosure sale and the upcoming November foreclosure sale declared invalid because respondent had not negotiated in good faith and had not given the requisite notice of mediation rights under Minn. Stat. § 581.05. Appellants also requested damages in excess of $50,000.

* * *

In the present case the trial court refused to issue the temporary injunction primarily because of its assessment that appellants had failed to show bad faith and therefore were unlikely to prevail on the merits in their underlying action which was also based on respondent's bad faith in mediation. Minn.Stat. § 583.27, subd. 1 provides:

> The parties must engage in mediation in good faith. Not participating in good faith includes: (1) a failure on a regular or continuing basis to attend and participate in mediation sessions without cause; (2) failure to provide full information regarding the financial obligations of the parties and other creditors; (3) failure of the creditor to designate a representative to participate in the mediation with authority to make binding commitments within one business day to fully settle, compromise, or otherwise mediate the matter; (4) lack of a written statement of debt restructuring alternatives and a statement of reasons why alternatives are unacceptable to one of the parties; (5) failure of a creditor to release funds from the sale of farm products to the debtor for necessary living and farm operating expenses; or (6) other similar behavior which evidences lack of good faith by the party. A failure to agree to reduce, restructure, refinance, or forgive debt does not, in itself, evidence lack of good faith by the creditor.

Minn.Stat. § 583.27, subd. 2, sets out a procedure for a mediator to report a party's lack of good faith in mediation by filing an affidavit with the director and the parties. In its accompanying memorandum, the trial court emphasized that the mediator had not filed an affidavit. As the trial court noted, mediation proceedings are unrecorded, and therefore without such an affidavit a determination of bad faith is very difficult.

Appellants claim, however, that an affidavit from the mediator is not necessary to prove their claim of bad faith because there are several aspects of respondent's conduct that prove the claim. First, appellants point to the fact that throughout mediation respondent continued to assert that if the supreme court reversed this court and determined that the mediation laws did not apply where debt enforcement proceedings had already been commenced, the April foreclosure sale would be valid. However, respondent did not use this argument to refuse to enter into mediation but only refused to waive the issue. Maintaining alternative legal positions is not unusual, especially in a case such as this where the law is in flux. Under the circumstances, respondent's approach does not necessarily evidence bad faith.

Appellants also argue that respondent's bad faith was shown because respondent believed it did not have to negotiate, could just wait out the mediation period and then foreclose. What respondent actually asserted at the hearing was that its physical presence was not even required at the mediation sessions and that by being present it had gone beyond what was required. Respondent's assertion is supported by Minn.Stat. § 583.28, subd. 1 (1986), which addresses instances when creditors need not attend mediation sessions. That section provides:

A creditor that is notified of the initial mediation meeting is subject to and bound by a mediation agreement if the creditor does not attend mediation meetings unless the creditor files a claim form. In lieu of attending a mediation meeting, a creditor may file a notice of claim and proof of claim on a claim form with the mediator before the scheduled meeting.

By filing a claim form the creditor agrees to be bound by a mediation agreement reached at the mediation meeting unless an objection is filed within the time specified. The mediator must notify the creditors who have filed claim forms of the terms of any agreement.

Respondent's stated positions regarding mediation are not sufficient to demonstrate that the trial court clearly abused its discretion in denying appellants' application for a temporary injunction.

Appellants also challenge the fact that respondent never served a mediation notice on the debtor and the director as required under Minn.Stat. § 583.26, subd. 1. However, appellants themselves requested mediation under Minn.Stat. § 583.26, subd. 2(c) which provides:

> (c) If a debtor has not received a mediation notice and is subject to a proceeding of a creditor enforcing a debt against agricultural property under chapter 580 or 581 * * *, the debtor may file a mediation request with the director. The mediation request form must indicate that the debtor has not received a mediation notice.

The farmer-lender mediation act does not impose a penalty when a creditor fails to serve a mediation notice. In the present case mediation did occur. While respondent did not follow the creditor notice provision of section 583.26, subd. 1, we can discern no prejudice to appellants that would justify granting a temporary injunction to halt the foreclosure sale.

* * *

KIMBERLEE K. KOVACH, GOOD FAITH IN ME-DIATION—REQUESTED, RECOMMENDED, OR REQUIRED? A NEW ETHIC
38 S. Tex. L. Rev. 575, 579–581, 610–611, 614–615, 618– (1997).

My focus is not, however, on the neutral mediator or her behavior. Rather, it is on the other participants, particularly the lawyer representatives. As the way we approach dispute resolution changed, literature became abundant with articles about the effect on courts and the legal system, the parties, and even the role of the lawyer as mediator. Although lawyers were given new methods for addressing the disputes of their clients, very little was provided in the way of guidance. It appeared that the advocates and other parties participating in a new and foreign process were expected to, almost automatically, change their behavior to conform to the nuances of the process. Such has not been the case.

* * *

Mediation provides a different paradigm for dispute resolution—one which includes collaboration, creativity, and often cooperation. Participants, and in particular attorney-advocates find that old behaviors are no longer helpful nor appropriate. In fact, previously learned tactics can often damage the potential for resolution. I recognize that changing, almost overnight, the mindset and behavior of lawyers, is a most formidable task. Yet if mediation is to survive as an alternative and fulfill any of the expectations, objectives, and goals of the process, which range from cost and time savings to satisfaction in settlement and empowerment, then the way the process is approached must be changed. The participants, the parties, and the lawyers must not be able to use the process to gain adversarial advantage which intentionally disadvantages other parties. This contradicts the goal of attaining a mutually satisfactory solution. Mediation, even within the context of the legal system, should maintain certain characteristics if it is to be a separate, viable alternative to adjudication.

* * *

B.   What Good Faith Is Not

Good faith in mediation does not mean not reaching an agreement. That is, I do not want to imply that in order to demonstrate good faith, the parties must settle the controversy or even that with mandatory good faith, agreements will be more likely. In fact, I am quite sure that there are many instances where neither party to the mediation demonstrated good faith in the process and yet were able to reach an accord. But settlement is not, and should not be, the absolute objective and goal of mediation. A mediation can be fruitful and beneficial even if no agreement is reached.

Good faith does not obligate the parties to possess a sincere desire to resolve the matter. While maintaining an open mind is certainly helpful to the mediation process, to judge a party's state of mind is too complex and subjective.

Good faith does not mean not having to disclose to the other participants or even the mediator everything about your case. Fears about mediation have been expressed by litigators in terms of "showing their hand" in advance of trial. While the merit in keeping secret something which probably is not that secret is questionable, especially if disclosing the information can realize the client's goals, nonetheless, if the parties refuse to share particular knowledge, they should not be compelled to do so. However, it is important that some information be exchanged that would provide an explanation for, or the basis of, the proposed settlement or lack thereof. In other words, since a primary focus of mediation, whether in a settlement or empowerment context is increased understanding and communication, disclosures are necessary. The scope of information to be disclosed, however, remains within the purview of the parties.

Just "being nice" is also not an element of good faith. One can be kind and cooperative, and yet do nothing to advance the ball in terms of resolution. Sometimes, of course, being "nice" is used as a tactic to throw the other unsuspecting party off guard, like the Mutt and Jeff or "good cop-bad cop" tactics. Just sitting and smiling at the other side does not constitute good faith. Some preparation and attempt to participate in a meaningful way should be exhibited.

C. Previous Definitions

Admittedly, some prior uses of the term good faith have proven problematic. Nonetheless, that should not, in itself, be the obstacle to the creation and implementation of such a requirement in mediation. The term good faith has been used in a number of contexts, ranging from transactional practice to litigation.

* * *

D. New Definitions and Perspectives

Good faith can mean a number of things as previously set forth. However, a more specific definition, at least initially, may help mediation participants know what to do; may aid the mediator, if and when a determination is to be made; and may assist the court should enforcement be necessary. Most individuals are familiar with common usage of the terms good faith and fair dealing. These include honesty in fact, truthfulness, as well as the absence of bad faith. But these elements have been applied primarily to actions which occur during the exchange segment of the negotiation. Yet the mediation process really begins earlier. Preparation and arrival for the mediation should be stages addressed by any good mediator. Moreover, courts can and do order attendance and exchange of information. This is an important consideration in creating a rule that is specific and directly specific to mediation. Prior criticism of good faith is, in part, based on the lack of objective standards; and that a demonstration of good or bad faith is dependant on one's state of mind. Some objective standards, which are not based upon the content of the proposals, are therefore necessary.

The following is a list of suggested factors which could be included in a rule or statute compelling good faith: Arriving at the mediation prepared with knowledge of the case, both in terms of the facts and possible solutions; taking into account the interests of the other parties; having all necessary decision-makers present at the mediation, not via a telephone; engaging in open and frank discussions about the case or matter in a way that might set out one's position for the other to better know and understand; not lying when asked a specific and direct question; not misleading the other side; demonstrating a willingness to listen and attempting to understand the position and interests of the other parties; being prepared not only to discuss the issues and interests of your client, but also to listen to the issues and interests of all other participants; having a willingness to discuss your position in detail; and explaining the rationale why a specific proposal is all that will be offered, or why one is refused. Many times a "hard" negotiator won't even know himself the reasoning behind what he is saying or the intractable position he takes. It's just a learned technique to be obstinate. Good faith includes coming to the mediation with an open mind, not necessarily a promise to change a view, but a willingness to be open to others. Although it may appear that there is a very fine line between not requiring a change of view, and a consideration of the requests of the others, the focus is on information. One party need not to agree with the other, but attempt to understand, and, at the very least, not summarily and without consideration immediately reject what the person has to say. From the lawyer's perspective, additional guidelines are applicable, such as allowing the client to discuss the matter directly with the other side and with the mediator. The purpose is again on the free flow of information between the disputing parties, a hallmark of the communication and participation necessary in the mediation process.

* * *

A good faith requirement in mediation could be established by legislation, court rule, rules of conduct for lawyers, or rules of practice in mediation. As a requirement, it is important that the necessity of good faith must be communicated to the participants prior to mediation.

* * *

Whether called good faith, "meaningful participation," or another similar term, some action to require a specific conduct conducive to the mediation process must be required. Whether by court rule, legislation, or a code of ethics, such an obligation should be constructed and implemented immediately. And the duty of good faith should extend to the parties as well as their attorney representatives . . . If mediation is to survive as a formidable, unique process with the characteristics remaining which has made it a process that results in party satisfaction, then practices and procedures with regard to lawyers' conduct in the mediation process must change. To require good faith is one suggestion and a step in the right direction. The road will not be an easy one, but the road less traveled initially can make all the difference.[32]

b.   Cost Considerations

There are a number of issues which surround a court's authority to make referrals which increase costs to the parties who are participating in a public justice system. A primary issue is whether the court can *require* parties availing themselves of a public service to incur additional cost. Because of the courts' sensitivity to the issue of paid mediators and the availability of nonprofit dispute resolution providers, such as dispute resolution centers, there has been little actual litigation surrounding this issue. Looking at the issue in the arbitration process can provide some guidance. When courts were faced with objections to arbitration based

32.   See Appendix C for the proposed   Rule of Good Faith.

upon the additional costs to the parties and attendant constitutional challenges, most resolved the matter in favor of the use of alternatives.[33]

Controversy about fees among providers is significant. For example, a litigant in either Harris or Travis County, Texas, who wishes to file a lawsuit must pay an additional ten dollar sum as part of the filing fee. This ten dollar "surcharge" constitutes the ADR fund for the county.[34] Some then argue that litigants should not have to pay again for a private mediation. A number of lawyers are now making a living mediating court referred cases[35] and want to restrict these litigant-funded centers to providing services for indigent individuals only. Payment to the mediator causes other concerns as well. One primary concern is that of neutrality. Difficulties may arise when one party, such as a large corporation, is a repeat player in the court and now mediation. This often more affluent party has the potential to refer a number of cases to the mediator. Moreover, in cases between a large corporation and an individual, where the company is in a better position to carry the cost of mediation, it may pay the entire amount of the fee, rather than the usual evenly split division. Mediators must be careful to not allow these matters to affect impartiality.[36]

Expenses associated with the mediation process include more than just the cost of the mediator. Penalties or sanctions for non-compliance with a mediation order are possible, and becoming more common. Fees for attorney time spent in preparation for, and attendance at, the mediation are additional cost factors. A few of these matters have been raised in court proceedings, and many are discussed regularly by the mediation and legal communities.[37]

Direct cost is not the only reason that persons with limited financial resources may not use mediation. Legal services or legal aid attorneys have been very hesitant to use ADR mechanisms, and they cite a number of reasons for their skepticism. Because lower-income individuals may be less educated or less sophisticated about the legal system, mediation, and other methods of problem solving, they may be intimidated by the experience. In these instances people may rather quickly accept a settlement in order to bring the process to conclusion. They may also be unaware that they could have bargained for more, or were entitled to it. Some of these issues could be remedied with legal representation, but not all parties to a dispute are going to have attorneys.

An individual left on his or her own may also lack skills in the negotiation process. Most mediators remain neutral even in this instance, for to assist one side in the process would likely forfeit neutrality.

---

33. For detail, see Rogers & McEwen, *supra* note 1, § 6:04 and Chapter 7, Mandatory Mediation and Settlement Pressure.

34. Tex.Civ.Prac. & Rem.Code Ann. § 152.004 (VTCA 1986 & Supp. 1999).

35. See Louis J. Weber, *Court–Referred ADR and the Lawyer–Mediator: In Service of Whom?,* 46 SMU L. Rev. 2113 (1993).

36. Neutrality and impartiality are considered in more detail in Chapter 7.

37. See Russell Engler, *And Justice for All–Including the Unrepresented Poor: Revisiting the Role of Judges, Mediators and Clerks,* 67 Fordham L. Rev. 1987 (1999).

Low-income persons, by definition, are in need of money. This is another reason low-income parties may be willing to settle their cases rather quickly. By doing so, they can obtain the money now, even though holding out may get them more in the long run. Finally, there is the concern about the inability to change the law through ADR mechanisms.

c. *Voluntary Participation*

Parties involved in litigation may voluntarily participate in mediation at any time during the pendency of the lawsuit. Factors which indicate why parties would be willing to do so have been previously enumerated. However, difficulties may arise when one party advocates mediation for a "wrong" reason, such as a disguised opportunity for unstructured discovery. In the instances where the case originally goes to mediation for the wrong reasons, but nonetheless is settled, it is likely that no harm results. However, in those cases where a request, and agreement by the other side, for mediation is made, due to fraudulent reasons, things become more complicated. This situation has not been routinely addressed by the courts. But without an agreement or court order requiring good faith participation, it does not appear that sanctions are available, particularly where there existed an apparent agreement to utilize the mediation process.

C. ISSUES OF TIMING: THE LIFE OF A DISPUTE

While issues of timing, or when to use ADR, are often discussed and debated, there is still little certainty. What is certain is that ADR use, regardless of the time of its intervention in a matter, usually results in a positive outcome. This has been confirmed by anecdotal information.[38] Although a positive outcome does not necessarily mean a completely final agreement, it does mean that the parties are pleased and satisfied with the process. In other words, there have been demonstrated benefits from ADR use, regardless of the timing. One interpretation is that there is no "wrong" time. Nonetheless, factors to consider when contemplating mediation merit examination.

Many have written of the nature of conflict and disputing, including the premise that "conflict lives." Conflict progresses through relatively predictable stages. Although the stages are distinct and recognizable, the timing or occurrence of each differs in each dispute. Many factors contribute to these differences. In the majority of cases, the parties begin with a recognition that a problem, disagreement, or dispute exists. If an immediate answer or resolution is not attained, the conflict escalates. In fact, the path of conflict has been likened to a snowball rolling downhill. As conflict continues, size and intensity increase. If stopped early, the growth is halted. Thus, the sooner a matter is resolved, the better.

---

38. While there is no specific study to establish this, the author reaches this conclusion after numerous discussions with a number of program directors throughout the United States, particularly those in court-annexed programs.

Sometimes, however, conflict dissipates on its own. The intensity of the dispute decreases. Time has intervened, and perhaps the subject of the conflict no longer holds the importance it once did. With time as an intervenor, the parties are better able to rationally examine the matter and work together to find a resolution. It is these two competing theories which contribute to the difficulty of prescribing the best time for mediation.

1. NON-LITIGATION MATTERS

In those cases where there is an ongoing relationship, whether personal or professional, a conflict or dispute can do harm. If time and energy are devoted to the dispute in a negative or destructive manner, people become more locked into their positions and close their minds to options. Thus in most cases, the sooner the conflict is resolved, the more positive the impact on the relationship. This is especially important when the parties have regular communication or interaction, such as working with each other or living in the same neighborhood.

Therefore, once individuals or entities realize that they are involved in a conflict, attempts at resolution through mediation are appropriate. Moreover, mediation is usually recommended prior to seeking legal assistance. In most cases little harm can result from mediation, even if no settlement is reached. The parties will still have all other options open to them. The only situation where it may be advisable to not adhere to the policy of "the sooner, the better" is where there is such hostility between the parties that any discussion would likely result in physical confrontation. Here, a "cooling off" period is needed.

2. LEGAL DISPUTES

By the phrase, *legal dispute*, it is meant that lawyers have become involved in representing the parties to a dispute. Of course, the sooner ADR intervention occurs, the greater the amount of monetary savings. These savings can be seen in a number of ways. One direct cost of a legal dispute is attorneys' fees. Another is management cost. In many businesses, time must be spent by key personnel dealing with the dispute. This is time away from managerial roles. Disputing may also cost a company in terms of its employee's productivity. Indirect costs to individuals include emotional costs expended not only in disputing but also in the court process.

Before everyone has become committed to full use of the legal system may be the time to look for creative options. Yet there is some debate about whether it is more conducive to a "better" resolution to attempt to resolve a legal dispute at an early stage. On one hand, if ADR treatment occurs very early, the individuals may still be hostile, and thus unwilling to negotiate. Alternatively, the longer the wait for mediation, the greater the possibility of the parties' becoming entrenched in their positions and unmovable. Clearly, each case varies.

When individuals first go to a lawyer, resolution by way of negotiated settlement is not usually one of the options anticipated. Yet, in many instances that is precisely when mediation is appropriate. This is even more true when the parties or entities involved have an on-going relationship—particularly one which depends upon direct communication. Examples include disputes between business partners, construction contracts, and franchise agreements.

After a lawsuit is filed and the defendant has been served, there is usually a period of distrust and hostility between the parties, and sometimes even between the attorneys. As the case progresses, this may decrease or increase. Through an exchange of information, the parties and their attorneys begin negotiating. If a settlement is not reached, but negotiations have commenced, it is clearly an appropriate time to participate in mediation.

In some matters, the attorneys will allege that discovery is necessary before the case can go to mediation. This may be true. Alternatively, the discovery process may cause the dispute to escalate, especially between the attorneys, which in turn increases costs. Because mediation has proven to be effective in all these instances, even if discovery is necessary, it may be possible for the participants to informally exchange information prior to the mediation. Moreover, several recent statutes have been enacted which toll the running of discovery deadlines or statutes of limitations during the time allotted for mediation. By the time most cases are set for trial, the conflict has decreased and a negotiated resolution is eventually reached. However, costs have been expended, and in some cases the costs are greater than the amount in controversy. Yet mediation has been successfully used even at the time of trial, particularly in those instances where the trial would have taken more than a day or two.

D. THE ROLE OF THE ATTORNEY–ADVOCATE IN THE REFERRAL PROCESS

Issues which surround the attorney's potential duty to advise the client about ADR have begun to be recognized. Currently the supreme courts of a few states strongly recommend, by way of professionalism mandates, that attorneys inform clients of alternative forums for dispute resolution.[39] The subject of the lawyer's duty with regard to ADR has been the subject of a spirited debate.[40] And now the American Bar Association, through it Ethics 2000 Commission, may consider within the Model Rules a provision requiring lawyers to advise clients about ADR processes.[41] Another approach, taken in Georgia, is a requirement

39. These include *Hawaii, Texas* and *Colorado.* For example, see Hawaii Rules of Professional Conduct 2.4 (1997) which provides "In a matter involving or expected to involve litigation, a lawyer should advise the client of alternative forms of dispute resolution which might reasonably be pur-sued to attempt to resolve the legal dispute or to reach the legal objective sought".

40. See Frank E.A. Sander & Michael L. Prigoff, *Should There Be a Duty to Advise of ADR Options,* 76 A.B.A.J. 50 (1990).

41. 84 A.B.A.J. 100 (August 1998).

that all members of the state bar be educated in dispute resolution.[42]

Clients may be aware of ADR and request it themselves. In some jurisdictions, courts are responsible for an ADR intervention. For instance, the judge may require ADR before setting the case for trial.[43] In other courts, local rules provide that by the time the case has been pending for a certain period, the parties must have participated in an ADR process. However, in the majority of cases, it is still going to be the attorney's role to suggest and discuss the possibility of ADR treatment with her client. In fact, some have argued that the failure to do so constitutes legal malpractice.[44]

The correct time for the attorney to discuss mediation touches upon many of the issues previously discussed. The client may have contacted the attorney because he is ready to fight, not settle. The client may think the suggestion of mediation or settlement is an indication of the attorney's lack of confidence in the case and become defensive. However, the attorney-counselor must remember that all options for disposition of a case should be discussed with the client.[45] While the initial interview may not be the right time, allowing the client to incur sizeable legal fees before suggesting mediation is not the best option either. Each case and each client is different. The various factors about each should be considered by the attorney and discussed with the client. The timing of these discussions with the client may be as important as the timing of actual mediation participation, particularly in terms of the client's attitude toward the process.

E.   SELECTION OF THE MEDIATOR

A discussion of the most appropriate mediator for each situation can be interesting and educational. Research has demonstrated that parties are more likely to be satisfied with mediation if it provides process control.[46] Therefore it has been urged that party satisfaction with mediation will be enhanced if the parties, rather than the court, control the selection process. As a practical matter, however, much of the decision regarding mediator selection will turn on the nature of the mediation community in each jurisdiction. A brief exploration of these considerations follows.

42. See Geor. R. ADR Rule 8 (1999).

43. This is known as the carrot approach, where the court induces a party to participate by providing a reward (an early trial setting) for participation.

44. Robert F. Cochran, *Legal Representation and the Next Steps Toward Client Control: Attorney Malpractice for the Failure to Allow the Client to Control Negotiation and Pursue Alternatives to Litigation,* 44 Wash. & Lee L. Rev. 819 (1990); Monica L. Warmbrod, Comment, *Could an Attorney face Disciplinary Actions or Even Legal Malpractice Liability for Failure to Inform Clients of Alternative Dispute Resolution,* 27 Cumb. L. Rev. 791 (1996–97).

45. *Id.* at 830. See also Mark Spiegal, *Lawyering and Client Decisionmaking: Informed Consent and the Legal Profession* 128 U. Pa. L. Rev. 41 (1979).

46. See Robert A. Baruch Bush, *What Do We Need A Mediator For? Mediations "Value–Added" for Negotiators,* 12 Ohio St. J. on Disp. Resol. 1 (1996).

1. MATCHING CASES AND MEDIATORS

Once case characteristics have been identified and prioritized resulting in the parties' referral or agreement to mediation, selection of the mediator is the next step. The process of matching case characteristics with mediator characteristics is not a scientific matter. Sometimes certain factors are obvious, indicating a need for a certain style of mediator. In other situations, the choice will not be as clear.

First and foremost in many clients' thoughts, is the cost of the mediator. Certainly the client's willingness and ability to pay, in light of the amount in controversy, is a primary consideration. At one end of the range of cost are those programs which offer volunteer mediators such as local dispute resolution centers (DRCs) and court-connected programs. Alternatively, the charge for private mediation service providers range from $100–$300 per hour to $1,500–$2,000 per day, per party or side. Because there is no regulation, the range is quite broad.

In technical or highly complex issues, employment of someone with particular expertise is needed—for example, in patent, engineering, and architectural areas where the discussion may turn on a very specific technical issue. Therefore, in those cases an examination of the mediators' backgrounds to determine if they have specific expertise is the first, and sometimes only, step taken.

In most lawsuits, previous legal experience of the mediator is considered. Some courts focus on attorney-mediators and assert that pending litigation should be mediated almost exclusively by them. However, many experts in the field, as well as some lawyers and clients, feel otherwise and, in fact, steer away from the lawyer-mediator, particularly when the dispute involves primarily non-legal matters.

Personality type is another mediator characteristic that crosses the mind of some litigants and lawyers. This is even more important when considering the personalities and relationship of the lawyers as well as the strengths or weaknesses of the personalities of the disputing parties. Where the mediation table is surrounded by strong verbose attorneys and parties, the mediator must be able to control the situation. Yet, a mediator must also be able to be quiet, especially at those times when a relaxed approach is more effective.[47] A mediator who primarily allows open discussion will be helpful if parties and lawyers are sophisticated enough to conduct their own negotiation. On the other hand, where the parties are unsophisticated, emotional, or lack familiarity with the bargaining process, then a mediator who is more directive would be appropriate. The background and training of the mediator may also indicate his flexibility. Many mediators can vary styles depending on the matter in dispute and on the personalities of the participants.

MEDEIROS v. HAWAII COUNTY PLANNING COMMISSION

Intermediate Court of Appeals of Hawaii, 1990.
8 Hawaii App. 183, 797 P.2d 59.

Property owners appealed from decision of the county planning

---

47. An examination of the variety of mediator *styles* is included in Chapter 15.

commission approving permit for drilling of scientific observation holes in geothermal resource subzone established by Board of Land and Natural Resources. . . .

The time constraints in the mediation process were in accord with the dictates of HRS § 205–5.1(e). However, Appellants argue that, although they were required to share the cost of mediation, they were not given a voice in the selection of the mediators. We do not believe it is essential to due process that Appellants participate in naming the mediator or mediators. Appellants' due process rights are protected so long as the selection process and the chosen mediator are unbiased. Appellants do not claim the mediators were biased or prejudiced and do not claim to have been prejudiced by the Commission's selection.

2. FINDING MEDIATORS

There are a number of methods for obtaining information about potential mediators. Several mediator organizations have lists of their members. Many incorporated private providers have brochures describing their services and backgrounds of the affiliated mediators. A number of courts, both state and federal, have established approved ADR provider lists.

Many mediators advertise their services. In fact, in many jurisdictions mediators may be found in the yellow pages section of the telephone book.[48] And, as with all service providers, word-of-mouth can be a helpful source of information about potential mediator selections. One state, Ohio, has published a Consumer's Guide to Selecting a Neutral. It's very likely other states or local mediation programs will produce similar publications.

Looking for a good mediator is probably much like looking for or finding a good lawyer, accountant, doctor or any other professional. Much depends on the specifics of the case, including the people and personalities involved. However, there are some distinct factors about a lawsuit or a dispute that attorneys and their clients may consider when looking for a mediator.

QUESTIONS FOR DISCUSSION

4–1. Since a primary basis for the use of mediation is saving money and time, how is this goal met where the court makes a referral to a private mediator who charges a substantial fee?

4–2. A California resident faced with a custody or visitation issue absolutely refuses to go to mediation. What would you advise? See Trina Grillo, *The Mediation Alternative: Process Dangers for Women*, 100 Yale L.J. 1545 (1991).

---

48. Search engines on the World Wide Web may also be helpful in locating mediation services.

4–3. Ruth Suttle sued her employer, Power Driver Tools, for alleged acts of sexual harassment by her immediate supervisor, Joe Caps. The case is pending in the federal district court for the Eastern District of Decree. This court has enacted rules which permit the court to order a case to ADR, including case evaluation, arbitration, and mediation. Defendant has filed its answer two months ago, and the parties are about to initiate the discovery process.

Plaintiff alleges that Power Driver Tools has a specific written policy against sexual harassment which the male supervisors have openly made fun of and "jokingly" violate. Power Driver's C.E.O., Matthew Principle, believes all sexual harassment claims are frivolous and has issued an edict that no such claims will be settled and all such cases shall be tried. Larry Werner, outside counsel in the Suttle case, has been contacted by Sam(antha) Carese, counsel for Ruth Suttle. Sam(antha) asked Larry about the possibility of referring the dispute to mediation, and suggested that mediation will save both sides great expense. It was hinted that Ruth might lower her demands if she had a chance to tell Matthew Principle what is going on at the factory.

Werner has contacted Matthew Principle about the mediation option. Principle's response was, "Tell them, hell, no."

Carese has, after consultation with Ruth, filed a Motion to Refer to Mediation with the court, including a request that Matthew Principle be ordered, as the person with ultimate authority to settle, to attend the entire mediation.

When Principle was furnished a copy of the motion by Werner, Principle roared, "File whatever it takes to oppose this. This is America. No judge can force me to attend a mediation."

Principle has also advised Werner he wants to attend the hearing and "testify and give that civil rights lawyer a piece of my mind."

District Judge Timid Hand has routinely signed agreed orders to mediate. Judge Hand has never been confronted with an opposed motion to Refer.

(a) You are Carese. Prepare a Motion to Refer to Mediation, along with a Brief in support of your Motion. Be prepared for your Oral Argument on this issue.

(b) You are Werner. Prepare a Response to the Motion, along with a Bench Brief supporting your position. Do you take your client to the hearing? Explain.

(c) You are Judge Hand. Upon receipt of the Briefs and hearing the oral arguments of counsel, write your opinion.

Chapter Five

PREPARATION FOR THE MEDIATION

The events leading up to a mediation can have a significant effect on what happens during the session. The mediation process consists primarily of interpersonal communication, and, as such, is not only flexible but also, to a degree, spontaneous. Nonetheless, preparation for mediation is essential. All participants in the process, including the mediator, the parties and their representatives and, in some cases, the constituents[1] of those at the table, must prepare for the session. The duration of the preparatory stage varies considerably, ranging from a few minutes to several months, depending upon the nature of the dispute. As the use of mediation increases, and the importance of preparation is realized, greater attention will be devoted to preliminary matters.

A. THE MEDIATOR

The mediator's preparation is frequently determined by the nature of the case and the method of its referral. In many cases, particularly where mediators serve on a pro bono basis, such as during a settlement week,[2] the mediator may receive information about the case only moments before sitting down with the parties. In such instances, the mediator has little time to prepare for the specific case. Such fast track preparation also occurs at community-based programs and dispute resolution centers. In the foregoing instances, the cases are assigned to a specific mediator only when that mediator arrives at the center. Likewise, during settlement week or in an ongoing, court-annexed program,

---

1. In large cases such as those involving public policy, not all affected individuals will be present at the mediation. See Chapter 17 for a discussion of public policy dispute resolution.

2. Settlement week is a program, sometimes mandated by statute, in which a high volume of pending lawsuits are strongly urged to settle by use of ADR. The ADR method is usually mediation. The courthouse is dedicated to this endeavor during a

one week period, such as a "dead week" where the courthouse would otherwise be shut down. For elaboration on settlement weeks, see Harold Paddock, *Settlement Week: A Practical Manual for Resolving Civil Cases Through Mediation* (1990) and James G. Woodward, *Settlement Week: Measuring the Promise,* 11 N. Ill. U.L.R. 1 (1990).

volunteer mediators usually know only the nature of the case prior to their arrival. These programs handle all pre-mediation details through a central administrative staff. Information is sent to, and received from, the parties without regard to the identity of the mediator. In some programs, the case is assigned to a specific mediator for the primary purpose of scheduling and completing a conflicts check.[3] The mediator is handed a case file or a summary of the case just minutes before beginning the mediation. In these instances, the preparation on the part of the mediator, of course, is minimal with regard to the specific case and facts. However, the mediator can prepare herself in a more global way in terms of being ready to listen carefully, analyze the case, remain neutral, and provide an environment for creative problem solving.

In a private mediation practice, the mediator can dictate the nature of the preparation. The mediator's preparation should begin with asking and answering two basic questions:

1.   What do you, as the mediator, want the participants to know prior to sitting down at the mediation table?

2.   What do you want to know about the case and the participants prior to beginning the mediation session?

An outlined response to these two questions provides the mediator the necessary steps she must follow in the preliminary stages. A third, related question concerns how the information exchange will be accomplished.

Preparation is both mechanical and mental. Mechanical preparation involves logistics, housekeeping and administrative details. First and foremost, the mediator should arrange to have the session held in a neutral location. A neutral site is not the office of one of the parties or a party's counsel. In most cases, the neutral location will be the mediator's office. In some instances, because of the number of parties or because the mediator is not serving in her jurisdiction, the location will be a hotel room, conference center, or another mediator's office. The mediator should be certain that there is sufficient room for the number of participants who will be attending, including additional rooms for break-out or separate caucuses.

Room decor is also an important part of the mediation session. As the mediation profession grows and individuals select offices with a primary focus on conducting mediations, additional attention should be given to the mediation environment. The way the room is arranged can affect the communication and behavior of the parties.[4] For instance, most communication is directed across a table, rather than around it. Moreover, seats at an end of a table often indicate a leadership and task orientation, while a center position suggests a more participatory role. Therefore, the mediator should give particular attention to the seating

---

3. Issues surrounding potential conflicts of interest, particularly for the attorney mediator, are examined in Chapter 14.

4. Chapter 3 provides a discussion of proxemics, concerning the effect of spatial relationships.

arrangements, especially in multi-party cases. Arrangements for items such as access to telephones as well as the necessities of food and beverages should also be handled by the mediator.[5]

Once the location is identified, the time for the mediation should be determined. Where courts are active in the referral process, the date is sometimes specifically set forth in the court's order. In most cases, however, these arrangements are left to the agreement of all participants and the mediator. Of course, if any of the participants is reluctant to attend, the entire scheduling process may require a mediation effort. Far more often, the mediator, by conference call herself or with the assistance of a coordinator, can work with the parties in hammering out these details.

One emerging problem for mediators in private practice is the cancellation or postponement of scheduled sessions. Most mediators, except those handling family cases, block out an entire day for a mediation. When cancellations occur, the mediator is left with down time and no income. If the session is merely postponed, the income is eventually received, but the previously scheduled day remains open. A few mediators require a non-refundable deposit at the time the mediation is scheduled, while others charge a cancellation fee. The policy with regard to cancellations should be addressed by the mediator at the time the mediation is arranged.

The amount of the mediator's fee should also be determined in advance. Private mediators' fees may vary significantly and are not currently subject to regulation. Most mediators charge either an hourly rate or a flat, per day fee.[6] The hourly rate is advocated by those who traditionally use this format, such as lawyers, accountants, and therapists. Such an approach is quite simple and straightforward, although it should be clarified in advance whether pre-mediation preparation is included. Others believe that the participants will constantly think about the mediator being "on the clock"; in order to avoid additional cost, they will rush to a settlement that they may not be satisfied with. The effect of each alternative has not been researched, but so far there does not appear to be a clear preference for one over the other. Fee structure is a matter of personal choice for the mediator. It is imperative that the structure, estimated amount, and billing practice[7] be clearly conveyed to all participants in advance. Most often the mediator or her administrator will include such administrative information in a pre-mediation letter to the participants.

This pre-mediation correspondence should also provide information about the mediation process and the mediator, herself. Where the

5. For more detail about an appropriate mediation environment, see Eric R. Galton, Representing Clients in Mediation 73–74 (1994).

6. A very limited number of mediators charge on a contingency fee basis. Most codes of ethics view contingency-fee-based mediation as a clear conflict of interest, and hence unethical.

7. That is, whether payment is expected in advance of the session or whether the bill will be sent subsequent to the mediation.

participants or their representatives select the mediator in advance, relevant information in terms of education and training may already be known. In cases of court appointment, participants may have been informed about the mediator by the court or other appointing entity. Even so, it may be helpful for the mediator to include a brief curriculum vitae in the materials provided to the parties although a complete life history is not necessary.

Just how much information the parties should receive and assimilate prior to the mediation is subject to debate. At one end of the scale are those who propose that very little education be provided, that the less the parties know about what will happen at mediation, the better. Although not often articulated, the presumption of such a mediator is that if the parties are completely familiar with the techniques and strategies that the mediator may utilize during the session, they may attempt to undermine her work. The theory is that the mediator is in control of the process and only she should know the intricacies of the process. Those mediators assume that most individuals go to a mediator because of her expertise and do not themselves want or expect to know much about mediation. On the other hand, some mediators believe that the more the participants know about the process in advance, the better. These mediators send the parties a very detailed outline of the process including all component stages, and possible modifications. Most mediators fall between these two extremes. They want the participants to know something about the process and what to expect, but they also believe that a detailed study of it by the participants is not necessary or appropriate.

Mediation is the facilitation of negotiation; the participants will be negotiating while the mediator facilitates. Therefore, most mediators conclude that it is important that the participants focus on the negotiation process and prepare accordingly. Some mediators will briefly describe negotiation as they see it; others will send each side either a loaner or complimentary copy of *Getting to Yes*[8] prior to the mediation session. In many instances, a two to three page outline of the negotiation or mediation process is sent out by the mediator. A typical pre-mediation packet of information for the parties would include this outline, the letter about administrative details, and any other items the mediator wants the participants to review. These other items may include a statement disclosing possible conflicts of interests, an agreement or contract to mediate, forms disclaiming mediator representation, waiver of potential mediator liability, confidentiality agreements, and evaluation forms.

In the correspondence sent to the participants, the mediator should also include a request for the information that she wants prior to the mediation session. Therefore it is important that the mediator determine how much information she thinks is necessary to have in advance of the session. In making this determination, the mediator must keep in mind

8. Roger Fisher, William Ury and Bruce Patton, Getting to Yes 2nd Ed. (1991).

that she is not making a decision about either the facts or the law of the case. Consequently, it is not necessary to know and memorize in advance, each factor or legal argument that the parties might propose at the mediation. It is imperative, however, where a lawsuit is pending, that the mediator know the status of the case along with any pending motions or deadlines. In some instances, these case variables affect how the mediation is approached. The mediator must be sure the parties consider these factors when looking at settlement options. Moreover, any resolution reached at mediation should not be in conflict with a court order.

Much of the theory and philosophy of mediation urges a move away from legalities and toward identifying the underlying issues and interests from the perspective of the parties. Many cases will be resolved by finding ways to satisfy those interests. When individuals set forth a legal position or written analysis of a problem, these underlying issues and interests are generally not stated. Parties usually first state their positions at an intake center[9] or by the filing of a lawsuit in a court. In either case, these statements are made in terms of the expected audience at that time. This is not the mediation audience. Therefore the mediator should be careful in reading this material. For similar reasons it is rarely advocated that the mediator look at all of the pleadings in the case. The goals to be achieved by pleadings differ dramatically from the goals of a mediation. The mediator does not serve as counsel or judge in the case, and therefore, should not review or analyze the pleadings from such viewpoints. Moreover, as mediation is a process through which the disputing parties can move away from the legal paradigm,[10] reviewing pleadings will only impede this goal.

Since it may expedite the session for the mediator to have some familiarity with the case, most mediators will ask the parties to provide a written overview of the case. These may be referred to as a "summary memorandum" or "pre-mediation submission."[11] Most mediators request that the parties submit these documents at least seven days prior to the session, although a few days in advance is usually sufficient. Many mediators ask that each participant provide a memorandum under separate cover which is not shared with the other parties. The mediator maintains the confidentiality of the contents. On the other hand, some mediators request that counsel exchange the documents as they would pleadings. In such cases, a provision for any confidential information may be made in a separate document. There is yet a third minority approach. Some mediators feel that the process might be expedited if the

---

9. *Intake* is the term utilized to describe the process by which a citizen involved in a dispute can be referred to mediation. Intake takes place at most community dispute resolution centers and court-annexed programs. A citizen meets with an intake specialist in a personal interview, and an attempt to find the most appropriate avenue to resolve the dispute is made.

10. For a discussion of the dichotomy of legalized paradigms and solutions versus those available in mediation, see Chapters 7 and 10.

11. These are but two terms that have been used to describe these documents. There are numerous other ways to refer to written information that the mediator receives prior to the mediation session.

lawyers are able to draft a form of joint statement, much like a joint pretrial order, with stipulations as to specific areas of agreement and disagreement. A fourth option is to request a combination of the foregoing documents.

In all cases the mediator should think through what type of information she is looking for and how much time should be spent in preparation for the session. For instance, in some cases the parties have sent the mediator video tapes. These can take hours to review. Since the mediator is not making a decision as to the outcome, elaborate pre-mediation submissions may not be necessary. The extent of detail in the submission may also depend on the complexity of the case.

Pre-mediation submissions serve other functions beyond educating the mediator. Mediation is a relatively new activity for lawyers, particularly litigators. The courthouse is familiar—the mediator's office is not. Preparation for court is common—preparation for mediation is not. Even in jurisdictions where court-annexed mediation is widespread,[12] it is not unusual to see lawyers arrive at the mediation session having never looked at the file or discussed the case with the client. By requiring each party's representative, usually an attorney, to submit a written memorandum in advance of mediation, the case is at least reviewed. In those instances where the submission is exchanged, advance education of the opposing parties can occur. If information about the matter previously not disclosed is revealed, it can be beneficial in opening discussions. As lawyers differ in their degree of preparedness for trial, likewise they differ vastly in how they prepare for mediation. It is up to the mediator to do what she can to encourage the participants to be prepared for the mediation and to assist her in preparation as well.

The mediator must also identify who will be participating and, if at all possible, assure that everyone who is necessary for a binding decision be present at the mediation table.[13] How the mediator will deal with lawyers and their clients is also something that should be considered by the mediator in this preliminary stage. It is important that the lawyers and their clients know in advance what role each will play in the mediation. Some mediators allow the lawyers to basically control the process and dictate what role the client will have. Most mediators, however, know that it is important that the client participate, and in fact, subscribe to the belief that the case belongs to the parties and not to their lawyers. Therefore, decision-making with regard to settlement options should be left with the client.[14] Most clients know more about the

12. For example, Florida and Texas courts refer thousands of cases a year to mediation.

13. This was discussed in Chapter 4, and is a very important element of the process. Getting all participants to the mediation table has been a difficult part of mediation. Many mediators claim this is one of the primary reasons why mediations do not result in an agreement. Any effort

the mediator can make in this regard prior to the actual mediation hearing is strongly advised.

14. See Robert F. Cochran, *Legal Representation and the Next Steps Toward Client Control: Attorney Malpractice for the Failure to Allow the Client to Control Negotiation and Pursue Alternatives to Litigation,*

subject matter of their dispute and are consequently in a much better position to evaluate alternatives. And, in some cases, the attorney's interest is in conflict with that of the client.[15] In order to reach a final resolution it is extremely important for the parties to fully participate in the mediation. Hence, some mediators will request that the lawyers take a back seat (sometimes, literally, in that they move them away from the table). In other cases, however, clients are uneducated and lack negotiating skills. It is important that these individuals be represented at the mediation. Other authorities have identified four distinct roles an attorney may play while representing a client at mediation. These are: a) attorney as non-participant, b) attorney as silent advisor, c) attorney as co-participant, and d) attorney as dominant or sole participant.[16] In cases where the attorney is a non-participant it is important that the client have adequate legal advice in advance of the mediation as well as that related to a settlement. As a silent advisor to his client in mediation, the lawyer is present at the mediation, but refrains from any active role.[17]

When the attorney is a co-participant with his client, they may be involved equally throughout the process, or alternately divide the roles and responsibility. And, in those mediations where the attorney is the dominant or sole participant, the client may not be present, though in most instances would still be available by phone.[18] While the merits of each approach can be argued, each mediator must make her own decision as to what expectations she places upon the participants. What is important however, is that these items are considered, determined and communicated to the participants in advance. Where attorneys are involved in the case, the mediator should inform them of their expected role at the session. In most court-annexed cases, mediators look for participation from both the client and his representative.

The mediator should explain to the participants how the opening statement will proceed. For example, the lawyer may speak first with subsequent comments by the client. In some cases, the client first presents the situation, followed by a legal analysis by the lawyer. If the mediator expects the lawyers to take a very limited role, she needs to share this information in advance. Complete exclusion of the attorney or representative is generally not advised. However, consider the following California rule.

§ 3182.　Authority of mediators; exclusion of counsel; exclusion of domestic violence support person[19]

(a) The mediator has authority to exclude counsel from participation in the mediation proceedings pursuant to this chapter if, in the mediator's discretion, exclusion of counsel is appropriate or necessary.

47 Wash. & Lee L. Rev. 819, 854–862 (1990).

15.　*Id.* at 854. See also Chapter 14, § B, which examines attorney-client conflicts in mediation in ethical terms.

16.　John S. Murray, Alan S. Rau and Edward F. Sherman, Mediation and Other Non–Binding ADR Processes, 150–151 (1996).

17.　*Id.* at 151.

18.　*Id.*

19.　West's Ann.Cal. Fam. Code § 3182 (1993).

(b) The mediator has authority to exclude a domestic violence support person from a mediation proceeding as provided in Section 6303.

The mediator is a neutral third party to a dispute before, during, and after the mediation. Throughout the mediator's preparation, and particularly while the mediator is reviewing the mediation submissions, she should avoid ex-parte telephone calls with any participant. Any telephonic communication should be done in a conference call format. This is to assure actual, as well as perceived, neutrality in the case.[20] In her preparation the mediator should also begin to identify possible areas of mutual concern or interest. These are much easier for the mediator, an objective party, to identify. Because mediation deals with human behavior, these interests are always subject to change. The mediator must maintain an open mind and be careful to avoid making any prejudgments about the case.

Mediation is termed a dispute resolution alternative; thus, mediation is usually seen as a method to resolve a dispute or conflict. However, the mediation process can also provide assistance in the negotiation of transactions. In these instances, the mediator's preparation will differ slightly. In the disputing context, determining possible solutions constitutes much of the mediation, and options are wide open. In the transactional context, the parties are more focused. They are aware of the goal they wish to accomplish, e.g., a lease agreement or an employment contract. In these instances, it is helpful for the mediator to be familiar with the business endeavor of the parties. In preparation she too will be more focused on assessing vehicles through which the parties might reach their goal, rather than on what past events occurred.[21]

Most of the foregoing dealt with the mechanical preparation for the mediation. It is also important that the mediator consider what has been termed the mediator's mental preparation. Just as with the mechanical, there are various elements included in the mental preparation. Each mediator will have to decide for herself the extent to which each is necessary, a determination likely to differ in each case.

First the mediator must rid herself of all preconceptions of opinion and adopt a non-judgmental state of mind. The mediator should remind herself that neutrality is the essence of being a mediator. She must also prepare to be patient. One example is to vow to not allow a desire for a faster pace to impact the disputants' full ability to express their feelings or describe the dispute. The mediator must also get ready to focus completely on the dispute and be able to avoid any other distractions or commitments.

The mediator should also anticipate and relish diversity. She must remember that all people are entitled to a respectful process. A commit-

---

20. For details on neutrality issues, see Chapter 7.

21. For more detail on the mediation of transactional matters, see Chapter 16.

ment to actively listen to the comments of all participants is vital. And very importantly, the mediator must pledge to search for underlying interests. She should also remember that the parties, beyond settlement, may desire conciliation or closure.

It is also important that the mediator not begin the process either overly optimistic or pessimistic. Each mediation is different. Anticipate that a resolution will be achieved, but also expect that impasse will occur and commit to work through impasse. And finally, the mediator should remember mediation is about the disputants—not the mediator.

B.   THE PARTIES AND THEIR REPRESENTATIVES

Recognizing that mediation is a relatively new field and in a state of continuous change, it is not surprising that participants might differ in their approaches to mediation or in their mediation strategies. In most lawsuits, the parties and their attorneys give a great deal of thought and attention to preparation for trial or other events which may result in a final disposition of a case, such as a hearing on summary judgment. In a large percentage of mediation cases settlement is reached,[22] which is often the final stage of the matter. Therefore, the degree of preparation should be appropriate to the likelihood of concluding the case.

Before the mediation, each side of the dispute should gather its representatives, decision makers, and legal counsel for a strategic planning session. The lawyer should not be picking up the file as he runs to the mediation session, although this has been the case on more than one occasion. In a matter where the representative attending the mediation represents other interests, such as in a large public policy case or where there is a hierarchy of authority, a meeting with all constituents should take place prior to the mediation. At the planning session, each side should review the factual dispute, create a condensed description of the issues, outline the manner of presentation, and identify options for settlement. As the attorney[23] and client prepare for the mediation, they should clarify their goals and objectives and discuss how to achieve them.

With regard to a presentation of the history of the dispute, participants should remember that no one is making a factual determination of right or wrong. One of the most important factors to remember—from a participant's view—is the difference between mediation and the courthouse. Unlike a trial where a decision based on past events is made, mediation is future oriented. Mediation's focus is on how the matter will be resolved. This resolution will entail some action by the parties which will take place in the future. That is not to say that mediation ignores

22. In pre-litigation as well as pending cases the national average indicates that about 80% of all cases that are mediated are settled at the time of the mediation.

23. In the majority of the cases, if participants have representation at a mediation, it is usually in the context of an attor-

ney-advocate. That is not to say that other representatives, such as a financial consultants or supportive friends or relatives would not attend. However, for purposes of simplicity, the words representative and attorney will be used interchangeably.

the past. Usually each side's opening statement includes a brief historical overview of the dispute.

Another key difference between a trial and a mediation which participants should note is the identity of the decision maker. Unlike the situation in a trial or arbitration where the decision maker is the neutral party, in mediation it is not the mediator who is the decision maker, but rather the other side. If persuasion or advocacy is to take place, it should take place across the table. It is important therefore that all decision makers be prepared to be present and listen to each other throughout. In planning for mediation, therefore, deciding who will make the opening statement can be somewhat complex. The party himself or herself, the advocate representative, or a combination may be the most effective choice. It is important to remember that it is the parties who own the dispute. It does not belong to the attorneys and certainly not to the mediator; therefore, the parties must participate in the process. Much of the philosophical basis of mediation stems from the concepts of self-determination and empowerment. Even in the event of active representation, the party to the dispute must be given an opportunity to speak and be heard.

Most mediations provide time for uninterrupted opening remarks[24] by each side, and this should be prepared by the participants in advance. While not scripted in detail, it should at least be outlined and its duration kept reasonable. Most mediators do not put time limits on the opening statements, but less than an hour is normally appropriate. Of course, where there are a large number of parties or where the cases are complex, time may be limited or more time may be allotted.

Parties should consider the use of any other documentation such as charts, graphs, or video tapes in advance. The mediator should be advised so that proper equipment, such as an overhead projector or VCR and monitor is available. A determination should be made as to whether these are to be used in the session as part of the opening statement or in a later segment.

As part of preparation for the mediation, the parties may be wise to determine what, in fact, are their underlying interests and issues. What are their ultimate goals in the case? Is it money; or, perhaps, are there non-monetary needs, interests and wants here? How might these goals and objectives be achieved? It is important to be cautious here. The mediator does not want to encourage the participants to come into a mediation with their minds made up. That would severely limit the possibilities for alternatives. On the other hand, the mediator would prefer that some thought had been given to options so that the participants have some idea of the direction in which the mediation might go. The participants should thus be encouraged to engage in a preliminary discussion of options. However, since mediation is premised on flexibili-

---

24. As the term "opening statement" is derived from the adversarial model, students of mediation have suggested using the alternate term *remarks*.

ty, listening to the other side, and options generated during the session, it may be helpful to remind parties to maintain an open mind.

A related and often overlooked part of preparation for the participants is to consider the goals, objectives and interests of the other side. While most disputing parties hope to go to mediation and obtain the best they can for themselves, the process is premised upon give and take; and without that exchange, no progress will be made. Any time there is a give and take situation, that is, a negotiation, both sides must be motivated. Therefore, in the preparatory stages some thought should be given to the possible interests and objectives of the opposing side. If possible, areas of mutual interest should also be identified. Likewise, in cases where the primary focus is on a monetary settlement, it is important to have a basic idea of a range of settlement, keeping in mind that all of the information has not been exchanged.

This leads to what is probably the most important aspect of mediation preparation from the standpoint of the parties and their representatives: the parties must be prepared to listen. While it is inherent in the process that participants attend a mediation to express their views, it is also critical that they listen to other views expressed at the table. It is only by the exchange of information that all parties are able to determine exactly what the main issues and interests are. Information exchange will also assist in identifying areas of mutual interest. True attentiveness thus makes resolution possible.[25]

QUESTIONS FOR DISCUSSION

5–1. You are preparing to mediate a dispute over a sales contract between parties who have been doing business together for over four years. One individual is the manager of a restaurant, and the other is the owner of a small but highly reputable fresh fruit and vegetable wholesale supply company. The dispute centers around alleged inaccurate deliveries, in terms of time and content. Although suit has not been filed, the attorneys for both parties will be attending the mediation. You have arranged your conference room so that the clients are closest to you. It is part of your strategy to engage them in a dialogue. As the parties enter, before you can direct them to the seats, the attorneys take over, sit at the head of the table closest to you, and direct their clients to take a back seat. What do you do?

5–2. West's Ann.Cal.Civ.Code § 3182 clearly allows exclusion of the lawyer from the mediation. How might this impact the attorney-client relationship? In the case where the mediator excludes an attorney during the session, what effect will this have on the mediation, and, in particular, with all participants' subsequent satisfaction with the process?

25. For a more detailed approach to the attorney-advocate and to client preparation for mediation, see Galton, *supra* note 5.

5–3. Some mediators arrange the chairs around a conference table and allow participants to pick their own places at the table, feeling that parties will sit where they are most comfortable. Comment on this approach.

5–4. You are the mediator in a medical negligence case. One participant, the Hospital Administrator (Defendant) arrives at the mediation with her attorney. Both appear to be fully prepared for the mediation. In fact, you received a twenty page bound mediation notebook as a pre-mediation submission from the attorney's office three days ago. The notebook contained both a summary of discovery as well as citations to and copies of the alleged controlling cases. The plaintiff, a relatively uneducated dock worker, arrives at the mediation with a lawyer he hired two days ago. You are told by the new lawyer that the plaintiff's previous lawyer withdrew from the case due to a change of employment. It appears that plaintiff's counsel is completely unfamiliar with the case. This is confirmed when, on the way into the mediation, plaintiff's counsel, within hearing of plaintiff, states in a joking manner that he hopes you will let him know what the case is about. The matter was referred to mediation and scheduled on the specific date by the court. What are your options? Which course of action would you choose, and why?

5–5. An agreement to mediate is essentially a mediation contract. What should be included in the contract? By whom should it be signed?

5–6. The Bargaining Bank

Nearly two years ago, the Bank of Alpha, located in Alphaberg, Pennsylvania, loaned the Harris Company, a Pennsylvania Partnership, $8,000,000. The loan was secured by a Deed of Trust on 100 acres of raw land owned free and clear by the limited partnership. The personal guaranty of two of the limited partners, Theodore Deltak and Catherine Zeff also secured the loan. Each spouse, Georgette Deltak and Harvy Zeff were also required to sign the guaranty.

In early June of this year, the borrowers defaulted on their required principal and interest payments of approximately $65,000 per month. The Bank sent a notice of default to the Harris Company along with notices to each of the four guarantors. Notice of acceleration in accordance with the loan provisions was included.

Simultaneously, in late June, the Bank entered into discussions with the Deltaks and the Zeffs regarding a potential restructuring of the loan. After several weeks of negotiation, the bank obtained approval from its loan committee to extend an additional $1.5 million loan, and take as additional collateral, deed of trust notes on the residences of the Deltaks and the Zeffs.

The restructured loan included scheduled draws over a two year period for construction of a residential development. During negotiations, the Harris Company submitted a budget to the bank. Loan documents evidencing the restructured agreement were prepared and included a provision which required the borrowers to comply with the budget and schedule as a condition of the loan.

After five months the borrowers have ceased to comply with the budget. The bank subsequently files a lawsuit seeking, among other things, foreclosure on the residences. The borrowers respond with a counter claim of "lender liability" alleging "bad faith" on the part of the Bank. The borrowers claim that during the period of the restructuring negotiations, they passed up an opportunity to obtain financing from another bank because an executive at Alpha Bank represented that the budget was only a "formality," and that the bank would be flexible and work with the borrowers to prevent default. The borrowers further maintain that since their spouses, Georgette and Harvey, had no involvement in the Harris company, the bank violated federal regulations in seeking and requiring the spouses' guarantees.

Two weeks after the suits are filed, lawyers for Alpha Bank and the Deltaks and Zeffs request that you mediate this dispute. In preparation for the mediation, which is scheduled in ten days, decide the following:

(a) What information do you want, and how will you obtain it?

(b) Who should be present at the mediation?

(c) What will you ask the parties to supply you with?

(d) What information, if any, will you provide to the parties?

Chapter Six

BEGINNING THE MEDIATION

The mediation session may be the first time that all participants in a dispute, including decision makers, their attorneys and representatives are gathered together at the same time and place. This is particularly true in matters involving a pending lawsuit. The mediator's handling of this initial meeting can greatly impact the remainder of the session. In most instances, the parties, after being greeted in the reception area, will be brought together in a joint meeting room where the mediator will begin his introductory remarks. There may, however, be situations which require deviation. Like most aspects of the mediation process, there are exceptions to the general rule.

For example, if the mediator has any advance information which indicates a potentially volatile situation should the parties come into direct contact with one another, he may alter the structure of the session. In this case the mediator should make certain that the receptionist or individual responsible for greeting everyone is aware of the problem, and that the parties are initially kept separate. While such situations represent a very small number of cases, if handled incorrectly, the mediation can be doomed before it begins.

A. THE MEDIATOR'S INTRODUCTION

The mediator's introduction establishes the tone and tenor of the entire mediation session. The introduction is the primary vehicle through which the mediator begins to build trust with the participants. Trust must be established if the participants are to share information, remain open to discussion and allow the mediator to facilitate the negotiation. Although the use of mediation has increased dramatically, the mediator can still safely assume that in the majority of cases mediation will be a new experience for the participants. This is particularly true for the parties, often involved in their first lawsuit. Therefore, while the introduction may become "old hat" for an experienced mediator, he should still give some thought and preparation to it in each case. The introductory remarks should be very familiar to the mediator; yet, they should not be so over rehearsed that the delivery results in a speech-like monotone. In fact, experienced mediators must be careful not to become so bored with the introduction that it becomes rushed; adequate time must be given to it.

The specific style of the mediator's introduction may vary a great deal. In family or other types of cases where emotional issues are paramount, an emphasis on relaxing and building trust with the parties is appropriate. In other cases, such as a construction matter, a more direct, businesslike tone may be used. Where conflict is overt, the mediator must exert control over the session and establish it during his introductory remarks. However, the mediator's introduction should more closely resemble a conversation than a speech or legal proceeding. The mediator can set the stage for the session by exhibiting an enthusiastic, positive, and encouraging attitude. The mediator's introduction serves a number of purposes. Likewise, the introduction should include specific items, although it can be modified in content, depending on a number of case variables.

1. PURPOSE

In general, the purpose of the mediator's introduction is to inform the participants about what is going to happen. Many people, having arrived at the mediation table for the first time, are nervous, apprehensive, and unsure of what to expect. Even though the mediator may have sent detailed information to the parties and their representatives in advance of the mediation, there is no guarantee that it has been read. Even in those cases where the information is reviewed, it may not be fully understood. Upon arrival at the place of the mediation, the parties may experience a sense of trepidation. The mediator can use this introductory time to provide the parties time to relax and feel more at ease with the surroundings, the mediator, and the process.

This is also the time during which the mediator can set the tone, and let the participants know that he is in control of the mediation process. The mediator also begins to build trust with all the participants. The mediator simultaneously establishes his credibility and demonstrates knowledge of the process. In terms of credibility, the mediator may provide the participants some information about his background, training, and previous experience. This is not the time, of course, for the mediator to go into great detail about the heritage of his great-grandparents; however, the mediator should at least let the parties know that he is well trained in the process.[1] He may also include any relevant expertise in the subject matter of the dispute.

The mediator's introduction informs the participants about why they are at mediation, and how, in general, the session will proceed. This provides them at least some idea of what to expect. The mediator should

---

1. Of course, background and experience may be a difficult subject for the novice mediator. The novice mediator might want to discuss any particular expertise that he may have with regard to either the content matter of the case or experience in another area that may add to his credibility. In cases where none exists, then the mediator may merely say that he is a trained mediator.

not be too specific, so that room for flexibility and modification remains. The mediator's introduction also serves as the vehicle through which rules of the procedure are introduced. These include how the parties will proceed to discuss their case. Any ground rules should be established during the introduction. Providing general introductory remarks also allows the mediator time to size up the participants. It is anticipated that during this introduction all parties at the table will begin to feel more comfortable with one another. As the mediator describes the process and its purposes, a positive atmosphere may be created, where, ideally, all participants acknowledge the benefits of a collaborative approach to problem solving.

2. CONTENT

The very first item that should be included in the mediator's introduction is a complete introduction of all the parties sitting around the table, including the mediator himself. In most instances, the mediator will ask the parties and representatives to introduce themselves, identify with whom they are affiliated and confirm that they have adequate authority to settle the matter. Any potential conflicts[2] which have been identified and disclosed should be restated, along with everyone's agreement to participate. Any documents, such as agreements to mediate, disclaimers of legal representation, or confidentiality agreements, should be finalized at this time, if not completed prior to the session.

The mediator should then spend some time discussing the mediation process. Even though some background information may have been given to the participants in the pre-mediation stage, the mediator cannot be sure that it was completely read or understood. Therefore, discussion of the mediation process, and especially its purpose, should be included so that the parties have a better understanding of the nature of the proceeding. A general discussion of the benefits of the mediation process should also be included in the introductory remarks. While this is not the ideal time to "sell" the process, some individuals may go to mediation still reluctant to participate. The mediator's role, in part, is to motivate the parties in the direction of a satisfactory resolution. During the introduction, the mediator can begin to positively reinforce their attendance at the mediation, and encourage their open-mindedness and determination to proceed with the process. Obtaining an affirmative commitment from the parties to listen to each other and to explore a variety of options for settlement can be of great assistance in establishing a positive tone which will further the mediation. In this manner the mediator can also begin to elicit cooperation and even a commitment to good faith participation[3] from all of the parties.

Once the mediator describes the process, he should move into a discussion of his role in it. This will clarify for the parties exactly what

2. See Chapter 14 for a discussion of potential conflicts of interest.

3. See Chapter 4 for the discussion of the parameters of good faith participation in mediation.

he will do. Some mediators choose to do this in terms of what the mediator is not, that is, they explain that they are not a judge, jury or fact finder. Others choose to describe the role in terms of the mediator's action in the session, such as assisting in communication, facilitating negotiation, pointing out areas of agreement, and searching for settlement alternatives. Yet other mediators include both aspects of role definition.

Next, the mediator should set forth a brief procedural outline of the process. This includes how the opening remarks will proceed, whether the parties will immediately move into separate sessions or remain together for a period of time to exchange information, and whether any documents or outside individuals will be brought in. Thereafter, specific ground rules should be explained. These might include rules against interruptions, suggested time limits, expected time commitments and rules governing confidentiality. The confidential nature of the session should be explained including any statutory, common law, case law, or contractual basis of confidentiality. The nature of the private session or caucus should also be explained. There is a great variation in the use of private sessions.[4] Some mediators structure of the mediation around the constant use of private meetings. A small minority of mediators almost never use them. The majority of mediators take a wait-and-see posture, which results in intermittent use of private meetings. Rather than waiting until the time a caucus is needed, however, the parties should be told in advance what can be expected from a caucus, including any confidential provisions which surround its use.[5] The mediator's introduction may conclude with a request for a commitment by the participants to a good faith effort at settlement.[6]

While some mediators wait until the introduction for the discussion and collection of fees, it is strongly advised that this be done as part of preliminary arrangements. The mediator's introduction should also include housekeeping details such as provisions for lunch, breaks, parking, telephones, and faxes. Lastly, before moving into the opening statements, the mediator should ask if there are any questions regarding the process. He is then ready to proceed to a discussion of the dispute. A few mediators begin by summarizing their understanding of the case. One advantage to this approach is an expedited process. However, unless there are strict time limits, this approach is not advised, since the participants should first be given sufficient time to discuss the matter in their own words.

4. See Chapter 10 for a more in-depth discussion of the use of caucusing.

5. While most caucuses are considered to be confidential, private meetings, some mediators begin with the premise that they plan to share the information learned in private session with the other side. Whatever the method, it should be specifically clear to the parties in advance. The mediator should discuss this, both during the introduction and at the time of moving into the caucus. This is further examined in Chapters 10 and 11.

6. Although a good-faith effort usually cannot be mandated, (see Chapter 4, § B) getting a personal commitment from the parties is nevertheless often helpful.

B. OPENING STATEMENTS

Once the mediator completes his introduction, it is time to hear from the participants. In most cases, the focus will be on the nature of the dispute that brings everyone to the mediation table. The dispute, however, may not be what the mediator assumes it is. The mediator must be careful not to bring into the session any presumptions about the case based on the information previously received. He may also want to stress this to the parties as a method of encouraging each person to listen to the others. The mediator may note that opening statements offer all participants the opportunity to take part in an information gathering process.

Where there is a pending lawsuit, most mediators will follow normal litigation procedure and ask the plaintiff, (attorney or client) to first present an opening statement. Exceptions to this general rule exist, such as when the defendant's claim, whether in terms of a counter-claim, cross-claim, or affirmative defense, is the primary focus of the mediation. In these instances it is appropriate to allow the defense to begin. In either instance, the rationale should be briefly explained to all participants so that the choice of who begins does not appear to be based upon partiality of the mediator. In the non-litigation context, often one party is the primary claimant, the one who is making a complaint and requesting a resolution to the dispute. It is then appropriate to begin the opening statements with this individual. It is also likely that one of the participants (and this is often the claimant) is responsible for getting the matter to the mediation table. In these instances, the mediator should explain that since this party is responsible for bringing the matter to mediation, it is proper and normal that the opening statements begin with this party.

The discussions in most mediation sessions are not limited to the nature of the case as previously described, but rather are open to all areas of controversy between the parties. These areas may include the primary and underlying causes of the conflict, as well as tangential issues and interests. Therefore, most mediators begin with a broad request for information by making a statement such as, "Tell us what brings us here today."[7]

1. IMPORTANCE OF OPENING REMARKS

In the majority of cases, the opening statement segment of a mediation is the first time that the parties actually listen to an uninterrupted statement of the case from the other side's point of view. It may also be the first time that the parties and their representatives have an

---

7. However, some cases, for a variety of reasons, may need more focus. Examples include victim-offender matters, which focus on restitution only, or complex cases with multiple parties, where specific matters may be discussed at specific times. In directing the focus of the opening statements, the mediator will somewhat control the content.

opportunity to provide a complete, uninterrupted statement of their perceptions of the case. The mediation, therefore, is often the first opportunity that the disputing parties have to "get off their chests" what the problem is, as they see it. Many times this is what the parties have been waiting for, and what they expected to get in court. Consequently, it is important for the mediator to be patient and model good listening skills, behavior which can encourage the other parties to listen as well. The mediator can gather information, not only about the case, but also about the reactions of the other, non-speaking participants. This is done by paying close attention to the non-verbal communication of the non-speaking parties.[8]

Neither the mediator nor the other parties should interrupt the speaker during the time reserved for the opening remarks. The opening statement provides each individual, whether the disputing party or representative, an opportunity to present the case in the manner and fashion desired. Each participant should be permitted to do so. But if the presentation is very confusing, or if another party begins to interrupt, or if the session begins to disintegrate into a negative exchange, then it is appropriate for the mediator to intercede and take control. To do so he might remind the participants of the ground rules and procedures. Other than those exceptions, an opening statement should proceed uninterrupted.

During the opening statements, the mediator will probably take notes, listening very carefully to what is said.[9] This is the portion of the mediation for which the participants are most prepared, and many important aspects of the case will be highlighted. The mediator should look for areas of agreement among the parties as well as note matters of perceived disagreement. It is important to emphasize perceptions at this point. Many times what is first perceived as a matter in conflict becomes a point of shared interests after information is exchanged.

Disagreement between the parties sitting across the table from one another is expected. However, it is quite possible that discord exists for those ostensibly on the same side of the case. Inconsistent goals can surface between a lawyer and his client, or between two parties on the same side of a table. While the mediator should refrain from calling attention to these potential conflicts in the joint session, he should be mindful of them and perhaps address them during a private session.

It is important for each party or entity represented at the table to have an opportunity to make an opening statement. There is some debate about this in those instances of a personal injury or products liability case, where there is often only one plaintiff with counsel, and four, five or six defendants, each with counsel. However, because of the variety of issues, claims, cross-claims, and counter-claims, it is recom-

---

8. While it takes an effort to maintain eye contact with the speaker, take notes and simultaneously keep an eye on the other parties, doing so can often provide important information.

9. The skill of combining note taking and listening is discussed in Chapter 3, § B.

mended that each defendant be given at least an opportunity to make an opening statement. Only through a complete exchange of information can the mediator acquire a thorough understanding of the case.

2. PARTIES

In most court related matters, the mediation is the individual's day in court and it should be treated as such. This is the time for the parties to explain in their own words how they feel and how they think they have been wronged, not only in a factual sense, but also in an emotional sense. This can also become a time of accusations and finger pointing. A few individuals will detail what they expect to get out of the proceeding. If the individual is well prepared by his representative or attorney, the statements may be structured and limited to the parameters of the lawsuit. Additional concerns or underlying interests may not be disclosed. However, if the mediator is listening attentively, the parties' true feelings and interests will often become apparent.

Ventilation, the expression of anger, frustration and other emotions, is a part of the mediation process and should be encouraged. Nonetheless, the mediator should be careful not to allow venting to become a direct attack on the other side. Where venting becomes destructive, the mediator must take control of the situation.[10]

The mediator should also keep in mind that the mediation is often the parties' first. If so, they are unfamiliar with the process. Unfamiliarity can itself evoke emotion, particularly if the parties are nervous. Unlike most mediators, educators, and legal professionals, many people are uncomfortable speaking publicly, particularly about something uniquely personal to them. Consequently, opening statements may be disorganized, repetitious, or even too brief. Rather than interrupt and clarify during the opening, the better practice is to allow the party to complete the opening statement. It is likely that the party's representative will provide clarification later. Alternatively, in an additional information gathering segment, the mediator can go back and fill in any information that is missing or confusing. Supplemental information will also be provided by the opening statements of others at the table.

3. ATTORNEYS

Ordinarily when an attorney attends a mediation, there is a lawsuit pending. It is important that the mediator determine the status or stage of the lawsuit in advance. Although a detailed analysis of the lawyer-client relationship is beyond this work, some consideration is appropriate.[11] The usual assumption is that the lawyer attends the mediation

---

10. A mediator's ability to deal with anger and other emotions is discussed in Chapter 3.

11. For detail about the lawyer-client relationship in terms of legal representation, see David A. Binder & Susan C. Price, Legal Interviewing and Counseling: A Client–Centered Approach (1977); James E. Moliterno & John M. Levy, Ethics of the Lawyer's Work, Chapter 3 (1993). For an in-depth examination of the role of the attorney in terms of settlement and ADR use, see Robert F. Cochran, Jr., *Legal Representation and the Next Steps Toward Client*

representing the best interest of her client. The lawyer has interests too, however, not only in representation of his client, but also in other terms which may conflict with those of the client. Possible conflicts include a financial interest and an interest in establishing a trial record. The mediator should be cognizant of this possibility.[12] Exactly what the mediator's role is in the event of direct conflict between a party and her representative is unclear. In cases of overt conflict some mediators will attempt to mediate between the lawyer and client, particularly where this is an impediment to settlement. Others will ask the lawyer and client to privately resolve the matter before coming back to the mediation table, and a few mediators will ignore the matter.

The lawyer-advocate attends the mediation on behalf of her client, and it is important that she be provided an opportunity to present the case as she sees it. Unfortunately, very aggressive presentations by advocates tend to obstruct settlement. As more lawyers become educated about and familiar with the mediation process, however, they realize that advocacy in mediation is not the same as advocacy in a trial or in arbitration. Where the neutral third party is a decision maker, the advocate's role is adversarial. But mediation is a non-adversarial approach to conflict resolution. Nonetheless, some lawyers still choose to utilize a competitive or adversarial approach in opening statements at mediation.[13] If possible, the mediator should attempt to constrain some of this prior to the presentation. For example, initial education about the appropriate structure of the opening statements can be included in the preliminary materials. The mediator can also reinforce the non-adversarial nature of the attorney's role at the end of his introduction. The mediator might first acknowledge the competence of the lawyers, and point out that while a very aggressive, adversarial presentation is appropriate in the courtroom setting, mediation is different. Many lawyers feel compelled to present the case in an adversarial manner because they assume that is what the client expects. And, in fact, many clients probably do expect this, not realizing the considerable difference between a trial and mediation. Part of the mediator's role, then, in making the transition to the lawyers' opening statements, will be to reduce the aggressiveness of the presentations by convincing the lawyers and clients that such an approach is not necessary.

The mediation session is likely the first time that the participants, particularly the parties, have heard the case presented by the opposing lawyer. Prior to mediation, there may have been meetings, depositions or motion hearings; but the client was probably not present. Moreover, there has likely not been a detailed presentation of the entire case. Therefore, not only should the mediator be attentive during the opening

---

Control: Attorney Malpractice For the Failure to Allow the Client to Control Negotiation and Pursue Alternatives to Litigation, 47 Wash. and Lee L. Rev. 819 (1990).

12. These potential lawyer-client conflicts are examined more closely in Chapter 14.

13. For a more complete examination of the role of lawyer representation in mediation, see Eric R. Galton, Representing Clients In Mediation (1994).

statements, but should encourage the other participants to listen to the other side as well. By listening to opposing counsel's presentation, a party may see the matter in a different light, or at least understand the other side, which may open up discussion and movement at subsequent stages of the process.

The lawyers should be careful to not use the opening statement at mediation as they would an opening or closing argument at trial, but they should use the time to set forth the specifics of the case. The mediator should refrain from requesting specific offers from the lawyers. Likewise, lawyers should not further aggravate the conflict by making unrealistic demands at this early stage of the case. However, general statements about goals and outcomes of the session can be encouraged by the mediator.

4. OTHER REPRESENTATIVES

In some instances, there may be non-lawyer representatives attending the mediation with the parties. This may be a friend or relative who, perhaps, has more expertise in the substantive matter. This individual may be more familiar with the court system or mediation process. Some representatives may be accountants or financial planners. Although uncommon, it is also possible for an individual's therapist or counselor to attend a mediation, particularly in family disputes. Some non-legal representatives attend in merely a supportive role, while others attend in an active representative capacity. The mediator should determine in advance the nature of the representative's role.

Representatives attending a mediation in a primarily supportive role usually do not take a direct or active role in the session. If, however, representatives are present to assist in the process, then they should be provided an opportunity to present opening statements. In these situations, the mediator should also learn how much decision-making authority the representative may have.

A particular problem arises where a representative is in the role of translator. Unfortunately, mediation has not grown to the extent that all mediators are multi-lingual, and many times translators are necessary.[14] While the ideal situation would be for the translator to be a neutral party, not brought by either side, at the current time, this is unrealistic. Therefore, on many occasions, the non-English speaking party brings his or her own translator. How the translator interprets what is said can impact the mediation. The mediator should be aware of this, and request that an accurate and direct translation be provided. And while the mediator may not understand the content of the statements of the non-English speaking party, he should still be attentive to paralinguistics and body language. While not a direct part of the translation, these are important aspects of communication.

14. For a thorough examination of mediation and interpretation, see Ileana Dominguez–Urban, *The Messenger as the Medium of Communication: The Use of Interpreters in Mediation*, 1997 J. Disp. Resol. 1.

5. USE OF DOCUMENTS, WITNESSES, AND EXPERTS

In complex cases, parties and their representatives may use documents, witnesses, and experts to clarify certain points. Normally, however, these are adjuncts to the process and should be kept to a minimum, particularly witnesses and experts. Mediation is not a fact-finding or decision-making process. In complicated, highly technical cases, however, some assistance may be necessary so that everyone has an adequate understanding of the case and the issues in controversy. Depending on the affiliation of the witness or expert, the timing and method of the presentation may vary. The specifics should be determined by the mediator in advance of the session, if possible.

In most instances, each side in the case should be given an opportunity to first complete its presentation. Additional information from "outsiders" should be avoided at the initial stage. Once all participants have been afforded the opportunity to present opening statements, additional parties may be introduced to the mediation. These witnesses or experts may provide a statement before or during the mediator's follow-up information gathering. During the questioning stage of the session, these experts can assist in clarification. The use of charts, graphs, or drawings for explanations is also encouraged during the follow-up stage, rather than as part of the opening statements, unless the visual aids are essential to the opening.

C. FOLLOW–UP INFORMATION GATHERING

Rarely in mediation sessions do the parties provide sufficient information during the opening remarks to fully identify the issues and move directly into option generation. This, however, is usually the first thing that a novice mediator wants to do; find an immediate solution. It is therefore imperative that the mediator keep in mind, and actually remind the participants, that not all of the information about the matter has been shared. In fact, where there is a pending lawsuit, the lawyers and clients may desire to withhold certain information.[15] While complete disclosure of every item is not necessary and should not be demanded by the mediator, there is still information that the mediator needs after the opening statements in order to assist the parties in generating their own ideas and options for settlement.

Information gathering is a significant stage of mediation and should not be overlooked or hurried through. Once parties begin to focus on issues and options for settlement, they become reluctant to share additional information. They stop listening, and become entrenched in positions. Therefore, the information exchange must occur early in the session. Information gathering in terms of questioning and clarification can be done by the mediator and the participants.

---

15. The use of this strategy of not showing the *entire hand* depends largely on the nature of each case and the individual lawyers.

1. EFFECTIVE QUESTIONING BY THE MEDIATOR

The mediator, rather than rushing to identify specific issues, should continue to gather more information from the participants. There are a number of reasons for this. The first, of course, is to clarify and understand any confusing factors or issues. It is acceptable for the mediator to act a bit uncertain about some of the matters in dispute in order to encourage the parties to disclose additional information. He should try, however, to avoid appearing completely bewildered lest credibility be lost. The mediator should let the participants know that additional information or clarification is needed for a complete understanding of the dispute. After all, this is usually the mediator's primary introduction to the case. This is probably also true for at least some of the parties, but, for a variety of reasons, they may not want to openly admit it. The mediator's role will be to continue to gather information, not only on his own behalf, but also on behalf of the other parties.

The mediator must not narrow the focus of the dispute too soon. After the opening statements, the mediator should ordinarily focus on the main areas of contention. He should also focus on areas of mutual or shared interests, as well. A request for general information, primarily by the use of open-ended questions is recommended. A helpful rule of thumb for obtaining general information is to begin by asking at least three open-ended questions. New mediators, especially those with a legal background, will often attempt to use leading questions aimed at specific facts and figures. Certainly this is appropriate and necessary where there is confusion. However, completion of the opening statements is still very early in the mediation session; it would be premature at this time to determine the primary issues and interests. Instead, this is an appropriate time to continue to obtain a broad picture of the dispute.

Most people are comfortable providing a narrative response to questions. More often than not, what is most important to an individual will become clear during such a response. Therefore, general, open-ended questions that search for areas of mutual agreement among the disputants are appropriate at this stage. Seeking background and historical information about the dispute can also be helpful in detecting areas of mutual concern and overlapping interests. For example, in a lease dispute, the mediator may ask general questions about the duration of the landlord-tenant relationship. When describing the relationship, a party may mention that, for the most part, it has been a good experience, and that this dispute is the first time that real problems have occurred. The mediator can easily determine that the parties have a mutual interest in maintaining the lease. On the other hand, if the relationship is recounted as one wrought with conflict, the mediator will realize that termination of the relationship is probably a shared interest.

The information gathering phase should include summarizing and reframing by the mediator. He should begin to use neutral language at this stage, in an attempt to rephrase areas of agreement and point out areas of mutual interest.

After an open-ended request for general information, the mediator may begin to use a variety of other types of questions. The specific combination of types of questions cannot usually be planned for in advance. However, the skilled mediator, like any skilled interviewer, becomes a master of asking the right question at the right time. A closer look at some of the forms of questions and their appropriate use follows.[16]

a. Open–Ended Questions

Open-ended questions allow for the broadest possible answer. They can be completely unfocused, such as, "What do you think?" or more focused on a specific topic. Examples include questions or requests for information that begin with phrases such as those below:

"Tell me more about . . ."

"Could you explain . . ."

"Please explain further about . . ."

"How did you feel when . . ."

"What happened?"

"Is there anything else that you believe is pertinent to . . ."

b. Open–Focused Questions

The open, but focused, question consists of requests for information similar to the general open question, but it is more directive:

"Between the time the cast was put on and the time it was taken off, did anything else happen that is related to this situation?"

"How did you feel when you first learned that . . . ?"

"Why do you want to continue a business relationship with X?"

"What happened after you first noticed . . ."

"Describe the kind of streets that are at the intersection."

c. Requests for Clarification

Requests for clarification are open to a degree but are even more focused than the two preceding types of questions:

"Could you explain to me how your product is not similar to product Y?"

"Help me understand why the lawnmower is not worth x"

"What specifically about your health is your main concern?"

---

16. These are examples of the most commonly used questioning techniques. For additional information on questioning in general, see David A. Binder & Susan C. Price, Legal Interviewing and Counseling: A Client–Centered Approach, (Chapter Four) (1974).

d. Leading Questions

Leading questions suggest the answer, often in terms of one or two words:

"What color was the car that hit you?"

"What type of traumatic experience has the accident caused your family?"

e. Either/or, Yes/No Questions

These questions are close-ended and ask for very short, specific answers:

"When you left the house was it one o'clock or two o'clock?"

"Were the headlights either too bright or too dim?"

"Tell me, *yes* or *no*, do you want to be friends with Steve?"

f. Compound Questions

Compound questions consist of more than one request for information at once, and should be avoided. Example:

"What type of party was it—social, professional, or was it just people from the neighborhood—and how did everyone know each other?"

———

Some trainers and authors have tried to identify particular times that are better than others to utilize some of these questioning techniques. For instance, open-ended questions are good in the early part of the session and can be followed by more focused questions. Close-ended and leading questions are used for later focus. Yes/no or either/or questions should be limited, but are useful when very specific information is needed. This will occur during the negotiation and review-of-agreement stages. More focused but still open questions can be used in the middle of the information gathering process.[17]

It is important that the mediator remain neutral in his information gathering. Thus he must be neutral in phrasing the question and in his tone of voice. For example, a party might say something that is somewhat unbelievable. The mediator must remember that as an impartial third party,[18] he is not in a role to make a judgment, including one on the credibility of the information. Questions should be as neutral as possible. Nevertheless, it is likely that some questions will elicit judgmental, value-laden information from the parties.

Judgmental language can be categorized into five primary areas. First, the "should or have to" language aimed either at the other side or at a party himself; second, limiting language, in which the party immedi-

17. Jay Folberg & Alison Taylor, Mediation: A Comprehensive Guide To Resolving Conflicts Without Litigation 113 (1984).

18. Although this can be debated. See Chapter 7.

ately closes himself to certain options or ideas; third, blame language with which one person blames another for an event; fourth, value judgments which assign value to an activity, such as right or wrong; and finally, assumptions based on inferences.[19]

It is essential that the mediator, particularly, remember that these judgments are not necessarily valid. Rather, these statements reflect the conclusions or opinions of the party; and as such, they are valid to that party. The mediator should refrain from commenting on judgmental responses. If the mediator begins a summarization, he may, to some degree, neutralize this language. This is often done by the restatement or reframing of the issues.[20] Neutralization can also be accomplished by the way a question is asked. The mediator's job here is to uncover the underlying basis for the judgmental statements by asking more specific questions. The mediator, however, in emotionally charged situations, should tread lightly. The participants may be very defensive. These matters are often better dealt with in a private session or caucus.

As the mediator asks questions or clarifies, he may also begin to reframe some of the issues. Ideally, the mediator should reframe or restate in as general a way as possible and yet retain accuracy. Accusatory language should be limited, but the accusing party needs to know that the mediator has heard what was said. The mediator can neutralize and acknowledge this information by highlighting the main issues and re-phrasing the statement in terms of the party's interests and needs.

2. ADDITIONAL INFORMATION GATHERING BY PARTICI-PANTS

In many mediations the parties are also present to gather information about the other side's view of the case. With this additional information, parties can better assess their cases for purposes of settlement. In most cases, the mediator should permit questioning to take place between parties across the table. A participant, whether it be the party or a representative, should feel free to ask the other side specific questions. However, the mediator must stay in control, so that the exchange does not disintegrate into a deposition-like question and answer session or an open discovery process. In a few cases there have been reports of one side requesting that a mediation be scheduled for the primary purpose of gathering information about the other side's case. If this intent is made clear, the mediator's role is to first remind the party of the purposes of the mediation process. If the party persists, the mediator will have to follow his instinct as to where to draw the line. If the session results in such an abuse of questioning that the other party becomes uncomfortable, a last resort is to terminate the session.

In most instances, despite the potential for abuse, an exchange of information can be very helpful. In fact, the mediator may wish to point

---

19. Lawrence J. Smith & Lorraine A. Mandro, Courtroom Communications, Strategies, Supp. 24–25 (January 1988).

20. This will be discussed further in Chapters 7 and 8.

out to the parties the benefit of exchanging information so that each side can begin to see the matter from a different perspective and consequently can be more open to a variety of settlement options. Thus the mediator can assist the process by encouraging questions, but he must simultaneously maintain control over the process.

DISCUSSION QUESTIONS

6–1. In a wrongful death case, the attorney for the defendant, an insurance carrier, refers in her opening statement to the deceased as a low-life alcoholic. She is alluding to the fact that at the time of his death, the twenty-six-year-old defendant was working odd jobs. He was at a construction site when an electrical explosion occurred, killing him instantly. Although the autopsy revealed a small amount of alcohol in the bloodstream, there has been no evidence submitted that this contributed in any way to the accident. Present during the opening statement are the deceased's mother and sister. What, if anything, should the mediator do?

6–2. Parties or lawyers unfamiliar with the mediation process sometimes refer to the mediator as "Judge" or "Your Honor." When this is done in the opening statement, what is the proper response of the mediator?

6–3. As part of an opening statement, the lawyer says "We're here only because we were ordered; we do have all the appropriate authority, but we do not intend to negotiate." What should be the mediator's response?

6–4. You are the mediator in a dispute over a car repair. During the opening statements made by the car owner and the manager of the repair shop, you learn the following:

The car owner had taken her automobile, a four year old Nissan, to The Repair Shop because of trouble with the transmission. When she left the car for repairs, the repairs took five days rather than the three that had been estimated. The estimated charge was $900; but when the car was ready, the owner of the car refused to pay an additional $480 charge. Consequently, The Repair Shop claimed a lien on the car and did not permit the owner to take possession of her car.

Both parties contacted their attorneys, who agreed that mediation should be tried before taking any formal legal action. Both attorneys advised their clients to attend without them, in an attempt not only to limit costs, but also to try to reach an amicable resolution.

(a) As the mediator, what are at least three appropriate follow-up questions?

(b) To whom will they be addressed?

6–5. A Case of Suite Sheets

You learn the following information in the general session:

Plaintiff is the manager of a small hotel named the STATELY SUITES. The hotel prides itself on offering suite and large hotel services in a friendly, personal, almost Bed-and-Breakfast manner. Defendant is Lum's Laundry, which has been the primary launderer for the hotel for the past several years.

Mr./Ms. Lum is the owner of the laundry. A few weeks ago on a Monday, the hotel, in anticipation of a large business meeting, took a majority of its linens to Lum's. Included were sheets, towels, and table cloths. Plaintiff claims that it was made very clear that the laundry HAD TO BE READY no later than Thursday morning, as all guests were to arrive that evening.

When the laundry was not delivered on time Thursday morning, Plaintiff called Defendant. Lum stated that there must have been a mistake; the laundry was on the truck and scheduled for early morning delivery.

When early afternoon arrived, still without laundry, Plaintiff stormed into Lum's irate. After some discussion, it was discovered that the laundry was "misplaced," so Plaintiff ran to the local department store to purchase the required linens. The cost was over $3,500, as all 30 rooms were booked for the conference. At approximately 5:30 p.m., on its last delivery, the truck stopped and delivered the original laundry to the hotel.

Plaintiff refused to pay its bill of $947.59 and has sued Lum's in small claims court for reimbursement of the other expenditures. Lum's alleges that the laundry was on time and has countered for the charges.

(a) As the mediator, will you continue a general meeting or meet separately with each party?

(b) What questions would you ask the hotel? The laundry?

6–6.   The Termination

This dispute involves a recent termination of employment at a general practice clinic located within the local medical complex. The claimant, Terry Totten, had been employed as a bookkeeper at a ten-physician general practice clinic, Daytime Doctors. Totten worked for about eight months until terminated by Dr. Greer, the managing partner. All employment related communication, including this termination, was by and through Dr. Greer. Reasons voluntarily provided for the employment termination included alleged continuous tardiness and carelessness on the job. Totten contends that s/he has not been late any more than most of the other employees, and that she performed all her assigned work with great care. In fact, she says, just three months ago s/he received an exceptionally high evaluation in the only performance review to date. The termination occurred almost four weeks ago, and the claimant has not yet been able to find employment.

The management committee of Daytime Doctors wants to end this silly matter and wants nothing more to do with Totten; but, it does not want to be sued. Totten, however, wants the job back, the missed month's salary, and a written acknowledgement of the wrongful actions which are alleged. While suit has not been filed, Totten's attorney has sent a demand letter. No attorneys are present at the mediation.

6–7.   Complaint of Threats

A neighborhood dispute has existed for about four months. The complainant, Steven Price, has attempted to file charges of threats against the respondent, Nancy Doss. The case has been referred to mediation and no charges have yet been filed.

The final incident happened last Sunday afternoon. Both parties are single parents and were inside when a fight ensued between their children out in the yard. (Price has two children, ages nine and seven, while Doss has one child, age eight.) Doss felt the two Price children were ganging up on her child, and ran out to break up the fight. Doss claims that when he appeared, Price shouted angry threats in front of all the children, using some rather colorful language.

Each parent wants the other family to leave the neighborhood. In the past few months the children have not been allowed to play with one another although they attend the same school.

Chapter Seven

NEUTRALITY

A. OVERVIEW

Neutrality is a central concept of mediation. As an intervenor in a dispute, the mediator is often referred to as the third party neutral, as are many of the other ADR providers.[1] In other ADR processes, such as arbitration and case evaluation, it is clear that the neutral will develop an opinion of the case during the process. In contrast, the mediator is expected to remain neutral throughout the mediation process: before, during and even after the mediation session. In fact, statements such as "neutrality is *the sine qua non* of mediation"[2] and "impartiality is key to the mediator's role"[3] are common.

Attempts to examine just what neutrality means, however, have proven to be quite difficult. Neutrality as a concept has been recognized as central to the theory and practice of mediation.[4] Neutrality is included in many contexts of mediation practice, such as in the professional standards of a number of mediator organizations. Yet as central as neutrality is, specific guidelines for its practice do not exist. Neutrality remains virtually unexplored in the scholarly literature.[5] In fact, it is suggested that because of this lack of research, neutrality functions more like a folk concept. Neutrality is discussed and even practiced rhetorically; yet, there is an absence of data demonstrating specifically what neutrality means.[6] Nonetheless, neutrality will be examined here because it is considered crucial to the role of the mediator and because of the divergence of opinions concerning the specific effect of neutrality upon the mediation process. Very different results may occur depending upon how the mediator approaches neutrality.

1. See Chapter 1 for a description of the various roles of the third-party neutral.

2. Barbara Filner and Michael Jenkins, *Performance Based Evaluation of Mediators: The San Diego Mediation Center's Experience*, 30 U.S.F. L. Rev. 647, 649 (1996).

3. Karen A. Zerhusen, *Reflections on the Role of the Neutral Lawyer: The Lawyer as Mediator*, 81 Ky. L.J. 1165, 1169 (1992–93).

4. Sara Cobb & Janet Rifkin, *Practice and Paradox: Deconstructing Neutrality in Mediation*, 16 L. and Soc. Inquiry 35 (1991).

5. *Id.* at 36.

6. *Id.* at 37.

Neutrality is often used interchangeably with a variety of other words and phrases: *impartiality*; *free from prejudice or bias*; *not having a stake in the outcome*; and *free from conflict of interest*. Other synonyms include *unbiased*, *indifferent*, and *independent*. There is dissension within the mediation community about whether all of these terms define neutrality, and, somewhat surprisingly, whether all, or any, are appropriate characteristics for the mediator.

While mediation practitioners often use the term *neutrality* interchangeably with *impartiality*,[7] some mediators claim that impartiality is a very different concept and should not be confused with neutrality. A code developed by family mediators states that mediators shall at all times remain impartial. Yet the same guide also implies that impartiality is not the same as neutrality, if neutrality means refraining from making any decision with regard to fairness of the outcome. For example:

> "While the mediator must be impartial as between the mediation participants, the mediator should be concerned with fairness. The mediator has an obligation to avoid an unreasonable result."[8]

Similarly, the Academy of Family Mediators also distinguishes between impartiality and neutrality:

> The mediator is obligated to maintain impartiality toward all participants. Impartiality means freedom from favoritism or bias, either in word or action. Impartiality implies a commitment to aid all participants, as opposed to a single individual, in reaching a mutually satisfactory agreement. Impartiality means that a mediator will not play an adversarial role.

> The mediator has a responsibility to maintain impartiality while raising questions for the parties to consider as to the fairness, equity, and feasibility of proposed options for settlement.

> Neutrality refers to the relationship that the mediator has with the disputing parties. If the mediator feels, or any one of the parties states, that the mediator's background or personal experiences would prejudice the mediator's performance, the mediator should withdraw from mediation unless all agree to proceed.[9]

These distinguishing characteristics, however, have been suggested in the context of family law mediation. It might be argued that in family cases the mediator's role differs from that expected in a business context. In divorce and child custody mediation, an underlying continuing relationship is present. Moreover, family mediation can affect third parties such as children who are unable to represent themselves. Even so, family mediators debate the specifics of the mediator's role with regard to impartiality.

---

7. *Id.* at 42.

8. Family Mediation Council Western Pennsylvania, Ethical Principles and Code of Professional Conduct for Mediators, (1984).

9. Academy of Family Mediators, Standards of Practice for Family and Divorce Mediation. (Format revised 1995).

Another Code of Conduct, directed at all mediators, provides separate sections for neutrality and impartiality, although a close examination reveals clear overlap.

Neutrality. A mediator should determine and reveal all monetary, psychological, emotional, associational, or authoritative affiliations that he or she has with any of the parties to a dispute that might cause a conflict of interest or affect the perceived or actual neutrality of the professional in the performance of duties. If the mediator or any one of the major parties feels that the mediator's background will have or has had a potential to bias his or her performance, the mediator should disqualify himself or herself from performing the mediation service.

Impartiality. The mediator is obligated during the performance of professional services to maintain a posture of impartiality toward all involved parties.

Impartiality is freedom from bias or favoritism either in word or action. Impartiality implies a commitment to aid all parties, as opposed to a single party, in reaching a mutually satisfactory agreement. Impartiality means that a mediator will not play an adversarial role in the process of dispute resolution.[10]

There has also been exploration of neutrality with regard to environmental disputes. Specifically, there is debate about whether the mediator has a duty or responsibility to assure a just and stable outcome. It is pointed out that in the environmental context, if the parties do not achieve all the benefits possible, then environmental quality and natural resources may be lost. Moreover, public health and safety could be jeopardized.[11] Consequently, the mediator should accept responsibility for ensuring that the interests of all stakeholders are met and that agreements are fair and indicated for the entire community.[12]

A very different view is that of the mediator who must be neutral with regard to outcome.[13] If a mediator is to be responsible for a particular outcome, it follows that she is not neutral, that, in essence, she becomes an advocate or moral judge.[14] In order to determine possible benefits, the mediator must take a position or view. In doing so, impartiality may be lost.

Obviously, a considerable amount of controversy surrounds the duties and responsibilities of the mediator with regard to neutrality, impartiality and fairness. Authors Rogers and Salem articulate this controversy in their discussion of the tension between fairness and neutrality.[15] While mediators are generally viewed as neutral, there may

10. Christopher W. Moore, CDR Associates, Code Of Professional Conduct for Mediators, 1982.

11. See Lawrence Susskind, *Environmental Mediation and the Accountability Problem*, 6 Vt. L. Rev. 1, 8 (1981).

12. *Id.* at 18.

13. Joseph B. Stulberg, *The Theory and Practice of Mediation: A Reply to Professor Susskind*, 6 Vt. L. Rev. 85, 96 (1981).

14. *Id.* at 116.

15. Nancy H. Rogers & Richard A. Salem, A Student's Guide to Mediation and the Law (Chapter Six) (1989).

be an underlying duty to be fair. In an attempt to be fair, neutrality may be abandoned.

Others contend that impartiality and neutrality signify merely that the mediator separates her opinion of the outcome of the dispute from the desires of the disputants. Thus, the mediator focuses on ways to help the parties make their own decisions. Specifically, the mediator is impartial and only helps the parties make their own choices, whatever they may be.[16] However, fairness is not mentioned. It has also been noted that informed consent is central to mediation with regard to self-determination.[17] In order that the parties are able to make informed decisions, mediators may have to provide information and educate them.[18] For example, Nolan–Haley has identified four models of autonomy:

> The exercise of autonomy in mediation may be understood through four models of mediator-party relationships: paternalistic, instrumentalist, informative, and deliberative. These relationships determine the kind of autonomous decisionmaking that occurs.
>
> In the paternalistic or "dictated autonomy" model, the mediator acts primarily as the parties' surrogate in assessing what outcome might be best. The parties' decisionmaking is supported by the mediator's presentation of selected information as well as by the mediator's explicit opinion of what should be done. Autonomy is exercised not only by the parties' agreement to mediate, but by their concurrence in the mediator's determination of what is best.
>
> In the instrumentalist or "limited autonomy" model, the parties' objective is simply to reach settlement. Their decisionmaking is strongly influenced by the mediator's presentation of selected information to each party to close the deal. The mediator highlights risks over any other kind of information—"You never know how the judge will rule." The presumption is that taking the offer would signal that the case would be over. Autonomy is primarily exercised by the parties' agreement to mediate because the mediator exercises subtle influence to close the deal to reach agreement.
>
> In the informative or "assisted autonomy" model, the mediator acts as an information conduit, providing parties with information that is relevant to their needs and interests. Receiving this technical expertise gives parties the means to exercise control. The mediator also assists parties in exploring individual values and in selecting outcome options that realize those values. The parties make the ultimate decision about what values matter and what outcome should be pursued. Decisionmaking is influenced by the factual and substantive information given by the mediator, and autonomy is max-

16. See Christopher W. Moore, The Mediation Process: Practical Strategies for Resolving Conflict 18 (2d Ed., 1996).

17. Jacqueline M. Nolan–Haley, *Informed Consent in Mediation: A Guiding*

Principle for Truly Educated Decisionmaking, 74 Notre Dame L Rev. 775, 840 (1999).

18. *Id.* at 810.

imized through the parties' use of information to control ultimate decisionmaking.

Finally, in the deliberative or "reflective autonomy" model, the mediator provides parties with the same factual and legal information described in the informative model, but also helps the parties understand, articulate, and finally, choose the values that should govern their ultimate choices. Disputing parties are encouraged not simply to examine personal preferences, but to consider—through consultative processes, deliberation, and dialogue—alternative choices, their worthiness, and their implications for settlement. Decisionmaking is influenced by activist mediator behavior in helping parties expand appreciation of values and then choose the values that are important in resolving their disputes.

The mediator engages in moral deliberation and helps the parties prioritize preferences. Coercion is avoided. Autonomy is expressed in self-understanding and moral self-development. Disputing parties come to know more clearly who they are and how the various outcome options affect their knowledge of self and their identity.

These models offer competing conceptions of autonomous decision-making and may operate in all the disparate conditions in which mediation occurs: with represented and unrepresented parties, in voluntary or mandatory, private or court-connected mediation programs.[19]

Other authors demand that mediators balance power by assuring that all interests are represented. This mandate directly collides with that of impartiality.[20]

The view of neutrality and impartiality as similar, if not synonymous, terms is reflected in a number of training and mediation texts. Others observe however, that there is also tendency to see them as different concepts.[21] This debate over the meaning of neutrality, impartiality, and fairness has only begun. Close examination of the issues is necessary, but easy answers to these issues do not currently exist.

Some of the early writers in this area looked to the overall theory of the mediation process. The theory posits mediation as an opportunity for individuals to come to their own decisions and determine the outcome of a matter. In a courtroom or litigation situation, decisions are made within the safeguards of procedural rules. Results are theoretically fair, based on social norms. This, by design, is not the case in mediation. In fact, it is clear that the mediation process is not concerned with achieving conformity to broader societal norms, but rather to creating individual norms for the parties themselves.[22] If this view of the mediation process is taken, then how should fairness be determined?

---

19. *Id.* at 815–16.

20. Sara Cobb & Janet Rifkin, Neutrality As a *Discursive* Practice, 11 Law. Pol. & Soc'y 69, 70 (1991).

21. Cobb & Rifkin, *supra* note 4, at 42.

22. Lon L. Fuller, *Mediation: Its Forms and Functions*, 44 S. Cal. L. Rev. 305, 308 (1971).

And what really is the meaning of *neutrality*? Each individual has certain values. These are established, developed, and shaped by the larger culture in which an individual is reared. In most instances, if a person remains within the same culture and subcultures (including location and family), these values or opinions are continually reinforced. Biases develop based upon strongly held values. People tend to forget that not everyone holds the same or similar values. People look at things differently and are motivated to make decisions for a number of reasons. The mediator's values may differ from those held by the parties. The difference may be slight or great. Herein lies the concern. How does the mediator demonstrate her neutrality? Should a neutral mediator be concerned that the mediation process and results be *fair*? And if the answer is *yes*, then in making judgments about fairness, whose values are to be considered? Those of the parties, the mediator, or some objective entity?

Concern about the mediator's impartiality and neutrality also stems from power imbalances and a perceived obligation of the mediator to balance the dialogue or the negotiation process. Power can be determined by a number of factors. Power is often seen in terms of wealth or money. Often, wealth and power go hand in hand. In mediation, wealth and power are most often apparent when the parties attempt to gain an advantage by hiring counsel or other experts. Some mediators feel a duty to provide the less financially able person with information or advice to equalize the balance.

Another form of power is provided by knowledge. In many cases one party will have greater or more sophisticated knowledge about the subject matter of the dispute or about the potential alternatives for its resolution. If one party is clearly more knowledgeable, should the mediator intervene and provide the requisite knowledge to the other party? In the alternative, should the mediator at least acknowledge this disparate knowledge and allow the less informed party the opportunity to obtain that information? Should the mediator merely encourage the party to gather that information?

Another source of power is that of community or numbers. One side of the table might seem more powerful because of the number of participants on that side. Does the mediator have any duty in these instances to compensate by limiting the amount of time for discussion to equalize the real or perceived imbalance?

These questions have been answered in a number of different ways in the variety of programs throughout the mediation community. At this point, this is something that still remains a personal choice for most individual mediators, but should be thought through and determined prior to the mediation.

B. DEBATING THE DUTY OF THE MEDIATOR

When moving from theory to practice, most of the literature assumes that the mediator has a duty to be neutral and impartial. And, even if these two terms mean something different, there remains the difficulty in determining specifically what those meanings are. Missing in much of the literature is a differentiation between the process and the content of the mediation. Looking at the issue of neutrality from these two different perspectives will provide a more complete examination of the controversy. For instance, does the mediator always remain neutral in the process and allow whatever occurs to occur? Or, should the mediator inject herself and modify her neutrality to assure a "neutral" result? Conversely, should the mediator be concerned only with issues of fairness in the process, or should she abandon process neutrality for fairness of the result?[23] These are the primary questions which, when answered differently, dictate a completely different role and action on the part of the mediator. Hence, establishing guidelines for the mediator is quite troublesome. Yet some try.

JACQUELINE M. NOLAN–HALEY, COURT MEDIATION AND THE SEARCH FOR JUSTICE THROUGH LAW
74 Wash. U. L.Q. 47 1994.

The trend toward court mediation is remarkable because our civil justice system has traditionally promised justice through law. The promise of mediation is different: Justice is derived, not through the operation of law, but through autonomy and self-determination. When mediation occurs in court, significant policy questions arise: What happens to law? To justice? Do they collapse in the experience of self-determination? If so, what then happens to the promise of justice through law, particularly where one or both of the parties are not represented by lawyers?

* * *

My inquiry focuses specifically on the role of law in mediation—how it affects the process, the outcome and, ultimately, the type of justice that parties achieve in court mediation.

* * *

The law's influence in the mediation process depends in large measure upon the individual mediator's approach to the mediation process. This unpredictable character affects the kind and quality of justice currently available in court mediation . . .

* * *

Parties choose the legal system to resolve disputes primarily because they want what courts have to offer, namely, a resolution of their

---

23. This is also examined in Rogers &   Salem, *supra* note 15, at 140.

disputes based on principles of law. When parties are required to resolve disputes differently, through the mediation process, their bargaining should be informed by knowledge of law. Thus, how legal rights are acknowledged or ignored determines in large measure whether parties achieve "equivalency" justice in court mediation.

* * *

There are, today, a number of differing views about the mediation process, and this, in turn, has generated a variety of opinions about the appropriate role of the mediator. The label "mediation" is attached to a wide variety of practices ranging from court conferences strongly suggesting settlement to exercises in moral development. At one end of the spectrum is the instrumentalist vision of mediation as an efficient means of managing court calendars—a perfunctory process which settles cases and clears dockets. At the other extreme is a more noble vision of mediation as a process of moral development which helps individuals realize their ends and develop a stronger sense of efficaciousness. Somewhere in between is the ethical pragmatists' view that mediation is a good method of resolving some disputes when it is responsive to human needs.

Depending upon one's philosophy of mediation, the cardinal virtues of this process can be self-determination, autonomy, empowerment, transformation, and efficiency. Mediation is thought to enhance parties' self-determinative capabilities because it permits them to structure and consent to the outcome of the bargaining process. Unlike decision making by a neutral third party in the adjudication process, decision making in mediation rests solely with the disputing parties. Some commentators consider mediation to be a fairer process than adjudication because the affected parties have complete authority in selecting what values will govern the resolution of their dispute. Finally, mediation is thought to result in greater litigant satisfaction than does judicial adjudication of disputes. There has been a significant amount of scholarly activity directed toward testing and validating these assumptions.

B.   The Role of Law in Mediation

Conventional wisdom concerning mediation holds that substantive law is not dispositive in the mediation process—it operates simply as a template to show what might be available in a more formal, legalistic setting. Instead of law, free-standing normative standards govern in mediation, and parties actually affected by a dispute decide what factors should influence the efforts to resolve that dispute. Thus, the moral reference point in mediation is the self, and individualized notions of fairness, justice, morality, ethics, and culture may trump the values associated with any objective framework provided by law.

Some scholars have argued that because mediation operates outside the supposed protection of law and the legal process, it has potential to do the most good. Disputing parties have the ability to resolve their problems in a wider framework than the limited confines of the legal system. Mediation does not silence the parties in ways that law does with rules of evidence, procedure, and the like.

* * *

D. THE PARADOX OF COURT MEDIATION

Litigants come to court for different reasons. Some seek justice through law; that is, a judge's decision based on the rule of law. Other litigants hope to coerce their opponents through legal means. Whatever their original purpose in seeking the court's intervention in their disputes, after referral to mediation, their dispute resolution activity takes place without the official power of law, but nonetheless under its aegis. When the court refers litigants to mediation, the litigants themselves are required to become the decision makers. This, then, is the paradox of court-based mediation: Despite the initial search for justice based on an objective standard outside of themselves, namely law, disputing parties are required by courts and coached by mediators to place the locus of decision making in themselves. The result is "individualized justice." The parties' original expectations for justice through law have been suspended. The court is now promising a form of justice which results more from individual preferences than from externally imposed standards. In addition to considering the law, parties are also invited to act creatively and pursue their personal sense of fairness based on nonlegal values such as culture, morals, and individual ethics.

But referral to mediation does not necessarily diminish the importance of law for those parties who sought its protection when they first came to court. In fact, law may have an exaggerated sense of value because of the feeling that the parties have lost the right to see a judge. Parties who choose to bring their conflicts into the public domain of the court system are likely to have strong beliefs about their legal entitlements. For them, law may be an important, if not predominant, value.

* * *

Parties will assert or disregard their legal rights in proportion to the value they place on them. For some litigants, conserving time may be more important than receiving an award of money. For others, the opportunity to vent may be more important than the right to void a contract. However, despite the choice of nonlegal values that may influence or determine the outcome of court mediation, law is still very much connected to the enterprise. Law motivates the choice of court as the forum for resolving disputes; law prompts the claims that are asserted; law determines the legality and enforceability of the outcome.

* * *

In short, balancing legal rights and nonlegal interests involves tradeoffs, and making informed decisions about tradeoffs requires knowledge of law. It is in this dualism that authentic self-determination is exercised and that the counterpart to justice through law is achieved. The reality of court mediation practice today is otherwise . . .

* * *

The fundamental questions about court mediation go well beyond the individualized justice which finds expression in autonomy, self-determination, and feelings of satisfaction. They go well beyond administrative efficiency and clearing dockets. Rather, the fundamental questions about court mediation concern fairness. What were the parties' reasonable expectations when they brought their dispute into the legal system? Did they achieve them in court mediation? The central inquiry in this analysis is whether parties who initially sought justice through law in court adjudication received the closest analogue to justice through law in court mediation.

Court mediation requires parties to place the locus of decision making in themselves; to become active participants in the resolution of their own disputes. In order to engage fully in this decision making process, disputants must be positioned to make conscious, informed choices. Thus, knowledge of legal rights is a necessary prerequisite to the exercise of self-determination in court mediation. Without such knowledge, the fairness of the mediation process and its outcome are suspect.

Presumably, parties represented by lawyers would have relevant legal knowledge, but most unrepresented parties—a growing population inside and outside the justice system—are at the "short end of the stick."

Despite the proliferation of mediation statutes in a wide range of subject areas, little attention has been focused on unrepresented parties as an identifiable group and on the mediator's responsibilities to them. The few rules and statutes that specifically refer to unrepresented parties require that mediators encourage them to consult with independent legal counsel. However, as discussed earlier in this article, the "independent counsel" rule is an illusory concept for the majority of Americans who cannot afford lawyers. Thus, there is no real system in place to protect unrepresented parties in court mediation. Should court mediators protect them?

There is considerable variance today in how mediators conceptualize their role. Moreover, much ink has been spilled by commentators who also differ on this question. The current divide lies somewhere between the vision of a mediator as a "disinterested referee" and as an "empowerment specialist." Locating the discussion within the context of court mediation and the role of law raises significant policy questions for unrepresented parties. Should mediators guarantee a fair agreement? Or, is it enough that the agreement be legal? What type of legal assistance, if any, should mediators offer? Legal advice? Legal information? Even though existing professional and ethical standards distinguish between these two forms of legal assistance, the distinction is not always clear in practice. Moreover, such inquiries cannot be neatly bundled into these two packages. Unrepresented litigants ask court mediators a wide variety of legal questions ranging from simple procedural matters to complex questions of law. Some questions can be answered quite easily by court clerks, some require legal counsel, and still others have no clear answers. Difficult policy questions remain.

The increased use of court mediation requires more guidance for mediators who work with unrepresented parties. Specifically, we need further empirical research of the kinds of legal assistance requested by unrepresented litigants in court mediation programs. This data can inform our thinking about the situations in which legal assistance by the mediator is or is not appropriate. As a beginning for this inquiry, I suggest four categories of legal questions that commonly arise with unrepresented litigants: administrative, informational, analytical, and strategic. Questions in the administrative category relate to issues such as amending a complaint, bringing a counter-claim, adding a third-party defendant, executing a judgment, suing in civil court without an attorney, or supporting specific claims with documentary proof. Information regarding these matters is often found in brochures distributed by the court and is regularly provided by court personnel. Mediators should be permitted to respond to such inquiries.

The second category of questions, informational, relates to information about specific areas of law. Examples from our clinic include inquiries related to the statute of limitations, admissibility of evidence at trial, enforceability of oral agreements, and availability of specific types of damages. Responding to these questions is problematic for the court mediator because they raise a host of additional, interrelated questions. How much information is enough? At what point does legal information fall under the rubric of legal advice? Is it ever possible to provide nonpartisan legal information without favoring one of the parties? Mediators should exercise extreme caution in responding to these inquiries, which, in my view, represent some of the most difficult questions in court mediation practice today.

Questions in the analytical category relate to ultimate issues and probable court outcomes. Am I liable under this contract? How would the judge rule if this case were in court? Is the defendant liable for any damages? Answering questions in the analytical category goes beyond the boundaries of legal information to the realm of specific legal advice. In my view, court mediators should not engage in this practice with unrepresented parties.

Finally, there are questions related to strategy and tactics. Common examples of such questions would be: What should I make for an opening offer? Do you think I should take his offer or try to get more? Do you think I am better off before a judge? Giving specific answers to these questions requires the mediator to act in a representational capacity, a role which is inconsistent with the nature of mediation.

* * *

Certainly, the mediation process allows litigants to acknowledge multiple human values that may not be recognized in law. Empirical studies show high settlement rates and suggest that both efficiency and individual satisfaction can be achieved. However, a closer look at what actually happens in court mediation tells a more unsettling story about the results of bargaining in ignorance of the law—the story of hit-or-miss justice ...

* * *

I believe that there are serious fairness concerns for the litigants who originally came to court seeking justice through law; many of them will settle in mediation and experience instead hit-or-miss justice. Those who are knowledgeable about their legal rights will receive a "hit," while the others will miss out. Thus, until there is a clearer consensus on goals other than efficiency, such as process and outcome fairness, we should question the imposition of court mediation on unrepresented parties with potentially unequal bargaining power.

* * *

Confronting the limits of court mediation means that in our desire to promote mediation as an enlightened vision of disputing, we must be careful not to devalue the parties' reasonable expectations for securing justice through law. Court mediation is a subculture operating officially within the main legal culture. The fundamental question it presents is one of fairness: Will those whose cases are shunted from the courtroom to the mediation room receive a fair shake? I believe they will if their bargaining is informed by law. If not, court mediation is an impoverished alternative to judicial adjudication that demeans both the courts and the mediation process.

———

Yet the mediator must concern herself with neutrality and impartiality in two distinct, but related, aspects of the mediation: one, the balance and the conduct of the negotiations which she facilitates throughout the mediation (i.e., the process); and two, the ultimate result or outcome of the mediation.

1. PROCESS

What specifically constitutes fairness in the mediation process? Fairness in the negotiation process has been identified as having four components: structural fairness, process fairness, procedural fairness, and outcome fairness.[24] Issues of structural, process and procedural fairness will be examined in terms of the mediator's conduct in the process, while outcome fairness will be looked at separately. Often there

24. Cecilia Albin, *The Role of Fairness* (1993).
in Negotiation, 9 Negotiation J. 223, 225

is overlap in these categories. The mediator should consider what action is appropriate, if any, in each case.

Structural fairness relates to the overall structure of the dispute and the relations between the parties. The mediator has little control over these variables. Yet some allege that the mediator should influence the structural fairness of the dispute. This would include, for example, providing advice to one of the parties. Others advise mediators to "take the parties as you find them." They argue that fairness in the process and procedure is where the mediator should focus. This includes focus on how the parties treat each other, the dynamics of the negotiation process, and the procedures used in arriving at an agreement.[25] If the mediator approaches the mediation by following an outline of the structure of the process, these variables will not be neglected. It is likely that procedural or process fairness can be achieved. But consideration and assurance of process factors alone does not assure fairness in the result.

2. THE RESULT

Should the mediator be concerned at all with the result of a mediation? Does the mediator have a duty to determine fairness in the outcome of a mediation? An imbalance of power at the table may lead to what the mediator perceives as an imbalanced result. Even though there is balance at the mediation table, the parties may reach an outcome that the mediator believes is unfair or unbalanced. Does the mediator have a duty to intervene in either instance?[26]

The issue of empowerment is also related. Mediation is often described as a process which empowers the parties to make their own decisions. If this is so, why then should a mediator intervene in the decision making? Some writers contend that a lawyer-mediator should specifically guarantee that the agreement reached is not one which a court would refuse to enforce. That is, she should ensure against an agreement tainted by fraud, duress, overreaching, imbalance in bargaining leverage, or basic unconscionability.[27] Since judges and juries differ, how could a mediator properly make this call? If such standards are established, will inaccurate predictions lead to an increase in claims of mediator malpractice?[28]

If the mediation process is, in fact, one of self-determination, then the parties ought to be able to make their own decisions. There are any number of factors that motivate people to make certain decisions. To ask the mediator to intervene and make judgments for those parties is to require conduct arguably outside the mediator's role. In the absence of strict guidelines, however, the individual mediator must make the

---

25. *Id.* at 230.

26. Clearly, if the result is something which offends the mediator's sense of morality or is illegal, the mediator should make that known and excuse herself from the case. These are not the instances discussed here.

27. Leonard L. Riskin, *Toward New Standards for the Neutral Lawyer in Mediation*, 26 Ariz. L. Rev. 329, 354 (1984).

28. See Chapter 15, § F for an examination of mediator liability.

choice. Basically, if the parties are satisfied, then absent illegality, the agreement should be executed.

Lastly, if there are instances where the mediator feels so strongly about an issue that she may attempt to influence the outcome, there is little doubt that she should not take the case. Likewise, where the parties *perceive* the mediator to be biased, most mediators voluntarily withdraw from the matter.

A number of other issues such as ethics, conflicts of interest, and standards of conduct overlap with neutrality and will be examined in more detail in subsequent chapters.[29]

PROBLEMS FOR DISCUSSION

7–1. Can the payment of a fee affect the mediator's neutrality?

(a) Most mediators split their fee for services, whether an hourly rate or a per diem charge, evenly between the parties. In a commercial landlord-tenant case, the tenant is a small start-up company with very little cash. Both parties want to participate in mediation and have agreed on James Lewis, a known businessman, as the mediator. The landlord agrees to pay 80% of the $2,000 per day fee. Might the mediator's actions with regard to treatment of the parties differ?

(b) Would the circumstances change if the fee were to be divided equally and billed at $280/per hour? How can the hourly rate affect the less wealthy party?

(c) Can the fact that the landlord may have a large number of other cases to refer to the mediator affect neutrality?

7–2. If a party conveys, in confidence, to you as the mediator, specific information, which, if known to the other side would negate an agreement, what is your duty? For instance, in a case over a sale of damaged goods, the Defendant has offered to convey to Plaintiff real estate in satisfaction for the debt. Just as the agreement is being finalized, the Defendant in caucus discloses to you, the mediator, that there are substantial tax liens on the property.

(a) Can you, should you, or must you disclose this new information to the Plaintiff?

(b) What are the potential consequences if you draft and finalize the agreement?

---

29. See Chapters 14 and 15.

Chapter Eight

IDENTIFICATION OF ISSUES AND INTERESTS

Once the mediator is certain that he has gathered sufficient information about the dispute or case, he should begin to identify the primary issues. Some trainers and writers refer to this stage as problem identification; however, the word "problem" has a negative connotation which can contribute to polarization of the parties. Issue identification or issue determination are more neutral ways of describing this stage of the process. During this phase, the mediator should also simultaneously attempt to identify the underlying interests of each party. These are often not the same as the issues which have been publicly stated.

Issues are those items which both sides are willing to openly discuss as the predominant points of contention, and about which the negotiation has been initiated. Parties take and defend their positions based upon those items. In most cases, each party also has certain underlying issues or interests. These matters are not likely to have been disclosed or identified at this stage of the process. Therefore, the mediator should initially focus on the identification and restatement of the main or apparent issues. He should keep in mind, however, that there may be other matters which should be discussed before a final resolution can be reached.

It is recommended that at this stage of the process, absent overt hostility, the mediator have the parties together. When identifying the issues, there should be mutual agreement on what they are, or at a minimum, an acknowledged agreement to disagree. If the mediator is gathering information in private meetings or caucuses, and in the process, identifies issues with each party separately, there is a significant risk that there will be misunderstanding or disagreement on specifically what the issues are. If the parties are not forthcoming with information, the mediator may need to meet privately with each party early on in the process. In these instances, specification of the issues in separate caucuses is necessary. The problem with this approach, however, is that what may be an issue for one party is not an issue for the other. Of course, this may occur even when the parties are together. But, in that situation, each party is likely to at least hear the other's issue expressed. They then will be in a position to better understand that different issues exist for each side.

If it is necessary to conduct this stage of the process in private sessions, the mediator's job becomes much more difficult. He will have to go back and forth to confirm exactly what issues need to be resolved. Explaining the issues from each person's perspective may also be necessary. Alternately, if the conflict and hostility is such that the parties cannot—or will not—hear the statements of the other, the mediator can bring a more neutralizing perspective to the communication. In this way, the mediator uses restating to allow the party to consider the position of the other. However, the fact that caucuses are commonly confidential presents another dilemma for the mediator: A party may disclose an issue to the mediator, but not authorize the mediator to share it with the other party. Of course, unless an issue is openly discussed, it cannot be resolved. In such situations, the mediator must then encourage, but not pressure, the party to allow disclosure of the information. In addition, when the privately disclosed issue is one of which the other parties were unaware, the mediator must confront questions such as "Why hasn't he told us that before?"

Once the issues are identified, the mediator should then restate and reframe them in such a manner that will leave the parties open to a variety of potential solutions. The mediator should utilize his listening skills to determine any issue and interest overlap or areas of potential agreement. Skill in the reframing and restating of these matters will assist in moving the mediation forward.

After the mediator has obtained the parties' agreement on the specific issues, he should determine an agenda for the mediation, particularly in complex cases. The agenda will dictate the order of discussion of issues for the remainder of the session. In simple cases, an elaborate agenda is not necessary. In others, the way the mediator approaches the agenda will determine how the negotiation proceeds. Restatement and ordering of the issues for discussion moves the mediation from information gathering to the problem-solving phase.

A.   IDENTIFY, REFRAME AND RESTATE: THE USE OF LANGUAGE

As the parties describe the dispute or conflict, the mediator begins to identify the primary issues of contention. The way these issues are described is considered to be how they are framed. The mediator may then restate the issue or reframe the problem. Restatement of what a party has said and reframing the way a party has related a problem, are two of the most effective tools the mediator uses. While some mediators see the terms as interchangeable, here *restate* connotes stating a few sentences in a way that reflects what the speaker said, but with a slight change of focus, or removing offensive language. *Reframing* connotes a statement about the problem or issues and is used to help the parties to view the problem or concern in a different light. There are several purposes behind restating and reframing. Not only does this let the party know that she has been heard and understood by the mediator, it may also assist the others at the table in hearing another point of view.

By using more neutral language, the mediator urges the parties to approach the dispute in a more neutral and positive manner. This technique is often effective in de-polarizing the parties. By restating, the mediator also begins to refocus the language used by the participants. After they hear statements made in a slightly different way, the parties may subsequently choose more precise words to explain themselves.

For example, rather than direct blame to the other party, reframing is also used to identify the main issues and points, and make a transition to the problem-solving stage of the process. By hearing neutral language and a broad view of the issues, the parties may become open to a more creative problem-solving approach.

Restatements may be used by the mediator at a number of times during the process. Some mediators have been trained to restate almost every thought or point that a party makes. Restating can be an effective tool: It conveys an empathetic understanding and helps separate the people from the problem.[1] Continual restatements, however, not only will become monotonous but will also cause the mediation session to take twice as long. Therefore, in most situations, the mediator should wait until the parties have completed their opening remarks and then restate the primary points in neutral, general terms. Where there are complex, or lengthy, opening statements, the mediator may need to restate the issues after each party makes his or her opening remarks. In less complex or lengthy cases, if the opening statements are brief, the mediator should wait to make primary restatements until all participants have delivered their openings and he has gathered some additional information about the issues. That is not to say, however, that single restatements are never necessary. Particularly in volatile situations, the mediator can defuse some of the hostility by restating each point made by the party. The mediator must be careful, however, not to engage in a constant parroting of the problem.

Exactly how much time is spent in this stage will depend on the nature and complexity of the dispute, and more importantly the parties' need for understanding and clarification of issues. There can be overlap between identifying the issues and setting the agenda. In some cases, these tasks can be performed simultaneously. In others they occur sequentially. And in still other cases, it is possible to identify an issue and completely resolve that issue before identifying others. While the single issue approach is not recommended in most instances, it can be effective, particularly if there is only one issue that the parties are

---

1. This is the first step of "Principled Negotiation", a concept first put forth by Roger Fisher & William Ury of the Harvard Negotiation Project in their book, Getting to Yes (1981).

initially willing to discuss. In most cases, however, the mediator will at least make an attempt to reach consensus on the nature of all issues as they are put on the table. Identifying most of the issues before initiating negotiation usually results in a number of items for discussion. Give and take is then possible, leading to a more integrative bargaining approach.[2]

Positive reinforcement is a powerful motivator for most individuals. The mediator should not overlook the use of pointing out the positive aspects which he sees in the dispute. Because the mediator sits in an objective chair, he is much more likely than any of the parties to see some middle ground, to observe that there is not as much disagreement as each side may initially perceive, and to identify areas of overlapping interests. When these overlapping interests are directly stated and obvious, they present the mediator with a logical starting point. Two common examples are the mutual benefits a landlord and tenant or a supplier and purchaser can gain by continuing their relationships. Once this is pointed out and acknowledged, renegotiating the terms of the contract is often much easier. In a family case, the mutual concern may be the best interests of the children. In personal injury litigation, parties want to conclude the lawsuit and get on with their lives. Where areas of common interest are more private or potentially embarrassing and not obvious, the mediator may choose to be less specific in his restatements, but he should keep these topics in mind (and in his notes) for later discussion.

Some mediators also ask the parties themselves to do some restating and reframing. The theory behind this approach is that the parties will better understand the other side and begin to acknowledge another view of the situation if they are required to restate it. Use of this method will depend primarily on the nature of the relationship between the parties and how comfortable they are with the idea. In some cases, after the mediator has restated some of the issues, he may ask each of the parties to restate what they think the other party has said. Other mediators may request that the participants do all of the restating. This may be done by asking each party to restate the opposing view before they put forth their response, position, or statement. Caution is advised in using this approach. Many individuals may be uncomfortable with this process. The mediator may lose the trust and cooperation of the parties.

New mediators often wonder how many issues there are in a case. Some mediators will go to great lengths to avoid single issue cases, as they are the ones most likely to lead to positional, distributive negotiation.[3] The mediator can try to fractionalize the issue, that is, break it into smaller components, to create more items for discussion and bargaining.[4] For example, a dispute over the payment of a sum of money is a

---

2. Negotiation theory and styles are discussed in Chapter 9.

3. For further detail on the types of negotiation and how to move the parties

away from positional, distributive negotiation, see Chapter 9.

4. For a discussion of reducing conflict by fractionalization, or breaking down the primary issue into sub-issues, see Joyce L.

typical single-issue case. While most negotiators (and some mediators) will discuss only the amount to be paid in an offer/counter-offer format, most mediators will look to find at least one other item for discussion. A mediator might fractionalize the money issue into the amount and the time of payment. This provides at least one more issue for negotiation.

Related to the strategy of numbering or fractionalizing issues are the concepts of linkage and non-linkage. More specifically, this refers to issues which are linked, or contingent upon each other. If there is a direct nexus, the resolution of one issue is contingent upon the others. The linkage may also be indirect: the issues are related, but resolution is not necessarily co-dependent.

In the case of unconnected issues, the items are not related, and one may be resolved while the other is not. There is no dependency. In these instances, it is possible to conclude the mediation with partial agreements.

The mediator, in gathering information and identifying the issues, will usually be able to determine which issues are linked and which are not. It is, of course, possible to have some of each in the same case. The more difficult task for the mediator is to decide whether he will attempt to link otherwise unlinked issues, or in the converse, unlink linked issues.[5] The specific technique the mediator uses here will depend upon the information he has regarding the interests of the parties.

The identification of issues is only the beginning of the problem solving process. As the parties begin to discuss the issues and generate options and alternatives, not only will the mediator be gathering supplemental information, but also additional issues and interests may come to light. Therefore, the mediator must be careful to not make a premature assessment that he has reached the conclusion of information gathering. Likewise, an early determination of the issues can be limiting. Since these items are subject to change, the mediator must never close his mind to additional issues as the process continues.

B.   SETTING THE AGENDA

Setting the agenda can be a strategic move for the mediator. When and how each of the issues is approached for discussion and resolution will influence the progression of the mediation. Conflicts can be defined so as to magnify or minimize the dispute. The mediator should approach agenda setting and the discussion of issues in a way which can minimize the dispute. Controlling what is perceived to be at stake is a method of preventing destructive conflict.[6] In some cases, the matter is not complex; it is not necessary for the mediator to spend time considering the

Hocker and William W. Wilmot, Interpersonal Conflict 194 (1991).

5. For further discussion of the linkage concept, see Christopher W. Moore & CDR Associates, Effective Mediation (1989).

6. Morton Deutsch, The Resolution of Conflict; Constructive and Destructive Processes 370 (1973).

variety of agenda options. If, however, there are a number of agenda items or issues to be discussed, the method of approach can set the tone for the negotiation. For instance, if the parties initially consider and resolve the easiest matters, they establish a positive tone, which may assist in resolving the remaining matters. Because the mediator is in control of the agenda order, he should give some thought to which items should be discussed first.

There are various approaches to agenda setting, each with its benefits and drawbacks. The mediator should weigh each method in light of the specific situation, considering both the subject matter of the dispute and the personalities of the parties. Of course, agenda setting is always subject to modification. If the mediator initiates discussion in a certain manner and finds that it is not working, it is appropriate to stop, rethink, and take a different approach.

A number of different approaches to agenda setting follow. The mediator should give thought to the use of these and not fear testing each to determine which work best.

The mediator may want to try several of the so-far identified approaches to the agenda: 1) ad hoc, 2) simple agenda, 3) alternating choices by the parties, 4) principled, 5) less difficult first, 6) most difficult first, 7) order of importance, 8) building-block or contingent agenda, and 9) tradeoff or packaging.[7] Each will be briefly described. The mediator should remain cognizant that if one approach does not seem to work, it is acceptable to change the strategy.

In an ad hoc approach, the mediator proposes examination of an issue as it is discussed. The parties analyze it thoroughly until they reach a resolution. The mediator moves through all issues in this manner, taking them in the order in which they were placed on the table. This may allow the more vocal party to exert control over the agenda and can be confusing. In less complex cases, however, it works quite well. The ad hoc approach calls for less direction from the mediator.

The simple agenda is very similar. In this approach, there is one main issue taken for discussion. Even if there has been some division of issues, or smaller issues arise, the primary item is dealt with and settled before discussion of others is commenced. This process works well in simple disputes where there is very little overt conflict. It is not applicable where there are a number of issues with varying importance. It is also inappropriate where issues are contingent upon one another. Neither the ad hoc nor simple agenda approach encourages compromise by exchange.

In some instances, the mediator may allow the parties to alternate choosing the topic of discussion. This method provides the parties more

7. Most of these were first set forth by Christopher W. Moore, The Mediation Pro-   cess 182 (1986).

control of the process. Choosing who goes first, however, can be problematic. The non-choosing party may refuse to participate in the discussion. Moreover, the mediator may lose control of the process. This approach may work well, however, where the parties are experienced negotiators and the level of conflict is minimal.

In a principled agenda, the mediator, with the assistance of the parties, establishes general principles that form the framework for settlement. The specific details of how these principles will be applied to specific issues then follows. This procedure requires that the parties be willing and able to negotiate at a fairly high level of generalization or abstraction. It is also appropriate where there is a strong desire for settlement by all parties. The parties are typically willing to defer decision making on minor issues until later in the bargaining process. One example is in the business context: the parties agree in principle to the renegotiation of a contract. The specific contents are then addressed. Another situation where an agreement in principle can be effective is in multi-defendant personal injury litigation. An agreement in principle is reached on the total amount to be paid to the plaintiff. The remainder of the mediation is devoted to how the defendants will allocate this amount.

In taking the less difficult items first, the mediator identifies those issues where probability of agreement is high. Reaching the agreement should not take a long time. Issues which appear to be less difficult are often less important matters, and the parties move quickly to resolution. These easy items constitute the beginning of the agenda. Reaching agreement on some matters early in negotiations promotes an atmosphere of agreement. Once these agreements exist, the parties are usually reluctant to forfeit them as the result of an impasse later on in the process. On the other hand, there can be drawbacks. The risk of dealing with the less important matters first is that if a final agreement is not reached, the parties will feel as if the mediation has resulted in a waste of time and money.

In other cases, the mediator may want to tackle the most difficult issues first. This is very closely related to the following approach of order of importance, particularly where there is agreement on the most important item. If agreement is reached on the most difficult agenda item, then it is likely the other issues will fall into place. On the other hand, beginning with the most difficult can result in an early termination of the session if agreement is not attained.

In the order of importance approach, the parties, with the mediator's assistance, choose the most important item for each of them. These issues are then placed first on the agenda. The assumption is that if these items can be agreed upon, the remainder of the less important items will follow suit. This procedure depends upon the parties' ability to agree on the most important issues and the order in which they will be handled. Of course, if all participants choose the same item as most important, it is likely the primary source of the conflict and hence the most difficult. If resolution can be achieved on this issue, the balance of the mediation will probably proceed easily.

In a building block agenda, the mediator identifies issues which must be dealt with first because they provide the groundwork or foundation for later decisions. In essence, the remainder of any agreement will be contingent upon the answer to the primary question. This approach can become fairly complicated. The parties must clearly express and understand the contingent nature of the issues. In cases where the issues are interrelated, however, this approach can prevent deadlocks due to incorrect sequencing of issues. An example from the business arena builds on the foundation issue of termination versus continuation of the joint venture. A similar example in the employment sphere is the initial issue of whether the employee will continue to be employed. On the other hand, some mediators may want to discuss each contingency and all of the potential ways to resolve each. For example, in an employment termination matter, one complete set of agreements are made contingent upon the rehiring of the employee. Another series of resolutions are made in the event of complete termination. The parties then, after considering all the possibilities, reach an agreement on the core issue— whether the employee will be rehired. This approach is also used in the family and divorce mediation context, for example to determine reasonable visitation schedules, without first establishing the primary custodial parent. Proponents of this approach (quite similar to the "A cuts the pieces of a pie, B selects which piece he wants) contend that such considerations prompt the parties to be more reasonable in their positions."

Another approach to agenda formation is issue trading or packaging. Parties unwilling to move on a single issue will often use combinations of issues. Offers are made in return for concessions. The mediator orchestrates this exchange. Issues may be traded one for another in such a way that mutual bargaining results. Trading can also be conducted on an issue-by-issue basis so that all issues are eventually resolved.[8] This is the basis of integrative negotiating. Packaging of proposals which contain multiple-issue solutions can be particularly effective where the issues are linked. The parties can see that mutual gain is possible. Because of the packaging, which is often done by the mediator, some of the reluctance involved in presenting alternatives for settlement is eliminated. The give and take does not appear so great since the proposal comes all in one package presented by the neutral mediator. The mediator must be careful, however, in utilizing this approach not to control the outcome.

As the mediator moves through agenda setting, he can do so in different ways. For example he may just initiate the discussion of each item. Alternatively he may first list the agenda for the parties on a flip chart or board. Regardless of the way the mediator sets the agenda, if problems should arise, movement to another issue or topic is appropriate.

8. Christopher Moore, The Mediation Process, 226–227 (2d Ed., 1996).

EXERCISES

8–1. The ability to hear a statement expressed in value-laden terms and restate it in more neutral language takes practice. There are a number of ways to rephrase these statements. Use the following statements as examples. First, restate the sentence with the intent to let the maker know she has been heard but without offending the other party. Second, try to reframe the issue in a manner which will move the parties to the option generation phase. Keep in mind that there are a variety of ways to restate and reframe. Much will depend upon the mediator's instinct during the mediation; nonetheless, an example follows.

Original Statement: "I can't believe that this hospital would continue to employ such practices that allow the patient's well-being to be jeopardized for the sake of money."

Becomes: "Mr. Smith, you are quite concerned about how your mother was treated by the hospital staff."

Becomes: "One of your primary concerns seems to be the policies of the hospital."

Original Statement: "I want $4,780 for the damage to my car that this stupid, inconsiderate, irresponsible, teenager caused."

Becomes:

Becomes:

Original Statement: "My hippie, punk neighbor had better stop having loud barbecue parties every weekend. Stereos play trash until the early morning hours."

Becomes:

Becomes:

Original Statement: "You arrogant, selfish, pin-striped bankers want to use the Taj Mahal for collateral on this loan when a merry-go-round from the local playground would do."

Becomes:

Becomes:

Chapter Nine

THE NEGOTIATION PROCESS

A. GENERAL OVERVIEW

It has been observed that negotiation is much like sex. It is something most of us do at various points in our lives—yet no one has taught us anything, nor is there much open discussion about it. But as the use of ADR has increased, so has awareness of the negotiation process. In fact, it is now viewed as a process, with its own stages and dynamics. The mediator's role is essentially to facilitate negotiation. Therefore, it is imperative that the mediator be intimately familiar with the negotiation process.

Negotiation is at the heart of all settlement; in fact, it is a part of everyday life. Although negotiation is often included as one of the dispute resolution procedures, ADR processes differ from negotiation in the existence of an intervention by one or more third party neutrals. Traditional negotiation, on the other hand, involves only the parties to the dispute and, if represented, their lawyers or other agents. Nonetheless, negotiation is a process, and like most processes, a variety of types and styles exist.

Informal negotiations take place all the time as we go about our everyday routines. Purchasing items on sale is, in essence, a negotiation. When family members decide which television program to watch on Tuesday evenings or where to order pizza, they negotiate. When there is a successful negotiation, there is no longer a dispute. Unsuccessful negotiations result in continued disputes. More formal negotiations also take place daily in more structured settings. Obtaining employment involves negotiation, as does selecting a place to live.

In the legal context, negotiation is the essence of transactional law. In the litigation arena negotiations may take place informally on an ad hoc basis, as the lawyers discuss aspects of the case. More structured or formal negotiations occur when there is a stimulus to settle the matter, such as a trial date.

Like other processes, negotiation is composed of various stages. How the parties in a negotiation pass through these stages may differ. In informal situations, the stages are often blurred. In more formal negotiations, the phases can be observed more easily. There are a variety of ways to label the stages of negotiation. One example is the six stage model:

(1) planning and preparation;

(2) establishing initial relationships between negotiators;

(3) opening offers or initial proposals;

(4) information exchange;

(5) narrowing of differences; and

(6) closure.[1]

A more detailed model provides additional information about the process.

Preparation and planning

Ice breaking

Agenda control

Information bargaining

Proposals, offers, demands

Persuasions/justifications

Concessions/reformulations

Crisis: resolution or deadlock

Closing

Memorialization[2]

While these have been depicted in the context of legal negotiations, they are applicable in all types of negotiations. Like any flexible process, there is overlap in the phases of a negotiation as well as movement back and forth between the stages.

B. NEGOTIATION THEORY

Negotiation is often examined and studied in the context of dispute resolution, since it is viewed as a method for resolving a dispute or problem. However, the use of negotiation in the context of a transactional matter should not be ignored. Negotiation takes place each time two or more individuals put together a deal, contract, or lease. The theoretical basis of the negotiation process in ordinary business transactions is very similar to that observed in dispute resolution. A primary difference in negotiation in these two contexts is that in the dispute resolution arena, feelings and emotions may be involved and are often negative. There is also a personal or professional history between the parties. On the other hand, in transactional cases there is not necessarily a prior relationship between the parties to the negotiation, although continuous

1. Donald G. Gifford, Legal Negotiation 8 (1989).

2. Thomas F. Guernsey, A Practical Guide of Negotiation 12 (1996).

negotiations are common among business associates. In transactional matters, however, the goal of the negotiation is to establish a relationship, whether it be short-lived, such as in the purchase of a car, or more lasting, such as in the creation of a business organization.[3] Despite these differences, in both the dispute resolution and transactional arenas, the underlying theories of the negotiation process are nearly parallel.

There are a number of basic theories which have been used to describe the negotiation process. The term *theory* is used in this context to refer to the underlying method of how the procedure or process of negotiation works. This is not to be confused with *style*, which is an individual matter of choice that the negotiator makes. Theory should also be distinguished from negotiation *strategy*, which has been identified as a specific set of negotiating behaviors.[4] This is not to say, however, that there is not overlap between the theoretical basis, types and styles of negotiation. For instance, a certain style of negotiator may prefer to use a particular type of negotiation strategy. On the other hand, when involved in a particular type of negotiation with a distinct theoretical basis, one might find certain styles more effective than others. Expert negotiators are able to change their styles depending upon the styles and strategies of the other parties, as well as upon the type of process. It is not as simple, however, to change the type of negotiation that is taking place.

In negotiation theory, some distinct types of negotiation have been identified. Most experts have identified these types by comparing and contrasting two methods of negotiation. Two primary theories of negotiation have been explored in detail: one is the dichotomy of negotiation as either distributive or integrative; the other views the negotiation process as either positional or principled.

In a distributive negotiation (also termed linear) negotiation, there is a fixed pie. There are limited resources (usually money) to be distributed or with which to negotiate. More for one necessarily means less for the other. This has also been described as a zero sum game. It is assumed, and is likely true, that where there is a fixed quantity of resources, one person's gain is necessarily the other's loss. In a distributive bargaining situation, there is a direct conflict of interest between the parties. Hence an adversarial, competitive style is most often observed.[5] Example: Two partners may negotiate how to split a monthly profit.

---

3. In many cultures, such as the Japanese, this focus on the future relationship is a primary, if not the main, point of the negotiation process. If a relationship is not established, the remaining part of the negotiation would not take place. For further information on cultural factors which influence negotiation and hence mediation, see Chapter 16, § K; Dean A. Foster, Bargaining Across Borders: How to Negotiate Business Successfully Anywhere in the World (1992), and Center for the Study of Foreign Affairs, National Negotiating Styles (Hans Binnerdijk, ed. 1987).

4. Gifford, *supra* note 1, at 18.

5. In fact, at least one author has identified the distributive phase of negotiation as the same as the competitive phase. See Charles B. Craver, Effective Legal Negotiation and Settlement 107 (1993).

On the other hand, integrative negotiations involve the exploration of a number of options, many of which are not in direct conflict with one another. There is an "expanded pie," which provides an opportunity for mutual gain in the negotiation. The interests of the parties are not necessarily in direct conflict, and therefore, there is not an inverse level of satisfaction inherent in the process. There is room for creativity, and a collaborative problem solving approach is usually observed in this type of negotiation. While some see these approaches as two completely discernable ways or methods of negotiating, others have viewed them as part of the same negotiation. In the latter view, the negotiation process proceeds from a distributive phase into an integrative one, unless, of course, the matter is completely settled while in the distributive phase.[6] For example, if our two partners settle on a 60–40 split in monthly profits, they may also decide that the partner with the smaller share gets the use of the company car.

The negotiation process has also been described as either positional or principled.[7] In positional bargaining, the parties align themselves to a position and spend effort defending it against attack. It is similar to the distributive approach, or the "more for me, less for you versus less for me, more for you" mode. However, in positional bargaining, the parties sometimes do not focus on what they really want. Rather, they remain stuck on their position, or the cause and support for the positions they take. The specific styles identified with positional bargaining are hard and soft. Hard style negotiators are adversarial and confrontational. A soft style in positional bargaining is a friendly, cooperative manner. But soft negotiators often yield and concede to avoid confrontation.[8]

Principled negotiators, on the other hand, attempt to identify underlying interests and come up with a number of alternatives for settlement. Rather than a single answer solution, the principled negotiator looks for possible solutions which might satisfy everyone's interest, with the objective being a final resolution with which everyone is satisfied. Specific styles are not as relevant. This looks very much like the approach in the integrative negotiation.

Negotiation can also be looked at as either interests-based or rights-based. These characterizations are similar to the principled versus positional approach just discussed. Interests-based negotiators look to the underlying interests of the parties and use essentially the same approach taken in principled negotiation. Examination of interests is a focus of an integrative approach as well. When underlying interests are considered, it is often possible for the negotiation to result in gains or satisfaction for all participants. Hence, interests-based negotiation is also known as mutual gains bargaining or MGB.[9] In a rights-based approach to a

6. *Id.* at 156.

7. These terms were first used by the Harvard Negotiation Project. See Roger Fisher and William Ury, Getting to Yes (1981).

8. *Id.* at 8.

9. Deborah G. Ancona, et al., *The Group and What Happens on the Way to "Yes,"* Negotiation J. 155, 156 (1991); see also Lawrence Susskind and Jeffrey Cruikshank, Breaking the Impasse: Consensual Ap-

problem, the negotiators look to the entitlement of rights between the parties in an attempt to determine a solution based on those rights. This is similar to the positional bargaining approach. Distributive negotiators also often look to rights to determine how to slice the pie.

Another way the negotiation process can be described is in a simple win-lose versus win-win approach. The win-lose approach is similar to the distributive or positional method where one party will win and get more, while the other party necessarily gets less. When approaching negotiation as an integrative, principled or interests-based process, joint gain and mutual satisfaction is probable, resulting in a win-win or "all gain" situation.

The preference for a specific type of negotiation in the mediation has often been discussed. Many mediation educators and trainers[10] strongly urge the integrative, principled approach. These proponents of integrative bargaining train mediators to constantly search for integrative potential when gathering information in the mediation. The theory is that not only will it be easier to achieve an agreement when engaged in an integrative negotiation, but the result will be also be one with which the parties are more satisfied; consequently the parties will comply with the terms of the agreement. One study has produced empirical data which convincingly supports this theory.[11]

When the parties are in a purely distributive negotiation, the mediator's task is to explore the possibility of a transition to an integrative or principled mode. Maintaining focus on interests and options are two primary methods the mediator should employ. In those cases where there is great difficulty in finding integrative potential or where the parties insist on remaining in a distributive negotiation, then the mediator may take an active role in helping the parties re-evaluate their positions. Re-assessment of one's chances at prevailing, considering both BATNA[12], or one's Best Alternative to a Negotiated Agreement, and WATNA, the Worst Alternative to a Negotiated Agreement, are key elements in moving the parties closer together and into resolution.

The mediator must be aware of all of these variables in negotiation. Her main task may be to change the type of negotiation or theory under which the parties negotiate. Far more difficult for the mediator, if not impossible and outside of her role, is to change or influence the specific stylistic approaches of the negotiators. Yet, in reality there is often overlap between the theoretical basis, the style and strategy used.

C. COMMON STYLES AND TACTICS

Within each of these types, the negotiator may vary his or her style. Negotiators' styles have often been described as competitive, adversarial,

---

proaches to Resolving Public Disputes (1987).

10. And I am one.

11. Raymond A. Whiting, The Use of Mediation as a Dispute Settlement Tool: A Historical Review and Scientific Examina-

tion of the Role and Process of Mediation (Dissertation)(1988).

12. Fisher and Ury, *supra* note 7, at 97–106.

cooperative, problem solving, or collaborative. At least one study has been conducted by Gerald S. Williams to gauge the effectiveness of some of these styles, particularly within the legal community.[13] He attempted to identify certain factors which would indicate that one negotiation style is more effective than another. Williams studied the traits of attorney negotiators and found that while there are distinct differences in approach between the competitive and cooperative negotiators, both types are rated as highly effective negotiators.[14] Common traits of both— such as preparation, adherence to ethical guidelines, trustworthiness, and honesty—were the factors which were indicia of effectiveness. Likewise, there were ineffective negotiators in both groups.

Some scholars have stated that both the cooperative and competitive styles are integral to the negotiation process,[15] and that both are to be used at different times and under different circumstances. Yet most individuals have not been educated in negotiation theory or practice and hence lack these specific skills. Most people rely on intuition and the legal process. An effective negotiator studies the various styles and strategies in order to choose those most effective in a given case. The mediator should recognize when the negotiators are unaware of strategy and when there is a specific, predetermined use of a style. In these two situations, the mediator's resulting intervention will differ.

In discussing negotiation, tactics or strategies used by negotiators have been identified. These maneuvers do not fall directly into specific types or styles of negotiation, but rather constitute recognizable behaviors which may be demonstrated in a given situation. While initially seen by many negotiators as advantageous, in reality, many of these tactics can easily backfire. Once recognized, the tactical negotiator is seen as no longer trustworthy. Hence, the negotiator should weigh carefully both the pros and cons of the use of these tactics. Some of the more common strategies are as follows:[16]

1. Use of additional individuals on the negotiating team;
2. Making an initial large demand or low offer;
3. Negotiating with limited authority;
4. Displays of real or feigned anger/intimidation;
5. Making false demands;
6. Proposing "Take it or leave it";
7. Creating/inducing guilt;
8. Acting like Mutt and Jeff;
9. Claiming alleged expertise/putting on a snow job; and
10. Using a Brer Rabbit-like reverse psychology.

13. For details of the study, see Gerald S. Williams, Legal Negotiation and Settlement (1983).

14. *Id*. at 25.

15. John S. Murray, *Understanding Competing Theories of Negotiation*, 2 Negotiation J. 179 (1986).

16. For elaboration see Craver, *supra* note 5, Chapter 10.

The mediator must be able to recognize the theory, the styles and the tactics to deal with them effectively. However, she must also be careful to avoid getting into the process, that is, she should not begin negotiating herself or position herself as the negotiating opponent. Each negotiator must stand on his or her own. As discussed in the next section, however, the mediator can control the climate and tenor of the process and provide an environment that increases the likelihood of an effective negotiation.

D. COMMON PROBLEMS IN NEGOTIATION

One of the primary problems for the negotiator is the lack of knowledge or skill about the process. Many negotiations in the business community, and even more in the legal arena, take a "seat of the pants" approach. Often in litigation, negotiation and settlement take place on the courthouse steps. In fact, legal negotiations are often like rolling the dice, not thought through at all. In a similar vein, if one is uneducated about the process, then preparation for the negotiation is virtually impossible. The lack of preparation and planning for negotiation contributes to a very haphazard approach to the process during mediation. The mediator must therefore encourage the participants to prepare in advance of the mediation. She may, for example, suggest the parties read a short overview of negotiating skills, or she may provide them with questions to answer that help them see potential approaches to negotiating their dispute. In fact, in some cases the mediation results in an education for the negotiating parties.

Another very common problem in the negotiation process is the parties' lack of specific focus or ability to keep on track. Many times the stages get muddled; people become disagreeable and are not able to stay focused on the main issues. This is less a problem in negotiation in the transactional arena, since all negotiators are present, and theoretically, have a common goal: putting the deal together. In the area of dispute resolution, however, the focus often gets lost once parties become preoccupied with a positional approach. Finding a workable solution is often sacrificed in order to be "right." The mediator can help the negotiators maintain the focus on interests.

Parties in a negotiation may have failed or refused to exchange information. Without information, informed decisions cannot be made. An intermediary may assist in this exchange. Furthermore, many negotiators are very reluctant to make the first offer. A longstanding myth has been that making the first offer is a sign of weakness. Such misperception persists even though much has been written to the contrary. For instance, many believe that putting forth the first credible offer is a sign of strength in a position or a case. Moreover, it has been established that the opening party can control the negotiations. Nonetheless, many still hold tight to the idea that making an unsolicited offer may appear, particularly in the legal context, as an admission of a weak position or case.

Another problem in the negotiation process is the inability of some parties to take responsibility for finding a solution. Some people mistakenly believe that there is a single "right" answer to any dispute or problem. Hence the parties are not compelled to negotiate. Also in the dispute resolution context, because there is a dispute, the parties lack the requisite trust of each other. They remain closed to proposals presented by the other side. The mediator can help the parties "own" the dispute, share responsibility, and therefore determine its resolution.

There probably are as many problems in negotiation as there are negotiators. The mediator must be aware of some of the more common situations if she is to effectively facilitate the negotiation process. Specifically how the mediator will enter a failed negotiation as a neutral third party and assist the parties in moving toward settlement will depend on the problems encountered.

ROBERT H. MNOOKIN, WHY NEGOTIATIONS FAIL: AN EXPLORATION OF BARRIERS TO THE RESOLUTION OF CONFLICT
8 Ohio St. J. Disp. Resol. 235 (1993).

* * *

A central question for those of us concerned with dispute resolution: Why is it that under circumstances where there are resolutions that better serve disputants, negotiations often fail to achieve efficient resolution? In other words, what are the barriers to the negotiated resolution of conflict?

* * *

. . . I will explore four such barriers. Each of these barriers reflect somewhat different theoretical perspectives on negotiation and dispute resolution. The first barrier is a *strategic barrier*, which is suggested by game theory and the economic analysis of bargaining. The barrier relates to an underlying dilemma inherent in the negotiation process. Every negotiation characteristically involves a tension between: (a) discovering shared interests and maximizing joint gains, and (b) maximizing one's own gains where more for one side will necessarily mean less for the other. The second barrier arises as a result of the *principal/agent* problem. In many disputes, principals do not negotiate on their own behalf but instead act through agents who may have somewhat different incentives than their principals. This work draws on research concerning the "principal/agent" problem in law and economics and transaction cost economics. The third barrier is *cognitive*, and relates to how the human mind processes information, especially in evaluating risks and uncertainty. My discussion here draws on recent work in cognitive psychology, especially the pathbreaking research of my colleague, Amos Tversky and his collaborator, Daniel Kahneman. The fourth and final barrier, "*reactive devaluation*," draws on the social psychological research of my colleague Lee Ross, and relates to the fact that bargaining is an interactive social process in which each party is constantly drawing inferences about the intentions, motives and good faith of the other.

As should be obvious, I am not attempting to provide a comprehensive list of barriers or an all-encompassing classification scheme. Instead, my purpose is to show that the concept of barriers provides a useful and necessarily interdisciplinary vantage point for exploring why negotiations sometimes fail. After describing these four barriers and their relevance to the study of negotiation, I will briefly suggest a variety of ways that neutral third parties might help overcome each of these barriers.

A. STRATEGIC BARRIERS

* * *

Because bargaining typically entails both efficiency issues (that is, how big the pie can be made) and distributive issues (that is, who gets what size slice), negotiation involves an inherent tension—one that David Lax and James Sebenius have dubbed the "negotiator's dilemma." In order to create value, it is critically important that options be created in light of both parties' underlying interests and preferences. This suggests the importance of openness and disclosure, so that a variety of options can be analyzed and compared from the perspectives of all concerned. However, when it comes to the distributive aspects of bargaining, full disclosure—particularly if unreciprocated by the other side—can often lead to outcomes in which the more open party receives a comparatively smaller slice. To put it another way, unreciprocated approaches to creating value leave their maker vulnerable to claiming tactics. On the other hand, focusing on the distributive aspects of bargaining can often lead to unnecessary deadlocks and, more fundamentally, a failure to discover options or alternatives that make both sides better off. A simple example can expose the dilemma. The first involves what game theorists call "information asymmetry." This simply means each side to a negotiation characteristically knows some relevant facts that the other side does not know.

* * *

Even when both parties know all the relevant information, and that potential gains may result from a negotiated deal, strategic bargaining over how to divide the pie can still lead to deadlock (with no deal at all) or protracted and expensive bargaining, thus shrinking the pie.

Strategic behavior—which may be rational for a self-interested party concerned with maximizing the size of his or her own slice—can often lead to inefficient outcomes. Those subjected to claiming tactics often respond in kind, and the net result typically is to push up the cost of the dispute resolution process ... Parties may be tempted to engage in strategic behavior, hoping to get more. Often all they do is shrink the size of the pie. Those experienced in the civil litigation process see this all the time. One or both sides often attempt to use pre-trial discovery as leverage to force the other side into agreeing to a more favorable settlement. Often the net result, however, is simply that both sides spend unnecessary money on the dispute resolution process.

B.   THE PRINCIPAL/AGENT PROBLEM

The second barrier is suggested by recent work relating to transaction cost economics, and is sometimes called the "principle/agent" problem. Notwithstanding the jargon, the basic idea is familiar to everyone in this room. The basic problem is that the incentives for an agent (whether it be a lawyer, employee or officer) negotiating on behalf of a party to a dispute may induce behavior that fails to serve the interests of the principal itself. The relevant research suggests that it is no simple matter—whether by contract or custom—to align perfectly the incentives for an agent with the interests of the principal. This divergence may act as a barrier to efficient resolution of conflict.

Litigation is fraught with principal/agent problems. In civil litigation, for example—particularly where the lawyers on both sides are being paid by the hour—there is very little incentive for the opposing lawyers to cooperate, particularly if the clients have the capacity to pay for trench warfare and are angry to boot. Commentators have suggested that this is one reason many cases settle on the courthouse steps, and not before: for the lawyers, a late settlement may avoid the possible embarrassment of an extreme outcome, while at the same time providing substantial fees.

* * *

C.   COGNITIVE BARRIERS

The third barrier is a by-product of the way the human mind processes information, deals with risks and uncertainties, and makes inferences and judgments. Research by cognitive psychologists during the last fifteen years suggests several ways in which human reasoning often departs from that suggested by theories of rational judgment and decision making.... I would like to focus on two aspects of their work: those relating to loss aversion and framing effects.

* * *

In other words, you can have a sure gain of $20 if you go out the north door, or you can instead gamble by choosing the south door where you will have a 25% chance of winning $100 and a 75% chance of winning nothing. Which would you choose? A great deal of experimental work suggests that the overwhelming majority of you would choose the sure gain of $20, even though the "expected value" of the second alternative of $25, is slightly more. This is a well known phenomenon called "risk aversion." ... many people will gamble, even if the expected loss from the gamble is larger. Their basic idea can be illustrated by changing my hypothetical. Although you didn't know this when you were invited to this lecture, it is not free. At the end of the lecture, the doors are going to be locked. If you go out the north door, you'll be required to *pay* $20 as an exit fee. If you go out the south door, you'll participate in a lottery by drawing an envelope. Three quarters of the time you're going to be let out for free, but one quarter of the time you're going to be required to pay $100. Rest assured all the money is going to the Dean's fund—a very good cause. What do you choose? There's a great deal of empirical research, based on the initial work of Kahneman and Tversky, suggesting that the majority of this audience would choose the south exit—i.e., most of you would gamble to avoid having to lose $20 for sure. Kahneman and Tversky call this "loss aversion."

Now think of these two examples together. Risk aversion suggests that most of you would not gamble for a gain, even though the expected value of $25 exceeds the sure thing of $20. On the other hand, most of you would gamble to avoid a sure loss, even though, on the average, the loss of going out the south door is higher. Experimental evidence suggests that the proportion of people who will gamble to avoid a loss is much greater than those who would gamble to realize a gain.

Loss aversion can act as a cognitive barrier to the negotiated resolution of conflict for a variety of reasons. For example, both sides may fight on in a dispute in the hope that they may avoid any losses, even though the continuation of the dispute involves a gamble in which the loss may end up being far greater. Loss aversion may explain Lyndon Johnson's decision, in 1965, to commit additional troops to Vietnam as an attempt to avoid the sure loss attendant to withdrawal, and as a gamble that there might be some way in the future to avoid any loss at all. Similarly, negotiators may, in some circumstances, be adverse to offering a concession in circumstances where they view the concession as a sure loss....

One of the most striking features of loss aversion is that whether something is viewed as a gain or loss—and what kind of gain or loss it is considered—depends upon a reference point, and the choice of a reference point is sometimes manipulable

* * *

... whether or not an event is framed as a loss can often affect behavior. This powerful idea concerning "framing" has important implications for the resolution of disputes to which I will return later.

D.   "Reactive Devaluation" of Compromises and Concessions

The final barrier I wish to discuss is "reactive devaluation," and is an example of a social/psychological barrier that arises from the dynamics of the negotiation process and the inferences that negotiators draw from their interactions. My Stanford colleague, psychology Professor Lee Ross, and his students have done experimental work to suggest that, especially between adversaries, when one side offers a particular concession or proposes a particular exchange of compromises, the other side may diminish the attractiveness of that offer or proposed exchange simply because it originated with a perceived opponent. The basic notion is a familiar one, especially for lawyers. How often have you had a client indicate to you in the midst of litigation, "If only we could settle this case for $7,000. I'd love to put the whole matter behind me." Lo and behold, the next day, the other side's attorney calls and offers to settle for $7,000. You excitedly call your client and say, "Guess what—the other side has just offered to settle this case for $7,000." You expect to hear jubilation on the other end of the phone, but instead there is silence. Finally, your client says, "Obviously they must know something we don't know. If $7,000 is a good settlement for them, it can't be a good settlement for us."

Both in laboratory and field settings, Ross and his colleagues have marshalled interesting evidence for "reactive devaluation." They have demonstrated both that a given compromise proposal is rated less positively when proposed by someone on the other side than when proposed by a neutral or an ally. They also demonstrated that a concession that is actually offered is rated lower than a concession that is withheld, and that a compromise is rated less highly after it has been put on the table by the other side than it was beforehand.

* * *

Ross has described a range of cognitive and motivational processes that may account for the reactive devaluation phenomenon. Whatever its roots, reactive devaluation certainly can act as a barrier to the efficient resolution of conflict. It suggests that the exchange of proposed concessions and compromises between adversaries can be very problematic. When one side unilaterally offers a concession that it believes the other side should value and the other side reacts by devaluing the offer, this can obviously make resolution difficult. The recipient of a unilateral concession is apt to believe that her adversary has given up nothing of real value and may therefore resist any notion that she should offer something of real value in exchange. On the other hand, the failure to respond may simply confirm the suspicions of the original offeror, who will believe that her adversary is proceeding in bad faith and is being strategic.

III.   Overcoming Strategic Barriers: The Roles of Negotiators and Mediators

The study of barriers can do more than simply help us understand why negotiations sometimes fail when they should not. It can also contribute to our understanding of how to overcome these barriers. Let me illustrate this by using the preceding analysis of four barriers briefly to explore the role of mediators, and to suggest why neutrals can often facilitate the efficient resolution of disputes by overcoming these specific barriers.

First, let us consider the strategic barrier. To the extent that a neutral third party is trusted by both sides, the neutral may be able to induce the parties to reveal information about their underlying interests, needs, priorities, and aspirations that they would not disclose to their adversary. This information may permit a trusted mediator to help the parties enlarge the pie in circumstances where the parties acting alone could not. Moreover, a mediator can foster a problem-solving atmosphere and lessen the temptation on the part of each side to engage in strategic behavior. A skilled mediator can often get parties to move beyond political posturing and recriminations about past wrongs and to instead consider possible gains from a fair resolution of the dispute.

A mediator also can help overcome barriers posed by principal/agent problems. A mediator may bring clients themselves to the table, and help them understand their shared interest in minimizing legal fees and costs in circumstances where the lawyers themselves might not be doing so. In circumstances where a middle manager is acting to prevent a settlement that might benefit the company, but might be harmful to the manager's own career, an astute mediator can sometimes bring another company representative to the table who does not have a personal stake in the outcome.

A mediator can also promote dispute resolution by helping overcome cognitive barriers. Through a variety of processes, a mediator can often help each side understand the power of the case from the other side's perspective. Moreover, by reframing the dispute and suggesting a resolution that avoids blame and stresses the positive aspects of a resolution, a mediator may be able to lessen the effects of loss aversion. My colleague Tversky thinks that the cognitive barriers are like optical illusions—knowing that an illusion exists does not necessarily enable us to see things differently. Nevertheless, I believe that astute mediators can dampen loss aversion through reframing, by helping a disputant reconceptualize the resolution. By emphasizing the potential gains to both sides of the resolution and de-emphasizing the losses that the resolution is going to entail, mediators (and lawyers) often facilitate resolution.

With respect to the fourth barrier, reactive devaluation, mediators can play an important and quite obvious role. Reactive devaluation can often be sidestepped if the source of a proposal is neutral—not one of the parties. Indeed, one of the trade secrets of mediators is that after talking separately to each side about what might or might not be acceptable, the mediator takes responsibility for making a proposal. This helps both parties avoid reactive devaluation by allowing them to accept as sensible a proposal that they might have rejected if it had come directly from their adversary.

* * *

E.   THE MEDIATOR AS CONDUCTOR FOR A NEGOTIATION DANCE

Negotiation can be seen as a dance. It takes two to tango and to negotiate; and in both instances some individuals go more willingly than others. Like two dancers, negotiators may proceed very quickly and deliberately, certain of their direction and steps. In other instances, they may hesitate or step on each other's toes.

The negotiation process itself may parallel a dance. The preparation stage is when one dancer is looking for a partner. The request and acceptance to enter the dance floor is the establishment of an initial relationship. The first steps, over which many dancers stumble, may be seen as the opening offers or initial proposals. As the dance develops, so does the negotiation; specifically, dancing is the information exchange; and as the differences narrow, the dancers become more synchronized. The length of the dance will often vary, depending on the energy of the dancers. Likewise, the speed at which the dance, or negotiation takes place, may change as well.

The mediator has a role in this dance, namely, to keep it going. She can first be seen as a conductor of the music, and where necessary, the choreographer. This role is more critical where the parties need assistance in their direction due to inexperience. The mediator may have to introduce the music as well as explain the steps to novice dancers. In this way, the mediator facilitates the negotiation process.

A mediator must also keep in mind that negotiation may be viewed as a ritual for many participants. Certain elements of the ritual must be experienced. And, the ritual unfolds over time. While the mediator cannot and should not completely change the ritual, by her intervention she can modify some of the stages, and in particular, the timing.

Parties often begin negotiating in good faith, but do not always continue on this path. Sometimes the music changes, and they are unaware of how to react. Or perhaps they are tired and lack motivation. The parties may be uncertain how to keep the process going. A mediator can help the parties continue with the negotiation or dance. In addition, it should be recognized that other neutral third parties are also used in negotiations.[17] For example, if a need for evaluation of risk is absolutely necessary, then one of the evaluative processes may be used.[18]

In the transactional area, the negotiators are often motivated to deal with each other. They have a common goal—to complete a transaction. However, in dispute resolution negotiations, the parties are frequently initially unwilling to dance because of the conflict itself, or because the negotiating environment has been inappropriate, or because the right music has not been played. A mediator may change the music. The environment may be modified to set a tone that provides a safe and more workable atmosphere for the parties. In dispute resolution, lack of trust between the parties is often a problem, since the disputants are at odds with one another. Thus, they hear completely different music and have no appreciation for another interpretation of the tune. The parties fail to see the other's offers in an objective light. And, in doing so, the disputants may pass over options to which they otherwise would agree. The mediator may assist the communication process by restating the

17. These were more fully examined in Chapter 1.

18. In the event the mediator is unable to assist the negotiation, or should her as-sistance not be sufficient to resolve the matter, she may want to urge the use of a different process.

offers or counter-offers to the parties. They may open their ears to the neutral.

The specific tactics the mediator uses to assist negotiation will vary, depending upon the variables of the dance in progress, if any. In many instances, the role of the mediator may be only to bring the dance partners together and begin playing the appropriate music. Thereafter, the disputants may be able to progress on their own until the process is completed. Such an approach is effective when the parties have an ongoing relationship or are sophisticated in the negotiation process; for example, two business partners. In these instances, they have danced together in the past. In other situations, the mediator will virtually have to lead each party, step by step, through the entire dance, selecting the type of music to be played and choreographing the steps the parties take. In this instance, the mediator has a very active and directive role in facilitating the negotiations. She must keep the process going or the negotiations will fail. Most mediators usually find themselves between such extremes. Many times the mediator will not know exactly what her role will be until she opens the mediation session, asks questions, listens, and learns just where the parties are in their dance. The mediator will figure this out by observing the dancers. Sometimes she will even directly ask each party, in confidence, what music is playing and further what their preference is.

In cases in which the parties have not made any movement, the mediator's first task will be to facilitate an information exchange. The scheduling of a mediation in and of itself can assist the parties in exchanging and gathering information about the case—their own as well as that of the other side. The mediator, in the initial stages of the mediation session, further encourages this exchange. The negotiations will not proceed unless and until such information has been exchanged.

Mediation also provides an environment in which an offer is not only acceptable, but also expected. This removes the negative stigma that unfortunately has been attached to making the first move. The mediator's role in this regard is to not only encourage movement by the parties, but also to encourage the parties to negotiate more reasonably. The tempo of the music, or timing of the offers, can also be directed by the mediator.

In a neutral, objective role, the mediator is more able to recognize alternatives or options as possible solutions which might be likely to satisfy all the parties at the table. Often, the parties may reject these ideas and refuse to continue dancing. The mediator may point out the similarities in the music and dance steps and help the parties continue. If the negotiators grow tired, the mediator can assist in moving them. She keeps the music playing.

Chapter Ten

FINDING A RESOLUTION

Once the mediator has identified the primary issues of the case and obtained confirmation from the parties, he should begin to guide the parties toward identifying and generating a variety of options and alternatives which may lead to a final resolution. The mediator at this juncture should also keep in mind the parties' underlying interests. A number of alternative solutions should be considered, rather than focusing on finding one specific answer. Generating options or solutions, however, is not a process with which most individuals are familiar. Many people do not see problem solving as a process. Therefore, the mediator should provide guidance.

The majority of mediation models have a separate stage that deals specifically with the attempt to identify or generate a variety of options for settlement. This stage of the mediation process is key to the goal of finding and agreeing on a solution with which all parties will be able to live, and in which all parties can find at least some satisfaction. Many times the negotiation process is seen as a win-lose situation; one party obtains what he or she has identified as a goal, and the other party has been "beaten."[1] Alternatively, in some negotiations there is compromise on both ends and a midpoint is reached. In both instances, however, the focus is narrow, and in many cases in which a midpoint is reached, both individuals are dissatisfied. Why? Throughout the negotiation, each party holds to a position or single solution; thus, once movement occurs, they feel as if they have "given up" something. In fact, some courts and judges have been known to say that a "good" settlement is one where everyone walks away unhappy or dissatisfied. Unfortunately, this is often a lose-lose negotiation.

One of the benefits of the mediation process is that participants are able to find and agree to alternative solutions. These solutions are generally more satisfactory to the disputants because they are crafted in a way that accomplishes the goals of both parties. Therefore, it is necessary that there be a stage or a time in the process devoted to searching for alternatives or resolution options. However, many people

1. For more on negotiation, see Chapter Nine.

do not know how to invent options, and, hence, are not familiar or comfortable with such a process. The mediator may, in fact, encounter some parties who are reluctant to generate ideas and alternatives. Therefore, the mediator's task is to assist the parties in overcoming their reluctance to participate in the search for alternatives.

A. OVERCOMING RELUCTANCE WITH PROBLEM SOLVING

Most individuals do not consciously think of problem solving as a distinct process. Rather, when they encounter a problem, a dispute or an uncomfortable situation, their instinctive response is to try to find an answer. Many times this immediate reaction is necessary. For example, if, as an individual is crossing the street, a car runs a red light, the individual's immediate and proper response is to jump out of the way. This problem necessitates a quick response. Likewise, if each situation a person encountered required a lengthy, mechanical, problem-solving process, he would make little progress. However, the expectation of an immediate solution has become so automatic that most people approach all situations as if equally easy to solve. Even in a more complex dispute, one that might require a more careful problem-solving process, it is common to fail to allocate time for such an analysis. Rather, people often assume that there is a single solution which can be found. The focus is narrow and restrictive. But disputes exist because two or more people have different feelings, views, perspectives, and needs. And, when each individual looks at the problem, each has his own idea for its solution. Collaboration in developing options does not come naturally to most people, particularly those involved in a conflict. The mediator's task, therefore, is to move disputing parties from their search for a single "right" answer and to broaden their perspectives.[2] He begins the transition by restating the disputed issues in broad terms.

An additional impediment to problem solving is the reluctance of the parties to share responsibility for a dispute, let alone its resolution. The most common reaction is an attempt to allocate blame. The mediator must get the parties to recognize that mediation is a problem solving process which uses collaboration, and that each person must share the responsibility for the process. The mediator should try to convince the parties that fixing blame for a past event is far less important than finding a solution that will work for both sides.

While it is important in the first few stages of the process to let the parties fully express their frustration and talk about the dispute, the mediator must then focus them on the future. One technique that is helpful in this endeavor is for the mediator to explain the differences between trial and mediation. It can be pointed out that in an adjudica-

---

2. This search for a single answer is one of several obstacles to invention of options that is pointed out in Roger Fisher, William Ury and Bruce Patton, Getting to Yes 58–59 (1991).

tive process the past is examined and a determination about it is made, whereas in the mediative processes, the focus is future oriented. Therefore, once the parties have been able to fully express their concerns about the past, the mediator can simply state that it is now time to look forward. He should recognize in a restatement that an activity or event has occurred, and then solicit ideas from the parties regarding possible solutions. The focus is on the future. The mediator may elect to be specific, asking the parties, for example, how they plan to deal with each other during the next six months or year. Such a technique is especially effective in situations where the parties have an ongoing relationship or where it may be mutually beneficial for a relationship to be established. Once focus is placed on the future, the parties usually begin working with one another to resolve the dispute.

An effective mediator thus has several tools at his command to help parties overcome their reluctance to begin solving the dispute. One, just by allocating "thinking" time, the mediator has moved them past the instinctive rush to answer. Second, by restatement in broader terms the mediator helps the parties see the problem from new perspectives. By encouraging them to collaborate on the solution he may get each party to assume responsibility for finding a mutually agreeable outcome. And, most importantly, the mediator can help the parties get past blame for the problem by focusing on future benefits of an amicable solution.

B. THE CAUCUS

The caucus describes that portion of the mediation session where the mediator meets privately with each party or combination of parties. A mediation often relies on candor of the parties. Yet, individuals involved in a dispute do not typically feel comfortable being completely candid in front of all the participants. Hence, in order to gather additional information or to explore alternatives, the mediator may need to meet separately with the parties. Other potential benefits of caucus include allowing a party to vent in private and avoid damaging the relationship between the parties. A caucus can also prevent one party, or an attorney, from manipulating another.

The mediator can also confront a difficult party and make forthright inquiries without causing the party to lose face. The parties may be more willing to open up and share secrets with the mediator in private. The mediator can also use the private session to educate the participants in negotiation skills and assist the parties in formulating an acceptable offer. A caucus also provides the parties some "down time" to relax, be calm or do "homework," that is, gather any needed or necessary information which will help move the matter to resolution.

Some mediators suggest caution in the use of caucus, particularly in community settings or when the disputing parties have an on-going relationship. Difficulties can arise from the possible perception of alliance or bias, particularly if the mediator spends more time with one party. Mediators also have a greater potential to become biased, and a party could attempt to manipulate the mediator. In a private confidential meeting, a party may be more inclined to not tell the truth, or a mediator could hear something he does not want to hear or know.

In many cases, it is important that the parties engage in joint problem-solving. Joint problem-solving involves interaction of the disputants. By contrast, in a caucus, the mediator and each party engage in separate problem-solving.[3] Studies indicate, however, that problem-solving occurs more frequently in caucus.[4] More information is likely to be disclosed in a private session, and the parties feel more comfortable in offering a number of alternatives. The mediator also takes a more active role in prompting options. It appears that where disputants are hostile and unable to generate options, the caucus is quite effective in overcoming these barriers.[5]

In most cases, each caucus is confidential,[6] and the mediator shares only that information which he has been given permission to divulge. In some cases, however, the opposite is true. The mediator will have the discretion to transmit any information he determines to be helpful to the process, unless specifically told otherwise by the party. It is therefore crucial that the mediator, in each private meeting, determine accurately that information which he is authorized to disclose to the other side and that which he is not. For these reasons, note taking is imperative. Many mediators have devised a system to distinguish between information that is permissible to disclose and that which is not. One example is to place an asterisk beside only those items which may be revealed. Sometimes a variety of pen colors are used to distinguish what can be revealed from that which cannot. Another approach is to circle the matters for general discussion. The approach taken need not be elaborate as long as it is accurate.

Private sessions with the parties are also used by mediators as times where certain conduct of the mediator, seen as inappropriate in a joint session, is necessary for the process. This conduct includes strategies such as: assisting the parties in evaluation of the case, urging the participants to take a realistic look at their objectives, and educating the parties about the negotiation process. When the parties are together, they may fear "losing face" in front of their perceived opponent. A private, confidential setting enables the parties and the mediator to be more direct.

C. IMPASSE, AND THE WAYS BEYOND

The impasse, or stalemate, is not encountered in each mediation; yet when it occurs, it can be an extremely frustrating situation for the

---

3. Neil B. McGillicuddy, et al., *Factors Affecting the Outcome of Mediation: Third-Party and Disputant Behavior* in Community Mediation 142 (Karen Grover Duffy et al., Eds., 1991).

4. *Id.* at 143.

5. *Id.* at 144.

6. See Chapter 11, which focuses on confidentiality.

mediator. As with most elements in this process, an impasse is defined in a number of ways. Authors and educators in the field have discussed the causes and solutions of impasse ad nauseam. Although impasses often occur, the mediator should not project the potential of impasse into every case he mediates. The mediator should not assume that just because the parties have declared their "bottom line," they are unwilling to move. Often these types of statements are part of negotiation strategy. However, the mediator should be open to the alternative of declaring an impasse for the purpose of terminating the mediation. The impasse in mediation is a situation best described as "you'll know it when you experience it!"

There are some methods that the mediator may employ when it appears the mediation is "stuck". Most involve changing the dynamics of the process. Some of these strategies are to be used alone; others in combination. And many times, if one doesn't work, try, try another. Some sample tools to get past a roadblock include the following:

- Change the focus or topic. If the negotiation gets stalemated on one issue or interest, move to another. Remember the mediator controls the process and the agenda.

- Start over. Ask the parties to make another opening statement with a different focus.

- Divide or break down the issues, if in a distributive negotiating mode. Remember integrative bargaining is usually more productive than distributive.

- Take a break. Often after a relaxing break or private time to reconsider, parties see things a little differently.

- Be silent. People are somewhat uncomfortable sitting silently. Complete silence in the mediation often "motivates" a party to say something new.

- Discover or remind parties of their BATNA (Best Alternative to a Negotiated Agreement) or WATNA (Worst Alternative to a Negotiated Agreement).[7]

- Use words of encouragement. If any progress at all has been made, acknowledge and positively reinforce it. This can go a long way in motivating further movement.

- Call a caucus. If meeting together is not productive, a separate meeting can provide the mediator information which may move the negotiation.

- Come back together. If in a caucus, or involved in a shuttle negotiation, bringing the parties back together often initiates productive discussions.

- Bring in snacks. If parties have been kept separate, this is a good way to reconvene the group.

7. First described in Fisher & Ury, Getting to Yes (1981).

- See if partial agreement can be reached. Emphasize this area of agreement.
- Use humor. While the dispute should not be made light of, appropriate humor can often ease tension.
- Turn to outside experts. Calling in a neutral expert can move parties away from their stalemated positions.
- Call it quits. Sometimes if the parties are told that the mediation is being terminated, they move off their positions. The mediator must, however, be prepared to end the session if neither party budges.

D. PROBLEMS IN GENERATING ALTERNATIVES

When involved in a dispute, most individuals hesitate to advance ideas for resolution. Part of this apprehension stems from a fear of rejection of the offered ideas. It is feared that ideas will be criticized and not accepted. Individuals refuse to make suggestions and worry that they may be exploited. Moreover, when people are involved in a dispute or conflict, the emotional aspects of the conflict often impair their willingness to hear or trust the content of any option or alternative suggested by the other party. The mediator's task, then, is to create an environment where the parties are no longer reluctant to generate or identify a variety of options for settlement. The mediator will also encourage them to be willing to explore those ideas suggested by the other parties at the mediation table.

The mediator can accomplish these tasks in a number of ways. The first is to explain that an essential part of the mediation process is to identify and consider all options; otherwise, a mutually satisfactory resolution may not be reached. The mediator must emphasize that this is a condition precedent to the selection of solutions or the decision-making segment of the mediation process. The evaluation and selection of alternatives for settlement must be separated from the stage of generating and creating those options. In other words, since judgment can hinder imagination, separate the inventing from deciding.[8]

By this point in the mediation, the parties will likely feel comfortable enough with the process and the mediator to share information. The mediator should nurture this atmosphere and continue to build trust so that the parties feel at ease in coming up with ideas that they otherwise might not suggest. Therefore, this critical stage should not be rushed. The parties must be provided sufficient time during the process to overcome their frustration or other emotion, and to develop a collaborative working environment, not only with the mediator, but also, in many situations, with each other.

8. Fisher, Ury & Patton, *supra* note 2 at 60.

E.   THE IMPORTANCE OF A NUMBER OF OPTIONS

When approaching a problem solving process, most people, including lawyers, will immediately gravitate to one idea or option and disagree or argue over the validity of that option. For example, the payment of money is often viewed as the only solution to a problem. In most cases, however, regardless of the type of problem or dispute, there are a variety of alternatives that might be suitable. This is particularly true in situations in which the parties have a number of interests to be met. Therefore, before rushing to finalize a solution, the parties should explore a number of alternatives. The mediator facilitates this process, and stresses that the parties should understand that any alternative, in whole or in part, may provide a workable solution to the problem. The mediator should suggest that to find only a single solution or to negotiate over a single item may obscure other more creative and satisfying options. Therefore, it is important that the parties be open-minded to the broad range of possible solutions.

Because the parties should consider a number of solutions, the mediator must be cautious not to ask for specific solutions or options too early in the process. Even though the parties may want to complete their opening statement with a demand, inasmuch as is possible, the mediator should explain to the parties that there will be a time later for examining a number of options. This explanation of the stages in mediation will minimize the likelihood that a party will establish a specific solution, and then become entrenched and unwilling to move away from it. Parties should not commit to a resolution until all options have been placed on the table. This maximizes the number of options for consideration, and thus increases the likelihood of agreement.

Mediation may be looked at as a creative problem solving process. As such, the parties are free to be creative in fashioning or designing their own solution. A phase of the mediation process should be devoted to allowing this exploration and creative thinking to occur. By generating creative alternatives during the negotiation, the parties are better able to fashion a resolution with which they are truly satisfied because they have had a direct hand in creating it. Such a process increases the probability that disputants will find solutions that will meet the needs of everyone at the table simultaneously. Experienced mediators have reported that a bright light may flash at the moment of such a convergence of ideas.

When moving into this stage, the mediator should emphasize to the parties that the creation or identification of options and alternatives is separate from the actual selection process. The parties, directed by the mediator, engage in a brainstorming session, after which they will begin to select the alternatives which are most likely to resolve the issue. The mediator will undoubtedly find a direct relationship between the number of options available and the likelihood of attaining a final resolution.

F. USE OF LATERAL THINKING

Understanding the creative process is an aid to the mediator who helps disputing parties find innovative solutions to their conflict. Many individuals take thinking for granted and assume that it is automatic. Like walking and breathing, many people believe thinking is an instinctive act, and there is nothing one can do about it. According to some scholars, however, thinking is a skill. And like most other skills, some people are better at it than others. Yet, everyone may acquire a reasonable amount of proficiency in the skill of thinking. Such proficiency requires desire as well as practice. Edward de Bono has written and lectured extensively about thinking skills.[9] As de Bono points out, we often think far too quickly. Thinking slowly and deliberately can increase the effectiveness of the thought process. Deliberation permits more focus on the subject matter.[10] This is especially useful in a problem solving process.

Certainly much of our thinking must be automatic or we would not get through the day. We cannot carefully consider and deliberate every piece of information which enters our thoughts. Instead, we rely on patterns of information that have become pre-recorded in our brains. These patterns permit us to almost effortlessly drive a car, cross a street, etc. In these situations, our actions are no longer contemplated but have become involuntary within our individual information systems. In problem solving, however, our thinking should be slowed down. Immediate, automatic responses do not often produce creative options and solutions.[11] Recognizing and emphasizing these principles, de Bono identifies a concept which he labels *lateral thinking*.[12] While the concept of lateral thinking is similar to creativity, de Bono distinguishes the terms because of value judgments already associated with the word *creativity*. *Lateral thinking* is now recognized and included in the Oxford English Dictionary, where it is defined as "pattern switching within a patterning system."[13]

Lateral thinking can be described as an attitude as well as a number of defined methods or skills.[14] At the very least, mediators must possess this attitude. Lateral thinking involves a way of looking at things, but also can be practiced as a re-patterning of the way the mind works. Specifically, lateral thinking will call on other processes that take place including insight, creativity and humor. Lateral thinking is used for the generation of new ideas or invention. It is related and similar to creativity, but more deliberate.

---

9. See, for example, Edward de Bono, Teaching Thinking (1976); De Bono's Thinking Course (1982); Lateral Thinking (1970).

10. Edward de Bono, de Bono's Thinking Course 10 (1982).

11. But not all problems require creative solutions.

12. See Edward de Bono, Lateral Thinking (1970).

13. See de Bono, *supra* note 10, at 58.

14. *Id.* at 59.

Perhaps the best way to define lateral thinking is to compare it to vertical thinking. Lateral thinking differs in a number of ways from vertical thinking.[15] Vertical, or traditional analytical thinking is described as a step-by-step logical thought process. Vertical thinking can be utilized in analyzing any situation. Vertical thinking uses sequential steps and considers only relevant data. A conclusion is reached by a series of organized steps.[16] In lateral thinking, on the other hand, one may consider irrelevant data. The lateral thought process may not proceed in a logical direction. In lateral thinking, one can be "wrong" at various stages or explore tangents and still achieve a correct, valid, and usable solution. In contrast, vertical thinking, most often used in logic or math, disallows irrelevant or tangential steps.

Lateral thinking can be provocative. It allows jumps in different directions. In lateral thinking, nothing should be excluded from consideration. With the use of lateral thinking, the final result is unpredictable at the beginning of the process.[17] Hence, particularly in those cases where there is a need for creative solutions, it is important that the mediator encourage the parties to employ lateral thinking.

Only in a rare case would the mediator actually tell the participants about lateral thinking. Rather, as the time approaches in the mediation session to search for alternatives, he will explain in general terms the concept of inventing options before making decisions. He may use the term *brainstorming*. Since most people tend to make judgments immediately after hearing an idea, the mediator may need to intervene during the option generation phase to strongly discourage judgmental remarks.

It is recognized that both vertical and lateral thinking are necessary processes; in fact, they are complementary. By the use of lateral thinking, a number of ideas and options are generated. When followed by a vertical thought process, the ideas or information which are most appropriate are selected and put to their best use. The use of these two complementary processes is important to the problem solving segment of the mediation process. The mediator can help the parties think in a lateral manner (if needed) by identifying or creating some options; thereafter, through the vertical thought process, an analysis can take place. The selection of the appropriate or workable alternatives will be made.

This sounds easier in theory than it is in practice. Often the mediator is anxious to think logically about the problem and its solution, and will rush to a conclusion. The mediator will, out of habit, employ vertical thinking. Therefore, the first step in the process for the mediator is to remember that most disputes can benefit by creative solutions. The mediator should create an environment that encourages lateral or creative thinking. He must be careful to avoid making statements that favor or focus on specific solutions prematurely. The mediator may want to

---

15. de Bono, *supra* note 12 at 12.   **17.** *Id.*
16. *Id.*

remind the parties that his role is to *assist* the parties in creating their own solutions.

It is not inappropriate, however, for the mediator to be thinking of options. The mediator should first encourage the parties to develop their own options and solutions since they own and know more about the dispute. But, as a last resort, if the parties have been unsuccessful, the mediator may indirectly suggest options and alternatives. The mediator should always come up with several ideas. If the mediator makes only one suggestion, it is likely that the parties, particularly where unrepresented, will see this suggestion as "the answer." The mediator will have then become an adjudicator. When suggesting alternatives, the mediator should not suggest them as correct solutions to the dispute, but only as possible ideas. When the mediator suggests options, phrases such as "what about . . ." or "some people have . . ." are appropriate. It should be made clear that these options do not belong to the mediator. To do otherwise may result in the mediator inadvertently becoming an arbitrator in the case. Ideally, the parties will consider the options as if they had suggested them, thereby developing ownership in the ideas.

The most basic principle identified in the lateral thinking process is that any particular way of looking at things is only one of any number of possible alternatives.[18] The option generation stage, rather than a search for the best approach, is the search for many different approaches. When lateral thinking is used in a creative process (for instance, in inventing, designing, or marketing) it is appropriate to come up with as many alternatives as possible. In a mediation, however, it is not always practical to spend a large amount of time generating an extensive number of alternatives. In most cases, the parties do not expect, nor have time to consider a hundred alternatives. The specific number of options will depend on the case and its appropriateness for creative solutions. The mediator may also need to point out to the parties that the options or alternatives that are first suggested do not need to be perceived as realistic. In brainstorming, one idea leads to more. It is during the subsequent evaluation and selection processes that judgments as to feasibility are made. It is important that the parties understand this so they refrain from making critical comments while ideas are being generated. Parties may hesitate to express an idea because they are fearful of what the others will think or say; likewise, their own decision making process may reject the idea as being inappropriate or even silly. By requesting that everyone suspend or postpone judgment, the mediator ensures that the parties become more comfortable with the process of suggesting options. And the suggestion of one idea (which is not judged) may stimulate another.

The mediator should also emphasize that just because one individual puts forth an idea, that person does not "own" it. That is, just because an idea is suggested by a party does not mean that the individual necessarily agrees with it. During the brainstorming process, it is accept-

18. *Id.* at 63.

able to suggest alternatives, which later even the suggesting party can reject. If judgment is suspended, the mediator will be better able to assist the parties in maximizing the available options. The mediator must also be careful not to indicate his feelings or judgment about any of the suggestions but rather to remain focused on facilitating the process.

Some mediators contend that to expect parties to act without judgment is unrealistic. Perhaps it is. Nonetheless, even if the parties do not completely "buy into" the process, a request from the mediator to postpone decision making may at least result in consideration of options that might be dismissed otherwise.

When proposing alternatives in a joint session, many mediators will sit and take notes of all suggestions in sequential order. Thereafter, the mediator will request a discussion of each, one at a time. Some mediators prefer to use a flip chart or chalkboard on which the ideas are written out as they are proposed. Another option is to ask each party to comment on those options he suggested. All of these are acceptable techniques for moving into the decision-making segment of the mediation.

When the mediator is conducting the entire session in a separate caucus format, option generation will not resemble traditional brainstorming where all parties work together. A disadvantage of this format is that it is very difficult to cross-stimulate the thinking; therefore, creativity may be more limited. Another downside is that the parties are forfeiting an opportunity to develop a collaborative working relationship between themselves. Cultivation of a cooperative working relationship between the parties is one by-product of mediation, which is particularly significant in cases where the parties will continue either a personal or professional relationship. Additionally, conducting separate meetings takes longer since the mediator will have to shuttle proposals back and forth.

There is a benefit, however, to using the separate caucus to generate settlement options. The parties may be more likely to disclose their true interests, and thereby bring out options which are workable and acceptable. They may also make suggestions that they would not propose if the other party were present.

The selection of ideas and alternatives for discussion and evaluation is also part of the mediator's role. The amount of input he has in that process is influenced in part by the degree of directiveness that the parties need from the mediator. Once there are a sufficient number of ideas to explore, the mediator should then proceed with the participants to the decision making stage.

One somewhat common non-monetary interest that arises in disputing is the need for an apology. This need, and the potential positive effects that result from its use is becoming more commonly recognized.[19]

---

19. See Jonathan R. Cohen, *Advising Clients to Apologize*, 72 S. Cal. L. Rev. 1009 (1999) and Denise R. Beatty, *Legal Conse-*

DEBORAH L. LEVI, THE ROLE OF APOLOGY IN MEDIATION

72 N.Y.U. L. Rev. 1165 (1997).

An employer and former employee, hoping to avoid a costly legal battle over the employee's discharge, enter mediation. During the morning of the first day, the parties state their positions in joint session, and the mediator shuttles back and forth between them. By lunch time, despite tentative progress on nonmonetary issues, the parties are still $200,000 apart in their settlement offers; the mediator is frustrated. Then, suddenly, the mediator thinks up a novel solution. He escorts the employer to lunch, takes him by the arm, and makes his proposal:

"You have the chance to wind up these negotiations and get the kind of settlement you want by performing one simple but difficult act. Nobody has so indicated from the other side, but I'd stake my mediator's fee on it. You do the right thing and this case might just fall in your lap."

"And the right thing is?" The employer and his lawyer look skeptical.

"Apologize for the way you fired her."

When the employer and his lawyer object, the mediator suggests that an apology could save the employer a great deal of money. He explains that the employee was hurt as deeply by the abrupt manner in which the employer discharged her as by the job loss itself.

Slowly persuaded by the mediator's expert framing, the employer agrees to apologize and privately expresses his remorse to the employee. When the parties reconvene, the employee wipes away tears, and the parties cooperate to reach an integrative solution.

It is easy to see how a story like this one, where an apology paves the way to resolution, could win adherents to the use of apology in mediation. This story, however, is far from typical. Because apology is a delicate interaction, it can only be effective when certain conditions are fulfilled.

* * *

Apologies, . . . alleviate tensions that lie at the core of public disputes and eliminate the fiction of translating emotional pain to dollars. Aside from directly compensating specific emotional harm, Professors Goldberg, Sander, and Eric Green have argued that apology can transcend discrete disputes to "repair . . . frayed relationships." Other advocates invest apology with greater potential than mere resolution of discrete conflicts. For example, Professor Deborah Tannen has argued that if Americans, particularly men, were more willing to apologize, "we'd do better as a society."

quences of Apologizing, 1996 J. Disp. Resol.   115 (1996).

Drawing in more detail, Professors Robert Baruch Bush and Joseph Folger connect apology to social change through their advocacy of "transformative" mediation. In a transformative mediation, parties, in the course of resolving a particular dispute, become empowered to define and express their interests and learn to verbally recognize their opponent's point of view. Learning to apologize, one form of such verbal recognition, makes the parties more responsible, better socialized community members. Thus, Professors Bush and Folger imply that citizens who know how to apologize improve our society.

While the dispute resolution theorists speculate about apology's potential, they have not focused directly on the mechanics of apology or described how an apology could aid in the resolution of a particular dispute. Meanwhile, lawyers often ignore the potential for apology to contribute to conflict resolution. Plaintiffs' lawyers are likely to shrug off a client's desire for an apology as secondary and even contrary to the goal of more tangible monetary or injunctive relief. Defendants' lawyers steer clear of any expression that might be construed as an admission of liability. Avoiding both conclusory idealization and complete dismissal of apology, this Note argues that, in some disputes, apology is a powerful means of moving parties closer to settlement. Though apology is probably not the direct substitute for monetary compensation depicted by the casebook employment scenario, it may facilitate agreements on compensation by alleviating the psychic injury that makes parties unable to settle. Because apology may improve the dispute resolution experience for both parties, lawyers concerned about client satisfaction should consider attending more carefully to demands for apology. Indeed, lawyers skilled in crafting language may aid parties to exchange sincere regrets without making specific admissions of liability and thus pave the way for more fruitful dialogue.

Contrary to some apology advocates, this Note recognizes that a simple "sorry" will not always save parties time and money, or mend relationships. Mediators and lawyers who wish to capitalize on the power of apology in a particular case must be sensitive to factors that may undermine apology's potential.

* * *

B. A Typology of Apology

The words "I'm sorry" and similar expressions of regret signal apology in its generic form. Yet, in the context of a bona fide dispute, a mere "I'm sorry" seems inadequate to the task of curing emotional harm or bettering society as set forth by advocates of apology. Close analysis of the potential for apologies to further dispute resolution requires a more precise vocabulary for differentiating apologetic gestures. Taking "I'm sorry" for a common denominator, this section proposes four variations of apology that might occur in mediation: the tactical apology; the explanation apology; the formalistic apology; and the happy-ending apology. Each of these apologies is distinguishable by its content and the response it is likely to elicit from the apologizee.

1. Tactical Apology

Perhaps the most common use of apology in disputes is rhetorical and strategic. For example, a savvy lawyer looks the plaintiff in the eye and acknowledges the plaintiff's suffering on behalf of himself and his client in order to gain credibility during negotiations. Defendants' lawyers include similar apologies in their opening statements. In Professor Dean Pruitt's anatomy of negotiating behavior, this type of apology might be called an "attitudinal structuring tactic"—an attempt to build a relationship in order to influence an opponent's bargaining behavior. While these tactics may soften the tone of negotiation interactions, the goal of "attitudinal structuring tactics" is fundamentally competitive, not cooperative. A tactical apology attempts to create an atmosphere of trust and good feeling in which an opponent is likely to make concessions without time-consuming wrangling. Thus, while the defense lawyer's expression of sympathy may get the attention of the other party, such expression is unlikely to elicit the plaintiff's forgiveness—particularly because "I'm sorry" is often followed by "but we did not do anything wrong."

2. Explanation Apology

The explanation apology employs mock regret to rebuff an accusation and then generates an account to defend past behavior. For example, a husband in a divorce mediation once apologized, "I'm sorry I've been slaving away, but I haven't been able to figure out how else to put food on the table." In other words, "my unavailability to my family should be excused because working was not an effort to avoid home but to provide for the family's comfort." The sarcastic apologetic gesture may acknowledge the other party's feelings, but, like the tactical apology, it avoids implicating the speaker in wrongdoing. Forgiveness may follow not because the speaker expresses sincere regret, but because the hearer credits the speaker's explanation.

3. Formalistic Apology

The formalistic apology occurs when an accused offender capitulates to the demand of an authority figure or offended party by pronouncing required words. Teacher admonishes student, "Johnny, say you're sorry for pulling Suzie's hair." Johnny groans, "I'm sorry," thus submitting to the school hierarchy and returning to the teacher's good graces without conveying heartfelt remorse. In settings where restoring social harmony is the most important goal of dispute resolution, well performed gestures of submission like the formalistic apology may result in absolution. In contrast, where the primary goal is repairing the offended individual's injury, a purely formalistic apology that does not indicate underlying remorse will not heal the breach. An acceptable apology in such an individualistic context requires a combination, often rare, of soothing words and wholehearted remorse.

4. Happy–Ending Apology

When this rare state of wholehearted remorse is achieved, parties may engage in the sort of tearful reconciliation that signals the happy-ending apology. In order for an apology to prompt true reconciliation, the hearer should be convinced that the speaker (a) believes she was at least partially responsible (b) for an act (c) that harmed the hearer and (d) feels regret for the act. The happy-ending apology requires that the apologizer identify personally with the offensive conduct and the injury it caused. Acceptance of the apology depends not on the apologizer's uttering of specific words, but on the injured person's impression of the apologizer's state of mind. When the advocates of apology call for a more prominent role for apologies in dispute resolution on the grounds that apologies compensate emotional harm or that they transform relationships, they seem to envision a proliferation of happy endings.

G. SELECTIONS OF ALTERNATIVES

> "You can't always get what you want … But if you try, sometimes, you just might find, you get what you need."
>
> —Mick Jagger & Keith Richards

In this phase of the mediation, the parties undertake to evaluate the alternatives previously put forth and make selections. This phase of mediation is not always clear cut. Additional information often comes to light during the evaluative process. New information may result in the modification of an alternative or an additional option.

The role of the mediator in the selection phase is to assist the parties in examining each of the proposed alternatives. There is no specific format for this process; it can be accomplished in a number of ways. For example, the mediator, with the input of the parties, can immediately eliminate some of the options that have been suggested because they are unrealistic or unworkable. Suppose there is a neighborhood dispute where the two parties live next door to one another. Neighbor A has suggested that Neighbor B sell his house and move from the neighborhood; but the economy is bad, houses are not selling, and neither party wants to leave the neighborhood. The mediator may first assist both parties in realizing that this is not a realistic alternative.

Once the unrealistic alternatives are discarded, others remain which merit further exploration. Some of these may be immediately accepted by the parties and will be items of agreement. Others can be modified for acceptance. There may also be partial acceptance of an alternative. A portion of an option can be extracted and used. The evaluation, negotiation, and selection process can take anywhere from just a few minutes to days, or even weeks. The longer time period is seen primarily in cases in which outside information (such as comment or ratification) is necessary.[20] In most cases, particularly where the mediator has successfully

---

20. While most mediations are a one time, one day intervention, some take place over a longer period of time. The consensus building process, used in public policy matters, involves input from a number of persons not at the mediation table. This necessarily involves a longer period to obtain input on the available options. Likewise, in

assisted the parties in identifying interests, decisions are made during the discussion of the alternatives. The mediator's role consists of directing and orchestrating the activity.

Another more deliberate way of approaching the selection of options is for the mediator to go down the list and have the parties discuss the pros and cons of each alternative. Although this method may take longer than the process of immediate elimination, a discussion of the pros and cons of each proposal may lead to additional options. This approach is recommended where there have been only a few alternatives elicited. The mediator should use his discretion in deciding whether to examine several options at one time, or to negotiate to a conclusion on one.

Once the parties have generated a number of alternatives, the analysis or evaluation phase will usually proceed quite naturally. What is somewhat more difficult, however, is the completion of details. After the alternatives have been evaluated, the parties are normally anxious to finalize the case. They accept the alternatives as final. The details with regard to the decision are, however, rarely complete. The mediator must ensure that all details are understood by all participants. If an option appears to be accepted by all parties, then the mediator must review it to ensure that all elements have been clarified and completed. He must also be certain that everyone has the same understanding about specific components of the agreement. Once the mediator has acquired all the details, he is ready to finalize the agreement.[21]

EXERCISES

10–1. Robert Roy and Dale Rogers have known each other for the past year. They have formed a partnership, and are interested in opening a drive-through vegetarian restaurant, ToFu ToGo. Robert has had extensive experience in growing fruits, vegetables, and seaweed, while Dale's experience has been as a cook. Neither has sufficient collateral to obtain a large business loan.

Last week they met with Cosmic Properties, a commercial landlord, to negotiate space. Both the location and the interior of the space were what Roy and Rogers had in mind. However, the rent is more than they can afford. What are some creative options for these negotiations?

10–2. You are the mediator in the following case. In the joint session, you learn:

Plaintiff, Micky Manor, has sued Vera Vend for breach of contract, dissolution of partnership, and for an accounting. The undisputed facts are as follows: Manor and Vend have known each other since high

divorce mediation, which generally takes place over weeks, each party is allowed the intervening time to make decisions and obtain advice from other professionals. For additional information on these two processes, see Chapter 16.

21. Details on the agreement phase of the mediation process will be further discussed in Chapter 12.

school. They served on the student council together at Copperfield High School. After graduation twenty years ago, they both attended college— Micky at CU and Vera at State. They both went into the real estate business; Micky went into commercial development while Vera sold primarily residential properties. They ran into each other, became reacquainted at their fifteenth year high school reunion, and decided to form a partnership.

An area about seventy miles from Copperfield was being developed as a resort. They thought that Micky's expertise in the commercial area, combined with Vera's knowledge of residential real estate, would enable them to buy, develop, and market the entire resort. The resort plan included commercial buildings for restaurants and hotels and the development of residential homes and condos. Since the resort was located in a mountain area, there could be skiing and other winter sports. A nearby lake could be stocked with fish during the summer months.

When the partnership was formed, no legal counsel was sought by either party. Consequently, there is very little documentation of the agreement. In fact, at a dinner party they orally agreed to split everything 50–50, shook hands, and named the partnership Property Acquisition and Leasing, PAL. In the first year, they found and leased an office building together and went to the bank to secure a loan. Micky, who was in a commercial business, already had a line of credit at First National. Although they both were present at meetings with the bank, Micky's background was not disclosed to Vera. Micky had debts of over $300,000 from previous and current ventures. All of the documents with regard to PAL, specifically, the lease agreement and the loans, were signed by both parties, individually.

The development of the resort area proceeded relatively well for about two years. A hotel that the partnership managed was built, and two restaurants were included on the property. A contract was established with a homebuilder, who began the process of constructing a small subdivision with two condominium complexes.

During the spring of the third year, there were severe storms which adversely impacted the resort. The mountainous area was partially washed away. The lake became contaminated as a result of runoff from a landfill which neither Micky nor Vera knew about at the time of the initial transaction. As a result, the resort area became unfit for its intended purposes. The individual homeowners who purchased the properties have threatened to sue PAL, stating that they were defrauded in the investment.

Though Micky and Vera both drew a decent salary as partners, neither has enough money to pay back the investors. This has strained the partnership, and, for the past six months, neither Micky nor Vera has spoken to the other. They have tried to concentrate on business but have been unable to do so. Finally, Micky, also fearful that his wife may file for divorce, has sued Vera for a partnership dissolution. The case has been pending for four months. Standard form interrogatories have been exchanged, and depositions for each party, along with environmental experts, are set for next month.

During individual caucuses you learn the following confidential information:

FROM PLAINTIFF'S CAUCUS

Although it appeared that Micky was in debt due to his previous commercial ventures, he actually owns properties in other countries. No one except Micky knows this. He therefore wants to stay out of litigation, and most particularly, out of bankruptcy court. He is afraid that through discovery other assets that he has hidden will be exposed.

Micky has also concealed his business affairs from his wife. He is fearful that if this case is not resolved, he will end up in divorce court as well. That is the last thing Micky wants, for his wife could learn about the other properties. Micky is afraid that because of his activities, she may be entitled to them. Although settlement is his goal, Micky is frustrated because he feels that it was Vera's sloppy work that got him into this mess.

FROM DEFENDANT'S CAUCUS

Vera is ready to file bankruptcy on a personal, as well as partnership, basis. The residential real estate business has not been that great, and she feels as though there is nothing to lose through bankruptcy. Nothing to lose, that is—except pride. Furthermore, if pushed to provide anything to Micky, Vera's choice would be to file bankruptcy. It is Vera's position that while there was not a written contract, she had outlined with Micky that the responsibility for the debts would be split 65–35 based on Micky's stated wealth. Even though they had been friends in school, Micky had always been the more popular, and Vera grew tired of it. Vera feels she did all the work during the partnership, and that her work was a major contribution. Therefore, in the dissolution of any assets, Vera's position is that she should get any remaining funds. She also thinks that Micky, as the primary deal-maker in the partnership, should take responsibility for preventing any further litigation against the partnership.

(a) As the mediator, how do you initiate the option generation stage?

(b) What are the specific questions you would ask?

(c) Would you conduct a search for alternatives in a joint session, or in individual caucuses?

Chapter Eleven

CONFIDENTIALITY

One of the most often cited benefits of the use of ADR processes is the confidentiality surrounding them. This is even more pronounced in terms of the mediation process than other ADR procedures. While the summary jury trial and arbitration may be subject to rules of disclosure, since these procedures occasionally take place in a public or open hearing, mediation has always been considered a confidential process. In fact, it has been noted that most people operate under the assumption that the mediation process is confidential, even if it is not.[1]

Yet, attempting to determine specifically what is meant by confidentiality can be very confusing. An initial consideration is whether confidentiality is thought of in its common or legal definitions. The parties are unlikely to see issues of confidentiality in the same light as the lawyers. And even within the legal definition there are differences which will be discussed in later sections of this chapter. Some parties are very concerned with confidentiality for a number of reasons including personal and professional issues. In contrast, a lawyer's concern with confidentiality is usually predicated on the possible effect it may have in future litigation.

While the use of mediation began with the assumption of a cloak of confidentiality, the validity of that assumption is not clear. With more analysis over the years, the issue of confidentiality in mediation has grown somewhat confusing. In today's mediation climate not all things are confidential. A mediator may have a duty to disclose certain matters discussed in mediation. Many of these considerations and conflicts have contributed to the dramatic increase in attention given to this aspect of mediation. Confidentiality has become such an important topic in mediation that in the effort to draft a Uniform or Model Act on Mediation, the National Conference of Commissioners on Uniform State Laws has determined that a primary focus would be on confidentiality.[2] However,

---

1. Lawrence Freedman & Michael Prigoff, *Confidentiality in Mediation: The Need for Protection*, 2 Ohio St. J. on Disp. Resol. 37, 42 (1986).

2. See Michael B. Getty, Thomas J. Moyer & Roberta Cooper Ramo, *Preface, Symposium on Drafting a Uniform/Model Mediation Act*, 13 Ohio St. J. on Disp. Resol. 787 (1998).

as is demonstrated throughout this chapter, the task is not an easy one. With a variety of challenging issues and conflicting interests, it has been noted that the drafters face a formidable task.[3] Before entering into a detailed analysis of what confidentiality in the mediation process means, consideration should be given to the general policies underlying this element of the process.

A. GENERAL POLICY CONSIDERATIONS

The law surrounding confidentiality in mediation is uncertain and constantly subject to change. Therefore, a survey of the policy considerations which underlie the concept of confidentiality in mediation is appropriate. Policy considerations are often considered by courts confronted with confidentiality issues, as undoubtedly will be the case in the furture.

Trust is an element of mediation closely related to confidentiality. For many proponents of mediation, establishing trust between the participants and the mediator is at the core of the process. Only when trust is established will persons disclose important information and personal needs. Because of the existence of a dispute, participants in a mediation often distrust one another and, hence, are unwilling to share information. Nevertheless, the mediator attempts to establish a trusting and safe environment; assuring participants of confidentiality assists in this task. In many cases the mediator must meet separately with the parties. In these separate and confidential caucuses, the parties often are less hesitant to share additional information. If they disclose new details, the mediator may be better able to facilitate a resolution based upon the parties' interests. Many mediators contend that the parties will be willing to make disclosures and openly discuss their underlying interests, needs, wants and desires only if the process is confidential and the items discussed are protected. Without this guarantee, they argue, mediations will not be productive.

The longstanding exclusionary rules surrounding compromise discussions is one of the stronger policy considerations for the establishment of confidentiality in mediation. The policy considerations for confidentiality in mediation are arguably very similar to those which underlie Federal Rule of Evidence (FRE) 408. Rule 408 and its state counterparts essentially prohibit the use of settlement offers as evidence of liability in a trial of a lawsuit, and in doing so, encourage the settlement of lawsuits.

Parties may be hesitant to engage in settlement negotiations if something stated could be used against them in a subsequent trial. With the assurance of confidentiality, parties and lawyers are more willing to openly discuss all matters and propose settlements. Offers to compromise disputed claims, as well as settlement agreements, have traditionally been inadmissible at trial in order to prove liability. Two reasons for

---

3. See Richard C. Reuben & Nancy H. Rogers, *Choppy Waters for a Movement To-* *ward a Uniform Confidentiality Privilege*, 5 Disp Resol. Mag. 4 (Winter 1998).

this exclusion are the lack of relevancy and the policy of favoring settlements.[4] It follows logically that the same treatment, for the same reasons, should be afforded to mediation participants. Historically, and to a lesser degree today, both mediators and mediation advocates rely on these grounds to assure a confidential setting.

Another policy which favors confidentiality of the mediation process is tied to the concept of mediator neutrality. The mediator is present to facilitate a negotiation as a neutral third party. If the mediator is either able or required to convey information to a decision maker, whether it be an agency or a court, the mediator may need to compromise her neutral role. She will be focused on what should be included in her testimony.[5] Further, if the parties are aware that the mediator may make a report to another entity, the mediator is perceived as affiliated with that entity, and perhaps not completely impartial. As a result, most participants would be reluctant to disclose all information pertaining to the dispute.

While confidentiality was initially seen as a protection afforded to the parties and their statements,[6] confidentiality in the mediation process can also serve to protect the third party neutral, the mediator. Most mediators work to facilitate a resolution or agreement and do not wish to be further involved in a case. Once the hour, day, or week of mediation is over, mediators see their role in a case as concluded. As with all facets of mediation, there are exceptions. In some instances the mediator continues to facilitate communication, discussions, and negotiations between the parties as part of implementing an agreement. This kind of continued mediator involvement is observed primarily in complex cases involving public policy issues, but it is the exception rather than the rule.[7] The mediator, however, maintains a neutral, facilitator role throughout. If mediators were regularly called to testify about events which occur during a mediation, they might spend so much time at the courthouse that there would be little time left to mediate.[8] If such testimony were permitted, it is likely that both sides would urge the mediator to testify on their behalf. Neutrality would again be threatened. Establishing and upholding confidentiality serves to limit the mediator's involvement in the continuation of the case and to maintain mediator impartiality.

Despite all of the benefits afforded to the mediation process by confidentiality, problems can arise. With the increased use of mediation, occasions for concern over misuse have become more apparent. A few years ago, a review of ADR literature would have revealed nearly

---

4. Charles T. McCormick, McCormick on Evidence § 266 (John W. Strong Ed., 4th ed. 1992).

5. While this was a premise of the court in an early case upholding confidentiality, *N.L.R.B. v. Joseph Macaluso, Inc.,* 618 F.2d 51 (9th Cir.1980), in some states mediators may now provide testimony to the court. See, for example, Cal. Fam. Code § 3175–3186, in Section F of this chapter.

6. The majority of the literature and discussion is focused in this manner.

7. More detail on public policy mediation is provided in Chapters 16, § F and 17 § A, 2.

8. While this may be an exaggeration, most practicing mediators do not want further involvement in the case. This is especially true for those who serve in a volunteer capacity.

universal agreement that confidentiality is necessary to the survival of mediation.[9] Although the policy considerations remain strong, an increasing number of situations provide arguments for exceptions to confidentiality. Situations that have exploited the confidential nature of the mediation process have been reported.

For instance, if a mediator is prohibited from disclosing anything that happened at a mediation other than the fact that the parties were in attendance[10] (and some would contend even the fact of attendance is confidential), then parties might misuse the session. One example of misuse is to cause delay by scheduling a mediation for the sole purpose of postponing a trial setting. Another tactic is for a party to attend a mediation and refuse to negotiate. Misrepresentations of fact during the mediation have also been reported and the confidentiality of mediation could encourage some participants to be less than honest in their negotiations. In fact, some attorneys, operating under the assumption that the mediation is completely confidential, have bragged about resolving the case by misrepresentation.[11] If a party relies on misrepresentations made by the other side during mediation, the injured party is left with little recourse to prove a contract defense of fraud if the mediation is strictly confidential. There would be no consequence for parties who abused the process and such actions would likely continue. Once injured, a party would probably choose not to participate in mediation again. The integrity of the process would eventually be eroded.

There are additional policy considerations against the enactment by courts or legislatures of an overbroad scope of confidentiality. When everything that transpires in mediation remains absolutely confidential, then there is no check on the mediator's conduct. If allegations of mediator misconduct are made, what information will be available to confirm or deny such matters? Some observers see only the before and after part of the mediation process have wondered if actions behind the closed door are like a "séance." Others have asserted that to maintain its integrity, the public ought to be able to observe the process.

In addition, it may be against public policy to preserve confidentiality in specific cases. For instance, in matters adversely affecting the environment, the general public should not be denied pertinent information. Where public agencies are involved, "sunshine" or disclosure laws may take precedence. Many states have Open Records Acts which allow the public access to governmental records. In these cases, the confidentiality needs of mediation may necessarily be secondary to the public need for information.[12]

9. Kent L. Brown, Comment, *Confidentiality in Mediation: Status and Implications*, 1991 J. Disp. Resol. 307, 308 (1991).

10. See, e.g. Tex. Civ. Prac. & Rem. Code Ann. § 154.053 (1997).

11. Where lawyers can be found to violate state disciplinary rules when they knowingly make a misrepresentation of a material fact about the case at any time, if there is no ability to disclose the information, no action can be brought against the attorney. This was the issue in *In re: Waller*, included in § G, 4.

12. See Thomas S. Leatherbury & Mark A. Cover, *Keeping Public Mediations Public: Exploring the Conflict Between Confidential*

There are yet other cases, where concerns for confidentiality are deemed less critical than the need to disclose information. One example is where individuals need to confront or call witnesses in their defense. The mediator may have a duty to disclose information when someone may be physically harmed. Another relatively well-established duty is the duty to report child abuse. When these duties clash with the need for confidentiality, the courts often apply a balancing test. But how far will the scales tip? Will the confidentiality exceptions become so numerous that they outweigh the arguments in favor of mediation confidentiality? This will be considered in more detail in the following sections.

Finally, there are other circumstances where confidences may not be routinely kept, at least to the degree anticipated by the parties. One is disclosure is an effort to seek advice.[13] In these situations a mediator may turn to a colleague to seek advice, either during or after the mediation. Other situations involve mediation education and research.[14] It is somewhat common for new mediators or those in a supervised setting to discuss the mediation with the instructor or supervisor. Empirical research also necessitates the disclosure of information about the mediation.

The Texas confidentiality provisions have caused additional consideration of these issues.

EDWARD F. SHERMAN, CONFIDENTIALITY IN ADR PROCEEDINGS: POLICY ISSUES ARISING FROM THE TEXAS EXPERIENCE
38 S. Tex. L. Rev. 541 (1997).

The scope of confidentiality in alternative dispute resolution proceedings has been one of the most contentious issues surrounding the spectacular rise of the ADR movement over the past few decades. The Texas Alternative Dispute Resolution (ADR) Act, passed in 1987, adopted perhaps the broadest ADR confidentiality provision in the country. The ten-year Texas experience provides an interesting context for evaluating the competing policy issues surrounding confidentiality in ADR.

The policy issues in the debate over ADR confidentiality seem to fall into two categories—"process" issues relating to what extent confidentiality is necessary to achieve the objectives of ADR within the context of the particular dispute, and "public access" issues relating to claims of overriding public interest in insuring public access to information communicated in the ADR proceeding.

The "process" issues focus on the need to encourage parties to speak freely in an ADR proceeding through a promise of confidentiality

---

Mediation and Open Government, 46 SMU L. Rev. 2207 (1993).

13. Christopher Honeyman, *Confidential, More or Less*, 5 Disp. Resol. Mag. 12, 13 (Winter 1998).

14. *Id.*

in order to promote a candid exchange that is considered desirable for settlement. A closely related concern is that the independence of the third-party neutral might be undermined if she were required to testify at some future time about what was said at the ADR proceeding.

On the other side of the process issues debate is our tradition that all relevant evidence should be available in judicial proceedings, subject only to certain very limited exceptions. Exclusion of ADR communications from evidence in a later trial or administrative proceeding arguably undermines the fairness and accuracy of the ultimate process for resolving the dispute. There is also a concern that spreading a cloak of confidentiality over all that occurs in an ADR proceeding could undermine the integrity of that proceeding, for example, by insulating from attack such improper conduct as fraud or third-party neutral malpractice, or by preventing clarification of what was meant by the parties as to unclear provisions of a settlement agreement. These process issues are central to the debate over whether confidentiality should be phrased broadly, as in the Texas statute, or with specific exceptions to allow breach of confidentiality when process values are at stake.

The second policy category—"public access" issues—focuses on whether, even if confidentiality would be desirable as a process matter, there is an overriding public interest in access to the information communicated in ADR. Proponents of confidentiality tend to view disputes as private affairs between the parties as to which the parties may choose to resort to a confidential ADR proceeding if that would promote settlement between them. Opponents maintain that there are good reasons that judicial proceedings are public: the glare of public scrutiny not only promotes proper procedures, but public access militates against settlements that are contrary to the public interest. In particular, they cite proceedings involving the government, public policy, and public health and welfare as to which, they claim, greater public access is warranted. These concerns are often expressed in statutes and court rules as to such matters as "open meetings," "open records," and "openness in litigation," which are potentially in conflict with broad ADR confidentiality.

There have been few occasions for the courts to interpret the Texas confidentiality provisions, and therefore these two policy issues are not much discussed in case law.

B. EXCLUSION OR PRIVILEGE

Until recently, a survey of case law revealed that, generally, where a statute provided for confidentiality in mediation, courts upheld it.[15] What is somewhat more problematic is a determination of the type and extent of confidentiality provided by such statutes.

15. For a detailed analysis, see Nancy H. Rogers & Craig A. McEwen, Mediation: Law, Policy and Practice (Chapter 9, Confidentiality) (1994 & Supp. 1999). Exceptions now provided in In re Grand Jury Subpoena date December 17, 1996, 148 F.3d 487 (5th Cir.) (1998), and Olam v. Congress Mortgage Company, 68 F.Supp.2d 1110 (N.D.Cal.1999) included later in this chapter.

Even though confidentiality in mediation is discussed a great deal, there is still confusion about its precise meaning. From the standpoint of a non-attorney, a statement that the mediation is confidential could be construed in a number of ways. Many people understand "confidential" to mean something secret: not to be disclosed to anyone—ever. Those individuals believe that absolutely no one other than those present in the mediation will know anything about what occurred. This is one extreme view. At the other extreme is the understanding that "confidential" means that the mediation is protected from disclosure to the court, but it can be disclosed to the rest of the world. A middle approach is that only the participants, plus individuals directly related to and affected by the dispute, will know about the case and the details of the mediation.

Lawyers are likely to understand confidentiality to have at least two contextually distinct meanings: one bearing on exclusion and one on privilege. Unfortunately, when discussing the confidential nature of a mediation session, many commentators and mediators, as well as many courts, fail to distinguish between the two. When confidentiality is mentioned, it is often not made clear whether the discussion is in the context of an evidentiary exclusion, which may prohibit certain evidence from the mediation from being admitted at trial, or whether it is a mediation privilege, which would prevent disclosure for other purposes.

1. AN EXCLUSION—SCOPE AND LIMITS

When considering an evidentiary exclusion, the rules of evidence determine what can be admitted as evidence at a trial. Federal Rule of Evidence 408 provides an evidentiary exclusion for settlement discussions. Most states have similar provisions. Rule 408 is silent, however, about whether information disclosed in a compromise discussion could be discussed with other entities, including, for instance, the press. The exclusion pertains only to the courthouse. Because of the similarity between settlement discussions and mediation in situations where there is a pending lawsuit, the policy supporting Rule 408 is relevant to mediation. The mediation process is a settlement device, and as such it would appear that Federal Rule of Evidence 408 applies.

Rule 408. Compromise and Offers to Compromise

Evidence of (1) furnishing or offering or promising to furnish, or (2) accepting or offering or promising to accept, a valuable consideration in compromising or attempting to compromise a claim which was disputed as to either validity or amount, is not admissible to prove liability for or invalidity of the claim or its amount. Evidence of conduct or statements made in compromise negotiations is likewise not admissible. This rule does not require the exclusion of any evidence otherwise discoverable merely because it is presented in the course of compromise negotiations. This rule also does not require exclusion when the evidence is offered for another purpose, such as proving bias or prejudice of a witness, negativing a contention of undue delay, or proving an effort to obstruct criminal investigation or prosecution.

Yet Rule 408 has limited application; all statements made during the settlement discussions are not covered by the rule.[16] However, a trend to extend the protection to all statements during a compromise has been noted.[17] Expansion of FRE 408 to apply specifically to mediation would be consistent with the general purposes and policies behind the rule. If all comments made during mediation were admissible at a later trial, there would be very little motivation on behalf of the parties and their attorneys to make any disclosures at the session.

It should be noted, however, that reliance on only Rule 408 in mediation is misplaced. Under Rule 408 and similar state rules, statements are excluded only if used to prove the validity or invalidity of the claim or amount. Statements can be admitted if they are offered for another purpose.[18] Additionally, much of what is stated at the mediation, particularly in the nature of options and ideas are not directly contingent upon one another. Thus, the statements might not be directly related to the "compromise" required by Rule 408. In mediations which are conducted in a caucus format, the mediator, as the intermediary, structures the exchange between the parties. Since the communication with each side is confidential, the offers are rarely contingent. These cases would not normally be protected by Rule 408. Of course state laws may provide a broader evidentiary exclusion applying specifically to mediation.[19]

An evidentiary exclusion only limits admissibility of information at a trial. Disclosures or testimony in other situations are possible, if not likely. Exclusions, however, do prohibit all parties from testifying. The information is excluded, regardless of whose testimony is sought: that of the mediator, an attorney, or a party. A privilege, on the other hand, may cover a greater number of situations but can be limited to prohibiting a specific individual from disclosure.

2. PRIVILEGE

In some respects, a privilege provides a broader scope of confidentiality. Although privilege is a legal concept operating generally to exclude evidence from trial or discovery, there may be protection against other disclosures as well.[20] Privileges involve parties in a relationship and generally prohibit the disclosure by one party of information revealed by

---

16. For instance, see *Thomas v. Resort Health Related Facility*, 539 F.Supp. 630, 637, 638 (E.D.N.Y.1982), which held that the evidence of an offer for reinstatement during a settlement meeting was deemed outside FRE 408 because it was not contingent upon compromise.

17. McCormick, *supra* note 4, § 266.

18. Fed. R. Evid. 408. Other purposes for example, might include "proving bias of

a witness," "motive or intent of a party," or "knowledge." Steven Goode and Olin Guy Wellborn, III, Courtroom Evidence Handbook at 97 (2d. ed., Student ed. 1997).

19. For example, see Me. R. Evid. 408(b) which excludes evidence of mediation discussions for any purpose.

20. McCormick, *supra* note 4, § 72.1.

the other. A privilege may prevent disclosure for any purpose, and in the mediation context this may even include the files and records of a mediation program.[21] Privileges are created by law in recognition of the sanctity of certain relationships which are built upon trust and the need for protected disclosure. While initially created by common law, most privileges are now statutorily mandated.[22] These laws may vary from state to state.

In most states, common or statutory law has established privileged relationships between doctor and patient, clergy and penitent, and between lawyer and client. In determining a claim of privilege against disclosure, courts have employed a four-part test, commonly known as the Wigmore test. In the case of the mediation, if a mediator claims a disputant-mediator privilege, it is possible that the court would employ the Wigmore test. The Wigmore test requires that:

The communications must originate in confidence that they will not be disclosed.

This element of confidentiality must be essential to the full and satisfactory maintenance of the relations between the parties.

The relation must be one which in the opinion of the community ought to be sedulously fostered.

The injury that would enure to the relation by the disclosure of the communications must be greater than the benefit thereby gained for the correct disposal of litigation.[23]

It is worthwhile to examine these elements to determine whether the mediator-disputant relationship would satisfy the Wigmore test. In most instances, the mediator describes the mediation as confidential; thus, the first part of the test is arguably met. Most mediation proponents would contend that the second and third elements of the test are clearly established by the nature of the mediation process.[24] Therefore, debate and discussion in the courts will likely center around the fourth element of the test. The fourth element requires a balancing test between the need for the "privileged" information in order to correctly decide the litigation and the need to protect the confidential status of the mediation process. This type of balancing has been performed by courts in the majority of the reported cases dealing with the issue of confidentiality in mediation.[25] Most likely this approach will continue.

In the cases where the courts have upheld the confidentiality of mediation, they have done so by enforcing a statute or agency rule. However, these cases do not indicate a trend toward a generic common law mediation privilege that courts would create and protect. Rather these cases have generally involved labor negotiations and seem to

---

21. Rogers & McEwen, *supra* note 15, Chapter 9, § 9:12.

22. *Id.*

23. John H. Wigmore, Evidence § 2285 (McNaughton rev. 1961).

24. See, for example, Freedman & Prigoff, supra note 1 at 37, 42, and *NLRB v. Joseph Macaluso, Inc.*, 618 F.2d 51 (9th Cir.1980).

25. Some of these are discussed in § G.

evidence the courts' recognition of legislative intent to encourage settlements through mediation.[26]

If courts and legislatures establish a mediation privilege, many questions should first be answered. Should there be an absolute privilege prohibiting any disclosure whatsoever? Or should a mediation privilege be qualified so that there is room for a balancing test? While *courts* generally have displayed a trend towards qualified privileges, based upon an utilitarian analysis,[27] at least half of the mediation privilege *statutes* appear to be absolute.[28] It appears that legislatures enacting these statutes fail to indicate an awareness of a need for a more balanced approach.[29]

Other important questions face those who establish such provisions. Where a mediation privilege is recognized, it is essential to determine the holder of the privilege. In other relationships which enjoy privileged communications, such as the doctor-patient or lawyer-client, there are only two parties. The holder of the privilege (the patient or the client) is the only person who can waive the privilege. In a mediation, however, there are always more than two individuals. Can the privilege be held by the mediator without regard to the parties? Or can the parties waive it?[30] In order to waive the privilege, must all parties agree? Another concern surrounding a liberal mediation privilege is the definition of mediation. In instances of established privilege such as that held by a penitent, patient or client, a relationship exists with a licensed or regulated professional. Mediation has not yet reached the stage where it is a licensed or regulated profession. Therefore, a party could assert a privilege to preserve the confidential nature of information by claiming that any third party present when the statement was disclosed is a mediator. Other important considerations include when the mediation begins, who is covered by the privilege, what later proceedings will be covered and the effect of conflict-of-laws issues.[31] These are a few of the concerns facing the creation and use of a mediation privilege.

C. CONFIDENTIALITY AGREEMENTS

Another means to secure confidentiality in mediation is through a confidentiality agreement. While most matters going before a court are not secretive or confidential, arguably when in mediation, there should be an exception.[32] In non-litigation matters, it is likely that courts would enforce a confidentiality agreement unless other laws mandating disclo-

---

26. Rogers & McEwen, *supra* note 15, see § 9:11.

27. *Developments in the Law—Privileged Communication*, 98 Harv. L. Rev. 1450, 1593 (1985).

28. Alan Kirtley, *Best of Both Worlds: A Mediation Privilege Should be Both Absolute and Qualified*, 5 Disp. Resol. Mag. 5 (Winter 1998).

29. Rogers & McEwen, *supra* note 15, see § 9:11.

30. Some of these questions have been at least preliminarily answered. See § G.

31. Key Question When Analyzing a Mediation Privilege Statute, 5 Disp. Resol. Mag. 8 (Winter 1998).

32. For reasons discussed earlier in this chapter.

sure take precedence. Because of the current confusion and difficulty surrounding issues of confidentiality in mediation, parties who wish to assure themselves and the mediator of protection should execute an agreement which provides for confidentiality. In fact, the American Bar Association's Standards of Practice for Lawyer Mediators in Family Disputes indicates that a mediator should ask the parties for such an agreement. These standards, however, place a duty upon the lawyer to inform the parties of the limited effectiveness of the agreement as to third parties.[33] Nevertheless, if the subject matter to be protected is not a matter about which testimony is compelled, it is likely that a court will uphold and enforce a confidentiality agreement.[34]

There are several other issues for consideration when contemplating contractual confidentiality as an avenue for protection. In the context of a judicial proceeding, courts generally weigh the issues of established public policy disfavoring confidentiality agreements against the potential harm resulting from disclosure. In most instances, it is likely that courts would enforce confidentiality agreements against those who sign the agreement.[35] If challenged, the circumstances surrounding the signing as well as the nature of the information protected will be considered by the court in a balancing test. If one of the signatories of the confidentiality agreement made the disclosure outside of the courtroom forum, there is little likelihood that the court could enforce the agreement. As a consequence, however, the injured party may sue for a breach of the agreement.[36]

Herein lies the problem with an agreement to not disclose: there must be at least a threatened, if not actual disclosure, before a court can intervene. Even though the agreement may be valid, there is no guarantee of protection. A cause of action for breach of the agreement may lie, but often the harm is already done. In response to this problem, some confidentiality agreements provide for liquidated damages.

Nevertheless, even in instances where enforcement by a court is questionable, there may be benefit in executing a nondisclosure agreement. The written agreement may serve as a deterrent. Individuals may maintain confidentiality because they have agreed to, not because they are legally bound to. With regard, however, to individuals not a party to the mediation, the effect of a nondisclosure agreement is very limited. In most instances, such an agreement will be viewed as suppressing evidence, against public policy, and therefore unenforceable.[37] Yet it may also deter third parties from seeking information.

D. COURT ORDERS

Courts can order the parties to maintain confidentiality, specifically through a protective order. Some courts routinely include in their order

---

33. *American Bar Association's Standards of Practice for Lawyer Mediators in Family Disputes* (1984).

34. See *Simrin v. Simrin*, 233 Cal. App.2d 90, 43 Cal.Rptr. 376 (5th Dist.1965), which enforced an agreement not to subpoena a rabbi who acted as marriage counselor.

35. Rogers & McEwen, *supra* note 15 at § 9:25.

36. *Id.* § 9.25.

37. *Id.*

of referral to mediation a provision that the process is confidential. Of course this protection appears to be limited to the litigation process. In cases of a challenge, the courts will likely apply a balancing test. Courts will place a greater burden to show compelling need for the confidential information on those who stipulated to the protective order than on outside parties. To increase the likelihood of enforcement of the order, it should include an acceptable, reasonable justification.[38]

E. DISCOVERY CONSIDERATIONS

Many situations in which issues of confidentiality and the subsequent need for information arise occur in the discovery process. While the balancing test previously discussed may be employed where no other guide is provided, many confidentiality statutes include exceptions allowing for discovery. These statutory exceptions are similar to those in FRE 408 which allow subsequent discovery of matters disclosed in compromise discussions.[39] For example, many statutes which provide evidentiary exclusions and privileges for communications in mediation include a clarification provision exempting from protection matters "otherwise discoverable." These statutes provide that if a matter is otherwise discoverable, then the fact that it is discussed in a mediation does not protect it from discovery.[40] This is consistent with the general rules of evidence with regard to compromise discussions, and Rule 408 specifically. The intent of the exception is to keep parties from discussing information during the mediation process in order to later exclude that information from the discovery or trial process by invoking the rule of confidentiality. Unfortunately, the result is an extremely confusing, mixed bag of protection.[41]

F. DUTIES TO DISCLOSE

Assuming that confidentiality is established as either an exclusion or a privilege, are there instances where the law establishes a duty on the part of the mediator to make disclosures? Some claim that the mediator's duty to preserve confidentiality is paramount, "There is no duty of the mediator greater than the duty to preserve the confidentiality of everything revealed to him or her during the hearing."[42] In this respect, mediation has been likened to the Roman Catholic confessional.[43] Yet some claim that, as in most other schemes to protect confidences, there are, or should be, duties of disclosure in certain situations.

---

38. *Id.* at § 9:21.

39. Kristina M. Kerwin, *Note, The Discoverability of Settlement and ADR Communications: Federal Rule of Evidence 408 and Beyond*, 12 Rev. Litig. 665 (1993).

40. Tex.Civ. Prac. & Rem. Code Ann. § 154.073(d) (1997 and Supp. 2000).

41. *Id.*

42. Peter Lovenheim, Mediate, Don't Litigate 44 (1989).

43. *Id.* at 34.

Under the evidentiary exclusion, there should be very few instances, other than a statutorily imposed one, where the mediator must disclose, that is, testify in a court. The California Trial Custody Program is one such exception. In this program (which some may claim is not true mediation), if an agreement is not reached between the parties, the mediator may make specific recommendations to the court concerning custody, visitation, investigations and restraining orders.[44]

Likewise, where a criminal defendant needs the testimony of a mediator as a defense, the court may require the mediator's cooperation.[45]

Statutes also mandate the disclosure of certain types of information. The most common is a duty to report child abuse. In some instances, the statutes which establish confidentiality in mediation include a specific provision which excepts from confidentiality matters otherwise required by law to be disclosed.[46] This clarifies potential conflict. In those cases where the confidentiality statute and a duty to report statute are in direct conflict, the mediator must make a personal judgment call. Where a case is pending, it is likely that the court would engage in a balancing test, and first review the matter *in camera*.

More difficult for the mediator are situations in which the mediator suspects wrongdoing, possible criminal action, or injury to one of the disputants or a third party. Is there a duty placed upon the mediator to disclose the information?

When considering the duty to disclose, a number of general issues arise. The first is determining to whom the mediator owes a duty. The second is identifying to whom the disclosure should be made. This may include the other party at the mediation, a third party or entity such as law enforcement, or the administrative staff of a mediation program. The third issue is the determination of what type and degree of disclosure should be made.

Defining what duties, if any, the mediator owes to parties not attending the mediation is a difficult task. In the area of family law, it has been alleged that the mediator has an affirmative duty to consider the interests of third parties not present, such as children or grandparents. There is also the counter-argument that the mediator is only responsible to facilitate the issues and items for discussion that are put forth at the mediation by the parties. If not advanced by anyone present, then the interests of any third party outside of the mediation should not be considered. Determining whether the mediator owes a duty to persons not present at the mediation is a critical threshold question.[47] If a duty of

---

44. Cal. Fam. Code § 3183 (Supp. 2000).

45. *State v. Castellano*, 460 So.2d 480 (Fla.App.1984).

46. See Tex.Civ.Prac. & Rem.Code Ann. § 154.073(d) (1997 and Supp. 2000) "If this section conflicts with other legal requirements for disclosure of communications or materials, the issue of confidentiality may be presented to the court ... to determine ... whether the facts ... sought to be disclosed ... are subject to disclosure."; Utah Code Ann. § 78–31(b)–7(3) (1996).

47. This issue is quite similar to that first examined in Tarasoff v. Regents of the University of California, 17 Cal.3d 425, 131 Cal.Rptr. 14, 551 P.2d 334 (1976).

any type is owed, it follows that information about the mediation may need to be disclosed to those individuals. The next concern might be the extent of the disclosure. For instance, if a mediator in a divorce action is found to owe a duty to the grandparents, must she disclose the entirety of the mediation session to them or only specific, directly relevant portions?

If a duty to outside third parties is established, how far should it extend? In instances of environmental concerns, should the mediator be responsible to the entire community? It is likely that in instances where the entire community is affected by the subject matter of the mediation, the mediation can no longer be confidential.

A few specific situations have been excepted from the confidentiality requirement. For example, the mediator may have a general duty to report crime. She may also have a duty to protect others from potential harm. Where the mediator learns information during the mediation that directly threatens the safety of one of the other parties, there is strong argument that she has an affirmative duty to protect that party. At a minimum, the mediator should not continue the mediation if harm will result. Whether she is under a duty to disclose the specific information to the party may depend on the nature of the potential harm and the likelihood of its occurrence.[48] The mediator's obligation is even more muddled when the potential harm is directed toward someone who is not a party to the mediation. Under a line of cases beginning with *Tarasoff*,[49] which established a duty of a psychiatrist to take reasonable steps to protect identifiable persons who are in danger, a mediator could be responsible to third parties. However, since the extension of these cases to other professions is currently unclear, this issue remains a matter of debate in mediation. Each mediator will have to make an independent judgment call on many of these issues.

G.   CURRENT LEGAL PARAMETERS

1. GENERALLY

Confidentiality which is invoked in a mediation may be established by law or by the agreement of the parties. Confidentiality in legal terms might be statutorily created or predicated on common law. If it is important to the parties that confidentiality surround the mediation, the mediator's first step is to determine the status of the law in the particular jurisdiction. Thousands of statutes currently exist which provide for confidentiality in the mediation setting.[50] Some of these laws pertain only to court-referred cases. Others protect only those mediations taking place within an established mediation or dispute resolution

48. Of course, judging likelihood is risky business.

49. 17 Cal.3d 425, 131 Cal.Rptr. 14, 551 P.2d 334 (1976).

50. For a complete listing, see Rogers & McEwen, *supra* note 15 at Appendices A, B, & C (1994 & Supp. 1999).

program. Some statutes purport to provide both an evidentiary exclusion and a privilege. A few are quite general. The variation in these numerous approaches causes confusion, and has been an impetus for the work to create a Uniform Mediation Act. An examination of court considerations and decisions provides an initial understanding of the issues.

Initial court consideration of confidentiality in mediation was primarily in the labor relations area.

NATIONAL LABOR RELATIONS BOARD
v. JOSEPH MACALUSO, INC.

United States Court of Appeals, Ninth Circuit, 1980.
618 F.2d 51.

Wallace, Circuit Judge:

The single issue presented in this National Labor Relations Board (NLRB) enforcement proceeding is whether the NLRB erred in disallowing the testimony of a Federal Mediation and Conciliation Service (FMCS) mediator as to a crucial fact occurring in his presence. The decision and order of the Board are reported at 231 N.L.R.B. 91. We enforce the order.

* * *

In early 1976 Retail Store Employees Union Local 1001 (Union) waged a successful campaign to organize the employees of Joseph Macaluso, Inc. (Company) at its four retail stores in Tacoma and Seattle, Washington. The Union was elected the collective bargaining representative of the Company's employees, was certified as such by the NLRB, and the Company and Union commenced negotiating a collective bargaining agreement. Several months of bargaining between Company and Union negotiators failed to produce an agreement, and the parties decided to enlist the assistance of a mediator from the FMCS.

* * *

In an effort to support its version of the facts, the Company requested that the administrative law judge (ALJ) subpoena Hammond and obtain his testimonial description of the last two bargaining sessions. The subpoena was granted, but was later revoked upon motion of the FMCS. Absent Hammond's tie-breaking testimony, the ALJ decided that the Union witnesses were more credible and ruled that an agreement had been reached. The Company's sole contention in response to this request for enforcement of the resulting order to execute the contract is that the ALJ and NLRB erred in revoking the subpoena of Hammond, the one person whose testimony could have resolved the factual dispute.

Revocation of the subpoena was based upon a long-standing policy that mediators, if they are to maintain the appearance of neutrality essential to successful performance of their task, may not testify about the bargaining sessions they attend. Both the NLRB and the FMCS (as amicus curiae) defend that policy before us. We are thus presented with a question of first impression before our court: can the NLRB revoke the subpoena of a mediator capable of providing information crucial to resolution of a factual dispute solely for the purpose of preserving mediator effectiveness?

* * *

The statute in question does not state that petitions to revoke subpoenas can only be made on the two grounds therein stated, or that the (ALJ) or (NLRB) may revoke only on those grounds. It does provide that a person served with such a subpoena may petition for revocation of the subpoena and the (NLRB) shall revoke it if one of the two specified circumstances exist (sic). Insofar as the statute is concerned, the (NLRB) may also revoke a subpoena on any other ground which is consonant with the overall powers and duties of the (NLRB) under the (NLRA) considered as a whole.

* * *

We must determine, therefore, whether preservation of mediator effectiveness by protection of mediator neutrality is a ground for revocation consistent with the power and duties of the NLRB under the NLRA. Stated differently, we must determine whether the reason for revocation is legally sufficient to justify the loss of Hammond's testimony.

* * *

The NLRB's revocation of Hammond's subpoena conflicts with the fundamental principle of Anglo–American law that the public is entitled to every person's evidence. *Branzburg v. Hayes*, 408 U.S. 665, 688, 92 S.Ct. 2646, 2660, 33 L.Ed.2d 626 (1972); *United States v. Bryan*, 339 U.S. 323, 331, 70 S.Ct. 724, 730, 94 L.Ed. 884 (1950); 8 Wigmore, Evidence § 2192, at 70 (McNaughton Rev. 1961). According to Dean Wigmore this maxim has existed in civil cases for more than three centuries, and the Sixth Amendment guarantee of compulsory process was created "merely to cure the defect of the common law by giving to parties defendant in criminal cases the common right which was already ... possessed ... by parties in civil cases ..." Id. at § 2191, at 68.

* * *

The facts before us present a classic illustration of the need for every person's evidence: the trier of fact is faced with directly conflicting testimony from two adverse sources, and a third objective source is capable of presenting evidence that would, in all probability, resolve the dispute by revealing the truth. Under such circumstances, the NLRB's revocation of Hammond's subpoena can be permitted only if denial of his testimony "has a public good transcending the normally predominant principle of utilizing all rational means for ascertaining truth." *Elkins v. United States*, 364 U.S. 206, 234, 80 S.Ct. 1437, 1454, 4 L.Ed.2d 1669 (1960) (Frankfurter, J., dissenting), quoted in *United States v. Nixon*, 418 U.S. 683, 710 n. 18, 94 S.Ct. 3090, 3108, 41 L.Ed.2d 1039 (1974).

The public interest protected by revocation must be substantial if it is to cause us to "concede that the evidence in question has all the probative value that can be required, and yet exclude it because its admission would injure some other cause more than it would help the cause of truth, and because the avoidance of that injury is considered of more consequence than the possible harm to the cause of truth." 1 Wigmore, Evidence § 11, at 296 (1940). We thus are required to balance two important interests, both critical in their own setting.

* * *

We conclude that the public interest in maintaining the perceived and actual impartiality of federal mediators does outweigh the benefits derivable from Hammond's testimony.

* * *

We conclude, therefore, that the complete exclusion of mediator testimony is necessary to the preservation of an effective system of labor mediation, and that labor mediation is essential to continued industrial stability, a public interest sufficiently great to outweigh the interest in obtaining every person's evidence. No party is required to use the FMCS; once having voluntarily agreed to do so, however, that party must be charged with acceptance of the restriction on the subsequent testimonial use of the mediator. We thus answer the question presented by this case in the affirmative: the NLRB can revoke the subpoena of a mediator capable of providing information crucial to resolution of a factual dispute solely for the purpose of preserving mediator effectiveness.[3]

UNITED STATES v. GULLO

United States District Court, Western District of New York, 1987.
672 F.Supp. 99.

[Author's note: Although the term arbitration is used interchangeably with mediation, it appears the initial process was mediation to be followed by arbitration.]

ELFVIN, DISTRICT JUDGE.

The above named individuals ("the defendants") have been charged in a one-count Indictment with participating in the use of extortionate means to collect, or attempt to collect, an extension of credit in violation of 18 U.S.C. §§ 874 and 2.

* * *

Gullo's motion to dismiss the Indictment arises out of his participation, as a party, in an arbitration hearing. In January 1986 he

---

3. The Company argued that revocation of Hammond's subpoena was improper because communications made to him during the course of the bargaining sessions were necessarily made in the presence of the opposing party and were not, therefore, confidential. Such a contention misapprehends the purpose of excluding mediator testimony which is to avoid a breach of impartiality, not a breach of confidentiality.

received from the Community Dispute Resolution Settlement Center ("the CDR Center") a notice indicating that a complaint or grievance had been lodged against him. The subject matter of the complaint was directly related to the events leading to the present Indictment. The complaint or grievance form identified the grievant, the nature of the dispute and the settlement sought, noted that the grievance had been referred to the CDR Center by the Jamestown (N.Y.) Police Department and described the CDR Center as "a project of the Better Business Bureau Foundation of Western New York, Inc., the Unified Courts System of the State of New York and County Youth Services and grants from the Erie County Legislature, and the City of Buffalo."

* * *

The CDR Center operates pursuant to the Community Dispute Resolution Centers Program established July 27, 1981 by sections 849–a to 849–g of New York's Judiciary Law. The statute states in part that there existed a

"compelling need for the creation of dispute resolution centers as alternatives to structured judicial settings. Community dispute resolution centers can meet the needs of their community by providing forums in which persons can participate in the resolution of disputes in an informal atmosphere without restraint and intimidation. * * * Community dispute resolution centers can serve the interest of the citizenry and promote quick and voluntary resolution of certain criminal matters."

The program is to be administered and supervised under the direction of the chief administrator of the courts. It provides funds for the establishment and continuance of dispute resolution centers. Grant recipients are defined as non-profit organizations organized for the resolution of disputes or for religious, charitable or educational purposes. To be eligible for funding, the Act provides that the neutral mediators have certain qualifications, that only certain costs be assessable to participants, that agreements or decisions be written, that monetary awards, which may not in any case exceed a certain amount, may be assessed only upon consent of the parties and that the dispute resolution center may not hear certain types of disputes of a more criminal nature. The centers are selected by the chief administrator of the courts from submitted applications. The state's share of any center's costs may not exceed fifty percent. The statute also imposes certain reporting requirements upon grant recipients. Importantly, the Act creates a privilege of confidentiality for the mediation of arbitration proceedings and decisions. Section 849–b, subdiv. 6.[2]

* * *

2. That subdivision provides: "Except as otherwise expressly provided in this article, all memoranda, work products, or case files of a mediator are confidential and not subject to disclosure in any judicial or administrative proceeding. Any communication relating to the subject matter of the resolution made during the resolution pro-

As to the first factor, there is a strong policy in favor of full development of facts and admissibility in criminal cases. As the United States Supreme Court has stated "[t]he need to develop all relevant facts in the adversary system is both fundamental and comprehensive." *United States v. Nixon*, 418 U.S. 683, 709, 94 S.Ct. 3090, 3108, 41 L.Ed.2d 1039 (1974). Suppression here would impinge on such policy.

Secondly, the policy sought to be furthered by the state promulgated privilege is the encouragement of participation in "the resolution of disputes in an informal atmosphere without restraint and intimidation." The confidentiality outlined under subdivision 849–b.6 is core to establishing an atmosphere "without restraint and intimidation." Although it is unclear whether the privilege acts in any primary sense to encourage participation in the program, it directly serves to insure the effectiveness of the program and thereby, secondarily, it serves to promote continued support for and existence of the program. It should be noted that abrogation of the privilege would place funding for the program in jeopardy. Subdivision 849–b.4; *People v. Snyder*, 129 Misc.2d 137, 492 N.Y.S.2d 890, 892 (S.Ct., Erie Co.1985).

With respect to the third factor, the United States has not shown any particularized need for the evidence. In fact, it concedes that, even without the evidence in dispute, the Grand Jury had more than enough evidence upon which to base its finding of probable cause. Government's June 8, 1987 Response to Defendant's Motion dated June 4, 1987, p. 3.

The final factor for consideration concerns the impact on local policy from not recognizing the privilege in this case. The privilege generally serves to foster participation in the program and serves to promote candor by those participating. Although, this Court grants that few potential parties will likely forego participation in the program because of knowledge that evidence adduced therein would be subject to presentation in a federal prosecution, the effectiveness of the program will nonetheless be reduced by compelled disclosure and its very funding will be called into question.

In balance, this Court finds that the privilege afforded by subdivision 849–b.6 must be recognized in proceedings before this Court. All statements made during the dispute resolution process and all terms and conditions of such settlement shall be suppressed.

* * *

HUDSON v. HUDSON

District Court of Appeal of Florida, Fourth District, 1992.

600 So.2d 7.

Per Curiam.

cess by any participant, mediator, or any other person present at the dispute resolu- tion shall be a confidential communica- tion."

The appellant husband has perfected this appeal from a final judgment of dissolution and from an order denying his motion to vacate said judgment.

It appears that, during the progress of the dissolution proceeding below, the trial court set the case for trial commencing April 1, 1991. In the interim, an order scheduling mediation was entered and a mediation hearing was set for March 27, 1991. At said hearing the parties arrived at what appeared to be an oral agreement settling the issues involved, but no written mediation settlement agreement was signed. Shortly thereafter, the husband apparently had second thoughts about the proposed settlement, and the parties never reduced the alleged oral agreement to writing. The trial date of April 1, 1991, came and the wife and her counsel showed up for trial but neither the husband nor his counsel appeared. The trial judge commenced the final hearing and heard the testimony of the wife and a residence witness.

The transcript of that hearing reflects that the wife apprised the court of the mediation proceeding, the negotiations toward settlement, and the proposed oral agreement. She even produced her written, unsigned version of what the parties had agreed to. Apparently to corroborate that, she had the mediator sign the back of her written version as a sort of certification that this was what the parties had agreed to at said hearing. In addition to these revelations of the "mediation agreements," the court took testimony from the wife relative to the marital property and other pertinent evidence generally submitted to arrive at a distribution of the marital estate and support needs of the parties. A final judgment was entered and in due course the husband obtained a copy. A motion to vacate the judgment was filed and a hearing held thereon, at which the trial court indicated that she did not hear a motion to enforce the oral mediation agreement, but that she tried the case on the merits and entered judgment thereon. The motion to vacate was denied.

Section 44.102(3), Florida Statutes (Supp.1990), the statutory court-ordered mediation provision, provides in pertinent part:

(3) Each party involved in a court-ordered mediation proceeding has a privilege to refuse to disclose, and to prevent any person present at the proceeding from disclosing, communications made during such proceeding. Notwithstanding the provisions of s. 119.14, all oral or written communications in a mediation proceeding, other than an executed settlement agreement, shall be exempt from the requirements of chapter 119 and shall be confidential and inadmissible as evidence in any subsequent legal proceeding, unless all parties agree otherwise.

The transcript of the dissolution trial leaves little doubt that the trial court was fully apprised of the mediation proceeding and exactly what the wife perceived to have been agreed upon between the parties, albeit there was no written executed agreement. It appears to us that the injection of the so-called agreement prepared by the wife and "certified" by the mediator, and the various testimonial representations of what transpired at said hearing vis-a-vis agreements between the parties, into the trial before the court violates the spirit and letter of the mediation statute. The confidentiality of the negotiations should remain inviolate until a written agreement is executed by the parties.

Therefore, we hold that the well was poisoned by the admission of the foregoing evidence of the "agreement" and so infected the judgment reached that it should be vacated and the matter tried anew.

Accordingly, except for the provision dissolving the marriage of the parties, the final judgment is reversed and the cause is remanded for a new trial on the remaining issues.

SCHNEIDER v. KREINER
Supreme Court of Ohio, 1998.
83 Ohio St.3d 203, 699 N.E.2d 83.

* * *

In December 1996, the Mediation Service mediated the case. Schneider and his former spouse agreed to perform and refrain from performing certain acts in exchange for the dismissal of the criminal charges against Schneider. The parties signed the Statement of Voluntary Settlement form indicating their agreement.

Subsequently, Schneider requested access to the entire mediation file from respondent, Cathleen Kreiner, director of the Mediation Service. Included in the file was a copy of the complaint form prepared by the mediator. Kreiner denied access to the file. Kreiner later offered to provide Schneider a copy of the Statement of Voluntary Settlement and a disposition report of the mediation service, both of which were filed in the office of the clerk of courts.

Schneider then filed a complaint requesting a writ of mandamus to compel Kreiner to provide him access to the complaint form. Schneider also requested attorney fees. This court granted an alternative writ and issued a schedule for the presentation of evidence and briefs.

This cause is now before the court for a consideration of Schneider's request for oral argument as well as the merits.

* * *

Moyer, Chief Justice. For the reasons that follow, we deny relator's request for oral argument and his request for a writ of mandamus.

* * *

Relator contends that he is entitled to a writ of mandamus under R.C. 149.43. We have construed R.C. 149.43 " 'to ensure that governmental records be open and made available to the public * * * subject to only a few very limited and narrow exceptions.' "

Among those exceptions in effect at the time of relator's request was former R.C. 149.43(A)(1)(k), 146 Ohio Laws, Part III, 4661, which provided that public records do not include "[r]ecords the release of which is prohibited by state or federal law." Respondent asserts that R.C. 2317.023 exempts the requested complaint form from disclosure as a confidential mediation communication. We agree with the respondent.

R.C. 2317.023 provides:

"(A) As used in this section:

"(1) 'Mediation' means a nonbinding process for the resolution of a dispute in which both of the following apply:

"(a) A person who is not a party to the dispute serves as mediator to assist the parties to the dispute in negotiating contested issues.

"(b) A court, administrative agency, not-for-profit community mediation provider, or other public body appoints the mediator or refers the dispute to the mediator, or the parties, engage the mediator.

"(2) 'Mediation communication' means a communication made in the course of and relating to the subject matter of a mediation.

"(B) A mediation communication is confidential. Except as provided in division (C) of this section, no person shall disclose a mediation communication in a civil proceeding or in an administrative proceeding."

Pursuant to the statute, the initial question is whether the complaint form sought by Schneider is a "mediation communication" as defined by the statute. R.C. 2317.023(A)(2) defines a mediation communication as "a communication made in the course of and relating to the subject matter of the mediation." The document sought here is a complaint form completed by the mediator. The mediator, in completing the form, describes information relating to the parties and the nature of the dispute. Significantly, the mediator also describes the disposition of the dispute under a section entitled "Hearing Disposition," and may make personal observations about the dispute under a separate section.

Under the statutory definition, it is clear that this form is a mediation communication. It is made in the course of the mediation by the mediator. The mediator compiles information on the form and then describes the outcome. The form is also related to the subject matter of the mediation. The form contains information about the dispute between the parties. It also reflects the thoughts and impressions of the mediator as to the outcome of the mediation, whether and what action shall be taken in the event of breach of the agreement, and the mediator's own observations about the mediation.

R.C. 2317.023(B) states that "[a] mediation communication is confidential." The words of this statute are clear. Mediation communications are confidential and may not be disclosed. "[A]n unambiguous statute means what it says." We give words in statutes their plain and ordinary meaning unless otherwise defined. Accordingly, having determined that the document sought by relator is a mediation communication, we are compelled by the words of the statute to conclude that the form is confidential and may not be disclosed, unless one of the exceptions enumerated in R.C. 2317.023(C) applies to the relator's cause.

Relator contends that the confidentiality requirement of R.C. 2317.023(B) does not apply because R.C. 2317.023(C)(1) and (4) preclude the application of R.C. 2317.023(B). We disagree.

R.C. 2317.023(C) provides:

"Division (B) of this section does not apply in the following circumstances:

"(1) * * * [T]o the disclosure by any person of a mediation communication made by a mediator if all parties to the mediation and the mediator consent to the disclosure;

" * * *

"(4) To the disclosure of a mediation communication if a court, after a hearing, determines that the disclosure does not circumvent Evidence Rule 408, that the disclosure is necessary in the particular case to prevent a manifest injustice, and that the necessity for disclosure is of sufficient magnitude to outweigh the importance of protecting the general requirement of confidentiality in mediation proceedings."

R.C. 2317.023(C)(1) does not prevent the application of R.C. 2317.023(B) to this cause. There is no evidence that either relator's former spouse or the mediator has consented to disclosure of the complaint form.

Similarly, R.C. 2317.023(C)(4) does not apply to allow disclosure of the complaint form compiled by the mediator. The plain language of R.C. 2317.023(C)(4) requires a hearing to determine whether this exception to confidentiality is applicable. The presence of a hearing requirement presupposes that the parties will argue the applicability of the exception at a hearing conducted solely for that purpose. There has been no such hearing or request for such a hearing in this cause.

Even applying the substantive provisions of this provision, the relator's arguments lack merit. Disclosure of the complaint form compiled by the mediator is not necessary to prevent a manifest injustice, nor is the necessity for disclosure of sufficient magnitude to outweigh the importance of protecting the general requirement of confidentiality. Relator's sole assertion for requesting the document is that he may face potential criminal charges if he does not comply with the agreement reached in mediation. However, the mere possibility that the relator may be involved in future litigation cannot possibly establish the presence of a manifest injustice, as required by the statutory exception. Such a conclusion does not comport with the common meaning of "manifest injustice," which is defined as a clear or openly unjust act. See Webster's Third New International Dictionary (1986) 1164, 1375. The plain meaning of the words of the statute requires more than a possibility of future litigation.

Likewise, the possibility of future litigation does not create a necessity for disclosure of a magnitude sufficient to outweigh the general requirement of confidentiality. Every agreement in mediation may be breached. Such a breach could result in future litigation. However, this possibility cannot outweigh the plain words of R.C. 2317.023(B), which establish a requirement of confidentiality. By those words, the General Assembly has determined that confidentiality is a means to encourage the use of mediation and frankness within mediation sessions. Were we to agree with the relator's argument, we would severely undermine that determination by the General Assembly, as reflected in the clear words of the statute. Accordingly, R.C. 2317.023(C)(4) does not apply to relator's request.

Finally, relator asserts that R.C. 2317.023(B) does not apply to this cause because the statute was not effective at the time that the record was created, i.e., when the mediation session occurred. R.C. 2317.023 became effective on January 27, 1997, which was after the record was created but before relator requested the form and filed this mandamus action. 146 Ohio Laws, Part II, 4033.

This contention also is meritless. R.C. 2317.023 was effective at the time of the request for the form. The date the form was created is not relevant for the purposes of R.C. 149.43. "Since the statute merely deals with record disclosure, not record keeping, only a prospective duty is imposed upon those maintaining public records."

Accordingly, there is no authority to overcome the confidentiality requirement of R.C. 2317.023(B). The complaint form sought by the relator is a mediation communication which is not subject to disclosure under R.C. 149.43 because R.C. 2317.023(B) clearly provides for its confidentiality. Therefore, we deny the relator's request for a writ of mandamus, and his request for attorney fees is also denied.

————

It is likely that courts will continue to uphold privileges where a statute exists, although there are exceptions in rare instances, such as where constitutional rights are at issue.[51] The federal courts, however, may see it differently.

CHARLES W. EHRHARDT, CONFIDENTIALITY PROTECTION: AN OPEN QUESTION IN FEDERAL COURTS
5 Disp. Resol. Mag. 17 (Winter 1998).

* * *

However, federal cases and federal courts are an entirely different matter that the practitioner should be aware of, regardless of whether one is mediating a case, or representing a party in mediation.

51. Rogers & McEwen, *supra* note 15, § 9:17; see also § 9:19.

In particular, federal courts do not currently recognize a general privilege that can be asserted to prohibit the introduction of evidence concerning mediation proceedings, even when a state statutory mediation privilege protects the communication. Since there is no federal statutory general mediation privilege, whether a mediation privilege would be recognized in the federal courts would be governed by Federal Rule of Evidence 501, the sole rule on evidentiary privileges. Federal Rule of Evidence 408, which covers settlement negotiations, may also provide some protections, along with some common law principles.

Rule 501 provides that the privileges applied in federal criminal prosecutions and in federal civil cases that are not based on diversity jurisdiction shall "be governed by the principles of the common law as they may be interpreted by the courts of the United States in the light of reason and experience."

In a federal criminal action, an Internal Revenue Service investigation or an action alleging a violation of Title VII of the Civil Rights Act of 1964, a state mediation statute will not be recognized even as to mediations that are ordered by a court of that state. In these cases, the question is whether the U.S. Supreme Court will recognize a "common law" mediation privilege under Rule 501.

In recent years, the Supreme Court has faced a number of cases involving new or novel claims of privilege. Rule 501 has been interpreted to provide the federal courts with flexibility to develop the rules of privilege on a case-by-case basis. However, the court has not been inclined "to exercise this authority expansively." New privileges are not created lightly because privileges are "in derogation of the search for truth" and the "duty to give what testimony one is capable of giving."

* * *

The court has applied the above principles in Rule 501 cases to reject new privileges against the disclosure of academic peer review and the disclosure of "legislative acts" by state legislators. The latter privilege was rejected even though the state constitution guaranteed the privilege in state criminal proceedings.

* * *

Almost certainly, if the privilege were recognized, the federal courts would also recognize that there are situations in which it should not be applied. Again, these exceptions should not be spelled out, but should be developed when appropriate cases arise. The *Jaffee* court observed that "there are situations in which the [psychotherapist-patient] privilege must give way, for example, if a serious threat of harm to the patient or to others can be averted only by means of a disclosure by the therapist."

So, too, if a mediation privilege is recognized under Rule 501, it is possible that the federal courts would also recognize exceptions when the interested of justice so require—for example, when disclosure is necessary because of a serious threat of harm to one of the parties.

IN RE: GRAND JURY SUBPOENA DATED DECEMBER 17, 1996

United States Court of Appeals, Fifth Circuit, 1998.

148 F.3d 487.

W. Eugene Davis, Circuit Judge:

The Government appeals an order of the district court quashing a grand jury subpoena served on the custodian of records of the Texas Agricultural Mediation Program ("TAM"), a state agricultural loan mediation program operated and administered by Texas Tech University, to the extent the subpoena sought documents relating to mediation proceedings involving appellees Gervase and Ira Moczygembas and the Poth Land and Cattle Company (collectively, the "Moczygembas"). The district court ruled that such documents are protected from disclosure to the grand jury by a federal mediation privilege. For the reasons set out below, we reverse and remand.

TAM is a state agricultural loan mediation program that receives federal funding under the Agricultural Credit Act of 1987, Pub.L.N. 100–233. The Agricultural Credit Act was passed in response to the growing problem of farm debt in the United States.

Among other things, the Act provides for financial assistance to states for the operation and administration of agricultural loan mediation programs to assist in resolving disputes between farmers and their agricultural lenders. See 7 U.S.C. § 5102. To qualify for financial assistance, a state must obtain certification from the Secretary of Agriculture. See 7 U.S.C. § 5101(a).

The Secretary will certify a state for qualification if the state has in effect an agricultural loan mediation program that, among other things, "provides that mediation sessions shall be confidential[.]" See 7 U.S.C. § 5101(c)(3)(D).

The state of Texas has received financial assistance for the operation and administration of TAM since 1988. Its proposal for certification provided that TAM would be operated in accordance with the confidentiality provisions of the Texas Alternative Dispute Resolution Procedures Act (referred to herein as the "Texas ADR statute"), Tex. Civ. Prac. & Rem.Code §§ 154.001 et seq.

The Texas ADR statute provides that "a communication relating to the subject matter of any civil or criminal dispute made by a participant in an alternative dispute resolution procedure . . . is confidential, is not subject to disclosure, and may not be used as evidence against the participant in any judicial or administrative proceeding." See Tex. Civ. Prac. & Rem.Code §§ 154.073(a).

However, if this provision "conflicts with other legal requirements for disclosure of communications or materials, the issue of confidentiality may be presented to the court having jurisdiction of the proceedings to determine, in camera, whether the facts, circumstances, and context of the communications or materials sought to be disclosed warrant a protective order of the court or whether the communications or materials are subject to disclosure." § 154.073(d).

In 1995, during the course of an audit of TAM, the Office of Investigator General ("OIG") of the United States Department of Agriculture ("USDA") discovered a number of irregularities and began to suspect criminal wrongdoing. The OIG's suspicions eventually led to a grand jury investigation of TAM. In November 1996, a grand jury subpoena was served on TAM's custodian of records. On December 16, 1996, one day before the return date of the subpoena, the Moczygembas moved to intervene and quash the subpoena on the ground that documents relating to mediation proceedings involving them are protected from disclosure by a mediation privilege.

The district court referred the matter to a magistrate judge. Before a hearing was held, Texas Tech fully complied with the subpoena and turned over documents relating to various mediation proceedings, including those involving the Moczygembas. The magistrate judge subsequently denied the Moczygembas' motion on the ground that federal law does not recognize a mediation privilege. The Moczygembas appealed the magistrate's denial to the district court, which held that the documents were protected from disclosure by a federal mediation privilege and vacated the magistrate's order. On remand, after making further findings as instructed by the district court, the magistrate judge entered an order quashing the subpoena to the extent it sought documents relating to mediation proceedings involving the Moczygembas. The district court denied the Government's appeal of the magistrate's order. The Government appeals that decision, which is final under 28 U.S.C. § 1291.

* * *

We turn now to the merits of this appeal. The Government argues that the district court erred in recognizing a federal mediation privilege that protects documents relating to mediation proceedings involving the Moczygembas from disclosure to the grand jury. The Moczygembas argue that the district court correctly recognized and applied a mediation privilege created by Congress. In ruling that the documents are protected from disclosure, the district court relied on three separate statutory schemes: 1) the Agricultural Credit Act; 2) the Texas ADR statute; and 3) the Alternative Dispute Resolution Act ("ADRA"), 5 U.S.C. § 571 et seq., a federal statute that authorizes federal agencies to use alternative dispute resolution proceedings to resolve certain disputes. The court first observed that the Agricultural Credit Act, at 7 U.S.C. § 5101(c)(3)(D), requires state agricultural loan mediation programs to provide that "mediation sessions shall be confidential" in order to qualify for federal funding. Because Texas represented that TAM would be operated in accordance with the confidentiality provisions of the Texas ADR statute and TAM was certified accordingly, the district court concluded that the Texas ADR statute "supplies the federal law of privilege in this case."

As set out above, the Texas ADR statute provides that "a communication relating to the subject matter of any civil or criminal dispute made by a participant in an alternative dispute resolution procedure . . . is confidential, is not subject to disclosure, and may not be used as evidence against the participant in any judicial or administrative proceeding." See Tex. Civ. Prac. & Rem.Code § 154.073(a). However, if this provision "conflicts with other legal requirements for disclosure of communications or materials, the issue of confidentiality may be presented to the court having jurisdiction of the proceedings to determine, in camera, whether the facts, circumstances, and context of the communications or materials sought to be disclosed warrant a protective order of the court or whether the communications or materials are subject to disclosure." § 154.073(d).

The district court determined that the statute's nondisclosure provision was in conflict with the ADRA, which provides that "information concerning any [mediation] communication" may be disclosed if a court determines that such disclosure is necessary to help establish certain violations of law. See 5 U.S.C. § 574(a)(4)(B). Relying on 5 U.S.C. § 574(e) the court concluded that before a court balances the equities to make such a determination in a particular case, the mediator must make reasonable efforts to notify the parties involved who must be given 15 days to offer to defend a refusal of the mediator to disclose the requested information. The court also concluded, relying on 5 U.S.C. § 574(c), that materials disclosed in violation of the ADRA's nondisclosure provisions are inadmissible in any proceeding relating to the issues in controversy with respect to which the communication was made. Because the district court was unable to determine from the record whether the Moczygembas were notified of the service of the grand jury subpoena on TAM but failed to offer to defend a refusal to comply within 15 days of receiving such notice, the court referred the matter to the magistrate judge, instructing the magistrate judge to grant the Moczygembas' motion to quash if TAM had not made reasonable efforts to notify the Moczygembas of the service of the subpoena. The magistrate ultimately determined that TAM had not done so and granted the motion to quash.

We review the district court's statutory interpretation de novo. We begin by observing that neither the Texas ADR statute nor the ADRA has any application in this case. The district court determined that the Texas ADR statute "supplies the federal law of privilege in this case" because § 5101(c)(3)(D) requires states to provide that mediation sessions shall remain "confidential" and Texas represented that TAM's mediation sessions would be kept confidential in accordance with the Texas ADR statute's confidentiality provisions. However, nothing in § 5101(c)(3)(D) or the Agricultural Credit Act's other provisions concerning state agricultural loan mediation programs suggests that the meaning of "confidential" is determined by resort to other sources.[3]

---

3. The Moczygembas do not argue that the Texas ADR statute in and of itself creates an evidentiary privilege that should be recognized in federal court. Rule 501 of the

The district court also concluded that the Texas ADR statute's nondisclosure provisions conflicted with the ADRA. The ADRA allows an "agency" to "use a dispute resolution proceeding for the resolution of an issue in controversy that relates to an administrative program." See 5 U.S.C. § 572(a). "Agency" is defined as "each authority of the Government of the United States," subject to certain exclusions. See 5 U.S.C. § 551(1), 571(1). An "issue in controversy" means "an issue which is material to a decision concerning an administrative program of an agency, and with which there is disagreement" either "between an agency and persons who would be substantially affected by the decision" or "between persons who would be substantially affected by the decision." See 5 U.S.C. § 571(8)(A), (B). There is no such "issue in controversy" involved in this case.

Accordingly, we are left to determine whether documents relating to mediation proceedings involving the Moczygembas are privileged and protected from disclosure to the grand jury under the Agricultural Credit Act. To reiterate, 7 U.S.C. § 5101(c)(3)(D) requires a state agricultural loan mediation program to provide that mediation sessions shall be confidential in order to qualify for federal funding. In imposing this requirement, Congress obviously sought to protect information relating to mediation sessions to some extent. Confidentiality is critical to the mediation process because it promotes the free flow of information that may result in the settlement of a dispute. In the absence of clear congressional intent to the contrary, however, we do not read § 5101(c)(3)(D) as creating an evidentiary privilege that protects information relating to mediation sessions from disclosure in grand jury proceedings. Section 5101(c)(3)(D) requires only that mediation sessions remain "confidential."

* * *

In the ADRA, by contrast, Congress explicitly provided that, subject to certain exceptions, a mediator "shall not voluntarily disclose or through discovery or compulsory process be required to disclose any information concerning any dispute resolution communication or any communication provided in confidence" to the mediator. See 5 U.S.C. § 574(a).

Federal Rules of Evidence governs the applicability of evidentiary privileges in federal court. Rule 501 provides that "[e]xcept as otherwise required by the Constitution of the United States or provided by an act of Congress or in rules prescribed by the Supreme Court pursuant to statutory authority," and except "with respect to an element of a claim or defense as to which State law supplies the rule of decision," the recognition of privileges "shall be governed by the principles of the common law as they may be interpreted by the courts of the United States in the light of reason and experience." When a party seeks to assert a privilege that does not exist at common law but is enacted by a state legislature, this court determines whether to recognize the privilege by "balancing the polices behind the privilege against the policies favoring disclosure." American Civil Liberties Union of Mississippi, Inc. v. Finch, 638 F.2d 1336, 1343 (5th Cir.1981). The Moczygembas have not argued that a mediation privilege exists at common law or that recognition of the privilege created by the Texas ADR statute is warranted.

Because privileges are not lightly created, United States v. Nixon, 418 U.S. 683, 710, 94 S.Ct. 3090, 41 L.Ed.2d 1039 (1974), we will not infer one where Congress has not clearly manifested an intent to create one. Thus, we hold that § 5101(c)(3)(D) does not protect documents relating to mediation proceedings involving the Moczygembas from disclosure to the grand jury. We observe, however, that due to the secrecy of grand jury proceedings, see Fed.R.Crim.P. 6(e), the confidentiality of the Moczygembas' mediation sessions will not be severely compromised by the disclosure of information relating to those sessions to the grand jury. Of course, if the grand jury returns an indictment, such information may become public. In returning an indictment, however, a grand jury indicates that it has found probable cause to believe that a criminal offense has occurred. We are satisfied that Congress did not intend that s 5101(c)(3)(D) be used to shield wrongdoing arising out of the state agricultural loan mediation process. Indeed, even the ADRA provides for disclosure where a court determines that disclosure is necessary to "help establish a violation of law ... of sufficient magnitude in the particular case to outweigh the integrity of dispute resolution proceedings in general by reducing the confidence of parties in future cases that their communications will remain confidential." See 5 U.S.C. § 574(a)(4)(B). Thus, if an indictment is returned, any interest the Moczygembas have in the confidentiality of their mediation sessions will have to give way to the public interest in the administration of criminal justice

For the reasons set out above, we conclude that the district court erred in ruling that documents relating to mediation proceedings involving the Moczygembas are privileged and protected from disclosure to the grand jury. We therefore reverse and remand this matter for further proceedings consistent with this opinion.

CHARLES POU JR., CONFIDENTIALITY IN FEDERAL AGENCY ADR: A TROUBLING DECISION
5 Disp. Resol. Mag. 12 (Winter 1998).

When Congress approved the 1996 amendments to the Administrative Dispute Resolution Act (ADRA), most observers believed the difficult issues involved in protecting confidentiality in federal alternative dispute resolution had been resolved. After all, the act's approach to confidentiality questions appeared clear and precise—indeed, its confidentiality section is the most detailed of any federal or state ADR statute.

As the Senate report for the original act stated, its confidentiality "... protections are created to enable parties to ADR proceedings to be forthcoming and candid, without fear that frank statements may be used later against them. Thus, documents produced during an ADR proceeding, such as proposals to resolve the dispute, are immune to discovery unless specific conditions are met."

* * *

It appears that the 5th Circuit erred in concluding the federal ADRA to be inapplicable in the Texas Tech agricultural mediation program.

Under the act's terms, it applies if an ADR process is employed to address any "issue of controversy" relating to any "administrative program." Moreover, the act defines these terms quite broadly.

The Texas Tech disputes would appear to raise such an "issue in controversy" for at least three reasons. First, the FSA was a party to nearly all of the cases mediated. Indeed, the USDA inspector general's interest in obtaining relevant communications was precisely *because* of the federal agency's involvement. Second, the issues in controversy relate directly to decisions and activities by FSA and other interested persons under the Agricultural Credit Act. Finally, the mediations were all conducted with the aid of funding from a grant program operated by a federal agency.

However, while the need for inspectors general to have access to government and grantee-related information to deter fraud, waste, and abuse may be clear, the fit between the confidentiality provision of ADRA and the data needs of inspectors general or grand juries has never been addressed.

———

Others may also share in Pou's concern.[52] However, one Court saw matters differently.

FOLB v. MOTION PICTURE INDUSTRY PENSION & HEALTH PLANS

United States District Court, C.D. California, 1998.
16 F.Supp.2d 1164.

PAEZ, DISTRICT JUDGE.

INTRODUCTION AND FACTUAL BACKGROUND

Plaintiff Scott Folb contends that defendants discriminated against him on the basis of gender and retaliated against him because he objected when Directors of the Motion Picture Industry Pension & Health Plans (the "Plans") violated fiduciary duties under the Employee Retirement Income Security Act of 1974 ("ERISA"). Defendants allegedly relied on a complaint that Folb had sexually harassed another employee, Vivian Vasquez, as a pretext to discharge him for his whistle-blowing activities.

The Plans allegedly promoted Folb several times while he worked for them. Folb became the Administrative Director in January 1996. After Folb took certain actions regarding Vasquez' access to the new computer software system, Vasquez allegedly filed a complaint about his management action. Folb claims Vasquez filed her sexual harassment complaint only after she was told plaintiff had discretion to make the managerial decision about which she had initially complained. Folb's

---

52. See Peter Marksteener, *How Confidential are Federal Sector Employment–Re-* *lated Dispute Mediations*, 14 Ohio St. J. on Disp. Resol. 89 (1998).

complaint describes in detail the events leading to defendants' decision to terminate Folb's employment, including the Plans' allegedly anomalous decision to hire Deborah Saxe, an outside attorney, to investigate Vasquez' sexual harassment claim.

Pending before the Court are Plaintiff's Objections to Order after Hearing of Magistrate Judge on Motion to Compel Production of Documents by Deborah Saxe, Esq. and by Hadsell & Stormer pursuant to Subpoenas ("Objections"). Magistrate Judge Woehrle denied plaintiff's motion to compel production of a mediation brief and related correspondence regarding settlement negotiations between the Plans and Vivian Vasquez, the employee who accused Folb of sexual harassment. In approximately February 1997, Vasquez and the Plans attended a formal mediation with a neutral in an attempt to settle Vasquez' potential claims against defendants arising out of the alleged sexual harassment. Vasquez and the Plans signed a contract agreeing to maintain the confidentiality of the mediation and all statements made in it. Vasquez' counsel prepared a mediation brief and provided copies to opposing counsel and to the mediator. The parties apparently did not reach an agreement during the mediation.

After the mediation, counsel presumably engaged in further settlement negotiations and the parties ultimately settled Vasquez' potential claims against the Plans. At some point, counsel for the Plans, Lawrence Michaels of Mitchell, Silberberg & Knupp provided Saxe with a copy of the mediation brief. Neither Vasquez nor her attorneys, Hadsell & Stormer, authorized the Plans to provide a copy of the mediation brief to Saxe.

Saxe refused to produce the mediation brief in response to Folb's subpoena, asserting that the confidentiality of the brief is protected under Fed. R. Evid. 408 and Cal. Evid. Code § 1119. Likewise, Hadsell & Stormer refused to produce either the mediation brief or documents relating to settlement negotiations with the Plans on behalf of Vasquez. Folb sought to compel production of (1) Vasquez' mediation brief; (2) correspondence between Vasquez' counsel and counsel for the Plans regarding mediation or other settlement discussions; and (3) notes to the file prepared by Vasquez' counsel regarding settlement communications. Folb argues that the Plans are trying to take a position in this litigation that is inconsistent with the position he believes they took in settlement negotiations with Vasquez. Folb suggests that the Plans will argue that he was properly terminated for sexually harassing Vasquez, despite the fact that they may have argued in mediation or settlement negotiations with Vasquez that she was never sexually harassed at all. Magistrate Judge Woehrle denied Folb's motion to compel production, and Folb filed the pending Objections.

Upon consideration of the parties' moving, opposition, reply and supplemental papers, Hadsell & Stormer and Saxe's separate oppositions to plaintiff's objections and supplemental papers, and the oral arguments of counsel, the Court considers Folb's Objections and modifies the magistrate judge's order in accordance with Fed. R. Civ. P. 72. While the Court concludes that the magistrate judge did not err in ruling that the motion to compel production of the mediation brief should be denied, the legal foundation for that ruling must comport with the analysis set forth in the Supreme Court's decision in Jaffee v. Redmond, 518 U.S. 1, 116 S.Ct. 1923, 135 L.Ed.2d 337 (1996) (recognizing psychotherapist-patient privilege under Fed. R. Evid. 501). In addition, the Court finds that Folb is entitled to discover information relating to any settlement negotiations conducted after the conclusion of the formal mediation session.

* * *

Because the mediation brief and the communications relating to settlement negotiations between the Plans and Vasquez are arguably relevant to both plaintiff's federal and state law claims, the Court must determine whether state or federal law controls disclosure.

* * *

The language of Rule 501 raises a difficult question regarding which law shall apply when evidence is relevant both to "an element of a claim or defense" controlled by state law and to a federal law claim. As the Supreme Court noted in Jaffee, "there is disagreement concerning the proper rule in cases such as this in which both federal and state claims are asserted in federal court and the relevant evidence would be privileged under state law but not under federal law." Jaffee, 518 U.S. at 16 n. 15, 116 S.Ct. 1923. That disagreement appears to center on the proper interpretation of Rule 501's mandate that the federal courts recognize state privileges only in cases in which "State law provides the rule of decision." Fed. R. Evid. 501.

In the Ninth Circuit, however, the question appears to have been resolved. "In federal question cases with pendent state law claims, the law of privilege is governed by 'the principles of the common law as they may be interpreted by the courts of the United States in the light of reason and experience.' "

* * *

Because the federal common law of privileges governs both federal and pendent state law claims in federal question cases, the Court must decide whether to adopt a federal mediation privilege under FED. R. EVID. 501.

3. *Federal Mediation Privilege*

The federal courts are authorized to define new privileges based on interpretation of "common law principles ... in the light of reason and experience." Jaffee, 518 U.S. at 8, 116 S.Ct. 1923. The general mandate of Rule 501 was substituted by the Congress for a set of privilege rules drafted by the Judicial Conference Advisory Committee on Rules of Evidence and approved by the Judicial Conference of the United States and by [the Supreme] Court.... In rejecting the proposed Rules and enacting Rule 501, Congress manifested an affirmative intention not to freeze the law of privilege. Its purpose rather was to provide the courts with the flexibility to develop rules of privilege on a case-by-case basis . . . and to leave the door open to change. Nonetheless, that authority must be exercised with caution because the creation of a new privilege is based upon considerations of public policy. In general, the appropriate question is not whether a federal mediation privilege should exist in the abstract, but whether "(1) the need for that privilege is so clear, and (2) the desirable contours of that privilege are so evident, that it is appropriate for this [c]ourt to craft it in common law fashion, under Rule 501." In re Grand Jury, 103 F.3d 1140, 1154 (3d Cir.1997) (quoting Jaffee, 518 U.S. at 35, 116 S.Ct. 1923 (Scalia, J., dissenting)), cert. denied, Roe v. U.S., 520 U.S.1253, 117 S.Ct. 2412, 138 L.Ed.2d 177 (1997).

The general rule is that the public is entitled to every person's evidence and that testimonial privileges are disfavored. Consequently, we start with the primary assumption that there is a general duty to give what testimony one is capable of giving. . . . Exceptions from the general rule disfavoring testimonial privileges may be justified, however, by a "public good transcending the normally predominant principle of utilizing all rational means for ascertaining the truth." To determine whether an asserted privilege constitutes such a public good,—in light of reason and experience, the Court must consider (1) whether the asserted privilege is "rooted in the imperative need for confidence and trust[;]" (2) whether the privilege would serve public ends; (3) whether the evidentiary detriment caused by exercise of the privilege is modest; and (4) whether denial of the federal privilege would frustrate a parallel privilege adopted by the states.

a. Need for Confidence and Trust

The existing Federal Rules provide an important backdrop against which to view the role of a mediation privilege in protecting confidentiality and trust between disputants. Fed. R. Civ. P. 26(b) provides that "[i]t is not ground for objection that the information sought will be inadmissible at the trial if the information sought appears reasonably calculated to lead to the discovery of admissible evidence." Recognizing the broad sweep of Rule 26, several courts have looked to Fed. R. Evid. 408 for protection of settlement negotiations, whether conducted with the assistance of a mediator or in private. See, e.g., Young v. State Farm Mutual Automobile Ins. Co., 169 F.R.D. 72, 76, 79 (S.D.W.V.1996) (weight of authority and Rule 26(b) impose greater burden to establish relevancy to gain discovery of inadmissible, non-privileged confidential settlement documents). Rather than applying Rule 501, the Young court and its progenitors have improperly established a heightened standard under Rule 408, and they apply that standard to provide a semi-privilege to confidential settlement agreements and negotiations.

Rule 408 provides that "[e]vidence of conduct or statements made in compromise negotiations is [ ] not admissible." Viewed in combination with Fed. R. Civ. P. 26(b), Rule 408 only protects disputants from disclosure of information to the trier of fact, not from discovery by a third party. Consequently, without a federal mediation privilege under Rule 501, information exchanged in a confidential mediation, like any other information, is subject to the liberal discovery rules of the Federal Rules of Civil Procedure, at least where jurisdiction is premised on a federal question and the material sought in discovery is relevant to the federal claims presented.

To determine whether there is a need for confidentiality in mediation proceedings, the Court looks first to judicial and Congressional pronouncements on the issue. No federal court has definitively adopted a mediation privilege as federal common law under Rule 501. In one of the leading cases on the treatment of confidential communications in mediation, however, the Ninth Circuit approved revocation of a subpoena that would have required a Federal Mediation and Conciliation Service ("FMCS") mediator to testify in a National Labor Relations Board ("NLRB") enforcement proceeding. National Labor Relations Board v. Joseph Macaluso, Inc., 618 F.2d 51, 52 (9th Cir.1980). Relying on United States policy favoring resolution of labor disputes through collective bargaining and on Congress' creation of government facilities for mediation, the Ninth Circuit in Macaluso concluded that "the public interest in maintaining the perceived and actual impartiality of federal mediators does not outweigh the benefits derivable from [the mediator's] testimony." *Id.* at 54 (citing 29 U.S.C. § 171(a)(b)).

The Ninth Circuit's conclusion that requiring a federal mediator to disclose information about the mediation proceedings would inevitably impair or destroy the usefulness of the FMCS in future proceedings is equally applicable in the context of private mediation. Admittedly, the express federal interest in preserving a labor mediation system establishes a stronger basis for a mediator privilege in the context of NLRB proceedings. Nonetheless, mediation in other contexts has clearly become a critical alternative to full-blown litigation, providing the parties a more cost-effective method of resolving disputes and allowing the courts to keep up with ever more unmanageable dockets.

Focusing on the role of the mediator, the Macaluso court emphasized that "the purpose of excluding mediator testimony . . . is to avoid a breach of impartiality, not a breach of confidentiality." Nevertheless, rules protecting the confidentiality of mediation proceedings and rules protecting the actual or perceived impartiality of mediators serve the same ultimate purpose: encouraging parties to attend mediation and communicate openly and honestly in order to facilitate successful alternative dispute resolution. [C]onciliators must maintain a reputation for impartiality, and the parties to conciliation conferences must feel free to talk without any fear that the conciliator may subsequently make disclosures as a witness in some other proceeding, to the possible disadvantage of a party to the conference. If conciliators were permitted or required to testify about their activities, or if the production of notes or reports of their activities could be required, not even the strictest adherence to purely factual matters would prevent the evidence from favoring or seeming to favor one side.

Whether information divulged in mediation proceedings is disclosed through the compelled testimony of a mediator or the compelled disclosure of documents conveyed to or prepared by the mediator, the side most forthcoming in the mediation process is penalized when third parties can discover confidential communications with the mediator. Refusing to establish a privilege to protect confidential communications in mediation proceedings creates an incentive for participants to withhold sensitive information in mediation or refuse to participate at all.

Today, the Court is faced with a somewhat more attenuated concern: whether the "imperative need for confidence and trust" that would support creation of a privilege protecting confidential communications with a mediator should extend so far as to protect all oral and written communications between the parties to a mediation. Before delving into the heart of the matter, we must also clarify what constitutes "mediation" for purposes of the Court's analysis today. Given the facts presented by the parties before the Court, we need only consider whether communications between parties who agreed in writing to participate in a confidential mediation with a neutral third party should be privileged and whether that privilege should extend to communications between the parties after they have concluded their formal mediation with the neutral.

Several commentators have suggested that successful mediation requires open communication between parties to a dispute. See, e.g., Alan Kirtley, "The Mediation Privilege's Transition from Theory to Implementation: Designing a Mediation Privilege Standard to Protect Mediation Participants, the Process and the Public Interest," 1995 J. DISP. RESOL. 1, 8, 16 (collecting sources indicating weight of scholarly authority suggests confidentiality is essential to mediation). Kirtley argues that [w]ithout adequate legal protection, a party's candor in mediation might well be 'rewarded' by a discovery request or the revelation of mediation information at trial. A principal purpose of the mediation privilege is to provide mediation parties protection against these downside risks of a failed mediation.

In general, however, the academic literature provides little analysis of whether communications disclosed to the opposing party in the course of mediation proceedings should be accorded the same level of protection as private communications between one party and the mediator.

One self-described "heretical" commentator has expressed doubt over the need for a mediation privilege to protect confidentiality in mediation. Although most mediators assert that confidentiality is essential to the process, there is no data of which I am aware that supports this claim, and I am dubious that such data could be collected. Moreover, mediation has flourished without recognition of a privilege, most likely on assurance given by the parties and the mediator that they agree to keep mediation matters confidential, their awareness that attempts to use the fruits of mediation for litigation purposes are rare, and that courts, in appropriate instances, will accord mediation evidence Rule 408 and public policy-based protection. Eric D. Green, "A Heretical View of the Mediation Privilege," 2 OHIO ST. J. ON DISP. RESOL. 1, 32 (1986) (arguing campaign to obtain blanket mediation privilege rests on "faulty logic, inadequate data, and short-sighted professional self-interest.").

Another author takes the position that, while a certain level of confidentiality may be necessary to make mediation effective, "it is wrong to assume that mediation needs absolute confidentiality." Kevin Gibson, "Confidentiality in Mediation: A Moral Reassessment," 1992 J. DISP. RESOL. 25, 26. * * * see also Note, "Making Sense of Rules of Privilege under the Structural (Il)logic of the Federal Rules of Evidence," 105 HARV. L. REV. 1339 (1992) (suggesting protection of communications in mediation should take form of confidentiality contracts, procedural limitations on discovery, and use of work product doctrine) [hereinafter "Structural Il(logic)"].

Legal authority on the necessity of protecting confidential communications between the parties to a mediation is sparse. In an early decision by the Second Circuit, the court stated: [i]f participants cannot rely on the confidential treatment of everything that transpires during [mediation] sessions then counsel of necessity will feel constrained to conduct themselves in a cautious, tight-lipped, noncommittal manner more suitable to poker players in a high-stakes game than adversaries attempting to arrive at a just solution of a civil dispute. This atmosphere if allowed to exist would surely destroy the effectiveness of a program which has led to settlements and withdrawals of some appeals and to the simplification of issues in other appeals, thereby expediting cases at a time when the judicial resources of this Court are sorely taxed.

At least one district court has concluded that confidential information disclosed in alternative dispute resolution ("ADR") proceedings is privileged. See United States v. Gullo, 672 F.Supp. 99, 104 (W.D.N.Y. 1987). In Gullo, the court found that the confidentiality provision in New York's Community Dispute Resolution Centers Program served to ensure the effectiveness and continued existence of the program. Looking to Rule 501, the court concluded, on balance, that the privilege afforded under New York law should be recognized by the federal court. Having concluded that the information was protected, the Gullo court suppressed evidence in a criminal proceeding of all statements made during the dispute resolution process, as well as the terms and conditions of the settlement.

Other New York district courts have impliedly approved a federal mediation privilege by sanctioning attorneys for disclosing information revealed during mediation proceedings conducted pursuant to the district court's mediation program. Bernard v. Galen Group, Inc., 901 F.Supp. 778, 782–84 (S.D.N.Y.1995) (sanctioning attorney for intentionally disclosing to the court settlement offers made in mediation proceeding); Cohen v. Empire Blue Cross & Blue Shield, 178 F.R.D. 385 (E.D.N.Y.1998) (sanctioning attorney for violating confidentiality provisions of court-annexed mediation program). Focusing directly on the need for confidentiality between parties to a mediation, another court applied state law to protect the confidentiality of disclosures made during participation in the district court's mediation program. Doe v. State of Nebraska, 971 F.Supp. 1305, 1307 (D.Neb.1997) (applying Nebraska law and district court's mediation plan). That court reasoned that: [i]f any comments about the dispute made during the negotiation process were later to be construed as admissions, or even to be used to show bias, as permitted in Fed. R. Evid. 408, the posturing of the parties in the negotiations could well reduce or eliminate any likelihood of settlement, or even serious negotiation, for the parties would be extremely cautious about advancing a settlement proposal that might be used against them. Thus, they may never get beyond their "positions," even if they both may genuinely want to settle their dispute.

* * *

Taking the foregoing authorities en masse, the majority of courts to consider the issue appear to have concluded that the need for confidentiality and trust between participants in a mediation proceeding is sufficiently imperative to necessitate the creation of some form of privilege. This conclusion takes on added significance when considered in conjunction with the fact that many federal district courts rely on the success of ADR proceedings to minimize the size of their dockets. Many jurisdictions make settlement proceedings, including mediation, a mandatory step in the litigation process. For example, in the Central District of California, Local Rule 23 requires the parties in every civil case to participate in one of the approved settlement procedures.

* * *

The proliferation of federal district court rules purporting to protect the confidentiality of mediation and the ADR Bill now pending before the United States Senate indicate a commitment to encouraging confidential mediation as an alternative means of resolving disputes that would otherwise result in protracted litigation. Academic authors differ on the necessity of creating a mediation privilege, but most federal courts considering the issue have protected confidential settlement negotiations and mediation proceedings, either by relying on state law or by applying the confidentiality provisions of federal court ADR programs.

Having carefully reviewed the foregoing authority, the Court concludes that the proposed blanket mediation privilege is rooted in the imperative need for confidence and trust among participants.

b. *Public Ends*

A new privilege must serve a public good sufficiently important to justify creating an exception to the "general rule disfavoring testimonial privileges." Jaffee, 518 U.S. at 9, 116 S.Ct. 1923. The attorney-client privilege encourages observance of the law and facilitates the maintenance of an effective adversarial system of justice; the spousal privilege protects the public interest in marital harmony; the doctor-patient and psychotherapist-patient privileges serve the public interest in providing appropriate physical and mental health care. The proposed blanket mediation privilege would serve public ends by encouraging prompt, consensual resolution of disputes, minimizing the social and individual costs of litigation, and markedly reducing the size of state and federal court dockets.

* * *

In an early, broad-based critique of the ADR movement, Professor Owen Fiss argues against rules that promote settlement, contending that settlement is a capitulation to the conditions of mass society and should be neither encouraged nor praised.... [W]hen the parties settle, society gets less than what appears, and for a price it does not know it is paying. Parties might settle while leaving justice undone.

* * *

While this critique has merit and, in an ideal world, we might prefer to allocate all necessary resources to public adjudication of civil disputes, we live in a world of ever-expanding court dockets and limited judicial resources. A privilege that promotes conciliatory dispute resolution and alleviates the press of cases on the formal judicial system also allows the courts to devote those limited resources to fairly adjudicating those cases that do result in protracted litigation. Rather than the hasty judgments born of overcrowded dockets, the courts are able to provide more carefully considered decisions in matters of sufficient public concern that the parties submit their disputes to a court of law, having found it too difficult to reach a mutually agreeable settlement.

Idealism aside, a mediation privilege would serve important public ends by promoting conciliatory relationships among parties to a dispute, by reducing litigation costs and by decreasing the size of state and federal court dockets, thereby increasing the quality of justice in those cases that do not settle voluntarily.

c. *Evidentiary Detriment*

In assessing the necessity of adopting a new privilege, the courts must consider whether "the likely evidentiary benefit that would result from the denial of the privilege is modest." Jaffee, 518 U.S. at 11–12, 116 S.Ct. 1923. In Jaffee, the Supreme Court reasoned that in the absence of psychotherapist-patient privilege, "much of the desirable evidence to which litigants ... seek access—for example, admissions against interest by a party—is unlikely to come into being. This unspoken 'evidence' will therefore serve no greater truth-seeking function than if it had been spoken and privileged." The same rationale applies with respect to party admissions in mediation proceedings. Where, as here, an employer is sued by one employee claiming wrongful termination based on false allegations of sexual harassment and by another employee asserting a claim for sexual harassment perpetrated by the other employee, a blanket mediation privilege might permit an unscrupulous employer to garner the benefit of the two employees' opposing positions. In open mediation proceedings, the employer would be forced to strike a balance between the two parties positions rather than taking one employee's side in the first case and then shifting to the other side when defending against charges by the second employee. Despite the potential moral implications of fostering such duplicity, however, there is very little evidentiary benefit to be gained by refusing to recognize a mediation privilege.

First, evidence disclosed in mediation may be obtained directly from the parties to the mediation by using normal discovery channels. For example, a person's admission in mediation proceedings may, at least theoretically, be elicited in response to a request for admission or to questions in a deposition or in written interrogatories. In addition, to the extent a party takes advantage of the opportunity to use the cloak of confidentiality to take inconsistent positions in related litigation, evidence of that inconsistent position only comes into being as a result of the party's willingness to attend mediation. Absent a privilege protecting the confidentiality of mediation, the inconsistent position would presumably never come to light.

Although the Court need not, and indeed may not, address the outer limits of a federal mediation privilege, it seems appropriate to note one potential limitation here. A federal mediation privilege may be attenuated of necessity in criminal or quasi-criminal cases where the defendant's constitutional rights are at stake. In a recent decision, a California appellate court discussed the scope of acceptable evidentiary detriment created by the mediation privilege set forth in Cal. Evid. Code s 1119. See Rinaker v. Superior Court of San Joaquin County, 62 Cal.App.4th 155, 74 Cal.Rptr.2d 464 (3d Dist.1998). In the context of a juvenile delinquency proceeding, the Rinaker court found that neither the witness nor the mediator had a reasonable expectation of privacy in inconsistent statements made by the witness during confidential mediation because it has long been established that, when balanced against the competing goals of preventing perjury and preserving the integrity of the truth-seeking process of a juvenile delinquency proceeding, the interest in promoting settlements (in this case through confidential mediation of a civil harassment action against the minors) must yield to the minors' constitutional right to effective impeachment. Id. at 161, 74 Cal.Rptr.2d 464.

Despite the potential need to limit a federal mediation privilege in certain types of cases, the matter before the Court is directly in line with the Supreme Court's conclusion in Jaffee that a new federal privilege results in little evidentiary detriment where the evidence lost would simply never come into being if the privilege did not exist. In fact, this rationale applies even more strongly in the context of mediation proceedings than in a psychotherapeutic relationship because mediation is part of an overall litigation strategy while psychotherapy is a response to health care concerns. The decision to seek out a therapist is often made without considering the potential impact on pending litigation. By contrast, anyone who attends a mediation, or decides not to use mediation to attempt to resolve a dispute, will consider the effect of disclosures on the pending or potential litigation.

d. Mediation Privilege in the 50 States

In assessing a proposed privilege, a federal court should look to a consistent body of state legislative and judicial decisions adopting such a privilege as an important indicator of both reason and experience. Jaffee, 518 U.S. at 12–13, 116 S.Ct. 1923. Put simply, "the policy decisions of the States bear on the question whether federal courts should recognize a new privilege or amend the coverage of an existing one." Practically speaking, the confidential status accorded to mediation proceedings by the states will be of limited value if the federal courts decline to adopt a federal mediation privilege.

Several years ago, one district court addressed the propriety of adopting a federal privilege protecting mediators from being compelled to testify. See Smith v. Smith, 154 F.R.D. 661, 670–71 (N.D.Tex.1994) (affirming magistrate judge's decision quashing subpoena served on court-appointed mediator). Because the parties in Smith had assumed that state privilege laws applied, that court ultimately declined to resolve the issue. Nonetheless, the Smith court—considering the somewhat different question raised there of whether a mediator should have protected status—commented at length on the importance of confidentiality to the mediation process. The court noted that "confidentiality appears to be widely accepted in state law as a desirable component of the mediation process[.]" At the same time, however, the Smith court suggested that the lack of uniformity and uneven protection of mediation in the states indicates "the absence of consensus concerning the scope of the right of confidentiality."

[A]t a time when state-law support for confidentiality in mediation is apparently increasing, the protections accorded are still characterized as uneven and lacking in uniformity.... The unsettled state of the law reflects disagreement among judges and legislators on the weight of competing interests[.] Although the Smith court reached no conclusion with respect to the propriety of adopting a mediator privilege, that court's reasoning suggests the federal courts should attempt to strike a balance or refrain from adopting a privilege when the states are in disagreement about the proper scope of the privilege.

At the forefront of the inquiry, however, is the fact that every state in the Union, with the exception of Delaware, has adopted a mediation privilege of one type or another. The District of Columbia's court rules on dispute resolution also provide that the mediation process is confidential.

* * *

The fact that the states have not settled on the scope of protection to provide should not prevent the federal courts from determining that in light of reason and experience we should adopt a federal mediation privilege. While the contours of such a federal privilege need to be fleshed out over time, state legislatures and state courts have over-whelmingly chosen to protect confidential communications in mediation proceedings in order to facilitate settlement of disputes through alternative dispute resolution. "Denial of the federal privilege ... would frustrate the purposes of the state legislation that was enacted to foster these confidential communications." Jaffee, 518 U.S. at 13, 116 S.Ct. 1923. Accordingly, this Court finds it is appropriate, in light of reason and experience, to adopt a federal mediation privilege applicable to all communications made in conjunction with a formal mediation.

e. Contours of the Privilege

Where courts are required to balance a number of factors to determine whether a privilege should apply to the particular factual scenario presented, the purpose of the privilege is severely undermined. [I]f the purpose of the privilege is to be served, the participants in the confidential conversation must be able to predict with some degree of certainty whether particular discussions will be protected. An uncertain privilege, or one which purports to be certain but results in widely varying applications by the courts, is little better than no privilege at all. Accordingly, in adopting any privilege under Rule 501, the federal courts must attempt to provide a clear rule of protection.

The mediation underlying the instant dispute was a formal mediation with a neutral mediator, not a private settlement discussion between the parties. Accordingly, the mediation privilege adopted today applies only to information disclosed in conjunction with mediation proceedings with a neutral. Any interpretation of Rule 501 must be consistent with Rule 408. To protect settlement communications not related to mediation would invade Rule 408's domain; only Congress is authorized to amend the scope of protection afforded by Rule 408. Consequently, any post-mediation communications are protected only by Rule 408's limitations on admissibility.

On the facts presented here, the Court concludes that communications to the mediator and communications between parties during the mediation are protected. In addition, communications in preparation for and during the course of a mediation with a neutral must be protected. Subsequent negotiations between the parties, however, are not protected even if they include information initially disclosed in the mediation. To protect additional communications, the parties are required to return to mediation. A contrary rule would permit a party to claim the privilege with respect to any settlement negotiations so long as the communications took place following an attempt to mediate the dispute.

Based on the foregoing analysis, although Magistrate Judge Woehrle erred as a matter of law by failing to strictly apply Rule 501, the ultimate decision to deny plaintiff's motion to compel is properly sustained. The Court also concludes that Magistrate Judge Woehrle neither erred as matter of law nor made a clearly erroneous factual determination when she concluded that Vasquez did not waive the mediation privilege when the Plans' attorneys disclosed the mediation brief to Saxe without Vasquez' consent. . . .

Because the Court has not had the benefit of in camera review of the documents at issue, certain documents at issue may fall outside the scope of the mediation privilege adopted today. Accordingly, as set forth in detail below, plaintiff may attempt to compel production of communications that took place between counsel privy to the mediation after the mediation was formally concluded.

III.

CONCLUSION

For the foregoing reasons, plaintiff's Objections to the Magistrate Judge's order are SUSTAINED with respect to the underlying legal reasoning and OVERRULED with respect to the magistrate judge's ultimate decision to deny plaintiff's motion to compel production of the mediation brief and communications between counsel privy to the mediation, at least to the extent that those communications were made in anticipation of or during the course of the mediation. Plaintiff may seek, by renewed motion before the Magistrate Judge within fifteen days of entry of this order, to compel production of any documents relating to communications between Vasquez and the Plans that were not made in conjunction with, or pursuant to, the formal mediation proceeding.

In short, the Court concludes that encouraging mediation by adopting a federal mediation privilege under Fed. R. Evid. 501 will provide "a public good transcending the normally predominant principle of utilizing all rational means for ascertaining the truth."

Note: The district court in the Northern District of California recently addressed this matter in Olam v. Congress Mortgage Company and specifically delineated where the protections must give way to the need for evidence.*

The exact nature of the privilege, as previously discussed, is not well-defined. Most commentators agree that the privilege binds only the mediator. The parties are free to disclose information as they desire. The nature of the relationship between the mediator and the parties is also unclear. How would specific duties owed to the parties affect confidentiality? Are these privileges so absolute as to prevent any discussions, such as those for teaching purposes? While policy reasons remain strong that matters in mediation should be confidential, there must be limits. An absolute privilege, preventing the mediator from discussing the matter with anyone, is probably what most people expect. A survey of the mediation confidentiality statutes and an interpretation of the case law, however, does not reveal support for an absolute privilege. Nevertheless, mediators routinely make promises and assurances to the parties

* See 68 F.Supp.2d 1110, 1999 WL 909731 (1999).

concerning confidentiality. The mediator must be careful not to create a situation where she may be liable for unauthorized disclosure or a breach of contract if she is required to testify later.[53]

In terms of privilege, there is some debate about who holds such a privilege. At least a few courts have allowed the mediator (or mediation center on behalf of the mediator) to claim the privilege, even though the parties waived it, and in fact, requested disclosure.[54] Statutes are beginning to provide clarification regarding the mediation privilege. At least one state has made it clear that the mediator holds the privilege only on behalf of the party, and only that party may effect a waiver.[55] A clear waiver, though to date not judicially tested, may be in terms of allowing the mediator to testify in his own defense in a malpractice case.[56]

The trend in mediation until recently was to assure participants of complete confidentiality. As this assurance of confidentiality increased, there was a slight tendency to misuse the process. Moreover, a broad blanket of confidentiality came into direct conflict with requirements for disclosure. Whether creating exceptions to confidentiality will change the nature of the mediation process is unknown, but courts and legislatures have begun to chip away at the confidentiality provisions for mediation. In some instances, confidentiality provisions may come into conflict with ethical considerations.[57] For example, attorneys have a duty to report unethical conduct of other attorneys.[58] In a mediation where the mediator is an attorney, is she obligated to breach a confidentiality agreement to report an attorney advocate's misconduct?

IN RE WALLER

Court of Appeals, District of Columbia, 1990.
573 A.2d 780.

PER CURIAM:

In this disciplinary proceeding, the Board on Professional Responsibility found that respondent had engaged in misrepresentation in violation of DR 1–102(A)(4) when, in response to a show cause order issued by the Superior Court, he falsely—and with intent to deceive—told the

---

53. For more on mediator liability, see Chapter 15, § F.

54. See, for example, *Fenton v. Howard*, 118 Ariz. 119, 575 P.2d 318 (1978) and Colo. Rev. Stat. Ann. §§ 13–22–301–313 (1997).

55. See Wyo. Stat. § 1–43–103 (Michie 1999).

56. A few states have provided explicit exceptions to confidentiality for these cases. 1995 Wash.Rev.Code Ann. 5.60.070(1)(g) and (2)(b) (1991); 12 Okla. Stat. Ann. § 1805(f) (1993).

57. For elaboration on this issue in the legal context, see Cletus C. Hess, Comment, *To Disclose or Not To Disclose: The Relationship Between Confidentiality in Mediation and the Model Rules of Professional Conduct*, 95 Dick. L. Rev. 601 (1991); Pamela A. Kentra, *Hear No Evil, See No Evil, Speak No Evil, The Intolerable Conflict for Attorney–Mediator Between the Duty to Maintain Mediation Confidentiality and the Duty to Report Fellow Attorney Misconduct*, 1997 B.Y. L. Rev. 715 (1997).

58. See, for example, the American Bar Association Center for Professional Responsibility, Model Rules for Professional conduct, Rule 8.3, Reporting Professional Misconduct. (1998 ed.)

court that he had previously lied to a court-appointed mediator about his representation of a third-party (a surgeon) and about his reason for that lie.

* * *

The pertinent facts in this matter, which are not in dispute, are as follows:

1. Respondent has been registered as an attorney with the District of Columbia Bar since 1971.

2. Sometime prior to October 1987 Respondent was hired by Yolanda Thorpe to handle a claim for damages arising from a medical bone implant procedure that failed. . . .

3. The suit joined the hospital where the implant had been done, as well as the tissue bank that supplied the bone tissue. The surgeon who did the implant was not named a defendant.

4. On March 29, 1988, before discovery began, the Trial Judge, Henry Greene, ordered the parties to attend a mediation session with Joel Finkelstein, a lawyer in private practice who would serve as mediator.

5. During the mediation session, it occurred to the mediator that "[t]here was a glaring vacuum in the pleading [i.e., complaint] in that the surgeon was not named as a defendant." At that time, Respondent told the mediator that he "was the surgeon's attorney." The mediator then told Respondent that, in the mediator's opinion, Respondent "had a conflict of interest in this case in that he represented the surgeon who could and probably should have been a named defendant because it was a meritorious malpractice claim." When Respondent disagreed with the mediator's assessment, the mediator told Respondent to bring the matter to Judge Greene's attention.

6. Thereafter, the mediator tried several times to reach Respondent by telephone to find out whether he had, in fact, alerted the Court to the possible conflict situation. The mediator never got through to Respondent.

7. Receiving no response from Mr. Waller, the mediator then contacted Judge Greene on his own. Judge Greene suggested that the mediator again attempt to reach Respondent in order to have Respondent himself contact the Court. This was attempted, again without success.

8. Still concerned, the mediator contacted Judge Greene once more and, for the first time, told him about the possible conflict of interest. The mediator felt he could do so despite the non-disclosure provision of the mediation order[4] because "it was a matter that had nothing to do

---

4. The order requiring mediation stated: ORDERED that no statements of any party or counsel shall be disclosed to the court or   admissible as evidence for any purpose at trial of this case . . .

with the negotiations between the parties but might affect the administration of justice in the Superior Court ..." ...

Judge Greene agreed and, on April 1, 1998, he issued an order requiring Respondent to show cause why his continued representation of Ms. Thorpe did not constitute a violation of the conflict prohibitions of DR 5–105(B)(2).

In response to the Show Cause Order, Respondent filed a document with the Court stating that, notwithstanding what he had said to the mediator, Respondent was not Dr. Jackson's attorney at the time of the mediation. Respondent admitted that the had told the mediator the opposite, but he explained that he had done so only to test whether remarks made during the mediation process would be held in confidence.

* * *

14. Shortly after he withdrew from representation of Ms. Thorpe, Respondent contacted Ms. Thorpe and tried to persuade her not to press claims against Dr. Jackson. He apparently told her that he didn't think Dr. Jackson had any liability and should not be included in the case.

* * *

We have pondered why Respondent took the unusual step of admitting to the mediator that the surgeon was his client. Perhaps he failed to realize that, by admitting the relationship with Dr. Jackson, he was effectively conceding a conflict of interest. Perhaps he believed, erroneously, that the mediator would not disclose such a startling revelation. For whatever reason, we feel that Respondent did lapse into candor in making the March, 1998 admission. In the Board's view, it would be truly ironic if, on the facts of this case, Respondent were disciplined for the one statement as to his relationship with the surgeon that came closest to the truth.

* * *

Because we have found a violation of the Disciplinary Rules, it becomes necessary for us to recommend appropriate discipline. In imposing sanctions, the Court in prior cases has looked to the well-settled factors that we now discuss in turn: ... Respondent has a record of prior discipline.

* * *

It can be seen that Respondent showed little awareness of the impropriety of his actions. At the hearing, Respondent continued to focus on his "abuse" at the hands of the mediator, who had disclosed to the Court what Respondent had told him.[5]

* * *

5. Respondent moved below to dismiss the charges based on the alleged violation of the non-disclosure requirement of the medi- ation order. We would agree with the Committee's recommended ruling that the motion be denied. We do not feel that the

Based on all of these factors, we believe that a 60–day suspension would be the appropriate sanction here . . . .

* * *

The most recent confidentiality statutes include provisions clearly addressing those specific situations where confidentiality conflicts with other reporting requirements. In most instances, other reporting requirements prevail.

But in many instances, uncertainty remains. As mediation is now in an adolescent state of development in the United States, to now lessen its confidential nature may result in distrust of the process. It is feared that a decrease in the use of mediation would follow. The establishment of clear guidelines for delineating the extent of confidentiality in the mediation process has become a necessity if the use of the process is to continue to increase. It is hoped that a Uniform Mediation Act, if and when enacted, will provide clear guidance for mediators, participants, legislatures and the courts.

H. CONCLUSION

The most important task for the mediator and the mediation advocate is to determine the status of the law with regard to confidentiality. The law of the jurisdiction where the mediation is being held should be reviewed, as should the law in the jurisdiction where the litigation is pending. Moreover, the mediator should be very careful to clarify the limits and extent of confidentiality with all participants. The advocates should ascertain from their clients whether there is a need or desire for confidentiality and its priority.

It is therefore important that not only the mediator and the lawyer representatives have a clear understanding of the law concerning confidentiality in each jurisdiction, but also that they explain it in clear and precise terms to the parties. In most cases, it is advisable that the understanding of confidentiality be in writing. Because mediation is a flexible and relatively young process, there are not yet strict rules and regulations concerning mediation and those who practice it. And since mediations run the gamut from a private mediation between two individuals, to one involving public funds and over one hundred parties, establishment of specific rules with regard to confidentiality may prove very difficult. Only time will disclose courts interpretations of those rules.

confidentiality requirement was intended to preclude disclosures such as that made by the mediator to the Judge in this case. In any event, the violation we have found is not based on a statement made during mediation, but one made in a document filed in open court records.

QUESTIONS FOR DISCUSSION

11–1. If "discoverable" information, or even information "leading to discovery," is exempt from protection of confidentiality, what specifically is confidential?

11–2. Many mediation programs have mediators, particularly novices, go through a debriefing session immediately following the mediation. How does confidentiality or a privilege affect those types of discussions?

11–3. In a mediation involving an ongoing landlord-tenant dispute, the landlord informs the mediator, in caucus, that she knows that the tenant has unpaid traffic tickets, and that she has alerted the county sheriff who is scheduled to arrive and arrest the tenant in about 30 minutes. What do you do as the mediator? Does it make a difference if the mediation is being conducted at the courthouse or at your private office?

11–4. In the efforts to draft a Uniform or Model Mediation Act, the National Conference of Commissioners on Uniform State Laws has discussed several exceptions to a broad provision of confidentiality. Current drafts grant a very broad privilege, which is followed by specific exceptions. One such exception reads as follows:

"If a court determines, after a hearing, that disclosure is necessary to prevent a manifest injustice of such a magnitude as to outweigh the importance of protecting the confidentiality of mediation communications."

(a) What difficulties does this present for a court charged with making this determination?

(b) Many mediators suggest deleting such a provision and, instead, enacting more specific exceptions. If this is the case, what should those exceptions be?

11–5. A number of private mediation providers offer to conduct mediations via the Internet. What problems regarding confidentiality are posed by such a practice?

11–6. Confidences of Colossal Computers

You represent the Colossal Computer Company in a case pending in the superior court of the State of Flax. Colossal Computer was sued by Jim Thomas, individually, and on behalf of his five year old daughter, Michele Thomas, for the alleged wrongful death of Margo Thomas, the wife and mother. Margo Thomas' death occurred when a Colossal truck collided with her automobile. Colossal Computer, from the inception, has taken the position that Margo Thomas was 100% responsible by failing to yield the right of way to the truck.

After the lawsuit was filed, Judge Hardly A. Wake ordered the case to mediation. The court order consisted of a one sentence referral. After four hours of mediation, a capable mediator declared a total impasse with the parties over three million dollars apart. Thereafter, the case went to trial. Two weeks into trial, and during the plaintiff's case, Judge Wake declared a mistrial when a plaintiff's expert mentioned insurance. Judge Wake, on his own motion, ordered the parties to mediate a second time. During the hearing on Colossal Computer's opposition to the second mediation, Judge Wake, after ordering the second mediation, commented, "I'll determine when to set the second trial, the extent of jury selection, and the amount of time for final argument based on who exercised the most good faith during the second mediation."

After nine hours, the second mediation reached a total impasse with no progress made from the status of the first mediation. The mediator issued a one page report to the Court which stated only "the parties appeared and the matter did not settle."

Judge Wake, after receiving a telephone call from the Thomas' counsel alleging Colossal Computer's bad faith in the second mediation, has set a hearing to determine who was "in good faith" at the second mediation. The judge has also ordered a bench subpoena for the mediator to appear at the hearing. Plaintiff's counsel also contacted the local press and described what happened at the second mediation; the newspaper wrote an article with the headline, "Colossal Computer Fails to Negotiate at Second Mediation."

Neither the statutes of the State of Flax nor the court's local rules directly address the issue of confidentiality.

You have the following assignments:

(a) Prepare a motion with a supporting brief for the court as to why the mediator should not testify.

(b) Prepare a motion for sanctions with a supporting brief regarding plaintiff's counsel's telephone call to the court and interview with the press.

(c) Prepare a motion to bar the press from the hearing and from writing about the mediations. Include a brief in support of your motion.

11–7. You are an attorney-mediator in private practice in California. You were contacted by the attorney for the plaintiff and agreed to mediate the case of Parker v. Secured Parking Systems, Inc. The case was a personal injury suit against Secured Parking for the aggravated sexual assault of Ms. Parker. The attorneys for the plaintiff, Kevin Blair and Gail Reedy of the firm Justice and Reedy, were present at the mediation along with their client.

When the mediation was first discussed, Mr. Blair requested that it be scheduled away from law offices and the courthouse. He stated that in his opinion a more relaxed environment would be better. A Saturday was also requested. As you are a flexible mediator, you complied. The mediation took place about a month ago at the conference center overlooking Malibu beach.

The case involves a claim against a parking garage and its management for the amount of 12 million dollars. Both companies and their insurers were present at the mediation. The case was eventually settled for approximately 3.8 million dollars. During the mediation both parties, for different reasons, stressed the need for confidentiality. Confidentiality was demanded not only for all discussions within the mediation session, but also for the contents of the settlement agreement. The defendants were hoping to avoid publicity and keep the amount paid quiet. Plaintiffs were so concerned with confidentiality that they agreed to dismiss the suit once the terms of the settlement were fully complied with. You thought this was a bit out of the ordinary, having not experienced a plaintiff so willing to maintain confidentiality of the settlement amount. You suspected that there were underlying issues that had not been disclosed. Despite your expertise in probing, however, the plaintiffs failed to disclose anything to you other than the need for confidentiality for protection of their client. A confidentiality agreement was executed by all parties, attorneys and the mediator. You facilitated all the other terms of the settlement and closed the mediation late that afternoon.

As they were leaving the mediation, the lawyers requested that you destroy your copy of a brief memorandum outlining the amount in settlement in a week. It also included the time and place of the exchange of the money. The exchange of money and documents was to take place between the counsels for each side within the following two weeks. The following week you were still somewhat puzzled, but you dutifully shredded your papers and closed the file.

About a week ago, at a pre-holiday season open house hosted by a local court reporting service, you ran into John Justice, one of the partners in the firm of Justice and Reedy. You knew that the attorneys for the plaintiff had a 40% contingency agreement in the case you mediated. Not believing an innocent comment to be within the realm of confidentiality protection, you casually slapped him on the back and said, "I bet you're going to have a wonderful holiday season figuring out how to spend all that money." Mr. Justice looked very puzzled and asked, "What are you talking about?" You responded, "You know, the cash from that big settlement." By the surprised and shocked look on his face, you were at once aware that he had no knowledge of the settlement of the lawsuit or of the mediation. You quickly mentioned that you needed to talk to someone else, and excused yourself from the conversation. You immediately left the open house.

The following week you receive a telephone call from Mr. Justice requesting your voluntary presence at a deposition. You learn during the brief conversation that at the time of the mediation, partner Reedy and associate Blair were in the process of leaving the firm. They purposefully failed to inform anyone, including support staff, of the fact that the mediation took place. In fact, it was their intent to take the client files with them and announce the settlement after leaving the firm.

Justice asks you to disclose everything that took place at the mediation, as well as the settlement amount. You turn white, request time to think about this, and quickly hang up the phone.

As the mediator, what do you do?

Chapter Twelve

THE MEDIATED AGREEMENT

In the majority of mediations, the parties and the mediator together will eventually arrive at a point where there appears to be agreement on most, if not all, of the issues. It is then time to finalize the elements of the agreement.

A final agreement may not be reached in every mediation. Yet, even in those cases that do not settle the mediation can often be termed an achievement. Neither a mediation nor a mediator should be judged solely in terms of whether or not an agreement is reached. There are other factors to consider. For instance, the parties may discuss the case a week later and reach a final agreement. In such a case, the mediation was effective. There may be times when the parties end the session by agreeing to disagree. Partial agreements are also possible. Agreements to reschedule the mediation are another option. Each of these results can be considered a successful mediation. Just as mediation is flexible, so are the results. Although complete settlement is some indication of the effectiveness of mediation, because of the variety of forms and styles of mediation, the types of cases and pressures to settle,[1] a final settlement should not be the sole measure of success.[2]

A. FINALIZING THE MEDIATED AGREEMENT

When the parties themselves engage in negotiation and exchange options directly, there may a tendency on the part of the mediator to take a back seat role. He may allow his listening skills to become less than efficient. Yet, the mediator should be very active at this stage of the process. It is clearly part of the mediator's role and task to continue to guide the parties in concluding their agreement. Often parties negotiating toward agreement include a number of details in their discussions. Lacking objectivity, and anxious to reach a final resolution, the parties

---

1. Issues of pressure to settle are discussed in § A, of this chapter.

2. This issue is also examined in terms of ethical issues in Chapter 14, and quality of practice in Chapter 15. See also Robert

A. Baruch Bush & Joseph P. Folger, *The Promise of Mediation: Responding to Conflict Through Empowerment and Recognition* (1994).

may inadvertently omit items previously discussed. The mediator, in his neutral role, should have notes identifying all of the interests, issues, options and agreements. It is important, then, that he be an active participant in finalizing the agreement and assuring that all of the items previously identified have either been addressed or purposefully disregarded.

After a number of hours at the mediation table, the parties are eager to end the mediation. In cases where relationships have been reconciled or established, participants may be willing to forego details. The mediator's task is to assure that all of the details are covered. A failure to fine tune the agreement could lead to further disputes.[3]

When approaching the finalization of the mediated agreement (actually at all points during the mediation) the mediator should keep in mind that there are three important elements of a satisfactory agreement: procedural, psychological, and substantive satisfaction. While these aspects of satisfaction are sometimes viewed in terms of negotiation, specifically the interest based model,[4] the mediation process itself assists in achieving these results. The mediator, when reaching the stage where the agreement becomes final, should determine from the parties, inasmuch as possible, whether all three elements have been achieved, recognizing the overlap between them. For example, if a party is satisfied with the procedure, that satisfaction will contribute directly to her psychological satisfaction. Likewise, when the substance of the agreement is satisfactory, psychological satisfaction is likely.

Procedural satisfaction is commonly achieved by participation in the mediation. When each party has actually participated fully in the process or feels that she has been provided the opportunity to participate without pressure, she usually feels satisfaction with the procedure. In fact, most studies report that the parties are satisfied with the mediation process, even in cases where a final agreement is not reached.[5]

Psychological satisfaction will be present if the parties have not only had an opportunity to be heard, but also to express their anger, frustration, disappointment, sadness, or other emotion. Many times it is important that parties express themselves, that is, vent their emotion. This will enable them to then focus on working out a resolution. The mediation process, by design, allows ventilation before cooperation is expected. In many mediation models, the time for expression and ventilation is a separate stage of the process. In many legal and business disputes, parties are required to present their dispute in the form of witness testimony. It is usually inappropriate to include emotional or psychological aspects of the dispute in the testimony. In the mediation

---

3. This is further discussed in this chapter at § A, 2.

4. Christopher W. Moore & CDR Associates, Effective Mediation 5 (1989).

5. Royer F. Cook, et al., Neighborhood Justice Centers Field Test, Executive Summary Final Evaluation Report 15 (1980). Anecdotal reports of this information are very common as well, and includes the author's personal experience.

process, however, expression of emotion is often encouraged.[6] Moreover, the mediator, by his actions—which include active listening—lets the parties know that they are being heard. This is not always the case in other types of dispute resolution procedures, particularly litigation. Therefore, the mediation process itself contributes to the psychological satisfaction of the parties. When reaching the final stages of the process, the mediator should take a moment to consider whether the psychological needs of the parties, within limits,[7] have been met.

The mediated agreement belongs to the parties, not to the mediator.[8] While acknowledging this, the mediator should still take a direct role in determining the substance of the final agreement. His role is not to dictate terms of specific content, but to assure that all pertinent items are handled. It is impossible for a mediator, as a neutral facilitator, to completely guarantee that all parties will be satisfied with the specific substance of an agreement. Nonetheless, if the mediator has identified the interests of each party and those interests are satisfied, the result will be an agreement with substantive satisfaction. Where procedural, psychological, and substantive satisfaction are substantially achieved, it increases the likelihood that the parties will completely comply with the agreement.

1. PRESSURES TO SETTLE

> There never was a good war, or a bad peace.
>
> —Benjamin Franklin

Most cases settle sooner or later. Mediation frequently moves later to sooner. In those cases in which the parties are unable to reach a final settlement, there is disagreement about the role of the mediator. This disagreement centers on how subtle or assertive the mediator should be in moving the parties to an agreement. This is also described in terms of mediator directiveness or pressure to settle. There are a variety of specific steps which some view as appropriate for the mediator to take, while others disagree. A push toward settlement may also come from outside sources that tangentially affect the mediation process.

In the context of mediation in a pending lawsuit, pressures to settle may come from at least three different avenues. One source is from the judge. The court—by its mere referral of a pending lawsuit to the mediation process—is usually exerting pressure upon the parties to settle. Even at court hearings, judges regularly hold judge-facilitated settlement conferences or require counsel to "go outside and talk." When referring a case to mediation, a judge sometimes makes obvious comments like, "This case ought to be settled," or "Can't you settle

---

6. Many mediators focus on asking questions such as "How did that make you feel?" for this reason.

7. By design, mediation is not the same as therapy or therapeutic counseling, and should not be a substitute process. See Chapter 3, § C.

8. For more on this point see, for example, Lon L. Fuller, *Mediation: Its Forms and Functions*, 44 S. Cal. L. Rev. 305 (1971). Compare however, Lawrence Susskind, *Environmental Mediation and the Accountability Problem*, 6 Vt. L. Rev. 1 (1981).

this?" In other situations, the judge's comment is not as direct, but the message is similar.

The referral system also provides incentives to settle. Some are not subtle. One method is a requirement that the litigants pay a penalty if they wish to avoid the settlement and go to trial. This is the procedure in "Michigan mediation." Although labeled *mediation*, it is not a mediation process at all. The process is essentially case evaluation, where the parties receive a recommended settlement from a panel of three lawyers.[9] If the parties do not wish to accept the recommendation of the panel, they can go to trial. However, if they do not achieve a result at trial which is at least 10% better than the panel's recommendation, they must pay the actual costs of the other party.[10] Other programs have imposed sanctions for failure to negotiate in good faith.[11] When pressures to settle have been challenged, the courts apply a balancing test: On one side is the desire to allow leeway in the administration of a program, on the other is the need to avoid placing an unfair financial burden on the parties or denying their constitutional rights.[12]

Another concern is with pressure from the mediator. While the mediator's role consists of facilitating an agreement, it is difficult to determine how far he should go in "motivating" the parties to settle. Many mediators, particularly lawyer mediators, discuss this in terms of being an advocate for settlement. The mediator is not an advocate for any party, but rather for the settlement process. In that role, some mediators have been known to engage in tactics which do not meet with universal approval. One such tactic is keeping the parties together despite an expressed desire to leave.[13] Agreements reached in this manner are more likely to be withdrawn, if possible, by the parties.[14] Many are critical of this tactic.[15] Other mediators stress that the case ought to be settled, and that the court will not be pleased to hear the matter. While some parties see this as pressure to settle, it can also be seen as an attempt by the mediator to assist the parties in reality testing. Another approach is to provide the parties with the mediator's proposal for settlement, which, in effect, transforms the mediation into a non-binding arbitration.

9. Kimberlee K. Kovach, *Neutral Case Evaluation*, St. Mary's ADR Institute (1989). See also Julie Heintz, *Mediating Instead of "Mediating"* 75 U. Det. Mercy L. Rev. 333 (1998).

10. Kathy L. Stuart, et al., *Settling Cases in Detroit: An Examination of Wayne County's Mediation Program*, 8 Just. Sys. J. 307 (1983).

11. See Chapter 4 for a discussion of good faith participation in mediation.

12. For an in depth examination of the issue, see Nancy Rogers & Craig A. McEw-

en, Mediation: Law, Policy & Practice, Chapter Seven (1994 & Supp. 1999).

13. See Randle v. Mid Gulf, Inc. 1996 WL 447954 unpublished (Tex.App.-Houston [14th Dist.]) which demonstrates that despite chest pains, the party was compelled to remain at the mediation until an agreement was signed.

14. *Id.*

15. See Allen v. Leal, 27 F. Supp. 2d. 945 (S.D.Tex. 1998) where the plaintiffs alleged that the mediator forced them to settle, Judge Hitner noted that coercion or "bullying" is not acceptable conduct for a mediator.

In any mediation, the parties will feel pressure to settle if the mediator has the ability to make a report to the court or other third party. The report may include reasons that the case did not settle.[16] It may also be in the form of a recommendation for final adjudication. For example, in California child custody mediation, the courts are permitted to obtain a recommendation from the mediator if the case does not settle.[17] On the other hand, to prevent such disclosures, some statutes actually prohibit any report to the court other than whether the case settled.[18] Conflicting messages are thus being sent to mediators, although most ethical advice which address this issue opposes or prohibits detailed reports to the court. Each mediator must use his best judgment when evaluating the degree of pressure to exert on the parties in "advocating" settlement. As a general rule, where guidance is limited, the mediator must recall that his role is to assist the parties in arriving at their own settlement.

2. CONTENTS OF THE AGREEMENT

The content of the agreement, just as the content of the entire mediation, belongs to the parties. That is not to say, however, that the mediator does not have a distinct role in assuring that all points raised during the mediation are dealt with in some fashion in the actual agreement. The mediator also plays a role in completing the details and fine tuning the mediation agreement. One of the primary reasons for the failure to comply with a mediated agreement is the lack of clarity in the final agreement.

When finalizing and drafting the mediated agreement, a mediator should ask the following question: **Can it be determined, from reading the agreement alone, who, will do what, when, where, how, and how much?** If this can be answered affirmatively, so that an individual, not present during the mediation and unfamiliar with the facts, would be able to read the agreement and determine specifically what is to happen, the mediator's job is complete. If any of these questions is not clearly answered by the agreement, then the mediator must continue to clarify issues before drafting the final agreement.

In determining the specific contents of the agreement, the mediator often engages in reality testing. That is, the mediator helps the parties discuss the specifics of implementing the agreement.[19] The mediator assists the parties in determining if what they are intending to agree to is really possible and how exactly it will be carried out. A simple example is the case of an agreement to make payments for a debt owed. A party is considering an agreement to pay $500 a month. The mediator learned

---

16. The report may, for example, identify the party, or side, that was uncooperative with the process.

17. Cal. Fam. Code § 3183 (Supp.2000).

18. Tex.Civ.Prac. & Rem.Code Ann. § 154.053(c) (1997).

19. Implementation is sometimes seen as a separate stage of the process. Christopher W. Moore, The Mediation Process: Practical Strategies to Resolving Conflict 301–304 2d ed. (1996).

from previous conversations that this individual nets only about $1,500 a month, and must pay apartment rent of $550 and a car payment of $380. Most trainers and educators agree that the mediator has a duty to raise a question of the feasibility of compliance with the agreement. That is, does the party have $500 of disposable income per month? On the other hand, some take the position that the parties should be free to make their own agreement, regardless of the content or ability to fulfill it. The minority position would suggest that in the preceding example the individual may have other means to fulfill the agreement, and the inquiry is beyond the mediator's role. If reality testing involves issues which might be sensitive, such as personal finances, the mediator should meet with the party privately.

Some propose that the mediator has a duty to assure that the agreement is a fair one.[20] This of course, places the mediator in a difficult role because his perception of fairness may differ from that of the parties. If the agreement is fair from the perspective of the participants, and they have had an opportunity to gather any information they deem necessary, the mediator's job is complete, absent, of course, illegality.[21]

Once the substantive elements of the agreement are determined, the specifics of implementation must also be finalized. In the preceding example, the following must be determined: a specific date for each monthly payment; the location where the payment is to be made; how the payment is to be made, e.g. by mail, in person, etc., and whether personal check, cashiers check, credit card debit, etc. is acceptable. Detailed implementation procedures help assure compliance with the agreement.

Although consideration of reality and implementation procedures are discussed as a separate stage of the process, they are often combined in the negotiation phase. This is particularly true in an integrative negotiation.[22] In that case, as a final agreement is being reached, any items which have not been included or determined should be raised by the mediator in an effort to provide a comprehensive agreement.

In many cases, when confronted with the task of determining specific implementation procedures, parties tend to call on a third party who may not be present to assist with the effort. The mediator must be careful to *not* include in the agreement a provision which requires an action on the part of someone who is not present at the session. In rare cases where no other alternatives exist, the mediator should require that the parties first obtain the consent of the third person before the agreement is finalized. This can often be done by telephone.

---

20. Leonard L. Riskin, *Toward New Standards for the Neutral Lawyer in Mediation*, 26 Ariz. L. Rev. 329, 354 (1984).

21. Also, see Chapter 7, which explored this issue in terms of the mediator's neutrality.

22. See Chapter 9 for a discussion of negotiation theory.

The mediator's role, insofar as finalizing the contents of the agreement, should also include an examination of contingencies. The mediator, as a neutral party, is more likely to see an indication that the agreement, as specified by the parties, may not be completely workable. In that instance, the mediator should assist the parties in identifying potential problems and finding alternative courses of action. Because the discussion of "what-ifs" could go on forever, the mediator must limit this discussion. This again, is a situation which will vary depending on the type and complexity of the case.

An item which should *not* be included in the agreement is a recital of fault. The mediation process is a forward looking process. Inclusion of matters such as blame, liability, or guilt is inappropriate in the mediated agreement. In drafting the agreement, the mediator must refrain from addressing these issues and avoid using phrases which begin: "because of" . . . "due to" . . . or "as a result of". Even where an acknowledgement of fault is demanded by one of the parties and agreed to by the other, it need not be included in the written agreement. Of course, there may be exceptions, for example, where a public apology is the essence of the agreement. This also raises questions about including a recital of consideration in the agreement and the subsequent effect on the enforceability of the agreement as a contract.

In most mediations, the final agreement is not unilateral. The majority contain reciprocal agreements by all parties. Therefore, as a practical matter, the concern with the consideration issue is minimal. Even so, many mediators, particularly lawyers, begin each written agreement with a phrase such as "for good and valuable consideration."[23] Most agreements naturally contain language describing a course of conduct on the part of each disputant—even if this includes an agreement to no longer pursue the matter. Some mediators include these in the agreement so that it appears that there is a balance of concessions.[24]

In terms of specific content, a recital or preamble which encourages positive and cooperative behaviors and attitudes may also be appropriate.[25] This may also assist with compliance. Statements reflecting the parties' commitment to the agreement may also be included with the general recitals of consideration.

3. PARTIAL AGREEMENTS

A mediator must keep in mind that, like all other stages of the process, the stage of finalizing the agreement must be flexible. This includes flexibility in the conclusion. In mediation, it is possible that instead of a complete settlement of the case, there will be one or more partial agreements. These normally take two different forms. The first is a partial agreement in terms of specific issues or parties to the case.

---

23. A discourse on general contract law is beyond the scope of this work. Since few mediators are also experts in contract, some mediators refuse to draft the agreement. See this chapter, §§ B & C.

24. Moore, *supra* note 19, at 312.

25. *Id.*

That is, the mediator will carve out certain issues to which the parties agree. These issues can be finalized without reaching conclusion on others. Partial agreement is also possible in multi-party cases where there is complete agreement among some parties, but not all.

The second type of partial agreement is a statement of a general intent to agree, or an agreement in principle, which leaves specific details to be worked out at a later date. Many times this is useful where there is a need for additional information. The mediator should be careful to specify exactly what the parties did agree to, and not make any implications.

The mediator should be able to recognize, identify, and clarify a partial agreement. He will often outline it for the parties. In cases of partial agreements, the parties, after a period of time, may obtain additional information, see things differently, and wish to reschedule the mediation. The partial agreement may thus include the specifics of the reschedule date.[26]

4. FORM OF THE AGREEMENT

The mediated agreement can take a number of forms. These range from the least formal, an oral agreement, to the most formal, a formalized legal document. There are many which fall between these two. The form of the agreement will often depend on the nature of the case and whether or not a lawsuit is pending.

It is also possible to have what is termed a self-executing agreement which is carried out completely at the time of agreement.[27] An example is the exchange of goods, or the payment of a sum certain. The item or cash is exchanged during the mediation, and the matter is concluded. Often a written agreement is not necessary.

In many cases, the form of the agreement is related to its enforceability. Issues of enforceability of a mediated agreement often rely on an understanding of general contract law. In some cases, it is specifically provided by statute that there must be a valid contract if the mediation agreement is to be enforceable.[28] In other instances, not only will the form of the agreement need to conform with general contract provisions, but it must include additional elements such as an acknowledgement that the party should consult with an attorney as well.[29] Therefore, in drafting the agreement it is important to consider the form, not only in terms of the parties and their needs, but also in light of enforceability issues. However, there is lack of consensus on whether it is part of the mediator's role to make determinations about enforceability.[30]

26. Rescheduling and following up after mediation are specifically dealt with in Chapter 13.

27. Moore, *supra* note 19, at 302.

28. See, e.g., Tex.Civ.Prac. & Rem.Code Ann. § 154.071 (1997).

29. Minn. Stat. Ann. § 572.35 (1998). Issues of enforceability are detailed in this chapter § C.

30. See also § B of this chapter for a discussion of drafting issues and the variety of mediator roles.

The least formal agreement is the oral agreement. In this instance, the mediator should restate what the terms of the agreement are, and perhaps even have the parties state to each other what they agree to do. Sometimes this is sealed with a handshake or other form of confirmation of the agreement. It is important, in these instances, that all the details are spelled out. Because the agreement is oral, there may a tendency on the part of the mediator, as well as the parties, to ignore or dismiss a need for details. It is assumed that everyone remembers from the negotiation what they have agreed to do, and therefore, no need exists for additional specificity or restatement. Unfortunately, this is usually not the case. The parties have probably not been taking any notes during this segment of the mediation. The mediator has a responsibility to take detailed notes so that he can rely on these notes to firm up all details. As previously stated, it is part of the mediator's job to review the agreement and assure that everyone concurs with the specific details. This is no different in the case where there is an oral agreement.

Another informal type of agreement is an agreement in principle. The parties arrive at a general agreement which includes further details that need to be worked out at a later time. If written, the agreement is usually in general outline form, in simple straightforward language, laying out what the parties have agreed to do. The agreement may even include lists. It is important that it is written so that all parties understand the terms. Sometimes, the form of the agreement is more complex, consisting of an original business contract or settlement documents for a lawsuit. In some instances the agreement can consist of a renegotiated contract, the final form of which may take days to complete. Finally, proposed legislation, rules, and regulations constitute yet another, albeit uncommon, form of a mediated agreement.[31]

The final form of the agreement may be influenced by whether litigation is pending. The sections that follow explain this impact.

a. Non–Litigation Cases

In matters where no lawsuit has been filed, attorneys are not often present at mediation. Consideration of court documents is not necessary. These are the cases where it is possible to utilize an oral agreement, although most mediation programs and mediators stress the advantages of a written agreement.[32] With a written agreement, the mediator must include all of the factors clearly, so that the parties are certain of what they are to do, including when, where, and how they are to do it.

Issues of enforceability are important here as well. The parties may want to be assured that they have a written contract. Just what a mediator can say and do in this regard is one of those items subject to

---

31. This once rare form is becoming more common where governmental agencies, along with regulatory and law making bodies, are using the mediation process to achieve consensus. See Chapter 16.

32. These include a permanent record of the specifics of the agreement and the ritualistic nature of agreement writing and signing. Such procedures may increase chances of complete compliance.

controversy.[33] If a mediator who is also a lawyer becomes directly involved in making certain the agreement is enforceable, then it is possible that he is providing legal advice. In the case of non-lawyer mediators, many may not know this information, or conversely, may be considered to be engaged in the unauthorized practice of law.

b. *Pending Lawsuits*

In mediations where a lawsuit is pending, the participants face additional choices with regard to the form of the mediated agreement. Prior to finalizing the agreement they must determine the effect of the mediated agreement on the lawsuit. A final settlement via mediation will take one of three primary forms: 1) a dismissal of the lawsuit, 2) a finalization of the lawsuit in terms of an agreed judgment, or 3) a continuation of the lawsuit with certain stipulations. All of these, of course, necessitate different forms for the agreement and subsequent documents.

If the lawsuit is to be dismissed, the remaining portion of the mediated agreement would most likely be drawn up as a contract. That assumes, of course, that all elements of the contract are present. In this instance, a dismissal or a non-suit will be filed, and the parties would then rely on the mediated agreement (contract) to indicate the action that will be taken.

In other instances, the parties do not wish to have the lawsuit dismissed, but prefer to incorporate the mediated agreement into the final papers or judgment of the case. In some cases the referring court or a statute may require that the agreement be submitted to the court.[34]

Court approval of the mediated agreement can be accomplished in several ways. The first is that the mediated agreement is, in fact, the final agreed or stipulated judgment of the court. All elements of the agreement are contained in the judgment proposed to, and signed by, the court. Another option is to incorporate the mediated agreement by reference into the final decree or judgment of the court. Many times in a divorce case, there is too much detail in the mediated agreement to be included in the final decree. Therefore, the agreement is either attached to the decree as an exhibit or incorporated by reference. An additional alternative is to include certain elements of the agreement in the court's order, along with a reference to separate agreement or contract which contains other items of agreement. All of these options have been used, with no widespread preference yet established. The key point is that the parties and the mediators are clear on what form the agreement will take before they enter into the finalization stage.

B. DRAFTING ISSUES

There are a number of issues surrounding the drafting of a mediation agreement. These, of course, include the form of the agreement, and

---

33. This is also discussed in § B, this chapter.

34. See, e.g., Colo.Rev.Stat.Ann. § 13–22–308 (1997); Me. Rev. Code Ann. § 251(3) (1998).

its contents, as well as its enforceability. The mediator plays a primary role in drafting the document, particularly in the physical production of the agreement. One important topic of discussion for mediators is whether the drafting of a mediated agreement is the practice of law. A related issue concerns providing advice regarding enforceability of the agreement.

For the lawyer mediator there is some question as to whether mediation is the practice of law. This issue overlaps with issues of mediator certification, regulation, and ethics.[35] There is no definitive answer, although, as a practical matter, charges for the unauthorized practice of law have not been routinely brought against non-lawyer mediators.[36] If mediating is practicing law, does the mediator commit legal malpractice when he drafts a faulty agreement? In most court-referred cases where parties are represented, mediators compose only a memorandum of agreement. It is then the lawyer-advocates' responsibility to draft the final documents, whether they be court documents (such as a judgment) or contractual in nature. If the parties are not represented by counsel and a lawyer mediator drafts the agreement, there is some concern that the parties may expect that the mediator is reviewing the agreement in terms of legal sufficiency. It is uncertain whether this is part of the mediator's role. Currently, in most instances mediators see it as beyond the scope of their role, and therefore, strongly urge that the parties have the agreement reviewed by their own counsel before finalization.

For the non-lawyer some issues are simpler, while others are more difficult. The mediator will probably not be expected or required to look at the agreement in terms of its legal sufficiency, but only to draft specifically what the parties request. His drafting is essentially the memorialization of the agreement. On the other hand, the mediator without legal training, if engaged in writing or drafting settlement decrees, might be viewed as engaged in the unauthorized practice of law. This very issue has been raised in the context of divorce mediation, with two conflicting results within two years of each other.[37]

Non-lawyer mediators, however, have been mediating cases for many years, in programs affiliated with the justice system and bar associations. It is common in the vast majority of these programs that the mediator draft the agreement. It is rare that issues of the unauthorized practice of law for drafting agreements will be raised, as in most

---

35. These will be examined further in Chapters 14 and 15.

36. However, these issues were raised in the mid-eighties in terms of ethical opinions. The question of whether mediation is the practice of law was answered both in the affirmative and the negative. See Nancy H. Rogers & Richard A. Salem, A Student's Guide to Mediation and the Law, 117–121 (1987) and more recently, Carrie Menkel–Meadow, Is Mediation the Practice of Law?, 14 Alternatives to High Cost Litig. 57

(1996), Bruce Meyerson, Lawyers who Mediate are not Practicing Law, 14 Alternatives to High Cost Litig. 74 (1996); National Institute for Dispute Resolution, Forum Issue, Mediation and the Practice of Law (June 1997). See also Office of the Executive Secretary, Supreme Court of Virginia, Guidelines on Mediation and the Unauthorized Practice of Law (1999) [Virginia Guidelines].

37. Rogers & Salem, *supra* note 36, at 27–28.

cases, the mediator is serving in a scrivener role. If however, a mediator is unclear about an issue, it is recommended that he advise the party to obtain independent legal counsel before finalizing the agreement.[38]

C. ENFORCEABILITY

In many of the community mediation models, the issue of technical enforceability of the mediated agreement is rarely raised. The theory is that individuals who take part in agreement formation have ownership in it, are psychologically committed to it, and, therefore, are likely to comply with the terms. Research supports this hypothesis. It has been demonstrated that not only are disputants satisfied with the agreement, but they perceive the outcome as significantly more fair than a court determination.[39] Consequently, there is a much greater likelihood that they will follow the terms.[40] Yet some agreements, particularly those which must be performed over time, contain compliance provisions. These may include a third party who will monitor compliance.[41] In litigation, this party is often assumed to be the court.

BARNETT v. SEA LAND SERVICE, INC.
United States Court of Appeals, Ninth Circuit, 1989.
875 F.2d 741.

* * *

Appellant contends that the district court erred as a matter of law by not allowing the introduction of evidence that a settlement had been reached during the mediation session. We review questions of law *de novo*.

Local Rule 39.1 of the Western District of Washington sets forth procedures for mediation, arbitration and special masters. The parties to the instant dispute participated in mediation under this rule. The provision which lies at the heart of the appellant's first contention is Local Rule 39.1(d)(3), which provides as follows:

> *Proceedings Privileged.* All proceedings of the mediation conference, including any statement made by any party, attorney or other participant, shall, in all respects, be privileged and not reported, recorded, placed in evidence, made known to the trial court or jury, or construed for any purpose as an admission against interest: No party shall be bound by anything done or said at the conference unless a settlement is reached, in which event the agreement upon a settlement shall be reduced to writing and shall be binding upon all parties to that agreement.

38. See Virginia Guidelines *supra* note 36, at 21.

39. Janice A. Roehl & Royer F. Cook, *Mediation in Interpersonal Disputes: Effectiveness and Limitations*, in Mediation Research: The Process and Effectiveness of Third Party Intervention 33 (Kenneth Kressel & Dean G. Pruitt, eds., 1989).

40. *Id*. at 34.

41. Moore, *supra* note 19, at 303.

Although the parties entered into mediation, the appellees refused to sign a settlement agreement prepared by the appellant after the mediation took place. At trial, the district judge refused to allow testimony by the mediator as to whether a settlement had been reached. Appellant contends that a settlement was reached.

Appellees argue that there was a mutual mistake and no settlement was ever consummated. Appellee argues that under Local Rule 39.1(d)(3), since no written settlement was consummated, none exists and therefore the district court was correct in not accepting evidence of a settlement.

We agree with the appellees' interpretation of the Local Rule. While appellant focuses on the language which provides that no party shall be bound unless a settlement is reached, we believe that the last phrase of Local Rule 39.1(d)(3) is controlling. It provides that once a settlement is reached it shall be reduced to writing and shall be binding upon the parties. We interpret this to mean that until a settlement is reduced to writing, it is not binding upon the parties. When a settlement is not binding no evidence may be introduced under Local Rule 39.1(d)(3). This ruling is reached only under the language of Western District of Washington Local Rule 39.1 and is not meant to be a general pronouncement on when binding settlements are reached in other cases, disputes, and forums.

RIZK v. MILLARD

Court of Appeals of Texas, Houston (14th Dist.), 1991.
810 S.W.2d 318.

PAUL PRESSLER, JUSTICE.

This Petition for a Writ of Mandamus challenges an order entered by respondent striking relator's pleadings and granting a default judgment against him in *Wesley L. Snyder v. Fred E. Rizk*, Richard Muriby and George Howard in the 189th Judicial District Court of Harris County, Texas. Relator requests that this court command respondent to reinstate relator's answers, set aside the default judgment and set this case for trial on the issue of liability. The petition is denied.

Relator was a member of a joint venture organized to subsidize certain patents on inventions developed by the plaintiff. The plaintiff is an inventor who developed a unique series of laser gun sight systems which were issued patents in both the United States and in numerous other countries in the world. The plaintiff claimed that relator and two other members of the joint venture had agreed to provide unlimited financial support. The level of support failed to meet the plaintiff's expectations, and he subsequently brought suit for breach of contract alleging damages of $200,000 as "prosecution" fees for preventing third parties from infringing upon the patents. Relator counterclaimed seeking recovery of all sums paid to the plaintiff under the agreement.

At the request of the parties, on October 1, 1990, respondent entered an Order of Referral for Mediation. The mediation was conducted on December 18. An oral compromise was negotiated and an initial draft of the settlement agreement was reduced to writing, but it was not signed by either the relator or the plaintiff. The mediator brought all parties into a conference room and repeated the terms of the settlement agreement asking each individual and his counsel to affirm, in the presence of each other, the specific terms of the agreement. All parties indicated that they agreed to the terms of the settlement agreement. No reservations or contingencies were orally expressed.

There is a difference of opinion between the parties as to why the settlement agreement was not signed the same evening it was drafted. According to the respondent, the agreement was not reduced to writing that night solely because counsel for the relator asked if he could attend his son's baseball game. Respondent points to the relator's deposition testimony where relator states that he made no statement that evening qualifying his agreement to the settlement. Relator claims that he equivocated at the conclusion of the mediation stating that he would have to obtain financing to meet his obligation before signing any settlement agreement. Relator's deposition does state that he had no intention of signing the compromise that day.

Relator later advised his counsel that he would be unable to meet his obligations under the compromise. Relator contacted the plaintiff, so informed him, and suggested the case be set for trial. The plaintiff responded that relator's actions violated the compromise and that he would seek all available remedies including a continuation of the litigation, a new lawsuit for breach of the compromise, and costs and expenses of the mediation as sanctions.

After hearing, on proper motions, respondent granted the plaintiff's Motion for Sanctions and on its own motion struck relator's pleadings and entered a default judgment for the plaintiff as to liability. Relator timely filed a Motion for Rehearing with a request for a hearing. Prior to the hearing, relator filed his petition for mandamus requesting that the respondent be directed to reinstate relator's pleadings, set aside the default judgment, and set the matter for trial on the issue of liability. This court stayed the scheduled hearing on the damages.

* * *

Relator argues that mandamus should issue because respondent's order constituted a gross abuse of discretion and is void. Relator contends that the unsigned settlement agreement was unenforceable and relator had an absolute right to revoke his consent to it under Tex. R.Civ.P. 11 since that rule, entitled Agreements to be in Writing, states:

> Unless otherwise provided in these rules, no agreement between attorneys or parties touching any suit pending will be enforced *unless it be in writing, signed and filed with the papers as part of the record* or unless it be made in open court and entered of record.

In *Kennedy v. Hyde*, 682 S.W.2d 525 (Tex.1984), the Texas Supreme Court held that Rule 11 is a *minimum* requirement for enforcement of all agreements concerning pending suits, including, but not limited to, agreed judgments. As a general rule, compliance with Rule 11 is a prerequisite for any judgment enforcing an agreement on a pending suit.

* * *

Relator also claims that since there was no pending motion to strike the pleadings before the trial court, he had no notice and that constituted a deprivation of due process.

* * *

Relator further argues that respondent had no authority to impose discovery sanctions under Tex.R.Civ.P. 215 for what the respondent believed was a willful and deceptive violation of good faith during mediation. Relator contends that there was no lack of good faith, but even if there were, the order was beyond the court's power. Respondent granted sanctions under Tex.R.Civ.P. 215. It claims these sanctions are available under the court's inherent authority pursuant to Tex.Gov't Code Ann. § 21.001. Respondent's theory was that mediation is a discovery tool and violation of the trial court's order for referral of mediation is therefore subject to Rule 215.

Repudiation of an unsigned settlement agreement forged in mediation is not subject to discovery sanctions under Tex.R.Civ.P. 215. The options available to a party are either filing suit on the agreement asserting that it is a valid agreement or, continuing with the original suit.

Relator's reluctance or refusal to sign a binding agreement the same day it was drafted is not a breach of good faith in mediation. Oral representations in arbitration are non-binding and privileged. Furthermore, there is no legal precedence for extending the court's inherent power to imposition of Tex.R.Civ.P. 215 sanctions without a violation of discovery.

Respondent asserts that mandamus is improper because relator has an adequate remedy at law. His motion for rehearing has not yet been heard. There was no hearing set on relator's motion for rehearing. At most, respondent merely denied relator's request for an immediate hearing on his motion. This court is confident that had the motion been set for hearing properly with the requisite notice sent to all parties affected, respondent would have heard the motion. The default judgment on liability is an interlocutory judgment and the relator's motion for rehearing can still be heard by the respondent. Thus, an adequate remedy at law remains available to the relator.

The petition for writ of mandamus is denied.

* * *

COLLEEN BENNETT v. LLOYD BENNETT

Supreme Court of Maine, 1991.
587 A.2d 463.

GLASSMAN, JUSTICE.

Lloyd Bennett appeals from the judgment entered in the Superior Court ... granting a divorce....

Lloyd first contends that the provisions of 19 M.R.S.A. § 665 (Supp. 1990) required the trial court to grant his motion to compel Colleen to sign and submit to the court the alleged agreement of the parties. We disagree. Section 665 provides: [t]he court may, in any case under this subchapter, at any time refer the parties to mediation on any issues. Any agreement reached by the parties through mediation on any issues shall be reduced to writing, signed by the parties and presented to the court for approval as a court order. When agreement through mediation is not reached on any issue the court must determine that the parties made a good faith effort to mediate the issue before proceeding with a hearing.... The provisions in section 665 governing the requirements of an agreement reached through mediation explicitly assure the court of the parties' consent to and willingness to be bound by the terms of their agreement. Absent such a signed, written agreement being submitted to it, the court makes a determination of the issues presented by an action for divorce based on the evidence adduced by the parties at the time of the trial of that action.

* * *

His contention is that because Colleen did not sign the alleged mediated agreement between the parties, section 665 mandates that the court order Colleen to sign the document and submit it to the court for its approval. To read such a mandate into the language of section 665 would of necessity require the trial court to engage in the time-consuming process of exploring what transpired between the parties during the course of the mediation in order to determine if they had reached any agreement and, if so, the actual terms of that agreement. Clearly, this is contrary to and would undermine the basic policy of the mediation process that parties be encouraged to arrive at a settlement of disputed issues without the intervention of the court. Accordingly, the trial court properly denied Lloyd's motion requesting that the court order Colleen to sign and submit to the court for its approval the alleged agreement of the parties.

Some state statutes which address the enforceability of mediated agreements acknowledge the contractual nature of such agreements. Other statutes work to modify existing contract law.

JAMES R. COBEN & PETER N. THOMPSON, MINNESOTA'S PHANTOM MENACE: THE CIVIL MEDIATION ACT

Vol. LVI, Bench and Bar of Minnesota, 33 September 1999.

. . . Certainly the drafters of the Civil Mediation Act were concerned about the fairness of the mediation process.

* * *

To "protect" the parties in mediations, the Act creates a series of technical and formalistic rights reminiscent of earlier days in the development of classical contract doctrine when formality and technicality prevailed over parties' expectations and reasonableness. With such a clear link to the distant past, it seems particularly fitting that the Civil Mediation Act, just like this summer's hit movie, is the "prequel" to its own unique trilogy, *Haghighi v. Russian American Broadcasting.*

THE HAGHIGHI TRILOGY

The *Haghighi* trilogy begins innocently enough in 1995 as a breach of contract dispute between Ali Haghighi, an international distributor of foreign language radio programming and Russian–American Broadcasting Company (hereinafter RAB), which provides ethnic radio and cable programming in Minnesota and other areas. RAB denied the breach and counterclaimed for alleged overdue payments. In an attempt to find peace, the parties agreed to mediate the dispute, and signed a written mediation agreement aimed at complying with the Minnesota Civil Mediation Act. After a day of mediation on Valentine's day in 1996, the parties reached agreement. Both parties were represented by counsel who drafted a handwritten three-page settlement document incorporating the terms of the agreement. The attorneys initialed each of the terms and the principals signed each page. The agreement had a clause that stated that it was a "Full and Final Mutual Release of all Claims" but did not have a clause that specifically said it was a "binding agreement."

Haghighi subsequently moved for an order "declaring" that the settlement agreement was valid and the defendant was in breach. In opposing the enforcement action, RAB relied on the Civil Mediation Act, which provided:

> A mediated settlement agreement is not binding unless it contains a provision stating that it is binding and a provision stating substantially that the parties were advised in writing that (a) the mediator has no duty to protect their interests or provide them with information about their legal rights; (b) signing a mediated settlement agreement may adversely affect their legal rights; and (c) they should consult an attorney before signing a mediated settlement agreement if they are uncertain of their rights.[1]

---

1. Minn.Stat. § 572.31 et seq.

RAB's argument was a short and airtight syllogism. The statute provides that mediated settlement agreements are not binding unless there is a clause that says they are binding. This mediated settlement agreement did not say it was binding; therefore, it is not binding. Much like the Jedi Knight Wui–Gon Jinn, who early in *Episode I* wisely notes, "things are not as they seem," Federal District Court Judge Donald Alsop took a step back.

Before him stood sophisticated parties who signed a settlement agreement drafted by counsel that said it is a "Full and Final Mutual Release of All Claims." If the parties believed at the time they signed the agreement that it was a valid agreement, surely, Judge Alsop reasoned, the agreement is not unenforceable simply because it lacks a formalistic recitation that would be meaningless in this context. Judge Alsop concluded the Minnesota legislature would not have intended such a result that would create a "trap for both the unwary and the wary" participants in mediations in Minnesota.

Subsequently, after an evidentiary hearing, Judge Alsop determined that the parties intended the document to be enforceable, that the agreement was enforceable, and defendant was in breach. On appeal, the federal court of appeals certified the following question to the Minnesota Supreme Court:

> "Whether a handwritten document prepared by the parties' attorneys at the conclusion of a mediation session conducted pursuant to the ... Act and signed contemporaneously on each page by the respective parties attending the mediation session but which does not itself provide that the document is to be a binding agreement, is rendered unenforceable as a mediated settlement agreement by virtue of Minn. Stat. § 572.35, subd. 1?"[5]

The Minnesota Supreme Court answered the question in the affirmative. In its opinion, however, the court made it clear that its decision is based on the issue certified and therefore assumes that the mediation was conducted pursuant to the Civil Mediation Act.

The Court bought into RAB's syllogism applying a literal interpretation of the statute. According to the Court, this is a simple case, assuming the Act is applicable. The Court found no ambiguity in the statute. The legislature said that the settlement agreement had to include certain "magic words;" these words were lacking; therefore, the settlement was not binding. Chief Justice Blatz writing for the court noted that this result is not necessarily an absurd result. The legislature may have intended that a settlement document must have the "magic words" so that parties can feel free to sign anything without fear that what they sign (even if it says it is a Full and Final Mutual Release of All Claims) can be used against them.

Back at the Eighth Circuit, the saga continued. Haghighi's attack on the sufficiency of the "Agreement to Mediate" was rejected as already

5.   577 N.W. 2d 927 (Minn. 1998).

implicitly decided by the nature of the question certified to the Supreme Court. The court also was not persuaded by Haghighi's argument that the Act was inapplicable because settlement was reached after conclusion of the mediation. And, with a foreshadowing of future conflict that even George Lucas would appreciate, the court declined to decide several additional arguments, specifically: 1) that the agreement's recital that it is a "Full and Final Mutual Release of All Claims" complies with the statutory requirement that the agreement state that it is binding; and 2) that in any event the court should reform the settlement agreement to conform to the intent of the parties. No doubt, the stage for Haghighi IV is set. Finally, the court rejected Haghighi's suggestion that RAB waived the Act's requirements because RAB failed to include binding language in later settlement proposals its counsel drafted. According to the appellate court, the trial judge's discussion of waiver was *dicta*, there was no direct evidence of waiver, and waiver would be counter to the public policy at the heart of the Act.

A Phantom Menace

Now, after some four years of litigation in three different courts with three published opinions and numerous hearings litigating the applicability of the Civil Mediation Act to a mediation that does not literally fit under the Act, the matter is back where it began, in front of the trial court. Perhaps this case with its multiple opinions could be cited as an example of the failure of the technical, slow and expensive litigation process, a further inducement to encouraging ADR processes as the preferred mechanism for dispute resolution. But the reality is that if the parties had not agreed to mediation and had engaged in private negotiation, this simple breach of contract case would have been settled or tried and appealed to conclusion years ago!

The case demonstrates the danger, the menace of including the worst of the litigation process—allowing formal technical rules unrelated to reasonable expectations—to take over the process of mediation. The mediation process, after all, was originally designed to avoid technical, formal rules in order that parties might act reasonably and reach reasonable accords. That menace—that phantom menace—is embodied in the Civil Mediation Act, an Act that was designed to encourage mediation in its goal of reducing costs and empowering parties to reach reasonable accords. While the litigation process is moving away from a highly technical and formal rights based approach to dispute resolution, the mediation process may well be going in the other direction.

* * *

Legislative Response

The Minnesota Legislature, in response to the Supreme Court's decision in *Haghighi*, recently amended the Act by adding a second clause to Minn. Stat. § 572.35, subd. 1: "or (2) the parties were otherwise advised of the conditions in clause (1)." Literally, the amendment renders mediated settlements binding if: 1) the written settlement agreement has a provision stating that it is binding (magic words); or 2) the *parties were advised that any agreement is not binding* if it lacks a clause saying it is binding. This amendment makes no sense. So if RAB were advised, which they were in their agreement to mediate, that mediated settlement agreements are not binding without a clause stating that they are binding, then the court would enforce the agreement without the clause in the settlement agreement itself.

Perhaps the legislature meant that the agreement without the magic words saying "it is binding" is enforceable if the parties were otherwise advised that the agreement was binding. According to the trial judge, the parties in *Haghighi* believed that the agreement was binding, but there is no evidence that anyone "advised" them that it was binding. Literally, to comply with the other conditions in the clause, if a mediated settlement agreement does not have a clause stating that the parties were advised in writing about the mediator's duties, the effect of signing, and right to consult counsel, the agreement can still be enforceable if the parties were advised (by someone) that they had been previously so-advised in writing.

Obviously, testimony about what the parties were advised may run into privilege problems. If a party is represented by counsel, private confidential legal advice may be privileged. If a party is advised by the adverse party, the communication may be privileged under the Mediation privilege. If the parties were advised by the mediator, then in addition to other privilege sources, the advice may be unavailable for evidentiary use because of the ADR neutral privilege/competency statute.

———

Minn. Stat. § 527.35 Subdivision 2. Debtor and creditor mediation.

In addition to the requirements of subdivision 1, a mediated settlement agreement between a debtor and creditor is not binding until 72 hours after it is signed by the debtor and creditor, during which time either party may withdraw consent to the binding character of the agreement.

———

Questions may also arise with regard to the ability or duty of a court to review or revise a mediated agreement.

Va. St. § 8.01–576.12 Vacating orders and agreements.

Upon the filing of an independent action by a party, the court shall vacate a mediated agreement reached in a dispute resolution proceeding pursuant to this chapter, or vacate an order incorporating or resulting from such agreement, where:

1.   The agreement was procured by fraud or duress, or is unconscionable;

2.   If property or financial matters are in dispute, the parties failed to provide substantial full disclosure of all relevant property and financial information; or

3.   There was evident partiality or misconduct by the neutral, prejudicing the rights of any party.

For purposes of this section, "misconduct" includes failure of the neutral to inform the parties in writing at the commencement of the mediation process that: (i) the neutral does not provide legal advice, (ii) any mediated agreement will affect the legal rights of the parties, (iii) each party to the mediation has the opportunity to consult with independent legal counsel at any time and is encouraged to do so, and (iv) each party to the mediation should have any draft agreement reviewed by independent cousel prior to signing the agreement or should waive his opportunity to do so.

The fact that any provisions of a mediated agreement were such that they could not or would not be granted by a court of law or equity is not, in and of itself, grounds for vacating an agreement.

The motion to vacate under this section shall be made within two years after the mediated agreement is entered into, except that, if predicated upon fraud, it shall be made within two years after these grounds are discovered or reasonably should have been discovered.

Minn. Stat. § 572.36   Setting aside or reforming a mediated settlement agreement

In any action, a court of competent jurisdiction shall set aside or reform a mediated settlement agreement if appropriate under the principles of law applicable to contracts, or if there was evident partiality, corruption, or misconduct by a mediator prejudicing the rights of a party. That the relief could not or would not be granted by a court of law or equity is not ground for setting aside or reforming the mediated settlement agreement unless it violates public policy.

IN THE MATTER OF THE MARRIAGE OF AMES
Court of Appeals of Texas, Amarillo, 1993.
860 S.W.2d 590.

* * *

In the first of four points of error, Raymond contends that the trial court erred in entering its decree of divorce on the basis of the settlement agreement because he had repudiated the agreement. We disagree. In its order of mediation, the trial court stated that "[t]his case is appropriate for mediation pursuant to Tex.Civ.Prac. & Rem.Code §§ 154.001 *et seq.*" Chapter 154 of the Texas Civil Practice and Remedies Code is entitled "Alternative Dispute Resolution Procedures." Section 154.071(a) states:

If the parties reach a settlement and execute a written agreement disposing of the dispute, the agreement is enforceable in the same manner as any other written contract.

Tex.Civ.Prac. & Rem.Code Ann. § 154.071(a) (Vernon Supp. 1993). We interpret this statute to mean, *inter alia*, that a party who has reached a settlement agreement disposing of a dispute through alternative dispute resolution procedures may not unilaterally repudiate the agreement.

* * *

If voluntary agreements reached through mediation were non-binding, many positive efforts to amicably settle differences would be for naught. If parties were free to repudiate their agreements, disputes would not be finally resolved and traditional litigation would recur. In order to effect the purposes of mediation and other alternative dispute resolution mechanisms, settlement agreements must be treated with the same dignity and respect accorded other contracts reached after arm's length negotiations. Again, no party to a dispute can be forced to settle the conflict outside of court; but if a voluntary agreement that disposes of the dispute is reached, the parties should be required to honor the agreement.[1]

Raymond argues strenuously, however, that section 154.071(a) does not apply in this case. Raymond maintains that section 154.071(a) conflicts with Tex.Fam.Code Ann. § 3.631(a) (Vernon 1993), and that the Family Code provision is controlling.

* * *

Even though section 3.631(a) is the more specific statute in this case, the Family code provision expressly states that an agreement may be repudiated prior to rendition of the divorce *"unless it is binding under some other rule of law."* Pursuant to section 154.071(a) of the Practice and Remedies Code, the settlement agreement is binding. Raymond could not unilaterally repudiate the agreement.

* * *

In his third point of error, Raymond, in the alternative, argues that if the agreement was not repudiated, the trial court erred in dividing the community property because the court's division differed significantly from the settlement agreement.

We agree with Raymond that there are several provisions of the divorce decree that are not found in the settlement agreement.

* * *

1. We are aware of the cases in which it has been held that a valid consent judgment cannot be rendered unless consent exists at the time the court undertakes to make the agreement the judgment of the court. *Vineyard v. Wilson,* 597 S.W.2d 21, 23 (Tex.Civ. App.—Dallas 1980, no writ); *Burnaman v.* *Heaton,* 150 Tex. 333, 338–39, 240 S.W.2d 288, 291 (1951). These cases are inapplicable to agreements reached pursuant to alternative dispute resolution procedures described in chapter 154 of the Texas Civil Practice and Remedies Code.

In her motion for rehearing, Nancy Jo Ames, appellee, concedes that the trial court's division of community property contains terms and provisions that are not found in the settlement agreement. Nancy now agrees with our conclusion that the court's judgment should have embodied the exact terms of the settlement agreement, said agreement being the only evidence before the court.

* * *

Rather, we are confronted with a decree of divorce that contains terms and provisions that were never agreed to by the parties. A trial court has no power to supply such terms and conditions. *Matthews v. Looney,* 132 Tex. 313, 317, 123 S.W.2d 871, 872 (1939). A final judgment founded upon a settlement agreement must be in strict compliance with the agreement. *Vickrey v. American Youth Camps, Inc.,* 532 S.W.2d 292, 292 (Tex.1976).

Therefore, the motion for rehearing is overruled.

PATEL v. ASHCO ENTERPRISES, INC.

District Court of Appeal of Florida, Fifth Dist., 1998.
711 So.2d 239.

ANTOON, JUDGE.

Viren A. Patel (Patel) appeals the final judgment and permanent injunction (final judgment) entered in favor of Ashco Enterprises, Inc., d/b/a Metro Services of Central Florida (Metro) in accordance with the terms of the parties' mediation agreement. Patel contends the mediation agreement was void and thus unenforceable because the parties entered into the agreement while the case was pending in county court which lacked jurisdiction over this matter. See § 542.30, Fla. Stat. (1995). However, the parties' mediation agreement was valid and enforceable. Therefore, we affirm the final judgment.

Metro filed a complaint in county court alleging that it was entitled to recover damages from Patel and Gary Keys for their breach of a noncompete employment agreement. While the case was pending in county court, the parties entered into a mediation agreement which provided that Patel would pay Metro $35,000 in monthly installments. The mediation agreement further provided that if Patel breached the agreement, the case would be transferred to the circuit court and a judgment would be entered against Patel for $100,000, plus $5,000 in attorneys' fees and costs. Additionally, the parties agreed that, upon default, a two-year injunction would be entered against Patel. When Patel failed to make the first installment, the case was transferred to the circuit court. The circuit court then enforced the parties' mediation agreement by entering a final judgment for $105,000, as well as an injunction against Patel.

Patel argues that the parties' mediation agreement was void ab initio, and thus the trial court erred in enforcing it, because the agreement was the result of a mediation which occurred while Metro's lawsuit was pending in county court. Specifically, Patel maintains the parties' mediation agreement was unenforceable because the county court lacked subject matter jurisdiction over Metro's noncompete claim pursuant to section 542.30, Florida Statutes (1995), which provides that Florida's circuit courts possess exclusive jurisdiction to enforce such agreements. We disagree.

While a settlement agreement may be the basis upon which a judgment may be entered, it is also a contract between the parties, the enforceability of which is governed by the laws of contract. This principle applies even when the court enforcing the settlement agreement lacks subject matter jurisdiction over the earlier action from which the agreement emanated. Id. Accordingly, the trial court properly enforced the mediation agreement entered by the parties' in the instant case even though it was executed while the litigation was pending in county court and the county court's jurisdiction to consider Metro's noncompete claim was subject to challenge.

AFFIRMED.

SILKEY v. INVESTORS DIVERSIFIED SERVICES, INC.

Court of Appeals of Indiana, 1997.
690 N.E.2d 329.

RILEY, JUDGE.

STATEMENT OF THE CASE

Appellants, Herschel J. Silkey and Wanda Louise Silkey (Silkeys), appeal from an order granting Appellees', Investors Diversified Services, Inc. and Mark Powers (Powers) (collectively referred to as the Brokers), amended Motion to Enforce Mediation Agreement and Request for Sanctions.

We affirm.

ISSUES

The Silkeys present two issues for our review which we restate as:

I. Whether the trial court erred in determining that an oral agreement reached during a mediation session was a final and binding agreement?

II. Whether the trial court erred in determining that the verbal agreement reached during a mediation session complied with the Indiana Statute of Frauds, Ind.Code § 32–2–1–1.

FACTS AND PROCEDURAL HISTORY

In early 1983, the Silkeys received a capital gain of $650,000 from the sale of their farm land to a coal company. They sought investment assistance from Powers, who was a registered representative of IDS and possessed all the necessary securities licenses to qualify for that position.

IDS is a securities dealer and brokerage firm with its principal offices located in Minneapolis, Minnesota, with an office located and doing business in Evansville, Indiana, and at other locations throughout the State of Indiana.

As a result of meetings and discussions, Powers recommended and the Silkeys purchased several investments, including a $100,000 investment in JMB Carlyle Real Estate Limited Partnership XII. This investment's performance did not meet the Silkeys' expectations, and on June 29, 1994, the Silkeys filed a complaint against IDS and Powers alleging misrepresentation, violations of the Indiana Securities Act, breach of fiduciary duty, and constructive fraud.

On August 16, 1995, the trial court ordered the parties to mediation. Mediation was held in Evansville, Indiana on January 17, 1996, five days before the scheduled trial date, with a mutually agreed-upon mediator. The mediator concluded the mediation with an oral recitation of the terms of the agreement and received verbal assent from all of the parties to the terms. This exchange was recorded on an audio tape. The tape was later transcribed by the mediator, and copies were sent to all parties. On January 18, 1996, the mediator filed with the trial court a Mediation Report which confirmed that a settlement had been reached, and the trial was removed from the court's calendar. On January 22, 1996, a typed transcription was sent to all parties by the mediator. On February 19, 1996, the Brokers forwarded to the Silkeys a Settlement Agreement and Mutual General Release (Agreement) which was prepared by counsel for the Brokers and signed by IDS and Powers. After receiving the Agreement, the Silkeys refused to sign it, and the Silkeys' counsel informed the Brokers of the repudiation. Subsequently, the Silkeys' counsel withdrew their representation, and the Silkeys obtained new counsel.

The Brokers filed a Motion to Enforce Agreement for Settlement on August 23, 1996. The trial court found that this was not a case where the parties were disputing whether the document accurately reflected the agreement, but rather the Silkeys were attempting to repudiate the agreement. The trial court concluded that an enforceable agreement was reached by the parties. The trial court ruled that the audio tape recording was a legally binding form of the agreement which set forth with reasonable certainty the terms and conditions and the parties' agreement to these terms and conditions. The trial court then directed that the terms of the audio tape recording be reduced to writing and that, when the writing fairly and accurately reflected the terms of the agreement, the parties would sign and file the agreement with the court. (R. 366).

DISCUSSION AND DECISION

I. Effect of the Oral Agreement

The central question in this case is what effect, if any, should be given to the oral agreement reached by the parties at the conclusion of the mediation. The Silkeys argue that the Rules of Alternative Dispute

Resolution control the disposition of this question. The rules provide that:

> (2) If an agreement is reached, it shall be reduced to writing and signed. The agreement shall then be filed with the court. If the agreement is complete on all issues, it shall be accompanied by a joint stipulation of disposition.

> (3) After the agreement becomes an order of the court by joint stipulation, in the event of any breach or failure to perform under the agreement, the court, upon motion, may impose sanctions, including costs, interest, attorney fees, or other appropriate remedies including entry of judgment on the agreement.

A.D.R. 2.7(E) (1996).

The Silkeys acknowledge that an agreement was reached and that it was reduced to writing. Appellant's Brief at 20. They also acknowledge that they have rescinded their verbal assent to the terms of the agreement. *Id.* They argue that because this agreement was neither signed by them nor filed with the court, there was no contract or breach; therefore, they argue neither enforcement nor sanction is appropriate. *Id.* We disagree.

The Silkeys present their appeal as one of statutory interpretation; therefore, we begin with consideration of the A.D.R. rules. The Indiana Supreme Court has noted in the preamble to the A.D.R. rules that the rules were "adopted in order to bring some uniformity into alternative dispute resolution with the view that the interests of the parties can be preserved" in non-traditional settings. A.D.R. Preamble. Mediation is a process to "assist [ ] the litigants in reaching a mutually acceptable agreement." A.D.R. 2.1. Although a court may order parties to participate in mediation and require that participation be in good faith, it cannot order them to reach agreement. *Id.* The ultimate goal of mediation is to provide a forum in which parties might reach a mutually agreed resolution to their differences. The A.D.R. rules provide a uniform process for negotiation, but they do not change the law regarding settlement agreements or their enforcement. Nothing in the text of the A.D.R. rules for mediation suggests the Indiana Supreme Court intended to change the trial court's role in enforcing settlement agreements. Thus, although the process of the mediation is controlled by the A.D.R. rules, the enforcement of any valid agreement is within the authority of the trial court under the existing law in Indiana.

"The judicial policy of Indiana strongly favors settlement agreements." Germania v. Thermasol, Ltd., 569 N.E.2d 730, 732 (Ind.Ct.App. 1991). Courts retain the inherent power to enforce agreements entered into in settlement of litigation which is pending before them. *Id.* Settlement is always referable to the action in the court, and the carrying out of the agreement should be controlled by that court.

The Silkeys argue that they were never compelled to agree and so should not be held to an agreement about which they have changed their minds.... Such a rule would clearly create a disincentive for settlement. Additionally, it would allow mediation to serve not as an aid to litigation, but as a separate and additional impetus for litigation. Neither the A.D.R. rules nor the law support such an interpretation.

The Silkeys are correct that a party has full authority over whether to settle his case or proceed to trial. Having decided to accept a settlement, however, the party is bound to that decision. "In the absence of fraud or mistake a settlement is as binding and conclusive of the parties' rights and obligations as a judgment on the merits." The Silkeys do not allege fraud or mistake in reaching this settlement agreement; in fact, they do not question the terms of the agreement at all.[4] Instead, they assert that they "no longer agree" to the terms of the settlement. Appellant's Brief at 21. This is not a sufficient ground to rescind a contract.

The Silkeys argue that the agreement was not final or binding because it is oral. A settlement agreement is not required to be in writing. Klebes, 607 N.E.2d at 982 (following Indiana Farmers Mut. Ins. Co. v. Walters, 221 Ind. 642, 50 N.E.2d 868 (1943)).

The trial court found that the terms of the agreement were not in dispute. In reaching this decision, it relied on the parties' affidavits, pleadings, and memoranda of law. At the hearing on the matter, the trial court admitted the tape recording of the recitation of agreement over the Silkeys' objection. It does not appear from the trial court's written findings that it relied on the tape recording of the agreement in reaching its decision, nor was it required to do so because neither the content nor the authenticity of the tape was in question. In fact, as noted, the Silkeys raise the issue that the agreement reached in the mediation was preliminary for the first time on appeal. Appellant's Brief at 22. Having failed to raise this issue before the trial court, it is waived. Franklin Bank and Trust Co., 563 N.E.2d at 553.

The evidence before the trial court clearly supports its finding that the parties entered an agreement at the close of the mediation session. The trial court had available to it a tape and a transcript which clearly indicated the parties had agreed in substance to the terms of the mediation. The Silkeys did not argue to the trial court that there were any changes or defects in the terms as they were reduced to writing by the Brokers. "If a party agrees to settle a pending action, but then refuses to consummate his settlement agreement, the opposing party may obtain a judgment enforcing the agreement." Having found that a settlement agreement had been reached, the trial court acted within its authority under the A.D.R. rules and the case law in Indiana in directing

---

4. In their brief, the Silkeys first assert that they agreed and then rescinded the agreement. Appellant's Brief at 19. Later in the brief, they argue that the terms did not constitute the entire agreement between the parties. Appellant's Brief at 22. Finally, in their reply brief, the Silkeys argue that "any agreement reached at or during the mediation session was preliminary, and, in any event, not complete on all issues." Appellants' Reply Brief at 22. Because they raise the question of the incompleteness of the terms for the first time on appeal, they are waived.

the parties to reduce their agreement to writing and sign and file it with the court.

The second issue raised by the Silkeys is that the verbal agreement is not in compliance with the Statute of Frauds and is, thus, unenforceable. They make three arguments on this issue: first, that the terms did not constitute the entire agreement; second, that the audio tape is insufficient to meet the requirements of a writing in order to take the agreement outside the Statute of Frauds; and third, that the agreement cannot be performed within one year of its making. Appellant's Brief at 21–22.

* * *

Thus, the agreement falls outside the Statute of Frauds. Because the Statute of Frauds is not applicable to this settlement agreement due to the fact that it could be completed within one year, we need not address whether it meets the other requirements of the Statute of Frauds.

The trial court acted within its authority to enforce a settlement agreement in a case pending before it where the parties clearly agreed to the terms, but later attempted to rescind their assent. The oral settlement agreement is enforceable, and the parties may be ordered to reduce their agreement to writing and file it with the court. Additionally, because the oral agreement may be performed within one year and there is no express stipulation between the parties that it will not be performed, it is outside the Statute of Frauds.

ALLEN v. LEAL

United States District Court, S.D. Texas, Houston Division, 1998.
27 F.Supp.2d 945.

HITTNER, DISTRICT JUDGE.

Pending before the Court are the Motion for Summary Judgment filed by the plaintiffs Noel and Rebecca Allen ("the Allens") and the Motion for Summary Judgment filed by the defendants Michael Leal, Carle Upshaw, and the City of Bellaire, Texas. Having considered the motions, submissions, and applicable law, the Court declines to exercise supplemental jurisdiction over the defendants' breach of contract counterclaim. Thus, the Court will not decide the motion for summary judgment. Instead, the Court determines that the defendants' counterclaim should be dismissed without prejudice to permit a state court determination of the counterclaim.

INTRODUCTION

This lawsuit arises out of the shooting death of Travis Allen ("Travis"). In the early morning of July 15, 1995, the Bellaire Police Department received a 911 call about a possible intruder at 4407 Acacia, Bellaire, Texas. When three police officers arrived at 4407 Acacia, they discovered Travis within the residence. Travis was lying on the ground, bleeding profusely. At that time, one of the officers, Daniel Shelor, departed, leaving only Leal and Upshaw. Travis subsequently was shot in the back by Leal and died from this injury.

This lawsuit was filed by Travis' parents individually and on behalf of Travis' estate and was originally brought in state court and later removed to this Court. The Allens bring the suit pursuant to 42 U.S.C. § 1983, alleging an intentional deprivation of Travis' constitutional rights.

* * *

THE MEDIATION PROCESS

Prior to the case proceeding as scheduled for a jury trial, the parties voluntarily attended mediation with M.A. "Mickey" Mills acting as the agreed mediator selected by the parties. The mediation took place on July 25, 1998. After a full day of mediating the case, the parties signed an agreement to settle all claims for the amount of $90,000.00. The Allens, who were represented by Graydon Wilson of the firm of Richard "Racehorse" Haynes & Associates, signed the agreement at the mediation. The Bellaire City Attorney represented the City at the mediation. The attorneys for the individual defendants were also present at the mediation.

According to the terms of the agreement, the settlement of the claims was:

> subject to the approval of the City of Bellaire City Council, at a meeting of 8/3/98, and within 20 days after plaintiffs have filed a stipulation of dismissal under Rule 41, F.R.C.P. the City of Bellaire agrees to pay Noel C. Allen, Rebecca Allen and the estate of Travis Allen the sum of $90,000.00 on or before 8/30/98.

See Settlement Agreement of July 25, 1998 at p 1.

Elsewhere, the agreement states: "Each signatory hereto warrants and represents that he or she has authority to bind the parties for whom that signatory acts, except that the parties agree that the City of Bellaire is not bound until such time as it has approved this agreement by a majority vote of its city council." Settlement Agreement at p 5.

On July 27, 1998 counsel for the Allens contacted counsel for the City of Bellaire and informed him that the Allens wanted to set aside the settlement agreement. Subsequently, the City of Bellaire City Council voted in favor of the settlement agreement on August 3, 1998.

On August 5, 1998 the Court conducted a hearing to determine the status of the case. At the hearing, Rebecca Allen informed the Court that she and her husband did not wish to be bound by the terms of the settlement agreement but rather, desired to proceed to trial. Mrs. Allen stated that she had concerns regarding the manner in which the mediation was conducted. Specifically, she stated that the mediator had "forced" her and her husband into settling the case and also misled them. The Court, therefore, released all parties from the confidentiality requirements of Rule 20I of the Local Rules for the Southern District of

Texas in order for her to discuss her concerns with the Court[1] and in order for the Court to evaluate the validity of the settlement agreement. Mrs. Allen testified that although her attorney, Mr. Wilson, was present during the entire mediation process, she felt "coerced" and "intimidated" by the mediator into signing the settlement agreement. She further informed the Court that the mediator stated that she and her husband would be responsible for paying all attorney's fees and costs if she did not agree to settle and that they would be "financially ruined." Apparently Mr. Wilson failed to advise the Allens of the pertinent federal statute and case law governing the award of attorney's fees and costs in federal civil rights cases in order for them to make a fully informed decision concerning settlement.

The mediator, Mr. Mills, was not present at the August 5, 1998 Court hearing. However, given that his name and reputation were publicly excoriated by the plaintiffs and plaintiffs' counsel, the Court determined that, in fairness to Mr. Mills, he should be given an opportunity to defend his professional reputation and integrity as a mediator. As such, the Court relieved Mr. Mills from his duty of confidentiality.[4] Mr. Mills appeared at a status conference conducted on August 7, 1998 at which time he was provided an opportunity to present his side of the matter. Mr. Mills stated that the mediation process was entirely proper and that he did not engage in coercive conduct.

After the above mentioned hearings, the Association of Attorney–Mediators ("AAM") filed a motion to appear as amicus curiae to present the AAM's position on the confidentiality of the mediation process and the enforceability of settlement agreements generally. The Court granted the AAM's request to appear as amicus curiae in this case and the AAM has filed an Amicus Curiae Brief. In its brief, the AAM argues that its "primary concern is the integrity of the mediation process; AAM is not taking a position with respect to the final outcome of this particular case." See Amicus Curiae Brief of Association of Attorney–Mediators at 3, filed September 24, 1998.

Notwithstanding the AAM's position concerning the "integrity of the mediation process," one of the authors of the amicus curiae brief, who is the president of the Houston chapter of the AAM, John Lee Arellano, was publicly quoted as saying in reference to this case: "[w]hat some people might consider a little bullying is really just part of how mediation works." See Charlotte Aguilar, No Decision in Allen Case, 14 Southwest News 1, 22 (October 6, 1998). This egregious statement, directed to the public, made by the president of the AAM, outside of the courtroom and in a local newspaper, is especially deplorable given that,

---

1. Local Rule 20I provides: "All communications made during ADR procedures are confidential and protected from disclosure and do not constitute a waiver of any existing privileges and immunities."

4. The Court fully recognizes the importance and gravity of the rules of confidentiality governing mediation. However, because the plaintiffs, in this particular situation, actually "opened the door" by attacking the professionalism and integrity of the mediator and the mediation process, the Court was compelled, in the interests of justice, to breach the veil of confidentiality.

pursuant to the standards governing the conduct of mediators in Texas, "[a] person appointed to facilitate an alternative dispute resolution procedure under this subchapter shall encourage and assist the parties in reaching a settlement of their dispute but may not compel or coerce the parties to enter into a settlement agreement." Tex.Civ.Prac. & Rem.Code § 154.053(a) (Vernon 1997).

Coercion or "bullying" clearly is not acceptable conduct for a mediator in order to secure a settlement, notwithstanding the statement of the president of the AAM.[5]

Breach of Contract Counterclaim

After the Allens informed the Court and the defendants that they would not file a stipulation of dismissal per the settlement agreement, the defendants sought leave of Court to amend their pleadings to add a counterclaim against the plaintiffs for breach of the settlement agreement. This request was granted. In the counterclaim, defendants argue that pursuant to Texas law, mediated settlement agreements constitute enforceable contracts.

According to the defendants, the Allens' attempt to withdraw from the agreement, which constitutes a binding, enforceable contract, constitutes a breach. See In the Matter of Marriage of Banks, 887 S.W.2d 160, 163–64 (Tex.App.—Texarkana 1994, no writ) A party who has reached a settlement agreement disposing of a dispute through alternative dispute resolution procedures many not unilaterally repudiate the agreement. If voluntary agreements reached through mediation were non-binding, many positive efforts to amicably settle differences would be for naught. In order to effect the purposes of mediation, and other dispute resolution mechanisms, settlement agreements must be treated like other contracts, reached after arms length negotiations.... No party to a dispute can be forced to settle the conflict outside of Court; but if a voluntary agreement that disposes of the dispute is reached, the parties should be required to honor the agreement.

The Allens, on the other hand, contend that the settlement agreement is not an enforceable contract for three reasons: (1) the agreement is indefinite; (2) the plaintiffs withdrew from the agreement prior to any contract having been formed; and (3) the agreement exists as a benefit for a third party (Grace Allen, Travis' minor sister), and the plaintiffs withdrew from the agreement prior to Grace's acceptance of the agreement.[6]

5. It is the Court's belief that the overwhelming majority of the mediators in Texas, as well as the nation, do not subscribe to the proposition that "bullying is really just a part of how mediation works."

6. The Court notes that Grace Allen, a minor, is not, nor has she ever been a party to this lawsuit. Further, the discussion of Grace Allen, as the intended third-party beneficiary of any recovery from this lawsuit, was brought to the Court's attention for the first time only after the plaintiffs attempted to withdraw from the settlement agreement.

For the reasons that will be more fully discussed *infra*, the Court will not reach the enforceability of the settlement agreement or whether fact issues exist which preclude a summary judgment determination.

* * *

In this case, the defendants' breach of contract claim and the Allens' claim under § 1983, concerning their son's death, are completely separate causes of action. The breach of contract claim arose well after the plaintiffs filed their suit against the defendants in 1996, and three years after the tragic shooting of Travis. The fact patterns for each cause of action are clearly distinct and separable. Specifically, each cause of action may be decided without any reference to the facts of the other cause of action. Therefore, as a matter of law and for the additional reasons stated *infra* the Court declines to exercise supplemental jurisdiction over the state law claim of breach of the mediation agreement. Accordingly, the Court determines that the breach of contract counterclaim should be determined by a state court.

The Court is gravely concerned with the plaintiffs' frontal attack on the mediation process itself. The mediation process has been responsible for the resolution of countless cases in this district, thereby avoiding the necessity for expensive adversary proceedings, including jury and nonjury trials. A significant amount of time and energy has been expended by the Court and the parties in this case as a result of the plaintiffs' actions. The conduct of the plaintiffs and their attorneys in attempting to upset a settlement of this case appears to constitute an abuse, even if unintentional, of the federal trial process. Considering the enormity of the loss of a child, the Court is perplexed that the Allens would have agreed to settle this case (even assuming arguendo that the mediator exerted pressure on the plaintiffs to settle the case) without being certain that such a settlement was appropriate. The Court is even more concerned that counsel for the Allens failed to advise his clients of the seriousness and finality of signing a settlement agreement if they had any reservations whatsoever. Moreover, the Court has not been advised of any actions taken by counsel for the Allens to protect them against any untoward pressure allegedly exerted by the mediator or the defendants. The Court therefore determines that it would be a further waste of federal judicial resources to proceed with the plaintiffs' 42 U.S.C. § 1983 claims before the defendants' breach of contract counterclaim has been decided by a state court.

Accordingly, the § 1983 matter will be administratively closed pending a final determination of the state law claim, i.e., the breach of contract claim, by a Texas court of appropriate jurisdiction.[7]

Therefore, based on the foregoing, the Court hereby ORDERS that the defendants' breach of contract counterclaim is DISMISSED WITHOUT PREJUDICE. The plaintiffs' 42 U.S.C. § 1983 cause of action is

---

7. In the Court's opinion, the delay of the resolution of this case in federal court is the sole cause and responsibility of the plaintiffs and the plaintiffs' counsel.

STAYED pending a final resolution of the breach of contract cause of action in a state court and this matter is ADMINISTRATIVELY CLOSED pending a state court judgment.

———

It should be noted that on February 22, 1999, a Texas state district court did grant a partial summary judgment in favor of the Leals and City of Bellaire enforcing the mediated agreement as a "contract pursuant to Texas law."[47] *It appears that affidavits were filed with the court as summary judgment evidence. The court's order was minimal, stating only that the contract was enforceable, and failed to grant further requests such as dismissal of the underlying suit and attorneys' fees or costs.*

———

And beyond the view of enforcement of mediation agreements as contracts, there has been some limited consideration of elevating a mediation agreement to "super-contract" status.[42] By this term it is meant that a court, without additional pleadings or evidence, would summarily enforce the mediation agreement, much like an arbitration award.[43]

* * *

QUESTIONS FOR DISCUSSION

12–1. Should there be a change in the Rules of Civil Procedure to provide for enforcement of mediated agreements, as distinguished from settlement agreements in the course of litigation? Does the mediation process offer additional safeguards to negotiation which should be taken into consideration when confronted with enforcement issues?

12–2. Are there occasions where sanctions should be imposed upon a party for reneging on a mediated agreement prior to its finalization by the court?

12–3. Should mediated agreements include a liquidated damages clause?

12–4. In the Allen v. Leal case referenced earlier, the state court action was concluded with the court ordering a partial summary judgment in favor of enforcement of the contract. Despite the multiple affidavits and court testimony alleging coercion in the agreement, the agreement was enforced. Was this a just result?

12–5. What should be the role of the referring court in reviewing a mediated agreement? See, for example, Kasper v. Board of Election

---

47. Signed order of court on file with author. According to one of the attorneys, as of December 1999, the case has been finally resolved.

42. See dissent in Cadle Company v. Castle, 913 S.W.2d 627 (Tex.App.–Dallas, 1995 writ denied).

43. *Id.* at 638–39.

Commissioners, 814 F.2d 332 (7th Cir.1987), where a trial court's refusal to enter a consent decree was affirmed.

12–5. A mediation has been underway in Columbus, Ohio for six hours. The dispute involves a suit by Woodrow and Sandra Bucki against Bea Fast, their architect, for alleged design defects in their home. The Buckis' primary allegation surrounds the pool area in the rear of their home. The pool was to be an exact replica of Ohio Stadium. Not only does it not look like Ohio Stadium, but, even worse, it resembles the stadium in Ann Arbor, Michigan. Fast, who, received a master's degree from the University of Michigan, disputes the claim and suggested in his deposition, that the Buckis might have spent too many hours at the V.C. watching re-runs of games.

Before the mediation, the Buckis' demand was $450,000.00 in actual damages for fixing and changing the design of their pool and an additional $2,000,000.00 in punitive damages for Fast's reckless conduct.

By the fifth hour of mediation, the Buckis were willing to accept $90,000.00 to fix the pool and a public apology by Fast at the 1995 Michigan–Ohio State football game in Columbus.

Fast, at mediation, agreed to the public apology. However, the insurance representative possessed only $25,000.00 in settlement authority. He requested three days to run trips to see if $90,000.00 could be raised. Fast's counsel, Will V. Reen has advised the mediator, in a separate caucus, that he would like three days to see if his client would respond favorably to the final proposal.

The Buckis were represented by Bruce Hayes. Hayes is outraged by his clients' willingness to even consider accepting $90,000.00 especially since the case is to be tried by a jury in Columbus. Nonetheless, Hayes tells the mediator that the three days are agreed to by the Buckis against his advice.

The mediator rejoins the parties in a joint session and confirms that Fast's counsel has three days to respond to the proposal; however, no written agreement is made. The mediation ends at 5:00 p.m. on Thursday.

On the following Tuesday, Fast's carrier agrees to pay the $90,000.00. Such "agreement" is communicated by Reen to Hayes at about 1:00 p.m. that day. Hayes responds that no agreement has been reached because the offer was not make "in three days." Reen contends three days meant three *business* days and files a motion with the court to enforce the verbal agreement. Reen further subpoenaed the mediator Newt Badger, to attend the hearing. Reen has also suggested that Badger's failure to reduce the "non-agreement" to writing may be mediator negligence.

(a) As Reen, what are your arguments for enforcement of the agreement. What are your other alternatives?

(b) As Hayes, what is your position?

(c) As Badger, do you attend the hearing? What does your testimony consist of?

(d) As the referring court, Judge Bruin, make your ruling on the issue of enforceability of the agreement.

Chapter Thirteen

CLOSURE AND FOLLOW–UP

Once the mediation is over, there may be a tendency on the part of the mediator, the parties, or the attorneys to rush out the door. However, formal closure to the mediation is important. In fact, it is suggested that in addition to the agreement, a formal or symbolic activity that signifies the termination of the conflict should occur.[1] Interestingly, lower animals have devised regular communication patterns that symbolize the end of a conflict, whereas human beings have not.[2] While most parties will assume, based on the written agreement, that the conflict has ended, it is appropriate that an additional symbol of conflict termination take place.

In business and legal disputes, handshaking combined with exchanging the executed agreement are the most common rituals. In other cultures, a meal is often held to signify the end of a dispute. Concluding the mediation with a champagne toast might be appropriate in some cases, although the mediator should use her discretion. In a large neighborhood dispute over deed restrictions, for instance, a backyard barbecue or block party has been an effective ending. These types of procedures, which can also indicate a peaceful resolution, enhance the likelihood of compliance with the agreement. Closure is particularly important in those cases where there has been a reconciliation between the parties.

Even if the closure activities are not this elaborate, and in most instances they are not, the mediator must be certain that the parties have achieved formal closure. In fact, complaints have been lodged against mediators who have not permitted time for the parties to complete closing remarks. Therefore, the mediator must see closure as a specific stage in the process, one not to be ignored. Closure can take very different forms, however, depending on the relationship of the parties, context of the dispute, and whether an agreement has been reached.

1. Christopher W. Moore, The Mediation Process: Practical Strategies for Resolving Conflict 316 (2d Ed. 1996).

2. *Id.* at 260.

In court-annexed mediation, many lawyers underestimate their clients' need for closure and may be unaware that such need even exists. Such lack of understanding may be a direct result of a lawyer's view that a settlement terminates a litigated case. However, emotional needs of the client may be important. Therefore the mediator must be vigilant that the parties may have real closure needs that their attorneys may be completely unaware of. The mediator should directly inquire about the clients' needs for closure and implement a process which meets the parties' needs. An illustration may help emphasize the importance of providing for closure.

A woman in her mid-fifties ran a red light and collided with another vehicle, killing the seventy-five year old driver in the other car. The woman, who had been a safe driver with a perfect driving record, was momentarily inattentive and made a mistake which caused a terrible result. At the time of mediation, two years after the collision, the woman remained terrified of driving, had not been behind the wheel since the collision, and was in therapy.

The adult children of the seventy-five year old deceased, the plaintiffs in the lawsuit, were still grieving the loss of their father and, despite countless depositions, could not understand how the collision could have happened. The mediation, during which the lawyers controlled the direct communications between the parties, produced a monetary settlement, but the resolution of a monetary exchange did not meet the closure needs of the parties.

In a private caucus, the daughter of the deceased expressed a real need to meet the woman. The daughter wanted to hear directly how the collision happened and also wanted to forgive a woman who she learned had been traumatized by the event. The woman, in private caucus, expressed the real need to meet with the family, apologize, and acknowledge their grief and loss.

The mediator asked the woman and the daughter to meet with him in another room. The woman explained to the daughter how she had re-reviewed the accident a thousand times in her mind and how, despite being a careful driver, her mind had drifted somewhere else. The woman expressed profound regret, acknowledged the loss, and told the daughter that she had been unable to drive since that terrible day. The daughter reached out to the woman, hugged her, and told the woman that the family forgave her and hoped that she would also find a way to get over the event. The daughter also offered the woman continued help and support and encouraged her to write or call her. In this important way, the parties' closure needs were met. The mediation process did more than deliver a monetary settlement. The process provided an avenue for conciliation and forgiveness and allowed all parties to leave with a sense of peace and hope.

Had the mediation process produced only a monetary settlement, other important needs of the parties would have been neglected and remained unmet. The mediation process provided an avenue for the very real human expression of the parties and their significant needs for closure. As a result, mediators must implicitly determine whether such closure is desired by the parties and make process decisions to meet such needs.

Despite the salient and necessary benefits of closure described above, closure may be very inappropriate in certain disputes. In certain instances, the parties may have no desire for conciliation based on the nature of the dispute. Typically, such cases involve allegations of fraud or purposeful, intentional acts. The mediator should not coerce parties to achieve closure if they have no desire for it. In sexual harassment cases, the victim may have obtained some closure by confronting the offender in the joint session but many have no desire for additional closure after a settlement is reached. The mediator's job is to determine the parties' desire for closure and provide a path for it if that is their wish. Similarly, the mediator should respect the parties' desires for no further contact or closure.

A.   CONCLUDING THE MEDIATION

Most mediations are set for a certain length of time. Whether this increment of time is set in terms of hours, days, or weeks, participants have an understanding of a time frame. Rarely do mediations continue indefinitely until an agreement is reached.[3] Where the time is not definite, reaching the agreement is the primary indication that the process is ending. In those cases which do not achieve settlement, the mediator must, nevertheless, close the session. Closing is a distinct stage of the process.

1.   CLOSURE WITH FORMAL MEDIATED AGREEMENT

In cases where agreement is reached, writing and signing the agreement is not necessarily the final part of the process. In some cases, however, all take place simultaneously. Execution of the agreement takes place at the session, if at all possible. In this instance, the agreement, closure, and implementation stages are contemporaneous. This situation, however, is not very common. The majority of mediated agreements result in a written document. Some closing remarks and rituals may occur while the mediator is drafting the agreement.

The mediator must remember that at all times—before, during, and after the mediation—she is a neutral third party. After an agreement is reached, written, signed, and distributed, the mediator should still maintain neutrality. This includes refraining from providing business cards to, or soliciting business from, either the parties or the attorneys.[4] Sometimes, particularly in cases where parties are not represented, the

---

3. Exceptions include the case of *international disputes*, such as those in the Middle East. Mediations of *class actions* also often lack deadlines.

4. An exception would be in the instance where the party inquires about the

mediator's services for other mediations in the future. In most instances, the mediator should still remain completely *neutral* in her remarks and information provided.

parties try to continue discussions about a point made in the mediation. The mediator should refrain from doing so. Not only will a post-mediation private conversation demonstrate a lack of neutrality, it may also cause the other party to question the mediator's neutrality during the session. When this occurs, the other party may then want to rescind the agreement. In other cases, in a later action for breach of contract or failure to comply with the mediated agreement, there may be an attempt to claim the mediator's lack of neutrality as a basis for invalidation of the agreement.[5]

In closing, the mediator should make sure of the following items: 1) the parties have exchanged any necessary information such as addresses and telephone numbers; 2) everyone has a copy of the agreement; 3) any follow-up between the parties or the mediator is clear and specific; and 4) that all dates, times, and places are clarified and preferably in writing. These points should also be covered in situations where there is an agreement to provide further information. After the signing of the agreement by all present, a copy is distributed to each party. The participants usually shake hands as a common means of bringing the mediation to an end.

2. CLOSURE WITHOUT FORMAL AGREEMENT

Often, a mediation closes without a formal agreement. Sometimes this is done with all participants together; and at other times, while the mediator is meeting separately with the parties. Some of these cases reach no substantive agreement, but the parties agree to continue negotiations or schedule a follow-up mediation.[6] Other cases end with no expectation of further negotiations, either between the parties directly or with the mediator's assistance.

In many of these cases, the reason for termination of the mediation will be obvious to the parties. As participants, they observe firsthand the stalemate. If no agreement is reached, the mediator need not explain to the parties in detail why the mediation is being terminated. She should explain only that it has reached an impasse, and should do so in a positive manner. In some cases, a mediator may declare an impasse to motivate the parties forward.[7] As the term impasse has become more widely used, it has developed an unfortunate negative connotation. Even in cases where an impasse has been declared, the mediator should positively reinforce any progress that was made during the mediation and encourage the parties to continue their negotiation. Nonetheless, it is recognized that in rare instances continued negotiation would be futile and should not be recommended.

Usually, the parties are amicable when leaving. In those occasional instances where there is concern about the safety of a party, or where

---

5. While this is an extreme case, it is a possibility, and thus the mediator should avoid even the appearance of *bias*. Also see Chapter 14 for further discussion of relevant *ethical considerations*.

6. The case of agreements to follow-up with mediation activity is discussed in § B of this chapter.

7. See Chapter 10, § C.

the mediation was volatile and face-to-face confrontation could be explosive, the mediator should take care to assure that the parties leave at different times. She might, for example, meet with one party separately while the other exits. It is imperative that neutrality be maintained at such times.

The mediator should be careful in recommending that the parties reschedule. Certainly all attempts to achieve a settlement should be made prior to the parties proceeding to trial or taking other action. A mediator might recommend rescheduling the mediation, however, motivated by self-interest in reaching an agreement. In most instances, the rule of thumb when considering whether to reschedule the mediation is to ask the question: Can something tangible be achieved by meeting again? Only if the answer is affirmative and specific should another session be scheduled.

B. POST MEDIATION FOLLOW-UP

In instances where the mediation terminates without an agreement, some mediators continue negotiations with both sides by telephone in order to achieve a settlement. While this should not be discouraged, the mediator should take care in how this is approached. She should not continually harass the parties in the hopes that they will be motivated to settle. In fact, some complaints have been lodged against mediators who continually called the attorneys for several weeks following the mediation. This type of follow-up is not recommended. In cases of unsolicited follow-up, it is suggested that initial telephonic communication be made by conference call, although if the mediation was conducted in a private session format, the telephone calls may be conducted separately as well.

Reasonable, non-coercive follow-up by the mediator is typically appreciated by the parties and viewed as evidence of the mediator's sincere commitment to the process. Sometimes, the parties need to leave a mediation session with some progress made and take stock of their situation before the negotiations may continue. The mediator, by keeping herself in the loop, may test the parties' new feelings about resolution and may obtain permission to extend new proposals.

When the mediation does not result in final settlement of the case, the parties may decide to return to mediation at a later date. A specific time may be predetermined at the original mediation. For example, where one or both of the parties need additional information or time to retrieve data, the mediator should write a memorandum or agreement to reflect that need, along with the time and place of the next meeting. Where there is not a definite time, and the session is not scheduled with the same mediator, a written agreement to continue is acceptable, though not necessary.

In cases of both rescheduling and follow-up, the mediator should have specific objectives in mind. Perhaps additional information is required. Perhaps the parties just need time to think about an offer or proposal on the table. A break may be necessary to allow one of the parties to obtain professional advice. In all cases the mediator should close the session with the goals and objectives for any follow-up meetings clearly understood by all participants.

Chapter Fourteen

ETHICAL CONSIDERATIONS

The term ethics as applied to mediation is almost impossible to define and dissect with precision. This is not because a wide range of definitions is not available, but rather is a result of the inherent variability of the process and the participants. One definition of ethics is "[t]he discipline of dealing with what is good and bad and with moral duty and obligation."[1] Ethical is also defined as "conforming to accepted professional standards of conduct."[2] A typical legal definition provides "of or relating to moral action, conduct, motive or characteristics conforming to professional standards of conduct."[3]

A discussion of ethics in mediation necessarily includes a variety of other considerations. There is clear overlap between ethics and standards of practice. The enforcement of ethical guidelines is one way to regulate a profession. Establishing ethics is a hallmark of becoming a profession.[4] Self-regulating professions typically require their members to adhere to a common set of ethical rules.

Distinguishing ethical behavior from a particular standard of practice for a mediator can be very difficult. For example, the issues surrounding confidentiality and neutrality are often considered ethical in nature. In many situations these are, in fact, termed "ethical considerations."[5] And although consideration of qualifications for mediators also includes ethical ramifications, there have been attempts to distinguish standards of practice from ethics.[6] Some of this cross-over discussion springs from the fact that the mediation "profession" is currently at a point where all issues are in the process of development and are ripe for examination. Perhaps as more of these issues mature, the lines between these matters will become more defined.

1. Merriam Webster's Collegiate Dictionary 398 (10th ed. 1993).

2. *Id.*

3. Black's Law Dictionary 573 (7th ed. 1999).

4. See Edgar H. Schein, Professional Education: Some New Directions 8–9 (1972).

5. See, for example, Robert A. Baruch Bush, *The Dilemmas of Mediation Practice: A Study of Ethical Dilemmas and Policy Implications*, A report on a study for the National Institute of Dispute Resolution (1992).

6. Jay Folberg & Alison Taylor, Mediation: A Comprehensive Guide to Resolving Conflicts Without Litigation 250 (1984).

Notwithstanding such difficulties, most educators, trainers, and practitioners agree that a definitive code of ethics is not only advisable, but also, at this stage in the development of the mediation practice, a necessity.

Equally important in the developing world of mediation practice are ethical guidelines for others participating in the mediation, especially for the disputing parties and their attorneys. Ethical considerations for the court or agency referring the matter to mediation may also be appropriate. Moreover, certain ethical duties and obligations might be established to guide the organizations or agencies that provide and administer mediation services.[7] At this time, the only significant development toward the establishment of ethical guidelines has been the creation of codes of ethics for the mediator. Work in the area of ethics for organizations is developing however, and as the use of mediation increases, it is likely that some consideration will be given to the others as well.

A. MEDIATOR ETHICS

Ethical codes and guidelines have historically been established in a variety of professions. A major obstacle in determining ethics for mediators is that mediation has not yet been formally established as a profession. Movement in that direction is apparent, however, as the development of ethical standards is occurring contemporaneously with the creation of the profession. But the task is not an easy one. There is a built-in inconsistency in the development of "standards" for mediators. The entire premise of mediation is its lack of rigidity. Mediation is a flexible process, and that flexibility is one of mediation's key benefits. There are no definitive standards of mediator competency, nor would testing for mediators in the traditional sense be advised. In order to encompass the variety of mediator styles, it would seem that mediator ethics must likewise possess elasticity. Yet, flexibility is not normally a component of ethics. Moreover, setting and enforcing guidelines of any nature seems at first antithetical to the mediation process. But because of the impact mediators can have on lives, there is a need for some type of guidance concerning mediator actions. The challenge is to create guidelines that are sufficiently specific in directing mediator conduct yet simultaneously allow for some individual leeway.

1. HISTORICAL OVERVIEW

The early development of ethical considerations for mediators was primarily for programs at the community level. In most of these programs, the mediators were volunteers from multiple disciplines. Mediation was, and still is, for the most part, an unregulated field;[8] yet many of the mediators felt a need for a set of mediation standards or guidelines.

7. Efforts here have developed and are outlined later in this chapter.

8. Some regulation has occurred in the court annexed mediation practice, for example in Florida and Virginia. See Chapter 15.

At the conclusion of a mediation, frequently one mediator would ask another, "Should I have done that?" Often what they wanted to know was if their conduct seemed ethical. Informal, generalized discussions between mediators would follow. As a result of these discussions, the staffs and boards of the mediation centers decided that a code of ethics (or at least a set of guidelines) was needed to provide some answers for the mediators.

Many recognized early on that because mediation is an interdisciplinary field, it was unlikely that any code of ethics from another profession would be directly applicable to the mediation context. First, it is not clear whether mediators continue to wear the hat of their primary or original profession during the mediation. Second, there is doubt whether the ethical considerations and guidelines of other professions are relevant to mediation.

Most ethical standards include discussions of avoidance of impropriety, fraud, conflicts, dishonesty, etc.; and there is little doubt that these would be applicable in mediation. Lawyers, however, also have specific duties premised on adversarial conduct. Ethics for social workers are geared toward a therapeutic approach. The practice of mediation requires skills and behaviors that differ from other professions. Consequently, many of the ethical standards of other professions are not suitable as standards for mediators. Moreover, ethical considerations important in other professions could be in direct conflict with the mediator's neutrality. But despite the difficulties, there have been attempts to create a code of ethics for mediators. Several are in existence, and efforts continue.

The Center for Dispute Resolution (now CDR Associates) in Boulder, Colorado was an early leader in the ethics effort. In 1982, CDR Associates pioneered the creation of a code of ethics by publishing a Code of Professional Conduct for Mediators. The Code was intended to be applicable to all types of mediators, and it was subsequently adopted by the Colorado Council of Mediators in 1982,[9] and later by a number of similar organizations.

Similarly, an interdisciplinary association, the Society of Professionals in Dispute Resolution[10] (SPIDR) has enacted ethical standards. The code adopted by the SPIDR Board of Directors in 1986 purports to govern all neutrals, including mediators.

In 1986 the Supreme Court of Hawaii established guidelines for both public and private mediators.[11] Indicative of the previously discussed problems in differentiating between ethics and standards of practice, the

---

9. Christopher W. Moore, The Mediation Process: Practical Strategies for Resolving Conflict 353 (2d Ed. 1996)

10. SPIDR is the largest interdisciplinary international dispute resolution membership organization.

11. Haw. State Jud., Program on Alternative Dispute Resolution, Standards for Private and Public Mediators in the State of Hawaii (1986).

guidelines were entitled Standards for Private and Public Mediators in the State of Hawaii.[12]

Many dispute resolution centers, likewise, have developed codes of ethics. In Texas, for example, all twelve community centers worked in conjunction with one another to achieve consistency among centers in the state. While the Hawaii Code is statewide and applicable to all mediators, the Texas model governs only those volunteer mediators in the centers. Some practitioners have attempted self-regulation. Since many mediators practice in the divorce area, the Academy of Family Mediators enacted a specific code: Standards of Practice for Family and Divorce Mediation.

As the use of mediation extended into the courts, additional concerns arose. Most of the mediators were lawyers, and assumptions were made that the lawyer's code of ethics[13] would apply. Yet it soon became apparent that fundamental differences in the roles of the advocate and the mediator prevent wholesale adoption by mediators of the lawyer's code of professional responsibility.[14] Attempts were then made to modify the Model Rules of Professional Conduct to provide guidance for the lawyer mediator. But there have not been any general changes thus far. The American Bar Association, however, is considering the inclusion of the lawyer's role as a neutral in the Ethics 2000 project[15] and an ethics commission has drafted such a model rule.[16] Changes have occurred in the family law area. Most lawyer mediators worked initially in the divorce area, and in 1984, the ABA adopted standards with regard to the lawyer mediator in family law matters.[17] Some state and local bar associations have also attempted to address the need for guidelines for the lawyer-mediator through their ethics committees. The result has been a segregation of the interests of lawyer mediators from those of non-lawyer mediators. Most individuals within the field believe that a code of ethics applicable to all mediators is preferable, although specific considerations for the lawyer neutral have also been advocated.[18]

2. CURRENT CODES

Currently, there are likely over a hundred separate codes of mediator ethics, many of which include standards of conduct. Mediators' duties

12. *Id.* (1995).

13. ABA Model Rules of Professional Conduct and Model Code of Professional Responsibility (1983).

14. For a very detailed examination of this issue, see Carrie Menkel–Meadow, *Ethics in Alternative Dispute Resolution: New Issues, No Answers from the Adversary Conception of Lawyers' Responsibilities*, 38 S. Tex. L. Rev. 407 (1997). See also Alison Smiley, Note *Professional Codes and Neutral Lawyering: An Emerging Standard Governing Nonrepresentational Attorney Mediation*, 7 Geo. J. Legal Ethics 213 (1993).

15. Feature, *Speakers Propose Model Rules Amendments to Ethics 2000 Commis-*sion, 9, No. 3, Prof. Law. 10 (1998). See also memorandum of Wayne Thorpe, Chair, Ethics Committee, ABA Section of Dispute Resolution (August 1999).

16. See CPR–Georgetown Commission on Ethics and Standards of Practice in ADR, Draft Model Rule of Professional Conduct for the Lawyer as Third Party Neutral, (1999).

17. Standards of Practice for Lawyer Mediators in Family Disputes, (Adopted by the House of Delegates of the American Bar Association, August 1984).

18. See Draft Model Rule, *supra* note 16.

may be determined by the type of case, the background of the mediator, the agency in which the case is mediated,[19] or the place of referral, such as a court. With so many codes in existence, it is very difficult for the mediator to determine exactly which code of ethics to follow. Fortunately, in most instances the code provisions are essentially consistent. Certain codes are narrow in focus. Other codes of ethics are more expansive and cover practice issues, since in reality it may be difficult to distinguish between the two.

In addition to advances made at local levels, many larger groups of mediators, such as the Academy of Family Mediators and the National Association of Social Workers, have enacted ethical guidelines for mediators. These organizations request that all members follow their code. Implicit in membership is an agreement to conduct mediations in accordance with the group's ethical standards. These standards, however, are purely aspirational. There is no method of inquiry or way to determine an ethical violation. Moreover, proving ethical violations is complicated by the confidential nature of mediation.

Some of the more widely distributed codes identified as ethical in nature are as follows: SPIDR's Ethical Standards of Professional Conduct; Association of Family & Conciliation Courts' Model Standards of Practice for Family and Divorce Mediation; Standards for Mediators in the State of Hawaii; Colorado Council of Mediators and Mediation Organizations' Code of Professional Conduct for Mediators; Texas Dispute Resolution Center Directors Councils' Code of Ethics for Volunteer Mediators; Oregon Mediation Association's Standard of Mediation Practice; and Standards of Professional Conduct for Certified and Court–Appointed Mediators in Florida. These codes cover a number of issues, and, as their titles indicate, most are considered a code of conduct which incorporates ethical guidelines. Only a few purport to provide exclusively "ethics."

A number of practice issues are consistently found within these codes. These include conflicts of interest, the mediator's role, impartiality, confidentiality, providing professional advice, fees, advertising, fairness of agreement, qualifications, training, and continuing education.[20] Other areas which some of these codes include are the mediator's responsibility to the courts, self-determination of the parties, interests of outsiders and absent parties, separate caucuses, and use of multiple procedures.

3. ISSUES SURROUNDING THE USE OF A CODE OF ETHICS

Several considerations present challenges to both the creation and implementation of a code of ethics for mediators. These include the

---

19. For example, these are Special Standards of Practice for Postal Service Mediations. See United States Postal Service, Mediating Postal Disputes 3–12 (1998).

20. Many of these topics will be examined in § 4 of this chapter, though the last three are seen as part of mediator competency, and hence included in Chapter 15.

interdisciplinary nature of the field, the inherent flexibility of the process, the lack of an enforcement authority, and even problems as basic as defining the process to be regulated.

Mediation is a flexible process. This is one of the attributes usually emphasized in training and teaching mediation. The process has quite broad applicability and has been effective in the resolution of an extremely wide array of disputes, largely because of this flexibility. The difficulty in defining the process and precisely how it works contributes to the complications in determining appropriate ethics and standards of practice. Moreover, it is feared that if rigid standards are established, the mediator's pliancy will be extinguished.

Mediators currently come from all walks of life. Until the profession is subject to some form of licensure or regulation, the ability to impact all mediators inclusively is impossible.

Many mediators are volunteers and arguably should not be overburdened by regulation. On the other hand, adopting a standard of ethics that excludes volunteers might send a message of a two-tiered approach to competency in mediation services.

Another dilemma arises when the mediator is bound to comply with other professional ethics. Which code regulates a mediator whose primary profession is accountant, doctor, lawyer, or therapist? While in most situations there will be more consistency than conflict, in the event of conflict, how will a decision be made concerning which code controls?

Just as troublesome in the creation of ethical guidelines is the determination of who is to enforce them. Some argue that the mere existence of ethical standards, in and of itself, is sufficient enforcement. Most individual mediators will voluntarily abide by them. Others, however, stress that there must be methods to enforce ethical conduct. These commentators would hold mediators responsible for more than voluntary compliance with guidelines: they would dictate standards.[21] As the majority of current codes of ethics were established as guidelines for mediators, in reality, no sanctions exist for violations. Thus, even mediators who knowingly violate ethical guidelines usually go unpunished, since there is no enforcement group.[22] Few mediators are currently prohibited from practicing mediation by the entity which enacted the violated standards. In addition to the lack of an enforcement authority is the lack of defined penalties appropriate to various ethical violations.

Another consideration is how to introduce ethical codes to new and experienced mediators. In many states, there is only a minimal, one time

---

21. This is the position of at least one Associate Justice of the Florida Supreme Court. When the Florida Supreme Court was enacting certification procedures, it was deemed necessary to establish an enforcement body. The Supreme Court of Florida was the first entity to assume the role of a regulating authority for the mediator profession. The State of Utah has provided that its Division of Occupational and Professional Licensing is authorized to deny or revoke certification of a dispute resolution provider. Utah Code Ann. § 58–39a–6 (1999).

22. This outside entity could be an organization of mediators, a mediation program, or a referring court or agency.

training requirement for mediators. Not surprisingly, training and educating mediators is far from standardized.[23] There is no consistency with regard to course content and it is difficult to ascertain whether trainings actually include ethical components. Although some mediator membership organizations provide ethical guidelines for their members, it is difficult, if not impossible, to determine whether the mediators are familiar with them. There is no standard testing of mediators. Consequently, many mediators may not even be aware of the existence of ethical guidelines or standards.

4. AREAS FOR ETHICAL CONSIDERATION

The variety of ethical issues facing mediators is considerable. The difficulty in determining which issues to address in a code of ethics is evidenced by the number of codes in existence and the variety among them.

An attempt to determine what issues mediators face in practice was made in the State of Florida. Research there included interviews with over eighty mediators, from varied backgrounds. Program and private practice mediators were included, and the cases were from the family, civil litigation and community fields of practice. The mediators were asked to describe situations in the course of their experience that presented "ethical dilemmas."[24] The findings indicated concern about several issues: confidentiality, conflicts of interest, competency, preserving impartiality, informed consent, preserving self-determination, provision of counseling and legal advice, and avoiding harm and abuse in the process.[25] Some of these issues admittedly overlap with standards of practice.

A survey of the literature and of current drafts of codes reveals a few primary ethical concerns for mediators. These include confidentiality and neutrality to which previous chapters are devoted.[26] The others, listed below, will be discussed here:

    a.   Conflicts of Interest

    b.   Impartiality

    c.   Role of the Mediator Versus Self–Determination

    d.   Providing Professional Advice

    e.   Advertising/Fees

In matters of conflicts of interest, the issue is just how neutral the mediator must be. For instance, should a mediator serve in a case where one of the parties is a former client if the matter is totally unrelated to that of the prior representation? Can a mediator mediate a case involving a former partner? A former roommate? Once a mediator serves in

---

23. This will be examined in Chapter 15.

24. Bush, *supra* note 5 at 6.

25. *Id.* at 9.

26. *Neutrality* is the subject of Chapter 7, while Chapter 11 addresses *confidentiality*.

the neutral role, is he forever barred from providing services (legal, accounting, etc.) to that individual?

Additional situations produce even more debate over the necessity for impartiality and freedom from bias. For example, if a mediator is divorced, should he be prohibited from mediating divorce cases? Should this bar last during some period before and after the divorce or forever? Likewise, if a mediator has been in a car accident, should he, for any period of time, refrain from mediating automobile accident cases? Impartiality and neutrality are often defined as "having no interest in the outcome." Yet, if a mediator is an advocate for settlement, it can be argued that he does have an interest in the outcome. This is especially troublesome in those cases where a settlement may result in additional business for the mediator.

Self-determination of the parties, many claim, is at the very core of the mediation process.[27] Yet some mediators may coerce parties into a settlement, claiming to have superior understanding of the best options for resolution of the matter. This coercive behavior likely occurs more often in court-annexed mediation.[28] The degree of mediator directiveness determines whether the parties' settlement is truly self-determined.

Considerations of party self-determination, mediator neutrality, and professional advice are linked. These interact and affect the role of the mediator in instances where a party is uninformed or uneducated about a matter. Should the mediator provide the missing information or advice, whether it be legal, financial, technical, or therapeutic in nature?

At least two competing ethical considerations drive this issue. These are the mediator's duty to be neutral, and the obligation he may feel to achieve a fair, fully informed settlement.[29] If the mediator is to empower the parties to exercise self-determination, however, it may follow that the mediator must ensure that decisions are made with adequate information and understanding.[30] Often this information and understanding is of a legal nature. Should the mediator provide this information? Once a mediator provides advice or information to a party, his role can be viewed as that of an advocate. Some view the mediator's duty not as one who directly provides the information, but rather one who advocates that the parties obtain independent legal counsel.[31] But doing so may result in increased cost to the disputants. Some mediators will provide the needed legal information. Others view providing any advice as unethical.

Mediator advertising and fee schedules have also caused some concern in the field. The general opinion is that the only guidance which should be provided to mediators is that fees be reasonable, and advertis-

---

27. Jacqueline Nolan–Haley, *Informed Consent in Mediation: A Guiding Principle for Truly Educated Decisionmaking,* 74 Notre Dame Law Rev. 775 (1999).

28. Allen v. Leal, 27 F.Supp.2d 945 (S.D.Tex.1998).

29. These issues were addressed in Chapter 7.

30. Robert A. Baruch Bush, *Efficiency and Protection, or Empowerment and Recognition?: The Mediator's Role and Ethical Standards in Mediation,* 41 Fla. L. Rev. 253, 278 (1989).

31. *Id.* at 280.

ing truthful and not misleading. Prohibitions against contingency fees are also common. This ban is based upon the premise that a mediator cannot have an interest in the outcome of the case. A minority view exists, and a handful of practicing mediators bill on a contingency basis.

5. JOINT CODE

JOHN D. FEERICK, TOWARD UNIFORM STANDARDS OF CONDUCT FOR MEDIATORS
38 S. Tex. L. Rev. 455 (1997).

* * *

In recognition of the growth of mediation, the American Arbitration Association ("AAA"), the American Bar Association ("ABA"), and the Society of Professionals in Dispute Resolution ("SPIDR") formed a joint committee in 1992 to develop a code of conduct for dispute mediators. A successful earlier joint effort by the ABA and AAA to develop a guide of ethical rules for arbitrators was a strong impetus for this collaboration. After two years of work, the latest effort culminated in proposed Model Standards of Conduct for Mediators ("the Standards").[32]

The purposes of the Standards are multifold: the promotion of integrity and impartiality in mediation, the handling of conflicts and the appearance of conflict of interest, and the treatment of fees in mediation, among others. The Standards encourage facilitative roles by mediators, assisting parties to arrive at voluntary resolutions of their problems. It has been said that the freedom of parties to reach the best solution on which they can agree must be preserved, and that mediation is a type of cooperation between parties and "not a combat to be won." The Standards are intended to invite comment, to increase consciousness of ethical issues in mediation, and to be adopted and tailored by different groups, as they feel appropriate. Further, the goal of the Standards is to encourage mediation of a high quality without drawing a distinction between the lawyer-mediator and other professional mediators.

In developing the Standards, the joint committee drew on a number of existing codes of ethics for neutrals, particularly codes developed in states such as Florida, Hawaii, Texas, Colorado, and Oregon. Additionally, ethical codes for mediators and arbitrators developed by various organizations were reviewed in drafting the Standards, namely from the following: American Arbitration Association/American Bar Association; American Arbitration Association and National Academy of Arbitrators and Federal Mediation and Conciliation Service; American Bar Association Center for Professional Responsibility; American Bar Association; Society of Professionals in Dispute Resolution; Academy of Family Mediators; Association of Family and Conciliation Courts; and Center for Dispute Settlement at the Institute of Judicial Administration.

32. These standards are included in this text as Appendix B.

The Standards are divided into nine sections and cover a broad range of topics: Self–Determination; Impartiality; Conflicts of Interest; Competence; Confidentiality; Quality of the Process; Advertisements and Solicitation; Fees; and Obligations to the Mediation Process. Each Standard states a broad principle so as to encompass varying situations and includes descriptive comments, stated both generally and specifically.

* * *

The Standards of Conduct for Mediators are intended to be a starting point in the development of national ethical guidelines for the practice of mediation. They do not deal with the role of party representatives in a mediation, or the responsibility of organizations and entities which appoint individuals to serve as mediators. These are, of course, subjects deserving of consideration. The Standards offer general considerations for people who take on the role of mediators. They are aspirational in nature and are intended to be guideposts toward the development of uniform standards of conduct for mediators. By attempting to encourage the development of national standards, the joint committee of the AAA, ABA and SPIDR hope to boost public confidence in a field that does not require certification, a license, or a law or other professional degrees. While discussion and application of these Standards is strongly encouraged, it is ultimately left to the participants in the field to determine if the Standards are appropriate for their use and, if so, how they will be applied and implemented, if at all.

There has been criticism of these standards. The primary complaint is that they are so broad that only minimal guidance is provided, and sources for interpretation are absent. Suggestions include a more limited, clearly defined framework, accompanied by an analysis of typical ethical dilemmas faced by mediators.[33]

Until specific codes are adopted or programs and courts institute mandatory ethical guidelines, many questions will remain unanswered for the practicing mediator. Determining what to do when faced with an ethical dilemma can be disconcerting. Each mediator should be familiar with the primary codes of ethics relating to his practice. And even though codes are adopted, each ethical quandary cannot be covered. When specific issues are not addressed by the code, individual choices must be made.

Inevitably, courts will confront these ethical matters. While many codes of ethics focus solidly on the mediator regardless of an individual's prior training and education in a profession other than mediation, there are times that the mediator's role will conflict with another professional role. In particular the courts have begun to address the issues that arise

33. Jamie Henikoff & Michael Moffitt, *Remodeling the Model Standards of Con-* *duct for Mediators,* 2 Harv. Negotiation L. Rev. 87 (1997).

when attorneys who serve as mediators remain with law firms and/or in the practice of law.

POLY SOFTWARE INTERNATIONAL, INC. v. SU
United States District Court, D. Utah, Central Division, 1995.
880 F.Supp. 1487.

WINDER, CHIEF JUDGE.

This matter is before the court on cross-motions to disqualify counsel. Plaintiff and Counterdefendant Poly Software International ("Poly Software") has moved for the disqualification of Lynn G. Foster and the firm of Foster & Foster. The current CEO of Poly Software is Xiaowu Wang ("Wang"). Defendants and Counterclaimants Yu Su, et al., ("Su") have moved for the disqualification of Berne S. Broadbent and the firm of Berne S. Broadbent, P.C. A hearing on these motions was held on February 16, 1995. Paul M. Durham and Berne S. Broadbent appeared on behalf of Wang and Poly Software, and V. Roland Smith, Lynn G. Foster, and Brett L. Foster appeared on behalf of Su, and Datamost Corporation ("Datamost"). Before the hearing, the court considered carefully the memoranda and other materials submitted by the parties. Since taking the matter under advisement, the court has further considered the law and facts relating to the motions. Now being fully advised, the court enters the following memorandum opinion and order.

I. BACKGROUND

Treatment of the disqualification motions at issue requires a brief account of the previous dealings of the parties. In 1989, Su was employed as a software engineer by Micromath, Inc., a company specializing in the development and marketing of mathematical software. Wang joined him in the same capacity in 1990. In the summer of 1992, both Su and Wang left Micromath, formed a partnership ("Polysoft Partnership"), and began producing their own line of mathematical graphing software. Micromath subsequently sued the Polysoft Partnership for copyright infringement. The focus of the Micromath litigation was a Polysoft Partnership product entitled "Techplot," later renamed "PS Plot," and then "PSI–Plot." Micromath claimed that Wang and Su had obtained user's handbooks and computer source code while working for Micromath, and illegally employed that information in their development of Techplot.

Soon after the complaint was filed the parties agreed to submit their dispute to mediation, a non-binding alternative to formal litigation, and chose Berne S. Broadbent ("Broadbent") to serve as mediator. Broadbent conducted a series of intensive meetings, conferring with the parties both individually and together. During Broadbent's private caucuses with the Polysoft Partnership both Wang and Su were present and openly discussed confidential aspects of their case, including detailed analysis of their source codes and handbook comparisons. At the conclusion of the mediation process Micromath and the Polysoft Partnership successfully negotiated a settlement of their dispute.

* * *

However, in December of 1993, Wang and Su dissolved the partnership. Under the terms of the dissolution, Su surrendered his ownership interest in the Polysoft Partnership to Wang, and received the rights to the PSI–Stat software. Wang retained the rights to the PSI–Plot and PSI–Math programs. Subsequently, Wang restructured the business as Poly Software International, Inc., and Su formed Datamost Corporation.

The present litigation was commenced on November 7, 1994, when Poly Software filed an action asserting copyright infringement and other related claims against Su and various other employees of Datamost. In substance, those claims asserted that "Statmost for DOS," Datamost's version of the program PSI–Stat (the rights to which had passed to Su upon dissolution of the Polysoft Partnership) illegally duplicated significant portions of the PSI–Plot User's Handbook, and incorporated source code unique to PSI–Plot.

Prior to commencing suit, Wang interviewed a number of attorneys for the purpose of finding a law firm to pursue his claim against Su and Datamost. One of those attorneys, Lynn G. Foster of the firm Foster & Foster, met with Wang in October of 1994. No fee was charged for this initial interview. Foster asserts that the meeting began at about 5:30 p.m., and lasted less than 30 minutes.

He also claims that Wang was given two options for the interview. One option would primarily focus on the fee schedule of the firm and outline the policies employed in pursuing litigation. Under this option, the potential client would give only a very general description of the litigation proposed. The second option would involve a much more significant interview, focusing on specific details of the potential client's case. Foster asserts that Wang chose the first option, and that Wang disclosed only that "he had a dispute against a former partner, software was involved, and there was some type of prior settlement agreement."

Wang, on the other hand, claims that the meeting was over an hour long, that he specifically discussed the evidence relevant to the proposed litigation, disclosed potential strengths and weaknesses of his case, displayed the user's handbooks printed by both companies, and compared a printout of portions of defendants' "materials" with those of Poly Software.

Wang testified briefly at the hearing before this court. He speaks and understands English, but his heavy accent nonetheless raises somewhat of a language barrier. In particular, Wang must often repeat what he says in order to make himself effectively understood. Foster claims that communication difficulties in his interview with Wang prevented them from discussing anything beyond the bare essentials of the case during the short time allotted.

* * *

When a federal district court is presented with a motion to disqualify, it relies on two sources of authority to guide the exercise of its discretion. The first source is "the local rules of the court in which [attorneys] appear." Rule 103–1(h) of the Rules of Practice for this district states that attorneys "shall comply with the rules of practice adopted by this court, and unless otherwise provided by these rules, with the Utah Rules of Professional Conduct, as revised and amended and as interpreted by this court." Additionally, "because motions to disqualify counsel in federal proceedings are substantive motions affecting the rights of the parties, they are decided by applying standards developed under federal law. . . . [and are thus] governed by the ethical rules announced by the national profession and considered 'in light of the public interest and the litigants' rights.'"

A. *The Motion to Disqualify Lynn G. Foster*

Rule 1.9 of the Utah Rules of Professional Conduct [hereinafter "Utah Prof. Conduct Rules"] governs Poly Software's motion to disqualify Lynn G. Foster and the firm of Foster & Foster. That rule forbids an attorney who has formerly represented a client from:

> (a) Represent[ing] another person in the same or a substantially factually related matter in which that person's interests are materially adverse to the interests of the former client unless the former client consents after consultation; or (b) Us[ing] information related to the representation to the disadvantage of the former client except as Rule 1.6 would permit with respect to a client or when the information has become generally known.

Hence, a party wishing to disqualify opposing counsel under Rule 1.9 must demonstrate three factors: (1) that a previous attorney-client relationship arose with the moving party; (2) that the present litigation is "substantially factually related" to the previous representation; and (3) that the attorney's present client's interests are materially adverse to the movant. In this case, Wang convened with Foster for the purpose of determining whether Foster would represent Poly Software in the very litigation for which Foster eventually was retained by the opposing side. Hence, the second and third factors are clearly demonstrated. The determinative question, then, is whether an attorney-client relationship ever arose between Wang and Foster.

* * *

This rule, however, may not adequately address the situation involving an initial interview (such as that occurring between Wang and Foster) where both parties understand that the relationship is potential, not implied or actual.

* * *

Balanced against these considerations, however, is the public interest of allowing clients (and attorneys) to freely choose their employment arrangements. It may often be necessary for potential clients to interview a number of lawyers before settling on the lawyer or firm that best meets their expectations. In this vein, it is critical to avoid a situation where a person, merely by arranging employment interviews, renders a large number of attorneys unavailable for the opposing party. The present conflict between Wang and Su may well be a case in point. Wang (quite understandably) visited a number of local attorneys who focus on intellectual property litigation before entrusting his proposed lawsuit to one of them. Although the Wasatch Front is a moderately-sized urban area, attorneys specializing in such fields are not overwhelmingly plentiful. If the ethical rules disqualified every attorney granting an initial interview, Wang, in a very short time period, could have (even unintentionally) forced his opponent to seek inexperienced or out-of-state counsel.

* * *

After carefully weighing the conflicting affidavits and testimony describing what occurred during the interview and how long it lasted, this court finds Foster's version to be the more credible of the two. As a result, this court also holds that the degree of confidentiality established in the interview was insufficient to preclude Foster's subsequent employment by Su and Datamost.

* * *

B.   The Motion to Disqualify Berne S. Broadbent

Su and Datamost have brought a similar motion to disqualify Wang's attorney, Berne S. Broadbent. That motion is based on Broadbent's previous role as a mediator in the Micromath litigation. With respect to the appropriate rule governing mediators, this case is one of first impression. In making their arguments on this issue, both parties have cited to the Utah Prof. Conduct Rules, Rule 1.12(a). That provision states that "a lawyer shall not represent anyone in connection with a matter in which the lawyer participated personally and substantially as a judge or other adjudicative officer, arbitrator or law clerk to such a person, unless all parties to the proceeding consent after disclosure." Su also cites to Nancy H. Rogers & Craig A. McEwen, Mediation: Law, Policy, Practice (2d Ed., 1994), and its proposed code of ethics for mediators, which provides that "[w]ithout the consent of all parties, a mediator shall not subsequently establish a professional relationship with one of the parties in a related matter." In substance, this proposal is analogous to Model Rule 1.9's proscription of subsequent employment on a "substantially related matter," or in the case of the more specific Utah Prof.Conduct Rules, Rule 1.9, "substantially factually related matter." Thus, Rules 1.9 and 1.12 promulgate a significant distinction in the scope of prohibited subsequent representation. This distinction becomes important in this case because the Micromath litigation mediated by Broadbent and the present lawsuit possess a common factual nexus, but are distinct legal disputes. With respect to "matter" as that term is employed by Rule 1.12, there is virtually no case law or other commentary. However, Rule 1.11 contains substantially the same provision as Rule 1.12 and, "as used in [Rule 1.11], the term 'matter' includes ... [a]ny judicial or other proceeding, application, request for ruling or other determination, contract, claim, controversy, investigation, charge, accusation, arrest or other particular matter involving a specific party or parties." Utah Prof.Conduct Rules, Rule 1.11(d).

* * *

In commenting upon the Utah Prof.Conduct Rules, Rule 1.9, the Tenth Circuit has observed that Utah's variation from the ABA model code [appears] to be a codification of our existing definition of substantiality by focusing on the factual nexus between the prior and the current representations rather than a narrower identity of legal issues. Substantial factual relation should not be read to require attorneys to have worked on exactly the same matter for both sides of the dispute before they are disqualified. SLC Ltd. V v. Bradford Group West, Inc., 999 F.2d 464, 467 (10th Cir.1993).

For the most part, [this difference] is due to the different purposes served by each rule. The purpose of rule 1.9 is to assure that the confidentiality and loyalty owed to the client is not compromised ... The purpose of [R]ule 1.11 is to prevent a lawyer from exploiting public office for the advantage of a private client. In this case the lawsuit between Su and Wang is legally distinct from the earlier Micromath litigation because it involves a separate dispute between differing parties, and thereby "lack[s] the discrete, identifiable transaction of conduct involving a particular situation and specific parties." Thus, it is not the same "matter" as that term is understood in Rule 1.12 or 1.11.

The present litigation is, however, "substantially factually related" to the Micromath litigation. Poly Software accuses Su and Datamost of impermissibly copying source code and handbook information from the PSI–Plot program. Micromath accused Wang and Su of pirating source code and handbook information to formulate an earlier version of the very same program. The complaints filed in the two cases are virtually identical in many respects, at times employing precisely the same phrasing. Moreover, as a mediator in the Micromath litigation, Broadbent examined in detail the disputed source code and elicited frank discussions in private caucus with Wang and Su as to which of them might be responsible for alleged illegal copying. Therefore, the determinative question on the issue of the ethical status of Broadbent's current representation of Poly Software is whether mediators should be governed by a same "matter" standard similar to that enunciated in Rule 1.12 and 1.11, or by a "substantially factually related" standard similar to that employed by Rule 1.9.

Preliminary to answering that question a brief discussion of the definition of "mediator," is necessary. For the purposes of this opinion, a mediator is an attorney who agrees to assist parties in settling a legal dispute, and in the course of assisting those parties undertakes a confidential relationship with them. Such mediation may often occur in the context of a court-supervised Alternative Dispute Resolution ("ADR") program. See generally, United States District Court: District of Utah ADR Program Manual s III [hereinafter "Utah District Court ADR Manual "]. "Mediator" in this particular context does not apply to circumstances already covered by the Utah Prof.Conduct Rules, Rule 2.2 where attorneys take on the role of intermediary between two or more clients with potentially conflicting interests. Rather, it applies to situations where litigation has already commenced, the parties subsequently agree to suspend their litigation, and also agree to the appointment of an attorney to facilitate settlement. The attorney who thus serves as mediator is a neutral individual who confers with each party in private caucus, learning what results are acceptable to each of them and assessing in confidence the strengths and weaknesses of their cases. The mediator also meets with all parties together to facilitate settlement of the case. In this regard, mediation may well be the most valuable ADR option. "Unlike the litigation and arbitration processes, mediation does not necessarily cast the parties in an adversarial relationship. Nor do parties emerge from the mediation process as clearly defined winners and losers."

* * *

These characteristics of mediation demonstrate that it differs significantly from more formal adversarial proceedings at which an adjudicative officer presides. Most importantly, the mediator is not merely charged with being impartial, but with receiving and preserving confidences in much the same manner as the client's attorney. In fact, the success of mediation depends largely on the willingness of the parties to freely disclose their intentions, desires, and the strengths and weaknesses of their case; and upon the ability of the mediator to maintain a neutral position while carefully preserving the confidences that have been revealed. The Utah District Court ADR Manual, for instance, encourages the parties to disclose to the mediator (in strict confidence) "[a]ll critical information, whether favorable or unfavorable to the party's position," and recommends that mediators "advise the parties and their attorneys that it is neither helpful nor productive to withhold information with the intent of gaining some tactical advantage." Adversarial proceedings, on the other hand, are characterized by vigorous attempts to maintain confidences. Attorneys who have received such confidential information are under a strict duty to avoid, without the consent of the client, any disclosures of that information. And because adjudicators do not occupy a relationship of confidence and trust with the parties akin to that occupied by the attorneys, they do not, for the most part, have access to those confidences. Thus, although mediators function in some ways as neutral coordinators of dispute resolution, they also assume the role of a confidant, and it is that aspect of their role that distinguishes them from adjudicators.

As a result, the appropriate ethical rule for mediators differs somewhat from the text of the Utah Prof.Conduct Rules, Rule 1.12. Where a mediator has received confidential information in the course of mediation, that mediator should not thereafter represent anyone in connection with the same or a substantially factually related matter unless all parties to the mediation proceeding consent after disclosure. This rule also takes into account some important policy considerations. If parties to mediation know that their mediator could someday be an attorney on the opposing side in a substantially related matter, they will be discouraged from freely disclosing their position in the mediation, which may severely diminish the opportunity for settlement. If, on the other hand, the disqualification net is thrown too wide, attorneys will be discouraged from becoming mediators. The "substantially factually related" standard best balances those two interests. It encourages parties to freely disclose their positions during mediation by assuring them that the specific information disclosed will not be used against them at a later time. It also limits disqualification to subsequent situations where there is a substantial factual nexus with the previously mediated dispute. Applying the "substantially factually related" standard to the present motion, it is evident that Broadbent received confidential information in the course of the Micromath dispute. It is also undisputed that Su and Datamost did not consent to his subsequent representation of Wang in a substantially factually related lawsuit. Therefore, his current representation constitutes a violation of the rule established by this opinion.

Nevertheless, because this is a case of first impression, the court wishes to make clear that in one respect this violation assumes a dramatically different posture than an infraction of a more clearly established rule. Given the paucity of literature on the issue and the tendency of many commentators to lump all ADR methods under the same ethical rubric, an attorney could have understandably selected the "same matter" standard of the Utah Prof.Conduct Rules, Rule 1.12, and thereby reasonably assumed that no violation would occur. Thus, imposition of sanctions or criticism of Mr. Broadbent's professional reputation is unwarranted in this case.

In any event, a finding that a violation has occurred does not necessarily end the inquiry. "The sanction of disqualification of counsel in litigation situations should be measured by the facts of each particular case as they bear upon the impact of counsel's conduct upon the trial.... The essential issue to be determined in the context of litigation is whether the alleged misconduct taints the lawsuit." In this case, Broadbent received a significant amount of confidential information during the mediation of the Micromath litigation. In particular, he was present while Wang and Su conducted heated conversations on the topic of which of them might be responsible for the copying alleged by Micromath. Poly Software argues that, because Wang was present whenever Su revealed anything to Broadbent, Poly Software does not gain access, by employing Broadbent in the present litigation, to any confidential information that it does not already possess. However, this argument ignores the fact that Broadbent's professional expertise afforded him a perspective on the legal significance of the confidences that

Wang himself could not possibly obtain or communicate to new counsel. In short his role as a mediator with experience in intellectual property litigation gives him an unfair advantage as an attorney in the present case. Moreover, given the posture of this case, the disqualification of Broadbent must be imputed to the other members of his small firm.

McKENZIE CONSTRUCTION v. ST. CROIX STORAGE CORPORATION

District Court of the Virgin Islands, Division of St. Croix, 1997.
961 F.Supp. 857.

RESNICK, UNITED STATES MAGISTRATE JUDGE.

THIS MATTER is before the Court on defendants St. Croix Storage Corp. and Sun Storage Partners, L.P.'s motion to disqualify the law firm of Rohn & Cusick as counsel for plaintiffs in this action. Plaintiffs filed an Opposition, defendant filed a Reply asserting new allegations. Plaintiffs responded further as directed by the Court and have requested "oral argument so that Attorney Moorehead can take the stand and inform the Court of the true nature of what occurred here."

Plaintiff McKenzie Construction is a local lumber retail company who brought this damages action against defendants St. Croix Storage Corp. for conversion of lumber. The Court ordered the matter submitted to mediation and later appointed Attorney Lisa Moorehead as mediator. (See Order Appointing Mediator dated May 26, 1994). Mediation was unsuccessful and the parties have resumed preparation for trial.

In seeking to disqualify the firm of Rohn & Cusick, defendants claim that the firm's hiring of Attorney Moorehead, who was the mediator appointed by the Court to settle this case, presents an irreparable conflict of interest in contravention of the rules governing the conduct of mediators and attorneys alike. Defendants reason that Moorehead's position as mediator allowed her access to "a wide range of confidential information derived from her private consultations" with the parties. Plaintiffs responded that although Moorehead may be subject to disqualification, she is simply "of counsel" to the law firm of Rohn & Cusick and that, under Virgin Islands law, the disqualification of the law firm is not automatic. Moreover, plaintiffs assert that although no confidences were exchanged in the mediation, the firm had created a "cone of silence" around Moorehead, insulating her from the case. However, defendants countered that since being hired by Rohn & Cusick in September of 1996, Moorehead had inserted herself into the case by meeting with an investigator for defendants concerning the investigator's contact with plaintiff about the case. The Court requested that plaintiffs file a direct response to defendants' allegation. In their response, plaintiffs submit an affidavit of Attorney Moorehead in which she avers that a "cone of silence" has been erected at Rohn & Cusick and admits that she met with the investigator in order to advise him that he could be civilly liable for attempting to settle a case with a represented party. She claims that she did not discuss the merits of the instant case. Defendants also seek the imposition of sanctions against plaintiffs' law firm for filing false affidavits.

After review of the record and the submissions of the parties, this Court concludes that there exists a sufficient basis for resolution of this issue on the pleadings alone. Accordingly, the request for a hearing is denied.

A motion to disqualify counsel requires the court to balance the right of a party to retain counsel of his choice and the substantial hardship which might result from disqualification as against the public perception of and the public trust in the judicial system.

* * *

This case presents the question whether a law firm must be disqualified from representing a party when it employs an attorney who was formerly the mediator in the identical litigation. Plaintiffs essentially concede that Attorney Moorehead should be screened from involvement in the case. Indeed, they "do not dispute that Ms. Moorehead, herself, may be subject to disqualification." Plaintiffs' Opposition, page 1. They argue, however, that the "cone of silence" erected around Attorney Moorehead is sufficient under the rules and case law, and that the facts do not warrant disqualification of the entire firm. Defendants maintain that Moorehead's contact with the investigator, subsequent to the date that the "cone of silence" was reportedly constructed, constitutes a violation of the relevant ethical standards and presents a more compelling case for disqualification.

* * *

The instant motion to disqualify differs somewhat from the cases cited above, in that it focuses on Attorney Moorehead's role as a mediator who was subsequently hired by the law firm in question. However, the analysis is the same. First, although it is arguable that mediation is not, technically, an adversarial process as is the traditional practice of law, where there is no specific rule that speaks to the issue, courts refer to the Model Rules as a guide to regulate the conduct of the attorney who serves as a mediator in Alternate Dispute Resolution [ADR] proceedings and is later involved in the matter in which he or she mediated. In both situations, the duty of loyalty is at stake. Defendants assert that as mediator Moorehead was privy to confidential information which would be relevant to the present litigation. They argue that under the existing local and ABA rules, her disqualification should be imputed to the entire firm. Mediation is defined as the private, informal dispute resolution process in which a neutral third person, the mediator, helps disputing parties to reach an agreement.

The recent case of Poly Software International, Inc. v. Su, 880 F.Supp. 1487 (D.Utah 1995), discusses the identical issue presented in the case sub judice. In that case, two parties agreed to mediate a copyright action which they were defending. However, soon after the mediated settlement the parties sued each other. One of the parties retained the mediator as his counsel. The other party moved to disqualify the mediator-turned-attorney in light of his prior status as mediator in the previous action. The District Court disqualified the attorney and his law firm from participating in the litigation and held that an attorney who serves as a mediator cannot subsequently represent anyone in a substantially related matter without the consent of the original parties. The court reasoned that mediators routinely receive and preserve confidences in much the same manner as an attorney. The court referred to the Model Rules of Professional Conduct and concluded that where the mediator was privy to confidential information, the applicable ethical rules imposed the same responsibilities as the rules relating to an attorney's subsequent representation of a former client. The court also considered the rule prohibiting judges and other adjudicative officers from representing anyone in connection with a matter in which he or she participated "personally and substantially." Model Rule 1.2.

Likewise, in Cho v. Superior Court, 39 Cal.App.4th 113, 45 Cal. Rptr.2d 863 (1995), a former judge and his law firm were disqualified from representing a party in an action in which the former judge had participated in settlement conferences. That court relied on ABA Model Rule 1.12 which prohibits a lawyer who has participated personally and substantially in a matter as a judge or adjudicative officer, from representing anyone in connection with the same matter. The Court compared the judge's role in the proceedings to that of a mediator, and found that the position necessarily involved the exchange of confidences going to the merits of the case. The court cautioned that "no amount of assurances or screening procedures, no 'cone of silence' could ever convince the opposing party that the confidences would not be used to its disadvantage." The Court concluded that based on the nature of the attorney's prior participation, there is a presumption that confidences were revealed, and the attorney should not have "to engage in subtle evaluation of the extent to which he acquired relevant information in the first representation and of the actual use of that representation." Thus, the rule of the cases is that a mediator should never represent a party to the mediation in a subsequent related or similar matter.

It is against this backdrop that this Court must determine whether Attorney Moorehead, who was the mediator in this identical action, may have received confidences which may be used to the disadvantage of defendant in this case, warranting her disqualification and that of her law firm. Guided by the case law and experience, this Court notes that the very nature of mediation requires that confidences be exchanged. Hence, Local Rule of Civil Procedure 3.2(c)(2) provides that a mediator appointed in this jurisdiction must be impartial and is required to disqualify himself or herself "in any action in which he/she would be required under Title 28, USC sec. 455 to disqualify him/herself if he/she were a judge or Magistrate Judge." Title 28, USC sec. 455 requires such a judicial officer to disqualify himself or herself (1) where the attorney served as a lawyer, the associate lawyer, a witness or a judge in the case;

or (2) where the attorney has served in governmental employment and participated in the case as a counsel, adviser or material witness.

John Landers, Vice President of defendant St. Croix Storage Corp., states by affidavit that he was present during the mediation conference and met with Attorney Moorehead separately and together with the other parties. He states that he openly discussed "the facts of the matter, the financial status and capability of Sun Storage to either pay a settlement figure or to pay a verdict, the status and degree of involvement of certain of the partners ... in the management and operation ... and the trial strategy that was to be employed in the absence of settlement of this matter." Plaintiffs claim that all discussions in the case were done in a group setting and not "confidential." They further argue that any information received would have been discovered during the normal course of litigation.

Plaintiffs' entire argument against disqualification lacks credibility, is unsupported by legal analysis, and completely ignores the existing standards governing attorney conduct. This Court finds, and many commentators agree, that during mediation parties are encouraged to disclose the strengths and weaknesses of their positions, in an effort to arrive at a settlement. Protection of confidences in such a setting strengthens the incentive of parties to negotiate without fear that the mediator will subsequently use the information against them. Additionally, the rules regulating attorney conduct place the onus on the attorney to "remain conscious of the obligation to preserve confidences and maintain loyalty." It is clear from the record that the parties met to negotiate a settlement. It is undisputed that the mediation lasted at least one hour. It is not unreasonable to assume that in light of the nature and purpose of the proceeding, that confidential information was disclosed by the parties. Notwithstanding Attorney Moorehead's statements to the contrary, the present situation presents such a serious affront to the policy that forms the basis of the rules, that this Court has no choice but to conclude that Attorney Moorehead must be disqualified.

Disqualification of the Firm

This Court further finds that disqualification of Attorney Moorehead should be imputed to the other members of the firm. The cases and Model Rule 1.10(a) require such disqualification. Here, the former representation and the present are one and the same, thus obviating the need to determine the existence of a "substantial relationship," and creating a stronger case for disqualification.

In addition, the Court is disturbed by Attorney Moorehead's contact with Mr. Pierre Tepie, an investigator associated with this case. Partly in response to a Motion for Sanctions filed by plaintiffs, Mr. Tepie, who is a self-employed investigator and process server, stated, via affidavit that he was hired by Shirryl Hughes, on behalf of a defendant in this case, to attempt to negotiate an out of court settlement. He further stated that after such attempted negotiation, he was contacted by Attorney Moorehead, who attempted to persuade him to discontinue his efforts. Attorney Moorehead responded, also via affidavit, that she contacted Tepie with regard to his attempted negotiation because she "thought it was wise to inform him that he could be civilly liable for contacting a represented party." She claims she did not know whom he worked for. Moorehead, who was reportedly excluded from the case, does not explain in her affidavit, the manner in which she learned about Tepie's involvement. In any event, this court finds that Moorehead's contact with an agent of the defendants in this very case, implicates the effectiveness of the measures allegedly adopted by her employer to avoid her involvement in this matter. Accordingly, disqualification of the law firm of Rohn & Cusick is necessary to safeguard the integrity of the ongoing litigation and to eliminate the threat that the proceedings will be tainted.

The Motion for Sanctions

Counsel for defendants also seek an order imposing sanctions on plaintiffs' counsel for filing false affidavits with the court. In particular, counsel refers to plaintiffs' attorneys' affidavits attesting to the exclusion of Attorney Moorehead from the case. Defendants' counsel submits that the evidence of Moorehead's subsequent involvement in the case renders the earlier affidavits false, exposing plaintiffs' counsel to sanctions ranging from suspension to disbarment. Federal courts have inherent authority to impose sanctions upon parties and counsel for filing false or seriously misleading affidavits. However, because of their effect, inherent powers must be exercised with restraint and discretion. A court's power to sanction attorneys should be reserved for those cases in which the conduct is egregious, and no other basis for sanction exists. Additionally, the sanctions should be tailored to address the harm identified.

The conduct under scrutiny, here, is the integrity of plaintiffs' attorneys' affidavits regarding Attorney Moorehead's involvement in this case after being hired by Rohn & Cusick. Specifically, the affidavits involved statements regarding Moorehead's contact with Mr. Tepie. It is clear from the record that the conduct of plaintiffs' attorneys is less than exemplary; however, in light of plaintiffs' final response, this Court finds that the sworn statements, taken together, are not patently false. Moreover, even absent such contact, there is ample material in the pleadings which would lead a court to conclude that Moorehead's association with the law firm of Rohn & Cusick creates a conflict of interest warranting disqualification. Accordingly, the Court's decision to disqualify the firm from litigating this action, including the loss of revenue that it portends, provides the intended result and embodies a sanction in and of itself.

Conclusion

Based on the foregoing, this Court finds that, as the mediator in this case, Attorney Moorehead is presumed to have received confidential information going to the merits of the case and must be disqualified. This Court also finds that in addition to the mandate of the Model Rules, the screening procedure reportedly employed at the law firm of Rohn &

Cusick failed to prevent Moorehead's subsequent involvement in this matter, further bolstering the court's conclusion that the law firm of Rohn & Cusick must also be disqualified. Finally, the Court finds that plaintiffs' affidavits herein do not warrant the imposition of sanctions.

FIELDS–D'ARPINO v. RESTAURANT ASSOCIATES, INC.

United States District Court, S.D. New York, 1999.
39 F.Supp.2d 412.

PAULEY, DISTRICT JUDGE.

This action involves claims of gender and pregnancy discrimination in violation of Title VII of the Civil Rights Act of 1964, 42 U.S.C. § 2000e et seq., N.Y. Human Rights Law § 296 and Title 8 of the Administrative Code of the City of New York. By letter memorandum dated January 15, 1999, plaintiff Shari Fields–D'Arpino seeks an order disqualifying the law firm of Dornbush Mensch Mandelstam & Schaeffer, LLP (the "Dornbush firm") from serving as counsel for defendants Restaurant Associates, Inc. and Maureen Hunt in this action. By letter memorandum dated January 22, 1999, defendants argue that disqualification of the Dornbush firm is unwarranted. Unless otherwise noted, the following facts are undisputed.

In January 1997, defendant Restaurant Associates promoted plaintiff to the position of Director of Recruitment for the company's Human Resources Department. On or about February 3, 1998, plaintiff wrote a memorandum to Lawrence B. Jones, Esq., in-house counsel for Restaurant Associates, advising him that plaintiff's supervisor, Maureen Hunt, was treating her unfairly. The plaintiff contends that the memorandum, which is not before the Court, stated her belief that Ms. Hunt was treating her differently because of plaintiff's pregnancy.

After Mr. Jones received plaintiff's memorandum, he contacted the Dornbush firm, outside counsel for Restaurant Associates, and spoke with Richard Schaeffer, Esq., a member of the firm. Mr. Schaeffer arranged to have another attorney at the firm, Cody Fitzsimmons, Esq., meet with the parties in an effort to resolve the dispute. Mr. Fitzsimmons contacted plaintiff and invited her to attend a meeting at his offices for this purpose. Plaintiff agreed.

The meeting occurred on February 5, 1998. Plaintiff was aware that the Dornbush firm served as Restaurant Associates' outside counsel, and she asked Mr. Fitzsimmons if Wendy Fields, Esq., her aunt and a partner in the Washington D.C. law firm of Katten Muchin & Zavis, could participate in the meeting via speaker phone. Mr. Fitzsimmons agreed. The meeting lasted between two and three hours. Ms. Hunt did not attend; only the plaintiff, Mr. Fitzsimmons and a paralegal from the Dornbush firm were physically present at the meeting.

Although the record is unclear, it appears that plaintiff filed an administrative charge of discrimination with the EEOC at some point subsequent to the February 5, 1998 meeting. By letter dated April 15, 1998, the Dornbush firm advised the EEOC that it represented Restaurant Associates in the matter. The letter submission to the EEOC refers to the February 5 meeting and states in relevant part:

> [O]n Thursday, February 5, 1998 and Friday, February 6, 1998, respectively, RA [Restaurant Associates] arranged for Ms. Fields–D'Arpino and Ms. Hunt, at their discretion, to meet separately with [Restaurant Associates'] outside counsel as a neutral third party in an additional effort to resolve their differences.

> . . . Ms. Fields–D'Arpino recounted her version of the disagreements that she had with Ms. Hunt on January 29 and 30, 1998, noting that prior to those dates she loved her job and enjoyed working with Ms. Hunt. Specifically, consistent with her letter to Mr. Jones of February 3, 1998 (which Wendy Fields, Esq. indicated that she assisted Ms. Fields–D'Arpino in writing), Ms. Fields–D'Arpino in no way stated or even implied during the meeting that she believed that she was being discriminated against or mistreated as a result of her pregnancy.

Pl.'s Letter Mem. at 2–3. The letter was apparently signed by Mr. Schaeffer. Plaintiff states, and defendants do not dispute, that Mr. Schaeffer's letter repeatedly characterizes his firm's role at the meeting as that of "neutral, third party." In their letter memorandum to the Court dated January 22, 1999, defendants state that they "intend to call Mr. Fitzsimmons as a witness at trial so that he may testify as to the purpose and content of the February 5, 1998 meeting."

DISCUSSION

Plaintiff argues that the Dornbush firm must be disqualified as counsel of record for defendants in this action based on EC 5–20, which provides:

> A lawyer is often asked to serve as an impartial arbitrator or mediator in matters which involve present or former clients. The lawyer may serve in either capacity if he first discloses such present or former relationships. A lawyer who has undertaken to act as an impartial arbitrator or mediator should not thereafter represent in the dispute any of the parties involved. N.Y.Code of Professional Responsibility EC 5–20 (McKinney's 1999).

Plaintiff also relies on Cannon 9 of the New York Code, which provides that a "lawyer should avoid even the appearance of professional impropriety", and DR 1–102A(4), which states that a lawyer shall not "engage in conduct involving . . . deceit, or misrepresentation." In this regard, plaintiff argues that she was lured into disclosing confidences to the Dornbush firm because it held itself out as a "neutral" mediator.

Defendants dispute that Mr. Fitzsimmons acted as an impartial mediator as contemplated by EC 5–20 because "his neutral role in attempting to resolve Plaintiff's concerns was much less formal." In addition, defendants argue that since Mr. Fitzsimmons has voluntarily withdrawn from representing defendants in this action, disqualification of the entire Dornbush firm is unwarranted. Defendants also point out that plaintiff was represented by her own counsel at the February 5 meeting. Finally, defendants submit that the Dornbush firm never misrepresented to plaintiff either its "identity or intentions."

Notwithstanding that the Dornbush firm did not conceal or misrepresent its relationship with Restaurant Associates, the record is clear that the firm held itself out to plaintiff as an impartial mediator for purposes of conducting the February 5 meeting. The Court rejects defendants' argument that EC 5–20 is inapplicable because the firm's role in the mediation effort was "informal." EC 5–20 does not draw such a distinction and the Court declines to do so. Mediation is inherently an informal approach to dispute resolution that lacks the exacting procedural rules of the judicial process.

As mentioned above, Mr. Fitzsimmons has voluntarily withdrawn from representing defendants in this action.

The only remaining question for this Court to determine is whether disqualification of the Dornbush firm is warranted.

Motions to disqualify counsel are generally viewed with disfavor because "disqualification has an immediate adverse effect on the client by separating him from counsel of his choice, and [because] disqualification motions are often interposed for tactical reasons." "[A] court's ultimate objective in weighing disqualification questions is to ensure that the balance of presentations in a litigation will not be tainted by improper disclosures ... Courts have been directed to take a 'restrained approach that focuses primarily on preserving the integrity of the trial process.' "

* * *

Defendants' argument, in essence, is that it never promised plaintiff or her counsel that it would not represent the defendants if litigation ensued. Under the circumstances, where the Dornbush firm held itself out to plaintiff and her counsel as a neutral, third-party mediator, that distinction rings hollow.

Two other courts have also disqualified law firms when one of the firm's attorneys previously served as a mediator in the litigated matter. In Poly Software International, Inc. v. Su, 880 F.Supp. 1487 (D.Utah 1995), two opposing parties had previously agreed to mediate a copyright action against them involving software products that they were marketing. The mediation was successful and the action settled. In the subsequent Poly Software action those same two parties had become adversaries, and the mediator-attorney from the earlier matter sought to represent one of them. The copyright infringement claims asserted in Poly Software involved the same software that had been the subject of the mediated action.

Drawing on applicable State disciplinary rules, the district court disqualified both the attorney and his law firm, holding that "[w]here a mediator has received confidential information in the course of mediation, that mediator should not thereafter represent anyone in connection with the same or a substantially factually related matter unless all parties to the mediation proceeding consent after disclosure." Poly Software, 880 F.Supp. at 1494.

* * *

More recently, in McKenzie Constr. v. St. Croix Storage Corp., 961 F.Supp. 857 (D.Vi.1997), the court disqualified both an attorney and her law firm under similar circumstances. The court rejected the firm's argument that it had created a "cone of silence" around the attorney in question, and found that the firm's disqualification was "necessary to safeguard the integrity of the ongoing litigation and to eliminate the threat that the proceedings w[ould] be tainted."

Two additional cases, Schwed v. General Electric Co., 990 F.Supp. 113 (N.D.N.Y.1998), and Marshall v. State of New York Div. of State Police, 952 F.Supp. 103 (N.D.N.Y.1997), are also instructive and warrant brief discussion. In both cases, law firms were disqualified because one of their attorneys had access to privileged information during a prior representation of an adverse party. The courts noted that under DR 5–105(D), a presumption arises that privileged information and confidences will be shared with other attorneys within a law firm.

* * *

The Dornbush firm has not even attempted to implement screening procedures that would prevent its attorney-mediator, Mr. Fitzsimmons, from sharing confidential information disclosed by the plaintiff during the mediation with other attorneys in the firm. On the contrary, in the administrative proceeding before the EEOC, the Dornbush firm attempted to exploit what Mr. Fitzsimmons learned during the mediation in order to rebut plaintiff's charge of discrimination. Even more troubling, the Dornbush firm intends to use Mr. Fitzsimmons as a witness at trial with respect to the purpose and content of the mediation. The Court will not permit the Dornbush firm to continue down this path. Under these circumstances, the Court finds that the presence of the Dornbush firm in this action perpetuates an unacceptable appearance of impropriety and raises the spectre that the litigation will be tainted by one side's "unfair advantage."

Conclusion

With the heavy caseloads shouldered today by federal and State courts alike, mediation provides a vital alternative to litigation. The benefits of mediation include its cost-effectiveness, speed and adaptability. Successful mediation, however, depends upon the perception and existence of mutual fairness throughout the mediation process. In this regard, courts have implicitly recognized that maintaining expectations of confidentiality is critical. Congress' view on the importance of alternative dispute resolution, and the need for confidentiality, is equally clear. The Alternative Dispute Resolution Act of 1998 requires each federal district court to authorize, by local rule, the use of alternative dispute resolution processes in all civil actions. See 28 U.S.C. § 651. The Act requires that ADR processes be confidential and prohibits disclosure of confidential dispute resolution communications, though it does not make mediation communications privileged. See 28 U.S.C. § 652(d).

In instances where public confidence in the Bar would be undermined, "even an appearance of impropriety requires prompt remedial action by the court." In light of the foregoing cases and strong public policy favoring mediation, the Court finds that the appropriate remedial action to be taken here is disqualification of the Dornbush firm. Accordingly, plaintiff's motion is granted and the Dornbush firm is disqualified from representing the defendants in this action.

Further, the Dornbush firm, including its employees, agents and members, is prohibited from discussing or revealing any information to the defendants or their counsel concerning the mediation it conducted with the plaintiff. In addition, neither Mr. Fitzsimmons nor any other attorney at the Dornbush firm will be permitted to testify concerning the mediation at any trial of this action. Finally, the parties are precluded from initiating any discovery with respect to the mediation. These prophylactic measures are necessary to level the playing field in this action and ensure that plaintiff's claims will be fairly adjudicated.

SO ORDERED.

However, the Georgia Dispute Resolution Commission advocates a different view of imputation. In an opinion issued in 1997, the Committee on Ethics of the Georgia Commission on Dispute Resolution addressed the issue. In looking at the rule which disqualifies entire law firms if a lawyer is disqualified, the Commission held that it should not be applied in the instance where the lawyer serves as a mediator. Noting that a mediator is pledged to confidence about the mediation, the lawyer-mediators' knowledge should not be imputed to the firm.[34]

B. ETHICS FOR THE ADVOCATES AND PARTIES

In the development of the mediation process, it is natural that the primary focus of ethics be on the mediator and his activities. The concern, initially, was that the mediator, as facilitator and conductor of the process, was perhaps in a position to reach too far, coercing the parties into an agreement. This was particularly true when the general public was unaware of the specifics of mediation and had no idea or expectations of the process. They were at the "mercy," as it were, of the

34. See Georgia Dispute Resolution Commission, Committee on Ethics, Advisory Opinion 4 (1997).

mediator. In an attempt to protect the parties, ethical standards of practice developed.

However, the mediator is not the only participant in the mediation session. In fact, often it is the participants, the parties and their representatives, who have the more active roles in the mediation. Hence, it seems appropriate that these participants should have ethical guidelines to follow. In fact, as previously discussed, some of the recent abuses or misuses of the process have been committed by the participants. Therefore, general guidelines for those participants should be examined, particularly as the roles of the parties and their representatives evolve.

The parties might be bound by certain ethical guidelines associated with their primary profession. For example, professionals such as accountants and physicians often participate in mediation as parties negotiating past due accounts in small claims courts. These professionals may also find their way to the mediation table in response to a claim of malpractice. Ethical concerns may arise in the course of the mediation, and could even be the subject of the dispute. For instance, doctors have specific ethical guidelines which must be adhered to when dealing with a patient. It is likely that these guidelines continue to be operable in the mediation session.

Many times the party in a mediation will be accompanied at the session by a representative. In most cases this will be an attorney. In some matters, particularly in the family area, a therapist may attend the mediation with his client. It can be assumed that individuals will abide by the ethical guidelines already established for their profession. In the majority of cases, these guidelines will be appropriate. However, those ethics were not determined with the mediation practice in mind. For instance, there may be a conflict between the primary role of the attorney in the courtroom and that of the attorney in the mediation. The obligation of the attorney to represent his client zealously means something very different in trial than it does in mediation. Moreover, attorney advocates may have duties in mediation not otherwise considered. Determining the fairness of a mediated agreement is one example. In the case of therapists, they may be bound to inject an opinion regarding the interests of the children during custody mediation. As the practice of mediation matures, increased involvement of these representatives may indicate or even necessitate a closer examination of their roles. Since there have been no changes to date, it can be assumed that the current operative standard of ethics remains that of the representative's primary profession. For example, the conduct of an attorney advocate in mediation would be examined using the lawyer's code of professional responsibility as if he were participating in a more traditional negotiation.[35]

---

35. However, changes have been advocated. See Carrie Menkel–Mealow, *The Trouble With the Adversary System in a Post Modern, "Multicultural World*, 38 Wm. & Mary L. Rev. 5 (1996); Kimberlee K. Kovach, *Good Faith in Mediation—Requested, Recommended or Required? A New Ethic* 38 S. Tex. L. Rev. 575 (1997).

There are also issues, primarily ethical in nature, which affect representatives prior to the mediation. One concern is whether or not an attorney has the duty to inform a client about the mediation option. In the legal profession, there is still some debate,[36] although most ethics experts would allege that the question has been settled. The attorney clearly has a duty, which has been legally established, to inform a client of settlement offers.[37] Argument has been made that this legal obligation should be expanded to discussing legal strategy, in particular settlement options and ADR with the client.[38] Some state and local bar associations and Supreme Courts, including those in Texas and Colorado, have enacted ethical obligations in the form of professional mandates which direct an attorney to inform a client about ADR, when appropriate. Most recently, the American Bar Association is considering the inclusion of such a provision in the Model Rules through its Ethics 2000 Commission at the urging of the ABA's Section of Dispute Resolution.[39] While companion requirements for other professionals such as therapists and accountants have not been established, it is conceivable that they too, should inform and refer their clients to the mediation process where appropriate.

C. ETHICAL CONSIDERATIONS FOR REFERRING AGENCIES OR ENTITIES

Most often, the agency or entity which refers parties to mediation is the court. Others may include institutions such as schools, universities and business organizations. As these entities establish comprehensive dispute resolution programs,[40] some ethical concerns should be addressed. They should, for example, consider the ethical obligation of the judge in making an impartial mediator selection. The courts, particularly, have been active in referring cases to mediation. In some instances the referral process can be conducted in such a way that the appearance of impropriety is clear. For example, if the majority of cases which are referred to mediation are sent to the judge's former law partner or son-in-law, ethical issues arise. Concern for the court's role in mediation resulted in the promulgation of standards which define the specific role of the court.[41] While only aspirational in nature, it is hoped that all state

---

36. See Frank E. A. Sander & Michael L. Prigoff, *Should There be a Duty to Advise of ADR Options*, 76 A.B.A.J. 50 (Nov. 1990).

37. See, Rizzo v. Haines, 520 Pa. 484, 555 A.2d 58 (1989).

38. Robert F. Cochran, Jr., *Legal Representation and the Next Steps Toward Client Control: Attorney Malpractice for the Failure to Allow the Client to Control Negotiation and Pursue Alternatives to Litigation*, 47 Wash. & Lee L. Rev. 819 (1990). See also Monica L. Wermbrod, *Comment, Could an Attorney Face Disciplinary Actions or Even*

Legal Malpractice Liability for Failure to Inform Clients of Alternative Dispute Resolution, 27 Cumb. L. Rev. 791 (1996–97).

39. 84 A.B.A.J. 100 (1998).

40. See Chapter 17 on Dispute Systems Design.

41. See National Standards for Court–Connected Mediation Programs, Center for Dispute Settlement and Institute of Judicial Administration, (1992). Executive Summary, Appendix D.

courts voluntarily adopt these standards. The standards, which touch upon ethical concerns, include a requirement for the court to determine that a mediator to whom a case is referred is competent, that the case is properly referred to mediation, and that the court does not receive confidential information from the mediator.

Another concern in the area of case referral with potential ethical ramifications is the issue of referral fees. If individuals or entities refer cases to a specific mediator, can the fee be split? In the alternative, would it be proper for the mediator to provide a referral fee to the person or agency which refers a case?

D. ETHICS FOR ORGANIZATIONAL PROVIDERS OF MEDIATION SERVICES

Organizational providers of mediation services include dispute resolution centers and statewide offices of dispute resolution. These are generally non-profit entities. There are also fee-generating private providers of these services. Both types of organizations employ administrative staff. In the not-for-profit area, agencies are publicly funded with the expectation that they will assist citizens in locating a mediator who will help resolve their disputes. These organizations should also abide by ethical standards, including those of impartiality and confidentiality. Likewise, conflicts of interest should be avoided. Some of these organizations have voluntarily applied the appropriate standards of mediator ethics to the manner in which they conduct business.

Private providers of mediation should not be exempt from established ethical guidelines. Ethical issues such as conflicts of interest, impartiality, advertising and fees have been traditionally discussed only in reference to the individual mediator. Extending ethical safeguards to the administrative organization may be proper, particularly in light of proposed changes with regard to law firms. For example, a committee of the Association of the Bar of the City of New York has recommended that law firms be liable for ethical violations of their lawyers.[42] The reasoning is that the entity—the firm—should have ethical obligations. Moreover, there are some matters over which the law firm has control, and it is the organization that should be responsible.[43]

Similarly, a private provider of mediation services should be held ethically accountable. The mediation organization should be responsible for the actions of its mediators that it can control, as well as be obligated to ethical standards in its own right. Recent focus on organizational providers has produced a draft of Principles for ADR Provider Organizations by the CPR–Georgetown Commission on Ethics and Standards in ADR.[44] The Draft provides several guidelines for provider organizations

---

42. Henry J. Raske, *Promoting Better Supervision*, 79 A.B.A.J. 32 (1993).

43. *Id.*

44. Draft 8/16/99—On file with author.

including providing quality and competence of service; duty to provide information; an obligation of fairness and impartiality; access for low-income parties; disclosure of conflicts of interest; the inclusion of complaint and grievance mechanisms; responsibility of organizations to require its neutrals to adhere to a code of ethics; a prohibition against false or misleading communication; and provisions of confidentiality. Although the implementation and enforcement of these guidelines will be challenging, this is clearly a step in the direction of the expansion of the professionalization of mediation.

QUESTIONS FOR DISCUSSION

14–1. The local court has referred a commercial litigation case to you for mediation. You recognize that the firm representing the defendant employs your ex-spouse, but do not see the name on the pleadings or correspondence. Should you disclose this to anyone? Who? Assume that you do not disclose this information, and much to your surprise, s/he arrives at the mediation representing the defendant. What should you do?

14–2. As a lawyer, you resign from your sixty lawyer firm to begin a full-time mediation practice. Should you be barred from serving as a mediator in all cases where your former partners and associates represent a party? Is any time limit appropriate?

14–3. You are an accountant for Sam Walt who is involved in a heated business dissolution. A variety of business and tax consequences concern your client. Moreover, of the five partners in this seven million dollar enterprise, two are related to Sam. One is a brother, and the other an aunt. These family issues have made the disputing parties even more tense. The attorney for Sam, has not mentioned ADR or mediation. You are familiar with the mediation process, having attended a mediation with a client in a real estate matter. What do you do?

14–4. You have a Ph.D. in clinical psychology with emphasis on child development and are in private practice as a therapist. You have been seeing Ralph, a ten year old child for the past four months. Ralph has demonstrated behavioral problems. You now learn that Ralph's parents have just filed for divorce. Each parent has called you. It appears that both have employed aggressive attorneys, as each attorney has called to schedule your deposition.

(a) How do you respond to the request for your deposition?

(b) Should you discuss mediation as an alternative for the divorce process? Should you initiate discussions with the lawyers? With Ralph's parents? With the court?

Chapter Fifteen

QUALITY CONTROL

The issue of regulation or assurance of quality control for mediators may seem, at first glance, a very simple endeavor—even unnecessary. After all, mediation is a voluntary process and the mediator doesn't make decisions. How can there be harm? Yet, the issue of quality control is a widely discussed and debated topic among mediators and other dispute resolution professionals.[1] It seems as if the seventies were the time for experimentation with mediation; the eighties for implementation of programs, and the nineties for regulation of the field. In fact, the largest organization of dispute resolution professionals, SPIDR (Society of Professionals in Dispute Resolution), has had two commissions review the matter.[2] Matters of "quality" in mediation encompass many aspects of the mediator's work. As pointed out in the preceding chapter, standards of conduct are related to, and overlap with, ethical considerations. The topic of quality control is even more expansive and is similarly problematic because of the variety of forms, functions and definitions of a mediator.

In this new and continually developing field of ADR, inquiries into matters of qualification, certification and evaluation of the mediator's work are now underway. Entities such as state and local bar associations, mediator organizations, and court administrative groups are beginning to examine these various issues. Yet, except for a few states which have enacted specific certification guidelines for mediators,[3] no other

---

1. See, for example Bobby Marzine Harges, *Mediation Qualifications: The Trend Toward Professionalization*, BYU L. Rev. 687 (1997); Deborah B. Gentry, *The Certification Movement: Past, Present and Future*, 11 Mediation Q. 285 (1994); Paul S. Spiegelman, *Certifying Mediators: Using Select Criteria to Include the Qualified— Lessons from the San Diego Experience*, 30 U.S.F. L. Rev. 677 (1996); Jay Folberg, *Certification of Mediators in California: An Introduction* 30 U.S.F.L.Rev. 609 (1996); Stephanie A. Henning, Note, *A Framework for* *Developing Mediator Certification Programs*, 4 Harv. Negotiation L. Rev. 189 (1999).

2. Society of Professionals in Dispute Resolution, Report of the SPIDR Commission on Qualifications, (hereinafter referred to as Report) (1989); Society of Professionals in Dispute Resolution, Ensuring Competence and Quality in Dispute Resolution Practice, Report 2 of the SPIDR Commission on Qualifications (1995) [hereinafter SPIDR Report No. 2].

3. See § D *infra*.

entity or organization has established strict regulations or licensing procedures.

Even though the profession is moving in the direction of quality control, debate about the need for regulation continues. The establishment of quality checks may serve the mediator, the profession and the public. For the mediator, qualifications provide guidance to those who are considering mediating as a career. With standardization of training comes enhancement of credibility with disputants, and a sense of professionalism. The establishment of qualifications will afford the mediation profession with legitimation of the field, with preparation for continued, organized growth of the mediation practice, and standardization of processes and procedures. The public will also benefit, since marketing and education about the differences in mediation may be provided, controls will be maintained, and a basis for redress of problems will be created.[4]

On the other hand, a contrary view expresses strong reservations about the establishment of mediation qualifications. There is fear that such "limiting" qualifications will retard the growth of ADR use. Furthermore, it is alleged that research has yet to demonstrate a real nexus between the mediator's skill and a successful outcome. Moreover, what constitutes *success* in mediation has not been determined. Finally, qualifications can raise costs and can certainly limit the mediator's work.[5] Even the SPIDR Commission has recognized that mandatory standards may provide inappropriate barriers to the field and limit the innovative quality of the profession.[6] Nonetheless, it appears that the profession is moving in the direction of establishing mediator qualifications. Determining specifically what those qualifications should entail is the focus of discussion. Research continues with additional inquiry strongly advocated.[7]

Many ways exist to ensure quality control in the practice of mediation. Such methods may be used separately or in combination with one another. Most existing quality control techniques have been tried in community or court-annexed programs. Quality control methods include the following: initial selection of individuals to become mediators; mediator training and education; testing and evaluation of the mediator's competencies, which may also be included in a certification process; regulation by a certification or licensing procedure; enactment of standards of conduct which must be followed; and establishment of liability. These elements, if correctly put into practice, can enhance the quality of the mediation practice.

4. Peter R. Maida, *Why Qualifications?* Qualifications Sourcebook Compendium (Society of Professionals in Dispute Resolution, Commission on Qualifications 1993) [hereinafter referred to as Compendium].

5. Christine Carlson, *Why the Practice of Mediation Should Not be Overregulated From the Perspective of a State Program Manager,* Compendium), *supra* note 4.

6. Report, *supra* note 2.

7. Margaret L. Shaw, Selection, Training and Qualification of Neutrals, A working paper for the National Symposium on Court–Connected Dispute Resolution Research (September 1993).

An initial impediment to implementation of the foregoing methods is the identification of a source which will make ultimate judgments of competency and quality. What entity should control mediator regulation? In court-connected programs, many strongly urge the courts to take this role.[8] In community centers, funding agencies or the boards of directors of the non-profit managing entities have assumed some responsibility for mediator quality. In other programs, and in the case of the open marketplace, who should assume the role of regulation and enforcement of standards is undetermined. Options range from the consumer to a mediator organization to a state agency.

With such a variety of entities attempting to assure quality control, there can be little consistency. In order to have consistent requirements for all mediators, one option is for each state to create a board of licensure or regulation for mediators similar to the state boards of other professions. The search for answers to these issues continues.

A. BACKGROUND

Complaints about mediators, though few and far between, have begun to surface. As more individuals participate in the process, there is fear that complaints will increase. In 1988, SPIDR, as the primary interdisciplinary organization of mediators and other third party neutrals, established a commission to examine issues surrounding the quality of neutrals. The commission quickly recognized that the task was not a simple one. SPIDR acknowledged both that there is no single way to promote quality in any professional practice, and that a number of options are currently used. The SPIDR report listed several current methods: free market; disclosure requirements; public and consumer education; "after the fact" controls, such as malpractice lawsuits; rosters; voluntary standards; codes of professional ethics; mandatory standards for neutrals; mandatory standards for programs; and improvements in training for neutrals, including apprenticeship programs.[9] The final report which summarized the commissions findings, was published in 1989 and provided general recommendations.

The Commission, striving to reach an appropriate balance between competing concerns, adopted three central principles:

A. that no single entity (but rather, a variety of organizations) should establish qualifications for neutrals;

B. that the greater the degree of choice the parties have over the dispute resolution process, program, or neutral, the less mandatory the qualification requirements should be; and

C. that qualification criteria should be based on performance, rather than paper credentials.[10]

8. Center for Dispute Settlement and the Institute of Judicial Administration, Standards for Court–Connected Mediation Programs (1992) (hereinafter referred to as National Standards (1992)).

9. Report, *supra* note 2, at 1.

The Commission recognized that the knowledge, skills and techniques needed to practice mediation competently may change depending upon a number of variables. The context of the dispute and its resolution, the particular process used, the issues involved in the case, and the institutional setting can all impact the neutral's actions. Therefore, there was no single entity to certify general dispute resolution competency.

The second principle attempted to balance the use of a free marketplace with mandatory programs. In this regard, SPIDR made three specific recommendations:

1. When parties have free choice of the process, program, and neutral, no standards or qualifications should be established that would prevent any person from providing dispute resolution services, as long as there is full disclosure of the neutral's relevant training and experience, the fees and expenses to be charged, and any financial or personal interest or prior relationship with the parties that might affect the neutral's impartiality.

2. Where public or private entities operate programs that offer no choice of process, program or neutral, an appropriate public entity should set standards or qualifications for such programs and for neutrals, in accordance with the principles set forth in this Report and make such standards and qualifications available to the parties.

3. When parties have some, but not a complete, choice of process, program or neutral, each program offering such services should establish clear selection and evaluation criteria and make such information available to the parties, together with its rules governing confidentiality, the means by which complaints may be lodged, and all relevant "full disclosure" information concerning the neutral selected for the particular case.[11]

The third principle, performance-based qualifications, included specific recommendations of performance-based testing, continuing education for the neutrals, and establishing qualifications for trainers.

The concern with this SPIDR report was that it raised more questions than it answered. In other words, it was just the beginning. The guidelines were not definitive, and since the report was issued in 1989, a more detailed analysis was completed. To complicate matters even further, some states, in direct contravention of the third principle, have enacted statutes which qualify mediators by the mere possession of a college or graduate degree.

A second SPIDR commission on qualifications was appointed to follow the work of the first. This second commission completed its task

10. *Id.* at 2.   **11.** *Id.*

and presented a final report in 1995.[12] In its work, the second commission attempted to distinguish and define with some precision the terms surrounding these issues of quality control. These are as follows:

Certification: Certification is an explicit recognition that a person has completed a specific level of education or training, or has achieved a particular level of skill in performing certain functions. Certification can be granted by public or private, professional or educational bodies. In cases where certification has been granted by a public body, the right to practice may be a consequence. Other times the right to use a professional title accompanies certification.[13]

Certification: a process whereby an individual is tested and evaluated in order to determine his mastery of a specific body of knowledge or some portion of a body of knowledge. As individuals are certified by groups expert in a certain field, it is generally viewed as voluntary.[14]

Licensure: permission to practice a particular activity, function, or profession. Licenses are generally granted by public authorities based on prescribed levels of education, experience, or performance. Licensure usually also carries with it a fee.[15]

Licensure is a process applied to individuals, granted by a political body to people who meet predetermined qualifications. It gives them the right to engage in a particular occupation or profession, use a particular title or perform a specific function. It is required.[16]

Regulation: the administration, direction, supervision, control or management of an activity, usually by a public authority. Administrative regulations generally are established by public bodies through open hearings and implemented through published rules and procedures.[17]

Often *certification*, *license*, and *regulation* are used interchangeably but as the mediation profession advances in its quest for uniformity, specificity in determining each quality control element becomes necessary.

This second SPIDR report, while very helpful in providing guidelines for consideration in designing certification programs, failed to establish specific requirements. Most recently, SPIDR has activated a third Committee on the subject, which is looking to be more specific in approach. This committee, known as 3CQ (Committee on Credentials, Competency

12. See SPIDR, Report No. 2, *supra* note 2.

13. Adapted from an early publication of the National Institute for Dispute Resolution and a 1991 report from the New South Wales Law Reform Commission. See Compendium, *supra* note 5.

14. Taken from an Information Background Kit provided by American Society of Association Executives to SPIDR, in Compendium, *supra* note 4.

15. Compendium, *supra* note 4.

16. Taken from an Information Background Kit, in Compendium *supra* note 4.

17. *Id.*

and Qualifications) will, as the name indicates, focus on reaching conclusions on precise and explicit qualifications.

B. QUALIFICATIONS

There are a number of ways by which an individual is selected to become a mediator. The term *qualification*, in this context, refers to the characteristics of an individual prior to participating in mediation training or education. These include the individual's educational background and any other acquired skill or training. Qualifications also include general innate tendencies, such as personality, communication abilities and conflict management style.

Some programs, courts, and statutory schemes provide that a college or graduate degree is required of all a mediators. Some specifically require additional training,[18] while others determine that a degree itself establishes sufficient competency.[19] As a practical matter, most mediators in court-connected programs possess college degrees, and the majority have received graduate degrees, usually in law.

Mediation trainers, educators and administrators have not reached consensus on which characteristics constitute necessary qualifications. Many assert that it is a combination of factors which indicate the individual's appropriateness for mediation training. In fact, preliminary research indicates that initial, innate qualities, such as one's predisposition for conflict management, are more important in determining a mediator's effectiveness than training or prior experience.[20]

Assuming that a determination of pre-training qualifications is necessary regardless of subsequent training or education, the problem of how these qualifications may be assessed remains. In the case of the requirement of a degree only, it is simple. In other instances, assessment of appropriate characteristics can be difficult. Several programs hold initial screening interviews before accepting individuals into training. Others require potential mediators to "audition" by conducting mock mediations. Some trainers require a number of years experience in a given field, primarily law. Pre-training appraisal via psychological inventories, such as the Meyers–Briggs type indicator,[21] may also be used.

Many of the factors used to determine mediator qualifications are subjective in nature, and consequently, some mediators claim they are unfair, particularly if applied inconsistently. Moreover, if mediation skills can be taught, there should be no necessity for initial screening.

---

18. See West's Fla. Stat. Ann. Mediator Rule 10.010 (Supp. 2000); Tex.Civ. Prac. & Rem.Code Ann. § 154.052 (West 1997) which, while recommending specific training, allow the court to waive the requirement; and Michie's Utah Court Rules Annotated, Utah Code of Judicial Administration, Judicial Administration Rule 4–510(3).

19. See Mich.Comp.Laws § 552.513(4) (Supp. 1999).

20. Shaw, *supra* note 7, at 14.

21. The Meyer–Briggs Type Indicator is a questionnaire which helps determine the taker's personality type. It is helpful in assessing one's character strengths and weaknesses, as well as compatible personalities. For an in-depth examination of the use of Meyers–Briggs in teaching negotiation, see Don Peters, *Forever Jung: Psychological Type Theory, the Meyer–Briggs Type Indicator and Learning Negotiation*, 42 Drake L. Rev. 1 (1993).

Most professions, however, have initial qualification requirements which must be met before a student can enter a professional school. If mediation is to be established as a "profession," pre-training qualifications may need to be defined and implemented.

C. TRAINING AND EDUCATION— TESTING AND EVALUATION

There is wide variation in the training and education of mediators.[22] While there was early consensus that some type of training or education for mediators was necessary, there was no consensus on the content of that training. Some programs and courts require nothing more than a three to four hour orientation to the mediation process. This is particularly true where a graduate degree such as a law degree, is used as the indicator of mediator competency. Other programs and projects recognize that specific training and education in the mediation process is necessary. Typically training programs range from a minimum of sixteen hours[23] to the maximum requirement of a forty hour training.[24]

In most other professions at least one year of schooling or education is necessary in order to be licensed or certified. Currently, the most training or education required to "become a mediator" is forty hours. Additional hours are sometimes required for specialty areas, such as in family matters.[25] Some colleges offer both undergraduate and graduate degree programs in conflict resolution that require a minimum of a year of study. If a mediation *profession* is established, it seems likely that the forty hour requirement will increase. Preliminary research, however, has not indicated that those who have more training necessarily perform better than mediators with less.[26]

Even in the instances where there is agreement as to the number of hours of required mediation training or teaching, there is no regulation as to the form of that education. Diversity exists in both the method and content of training. Some mediation training programs consist of no more than viewing videotapes of mediations. Others consist primarily of lectures. Some training programs encourage continuous participation by the trainee. Most educators recognize that it is a combination of activities that provides the best learning experience. Most of the ongoing forty hour trainings do, as a rule, have a combination of these activities, although each varies in the proportion devoted to the various teaching methods. For mediators who will work in court programs, it is recom-

22. For an in-depth examination of training issues see Joseph B. Stulberg, *Training Interveners for ADR Processes*, 81 Ky. L. J. 977 (1992–93). Also see John Ferrick et al., *Standards of Professional Conduct in Alternative Dispute Resolution*, 1995 J. Disp. Resol. 95.

23. For example, Columbus, Ohio, Night Prosecutor Program, (1980), Washington D.C. Multi–Door Training Agenda,

(1992), and New Orleans Civil Courts Pilot Project (1993).

24. See, for example, Tex. Civ. Prac. & Rem. Code Ann. § 154.052 (1997); Fla.Stat. Ann. Mediator Rule 10.010 (1999).

25. See Tex. Civ. Prac. & Rem. Code Ann. § 154.052(b) (1997) and West's Fla. Stat.Ann. Mediator Rule 10.010 (1999).

26. Shaw, *supra* note 7 at 13.

mended that the training includes role-playing with feedback.[27] Although some instructors and trainers voluntarily share information and methodology, few standards exist for those who train mediators. This lack of a standard curriculum ensures that mediators will emerge from training programs with very different ideas as to what their "profession" requires. They may share no "core competencies" with other mediators.

An even greater difficulty for the mediation trainer is the determination of whether a trainee has "passed" the course. How will successful completion be determined? Some mediation courses and trainings, particularly those in law schools or other educational institutions, administer tests to the students. These range from traditional written examinations to performance-based assessments. Court-based programs have experimented with performance-based testing,[28] but have found the time and effort involved in doing so overwhelming. Where evaluation is required, as in an academic setting such as a law school, performance-based testing is often combined with the more traditional written examination. The use of video has been quite helpful in this regard as well.[29] Others continue to test the evaluation process.[30]

In addition, there are different times at which the evaluation or testing can be conducted. A number of trainers test mediators within a year of training, since it has been noted that experience increases the mediator's skills.[31] Therefore, some programs include an apprenticeship requirement. Other methods of evaluation which have been used include settlement rates, user perceptions, including satisfaction, and opinions of judges, attorneys and peers.[32]

Most training programs, whether at the volunteer-community or the private provider mediator level, do not provide a formal evaluation of the trainee at the conclusion of the session. Trainers often do evaluate the trainees during the training and provide direct feedback. Such assessment may consist only of informal conversation, or it may involve the use of more sophisticated tools, including forms and charts for evaluation. Few training programs will directly tell a trainee that he did not "pass" the mediation training. Since there is currently no licensure, even if individuals do not receive letters or certificates of completion, they may still mediate. Only the state of Minnesota imposes a requirement that mediators who are compensated disclose to the parties in writing their qualifications prior to mediation. Failure to do so is a crime, a petty misdemeanor.[33]

---

27. National Standards, *supra* note 8, at 6–4.

28. Brad Honoroff, et al., *Putting Mediator Skills to the Test*, 6 Negotiation J. 37 (1990).

29. For a detailed look at the use of video, see Kimberlee K. Kovach, *Virtual Reality Testing: The Use of Video for Evalua-* *tion in Legal Education*, 46 J. Legal Educ. 233 (1996).

30. Christopher Honeyman, *On Evaluating Mediators*, 6 Negotiation J. 23 (1990).

31. Shaw, *supra* note 7, at 17.

32. *Id.*

33. Minn. Stat. Ann. § 572.37 (West 1998).

Many programs,[34] courts[35] and a few states[36] have continuing education requirements for mediators. Regardless of any actual requirements, because of the infancy of the field and its rapid change and expansion, active mediators will find it a necessity to continue the educational process.

D. REGULATION, CERTIFICATION, AND LICENSURE

It is very difficult to predict just what the regulation of the mediation profession will be and who will administer it. In many professions, regulation is achieved by a board and is administered on a state-wide basis. Such boards have not been established in the mediation profession, although the Supreme Courts of Florida and Virginia have attempted to fill that role. In Utah, the job had been delegated to the State Division of Occupational and Professional Licensing, but the legislature has now created an Alternative Dispute Resolution Providers Certification Board.[37] Mediators are still attempting to determine who the certifying or regulatory authority should be.

There is currently no type of licensure required for mediators. The terms "certification" or "certified mediator" are widely mentioned, although the "certification" procedure consists, in most instances, of the receipt of a certificate which provides that the individual has completed a specific number of hours in mediation training. The certificate itself has no bearing on the individual's competency as a mediator.

Some regulations exist in specific programs. For instance, many community based centers regulate mediators by allowing them to mediate only in a team or co-mediation format. In other instances, regulation is accomplished by a staff person or experienced mediator observing the mediators. Some mediator trade organizations have been formed which attempt self-regulation by enacting specific requirements for membership.

In 1992, the Supreme Court of Florida became the first organization in the United States to enact comprehensive guidelines for mediator certification and decertification.

FLORIDA RULES FOR CERTIFIED AND COURT–APPOINTED MEDIATORS
(1994).

PART I. MEDIATOR QUALIFICATIONS

RULE 10.010 GENERAL QUALIFICATIONS

(a) **County Court Mediators**. For certification a mediator of county court matters must be certified as a circuit court or family mediator:

---

34. For example, many Dispute Resolution Centers require all volunteer mediators to complete a number of hours of "continuing *mediator* education" to remain active with the center.

35. See, for example, U.S. Dist. Ct. Rules S.D. Tex. Rule 20E(3) (1994).

36. West's Fla.Stat.Ann. Mediator Rule 10.120(b) (1999).

37. Utah Code Ann. § 58–39a–2 (1998).

(1) complete a minimum of 20 hours in a training program certified by the supreme court;

(2) observe a minimum of 4 county court mediation conferences conducted by a court-certified mediator and conduct 4 county court mediation conferences under the supervision and observation of a court-circuited mediator; and

(3) Be of good moral character,

(b) **Family Mediators**. For certification a mediator of family and dissolution of marriage issues must:

(1) complete a minimum of 40 hours in a family mediation training program certified by the supreme court;

(2) have a masters degree or doctorate in social work, mental health, behavioral or social sciences; or be a physician certified to practice adult or child psychiatry; or be an attorney or a certified public accountant licensed to practice in any United States jurisdiction; and have at least 4 years practical experience in one of the aforementioned fields; or have 8 years family mediation experience with a minimum of 10 mediations per year;

(3) observe 2 family mediations conducted by a certified family mediator and conduct 2 family mediations under the supervision and observation of a certified family mediator; and

(4) be of good moral character.

(c) **Circuit Court Mediators.** For certification a mediator of circuit court matters, other than family matters, must:

(1) Complete a minimum of 40 hours in a circuit court mediation training program certified by the supreme court;

(2) be a member in good standing of the Florida Bar with at least 5 years of Florida practice and be an active member of the Florida Bar within 1 year of application for certification or be a retired trial judge from any United States jurisdiction who was a member in good standing of the bar in the state in which the judge presided for at least 5 years immediately preceding the year certification is sought;

(3) observe 2 circuit court mediations conducted by a certified circuit mediator and conduct 2 circuit mediations under the supervision and observation of a certified circuit court mediator; and

(4) be of good moral character.

* * *

(e) **Special Conditions**. Mediators who have been duly certified as circuit court or family mediators before July 1, 1990, shall be deemed qualified as circuit court or family mediators pursuant to these rules. . . .

PART II.   STANDARDS OF PROFESSIONAL CONDUCT

RULE 10.020   PREAMBLE

(a) **Scope; Purpose**. These rules are intended to instill and promote public confidence in the mediation process and to be a guide to mediator conduct. As with other forms of dispute resolution, mediation must be built on public understanding and confidence. Persons serving as mediators are responsible to the parties, the public, and the courts to conduct themselves in a manner which will merit that confidence. These rules apply to all mediators who are certified or court appointed. These rules are also intended to serve as a guide to mediator's conduct in discharging their professional responsibilities as mediators.

(b) **Mediation Defined**. Mediation is a process whereby a neutral third party acts to encourage and facilitate the resolution of a dispute without prescribing what it should be. It is an informal and nonadversarial process with the objective of helping the disputing parties reach a mutually acceptable agreement.

(c) **Mediator's Role**. In mediation, decision-making authority rests with the parties. The role of the mediator includes but is not limited to assisting the parties in identifying issues, reducing obstacles to communication, maximizing the exploration of alternatives, and helping the parties reach voluntary agreements.

(d) **General Principles**. Mediation is based on principles of communication, negotiation, facilitation, and problem-solving that emphasize:

(1) the needs and interests of the participants;

(2) fairness;

(3) procedural flexibility;

(4) privacy and confidentiality;

(5) full disclosure; and

(6) self-determination.

RULE 10.030   GENERAL STANDARDS AND QUALIFICATIONS

(a) **General**. Integrity, impartiality, and professional competence are essential qualifications of any mediator. Mediators shall adhere to the highest standards of integrity, impartiality, and professional competence in rendering their professional service.

(1) A mediator shall not accept any engagement, perform any service, or undertake any act which would compromise the mediator's integrity.

(2) A mediator shall maintain professional competence in mediation skills including, but not limited to:

(A) staying informed of and abiding by all statutes, rules, and administrative orders relevant to the practice of court-ordered mediation;

(B) if certified, continuing to meet the requirements of these rules; and

(C) regularly engaging in educational activities promoting professional growth.

(3) A mediator shall decline appointment, withdraw, or request technical assistance when the mediator decides that a case is beyond the mediator's competence.

(b) **Concurrent Standards**. Nothing herein shall replace, eliminate, or render inapplicable relevant ethical standards, not in conflict with these rules, which may be imposed upon any mediator by virtue of the mediator's professional calling.

* * *

PART III.   DISCIPLINE

RULE 10.160   SCOPE AND PURPOSE

These rules apply to all proceedings before all panels and committees of the mediator qualifications board involving the discipline or decertification of certified mediators or non-certified mediators appointed to mediate a case pursuant to Florida Rules of Civil Procedure 1.700–1.750. The purpose of these rules is to provide a means for enforcing the Florida Rules for Certified and Court–Appointed Mediators.

RULE 10.170   PRIVILEGE TO MEDIATE

Certification to mediate confers no vested right to the holder thereof, but is a conditional privilege that is revocable for cause.

* * *

RULE 10.190   MEDIATOR QUALIFICATIONS BOARD

(a) **Generally**. The mediator qualifications board shall be composed of 3 standing divisions that shall be located in the following regions: . . .

. . . Other divisions may be formed by the Supreme Court based on need.

(b) **Composition of Divisions**. Each division of the board shall be composed of the following members:

(1) three circuit or county judges;

(2) three certified county mediators;

(3) three certified circuit mediators;

(4) three certified family mediators, at least 2 of whom shall be non-lawyers; and

(5) three attorneys licensed to practice law in Florida who have a substantial trial practice and are neither certified as mediators nor judicial officers during their terms of service on the board, at least one of whom shall have a substantial divorce law practice.

* * *

RULE 10.220 COMPLAINT COMMITTEE PROCESS

(a) **Initiation of Complaint**. Any individual wishing to make a complaint alleging that a mediator has violated one or more provisions of these rules shall do so in writing under oath. The complaint shall state with particularity the specific facts that form the basis of the complaint.

* * *

RULE 10.240 SANCTIONS

(a) **Generally**. The panel may impose one or more of the following sanctions:

(1) Imposition of costs of the proceeding:

(2) Oral admonishment:

(3) Written reprimand:

(4) Additional training, which may include the observation of mediations:

(5) Restriction on types of cases which can be mediated in the future:

(6) Suspension for a period of up to one year:

(7) Decertification or, if the mediator is not certified, bar from service as a mediator under Florida Rules of Civil Procedure.

(8) Such other sanctions as are agreed to by the mediator and the panel.

* * *

(c) **Decertified Mediators**. If a mediator has been decertified or barred from service pursuant to these rules, the mediator shall not thereafter be certified in any circuit nor assigned to mediate a case pursuant to Florida Rule of Civil Procedure 1.700 nor be designated as mediator pursuant to Rule 1.720(f) unless reinstated.

(d) **Decision to be Filed**. Upon making a determination that discipline is appropriate, the panel shall promptly file with the center a copy of the decision including findings and conclusions certified by the chair of the panel. The center shall promptly mail to all parties notice of such filing, together with a copy of the decision.

(e) **Notice to Circuits**. The center shall notify all circuits of any mediator who has been decertified or suspended unless otherwise ordered by the Supreme Court of Florida.

(f) **Publication.** Upon the imposition of sanctions, the center shall publish the name of the mediator, a short summary of the rule or rules which were violated, the circumstances surrounding the violation, and any sanctions imposed.

(g) **Reinstatement**. A mediator who has been suspended or decertified may be reinstated as a certified mediator. Except as otherwise provided in the decision of the panel, no application for reinstatement may be tendered within 2 years after the date of decertification. The reinstatement procedures shall be as follows:

(1) A petition for reinstatement, together with 3 copies, shall be made in writing, verified by the petitioner, and filed with the center.

(2) The petition for reinstatement shall contain: . . .

(3) The center shall refer the petition for reinstatement to a hearing panel in the appropriate division for review.

(4) The division shall review the petition with or without hearing and, if the petitioner is found to be unfit to mediate, the petition shall be dismissed. If the petitioner is found fit to mediate, the division shall notify the center and the center shall reinstate the petitioner as a certified mediator; provided, however, if the decertification has continued for more than 3 years, the reinstatement may be conditioned upon the completion of a certified training course as provided for in these rules.

————

But once certified or licensed, what is to guide the mediator's conduct on a day to day basis?

E.   STANDARDS OF CONDUCT

Acceptance and adherence to common standards of practice is often one component of the definition of a profession.[38] What are considered standards of conduct within each profession varies. Many published standards of conduct include specific ethical considerations. As examined here, however, standards of conduct address the mediator's activities in a practical sense. Standards provide guidance to the mediator about skill and practice actions as opposed to ethics, which cover moral, or right and wrong, issues. These standards of conduct operate in some instances to regulate the practice, not in the sense of who may practice, but in terms of expectations of mediator conduct.

One problem in the enactment of these standards is that there are many stylistic differences in mediators. While some styles are seen by the majority of mediators as standard, other mediators may have difficulty conforming to specific patterns of action. The enactment of standards might imply that only some mediator styles will be deemed proper. For instance, Folberg and Taylor[39] identified a number of distinct mediation styles. They did so recognizing that there can be overlap, that the

38.   Jay Folberg & Alison Taylor, Mediation: A Comprehensive Guide to Resolving Conflicts Without Litigation 258 (1986).

39.   *Id*. at 130–145.

distinctions are not always clear, and that often a single mediator will blend styles. Perhaps the true mediator is a chameleon. Nonetheless, brief descriptions of some of the more common of mediation styles as identified by Folberg and Taylor follow.

1. **Labor Mediation**: The labor style uses separate meetings between the mediator and each side to explore minimum settlement positions, procedural traditions, and regulations. In the traditional model, each side has experienced representatives in labor negotiations as participants, typically representing either workers or management. Since all decision makers may not be present, it is common to need ratification of the agreement.

2. **Therapeutic Mediation**: While mediation proponents allege that mediation generally has a therapeutic value, this type of mediation is usually conducted by one with specific training in the psychotherapeutic or mental health field. In this process, emphasis is placed on understanding the underlying conflict and resolving the emotional aspects of the matter. The parties' psychological needs and acceptance of the solution is often stressed by the mediator.

3. **Legal Mediation**: In legal mediation, the focus is on the dispute. Little attention is paid to the underlying conflict. This style of mediation usually involves a legally trained mediator who discusses certain views of what the law is, and the legal parameters within which the parties' positions may be stated. The tendency is to focus only on the "legal" solutions as possible outcomes. The mediator may also provide legal analysis. It is the practice of this style of mediation which is, in part, responsible for the development of the evaluative aspect of mediation.

4. **Supervisory Mediation**: This mediation technique involves a mediator with some inherent authority, either assumed by the mediator or provided by the parties. There is a realization that if the parties do not arrive at their own settlement, the mediator may use this authority to decide for them.

5. **Muscle Mediation**: Muscle mediation has been used to describe the cases where a mediator strongly urges or coerces parties into accepting a settlement.[40] The muscle mediator is not a mediator in the classic sense of the word, since the mediator's role is to direct the parties to what their "best voluntary resolution" might be. This directive nature runs contrary to historic mediation practice, but is nevertheless observed today.

6. **Scrivener Mediation**: The scrivener mediator reports thoughts and ideas expressed by others and does little else. One of the most passive styles of mediation, a scrivener mediation relies on the ability of the parties to resolve their own conflicts. No active intervention is provided. The mediator's presence provides a safe and peaceful

---

40. In fact, the term "bullying" has been used to describe mediator conduct. See Allen v. Leal, 27 F. Supp. 2d 945 (S.D.Tex.– Houston Div. 1998)

setting, an expectation of reasonableness and the presence of someone who can clarify and record the agreement. This style is often used intermittently with the others.

7. **Structured Mediation**: This is the most rigid form of mediation; it is used primarily in divorce cases where the mediation takes place over a period of time. A set of rules specify such things as goals to be accomplished at each session, the role of the mediator, the session length, ordering of the issues, permissible conduct between sessions and the use of outside attorneys or consultants.

8. **Shuttle Mediation**: This brand of mediation involves separate caucus sessions that are connected by a "shuttling" mediator. Techniques taken from the labor field are used to narrow issues and explore positions.

9. **Crisis Mediation**: This is a formal mediation used in disputes which are "active"; that is, the parties are in the process of disputing. The mediator intervenes in the crisis in an attempt to reach a calming point; thereafter the underlying cause of the crisis is explored in an attempt to obtain a resolution.

10. **Co-Mediation**: This involves the use of two mediators simultaneously. This is particularly useful where the conflicts are multi-dimensional and require expertise of various types. Two mediators specifically trained in relevant fields save time, promote trust and more quickly narrow issues. Working together, co-mediators are better able to conduct the mediation. There can be disadvantages as well, however, including additional cost, scheduling difficulties, inability of the mediators to work as a team, and confusion of the parties. It is important that co-mediators share a similar vision of mediation.[41] It is also important that they communicate well before, during and after the mediation. Aspects of mediation such as seating arrangements and division of responsibilities such as the introductory remarks should be discussed and agreed upon in advance. It is also important that during the mediation session itself co-mediators do not compete with one another, consult with each other before making important decisions, maintain a unified focus, support each other and remain flexible.[42]

Although court-connected mediation was previously identified as a distinct style,[43] it is currently more accurate to distinguish the styles of mediators in pending litigation. When Florida's court program was studied, three approaches to mediation emerged. These were "trashing," "bashing," and "hashing it out."[44]

The "trashing" methodology involves tearing apart the case in a legal sense. Thereafter the mediator assists in building the case back

---

41. See Lela P. Love and Joseph P. Stulberg, *Practice Guidelines for Co–Mediation: Making Certain That "Two Heads Are Better Than One,"* 13 Mediation Q. 179 (1996).

42. *Id.*

43. Folberg v. Taylor, *supra* note 38.

44. James J. Alfini, *Trashing, Bashing and Hashing It Out: Is this the End of "Good Mediation"?*, 19 Fla. St. U. L. Rev. 47 (1991).

with a more realistic settlement figure on the table. Direct communication between the parties is discouraged.[45] This process resembles a case evaluation approach to dispute resolution.

The "bashing" technique was the second style identified in the study. Rather than engage in case evaluation aimed at getting the parties to offer more realistic monetary figures, bashers focus on the actual settlement offers. Generally, they then "bash" away at them until the parties agree to a figure somewhere between the two originally proposed. Mediators who bash permit direct communication between the parties.[46] Because of the distributive bargaining implicit in this style, the final settlement figure is predictably near the middle of the first offers.

The third style is "hashing it out." "Hasher" mediators take a more flexible approach to the process. Their styles and techniques vary depending on the needs and interests of the parties. Direct communication between the disputing parties is encouraged, permitting more party control of the process, and a focus on the interests and issues of the parties.[47]

Approaches to mediation have also been categorized as either problem-solving or predictive.[48] In predictive settlement procedures, the mediator attempts to influence the parties' concepts of what will happen at trial, thereby encouraging settlement. While there are other ADR processes such as neutral case evaluation, moderated settlement conference, and summary jury trials which provide this evaluation, some mediators opt for this approach. In fact, evaluative mediation has been labeled an emerging form, in which the mediation streamlines the exchange of information so to reduce the amount of time necessary for the parties to present positions.

Conversely, the problem solving approach does not rest on predicting what a court might do. The focus is not merely on arriving at a monetary settlement, but rather on the needs of the parties and their underlying interests. There is increased opportunity for integrative bargaining. Also in the problem solving approach, there is room for exploration of creative solutions. This dichotomy, whether real or perceived, has been the source of some conflict with the mediation community itself.

LEONARD L. RISKIN, UNDERSTANDING MEDIATORS' ORIENTATIONS, STRATEGIES, AND TECHNIQUES: A GRID FOR THE PERPLEXED
1 Harv. Negotiation L. Rev. 7, 8, 16, 1996.

* * *

The largest cloud of confusion and contention surrounds the issue of whether a mediator may evaluate. "Effective mediation," claims lawyer-

---

45. *Id.* at 67.

46. *Id.* at 69.

47. *Id.* at 72.

48. Craig A. McEwen, *Mediator as Predictor or Problem Solver*, 19 Fla. St. U. L. Rev. 77, 78 (1991).

mediator Gerald S. Clay, "almost always requires some analysis of the strengths and weaknesses of each party's position should the dispute be arbitrated or litigated." But law school Dean James Alfini disagrees, arguing that "lawyer-mediators should be prohibited from offering legal advice or evaluations." Formal ethical standards have spoken neither clearly nor consistently on this issue.

* * *

The system I propose describes mediations by reference to two related characteristics, each of which appears along a continuum. One continuum concerns the goals of the mediation. In other words, it measures the scope of the problem or problems that the mediation seeks to address or resolve. At one end of this continuum sit narrow problems, such as how much one party should pay the other. At the other end lie very broad problems, such as how to improve the conditions in a given community or industry. In the middle of this continuum are problems of intermediate breadth, such as how to address the interests of the parties or how to transform the parties involved in the dispute.

The second continuum concerns the mediator's activities. It measures the strategies and techniques that the mediator employs in attempting to address or resolve the problems that comprise the subject matter of the mediation. One end of this continuum contains strategies and techniques that facilitate the parties' negotiation; at the other end lie strategies and techniques intended to evaluate matters that are important to the mediation.

* * *

At the extreme of this evaluative end of the continuum fall behaviors intended to direct some or all of the outcomes of the mediation. At the other end of the continuum are beliefs and behaviors that facilitate the parties' negotiation. At the extreme of this facilitative end is conduct intended simply to allow the parties to communicate with and understand one another.

The mediator who evaluates assumes that the participants want and need her to provide some guidance as to the appropriate grounds for settlement—based on law, industry practice or technology—and that she is qualified to give such guidance by virtue of her training, experience, and objectivity.

The mediator who facilitates assumes that the parties are intelligent, able to work with their counterparts, and capable of understanding their situations better than the mediator and, perhaps, better than their lawyers. Accordingly, the parties can develop better solutions than any the mediator might create. Thus, the facilitative mediator assumes that his principal mission is to clarify and to enhance communication between the parties in order to help them decide what to do.

KIMBERLEE K. KOVACH, LELA P. LOVE, MAPPING MEDIATION: THE RISKS OF RISKIN'S GRID
3 Harv. Neg. L. Rev. 71 (1998).

* * *

Recently, Riskin published a map of the mediation universe—the Riskin Grid. The Grid divides mediation into four quadrants, each defined by a mediator's orientation with respect to two continuums: evaluative-facilitative role and narrow-broad problem definition. The Grid has made a substantial contribution both by clarifying the state of mediation practice today and by sparking a vigorous debate about the direction the practice should take in the future.

The question remains, however, whether users should rely on a map that characterizes one-half the mediation universe as evaluative, whether the boundaries of mediation practice should include the option of an evaluative orientation.

Since its introduction, the Grid has tended to legitimize evaluative activities conducted under the banner of mediation. Trainers and teachers discuss and explore the evaluative aspect of mediation, and some focus on how better to evaluate. A self-assessment tool has been developed for mediators to aid them in determining where their orientation fits on the Grid. Neutrals who essentially perform case evaluation feel comfortable calling themselves "mediators." This trend should stop.

An evaluative role fits a neutral serving in dispute resolution processes where the neutral assists by deciding or opining. That orientation comports with a philosophical map that instigates adversarial advocacy before a decision-maker who applies rules to "facts" and offers an opinion either to influence or spur party decision-making and settlement (e.g., summary jury trials, early neutral evaluation, and non-binding arbitration) or to generate "win-lose" outcomes (e.g., arbitration, private judging, and traditional litigation). However, if mediation is to remain a unique alternative to these processes, one that fosters party autonomy and decision-making, a mediator with an evaluative role could undermine those goals and align mediation with the evaluative-adjudicative processes. Consequently, we contend that the Riskin Grid, if used as a guide to what mediation should and can be and what mediators should and can do, will lead its users astray.

* * *

As Riskin's Grid indicates, many mediators in practice evaluate the fair or likely court outcome when necessary to move forward on a particular issue or on the entire dispute. While this Article addresses the dangers of such evaluations, in certain instances "mixed" evaluative and facilitative processes nonetheless can prove useful. Some mediators who mix mediation and case evaluation effectively help disputing parties. While functionalists would dismiss the importance of naming the process so long as it works, accurate labels, maps, and guides have significance.

* * *

The Riskin Grid accurately depicts the existence of evaluative orientations as part of current mediation practice, particularly in the context of court-connected cases or "legalized" disputes. However, mere existence of a practice does not legitimate that practice. Although professionals may conduct themselves in a manner outside of established norms or rules, such conduct does not thereby become legitimate or redefine the profession.

* * *

The debate over whether an evaluative orientation should exist in the mediation universe goes beyond a "terminological quibble." Professor Joseph Stulberg observes:

> In its rich, widespread history, mediation is not a process designed for having an expert apply some external criteria to assess the strengths and weaknesses of the parties' cases. Mediation is neither a process designed to marshal evidence leading to an advisory opinion by a third party, nor a rehearsal trial in front of judge or jury. Rather, mediation is a dialogue process designed to capture the parties' insights, imagination, and ideas that help them to participate in identifying and shaping their preferred outcomes.

> Proponents of "evaluative mediation" assert the utility of a neutral assessment to help parties overcome impasse. Few, if any, debate the usefulness of a credible evaluation to provide a reality check and to help disputing parties reach agreement. These purposes underlie several dispute resolution processes, including non-binding arbitration, summary jury trial, and early neutral evaluation. We maintain, however, that when a neutral offers a requested evaluation—even as a "last step" in the mediation process—he moves beyond the boundaries of the mediation map, crossing over into a different process that should have different governing guideposts.

* * *

A mediator is being "evaluative" in the sense of being off the mediation map when the mediator has an attitude or identity of being an evaluator (evaluative orientation) or when he asserts an opinion or judgment as to the likely court outcome or a "fair" or correct resolution of an issue in dispute (evaluative conduct). Such an orientation or such conduct may usurp the parties' role as evaluators of their own alternatives to negotiation (i.e., their "BATNA," "WATNA" or "EATNA") and of the best or the most fair outcome for the conflict. The line is fine between a mediator's proposing a fair outcome or the likely outcome at trial, and "reality testing" a party's proposal or assertion about the likely court outcome.

* * *

The "map" below depicts the neutral's orientation in various dispute resolution processes and their related tasks and outcomes.

On this chart, a Great Divide separates processes which require an evaluative orientation on the part of the neutral from those that require a facilitative orientation. In processes where the neutral ultimately

renders a judgment, decision, or opinion, the neutral has an evaluative role. In consensus-building processes, the neutral has a facilitative role. The neutral's orientation ultimately determines whether the process supports third-party decision-making, reflecting social rules and norms, or whether the process supports party decision-making, reflecting the parties' priorities and sense of justice.

Crossing the Divide has several implications:

1. Travelers must have the qualifications and equipment for the challenges they will face. A neutral should not take on a role without preparation and training. Some evaluations require quite substantial qualifications. Beyond understanding norms of credible evidence, fact-finding, burdens of proof, and appropriate legal research and analysis, in legal contexts, evaluators should be lawyers, constrained by codes of professional conduct and vulnerable to suits for malpractice. In other contexts, evaluators should have appropriate substantive expertise concerning the disputed issues to render high-quality decisions or opinions.

2. A traveler must pack appropriately for the journey and discard extra luggage that will not be helpful or welcome, keeping in mind the climate and customs of the destination. For example, in a facilitative terrain, a mediator uses the caucus as a tool, a tool he could not use as an evaluator or adjudicator. Also, in a facilitative setting, a mediator elicits information about assumptions, feelings, and perspectives, welcoming "hearsay" so that misunderstandings and erroneous perceptions can be brought to light and rectified. In an evaluative or adjudicative terrain, however, hearsay is prohibited, limited, or discounted as a source of improper influence on the neutral decision-maker.

A talented, resourceful intervenor can mix processes on occasion. We acknowledge and applaud the "mixed processes" that have developed. But when traveling across the Great Divide, for example in med-arb or in med-neutral evaluation, the neutral must alert the parties to the shift from mediation to evaluation, and the neutral must discipline himself to use the particular tools appropriate to the particular task. And, of course, all participants must elect with full knowledge to go on the particular journey being proposed.

Without a common understanding of mediation, we will experience trouble developing codes of ethics, finding qualified neutrals, or designing appropriate training programs.

Giving the same label "mediation" to activities which involve different levels of intervention into conflict—evaluation and facilitation—misleads and cripples with confusion the genius of an otherwise dynamic and powerful process. Mediation's core concept and motivating idea must remain simple and clear. Otherwise we will fall back on the adversarial paradigm because it is simple and clear.

A facilitative orientation on the part of a mediator does not deprive disputants of critical information about their rights or other social norms. It does not deprive parties of the expediency of having one neutral preside as both facilitator and expert advisor. Mediators do (and should) urge parties to "play with a full deck," to obtain critical information about legal rights, likely court outcomes, tax considerations, design and engineering matters or any other area pertaining to a dispute. Frequently, legal advocates and other experts educate mediation participants about the strengths and weaknesses of espoused claims and positions. Where the parties, after deliberation and consent, want the mediator to function as an expert or evaluator, the mediator can "change hats" and engage in a mixed dispute resolution process. By requiring that evaluative activity be called something other than "mediation," we highlight that in such processes the parties' roles shift to persuading the neutral, and that a neutral intervenor acting in the capacity of an evaluator assumes different qualifications, skills, and tasks.

[Where disputes settle in "mediation" primarily due to the influence of third party evaluation and recommendation, the process does not fundamentally differ from non-binding arbitration. Both arbitration and mediation, if unchecked, have a tendency to move towards the dominant paradigm of litigation with increased formality, less party participation and control, and higher cost]. Assimilation threatens the visionary promise of ADR as a panoply of different processes. It is deeply ironic that Leonard Riskin, who so lucidly articulated the radical difference in a lawyer's standard philosophical map and a mediator's standard philosophical map, has given us a new map—the Grid—which potentially locates mediation as a familiar landmark on the lawyer's standard map. Let us use Riskin's Grid as a warning descriptor of where the mediation field is today, and create an alternative map of the mediation terrain—a map that keeps the promise of ADR.

———

Thus, due to the variety in mediation practice, enacting standards has been 12 difficult. Strict standards would impose unnecessary restrictions on the mediator's activities. Specific standards which dictate the mediator's activities may conflict among themselves. The mediator must decide which approach to follow. Moreover, some standards obligate the mediator to do that which he should not do—make a decision.[49] Implementation is also problematic. Who will be present to monitor the mediator's actions?

Most standards encompass areas such as neutrality, impartiality, and confidentiality.[50] Most of the standards that have been established to date require that the mediator abide by confidentiality. Many provide that the mediator remain neutral and impartial. However, exceptions are then carved out. One such exception is with regard to imbalances of power or knowledge. For instance, the Oklahoma Supreme Court Rules require, in court cases, that the mediator avoid the bargaining imba-

---

49. For example, one program urged that the mediator terminate a session if a party is being *harmed*. Yet harm was not specifically defined.

50. Since these matters were covered in previous chapters, they will not be examined in detail here.

lances that one party may have in legal knowledge or negotiating skill. The mediator must provide assistance to one party if the other party is represented.[51] The mediator must recognize a power imbalance, which requires a judgment on the part of the mediator. Farmer-lender mediation programs often require mediators to provide expert advice ranging from legal aid to financial assistance[52] to the farm owner. These programs have pre-determined that the lender possesses an advantage.

Standards of conduct are difficult to define with precision, and although the more recent enactments take the position that evaluation is not part of the mediator's role.[53] In many instances, the behavior chosen by the mediator at a specific time may be a matter of personal choice. She will need to make decisions on her own, unless otherwise dictated by the training or practice requirements of a program, project or court through which she is mediating.

F. MEDIATOR LIABILITY

One option to assure quality control in the profession is the "after the fact" control method of establishing liability through malpractice suits. Even though mediation is a new profession with a great number of unanswered questions, there have been a few cases filed against mediators. While the number is not large, it is anticipated that such filings will continue. At the end of 1993, a primary insurer of arbitrators and mediators[54] reported that the current number of claims against mediators and arbitrators average five per year. The majority of these involved either general negligence, conflicts of interest, or breaches of confidentiality. The remaining were divided among other theories of liability.[55] Updated information demonstrates the anticipated increase. In 1998, there were eight claims, in 1999 thirteen, and by January 28 already 2 for 2000.[56] The mediator should examine the following list of potential issues in malpractice cases with a focus on how she might prevent such an occurrence.

1. CAUSES OF ACTION

A number of legal theories exist through which one can allege mediator malpractice. The theory with the broadest ramifications is general negligence. Depending on the nature of mediation practice, others include Deceptive Trade and Practices Act (DTPA), breach of contract, fraud, false imprisonment, libel, slander, breach of fiduciary duty, and tortious interference with a business relationship.

In fee generating mediations, the disputing parties may qualify as consumers under the breach of contract or DTPA theories. The mediator should be cautious in advertising and guard against making promises or guarantees. It may be advisable to put any information provided to the

---

51. Okla. Stat. tit. 12, § 37, App., Rule 1 et seq. (Supp. 1999).

52. Wyo. Stat. Ann. § 11–41–105(a), (b) (1999).

53. See Joint Standard, Appendix B at 378.

54. Complete Equity Markets, Inc.

55. Telephone conference with Gracine Huffnagle, January 3, 1994.

56. Telephone conference with Betsy Thomas, Complete Equity Markets, and

parties in writing and design a method to verify what information was received by the parties.

Matters such as libel and slander may fall within a claim of breach of confidentiality. The extent of confidentiality in the mediation process is not clear. Confidentiality, in the legal sense, varies depending on the jurisdiction, type of mediation and nature of dispute.[57] Recognizing this variation, the Joint Code states that the mediator's duty is only to meet the parties' expectations with regard to confidentiality. The code, by design, does not specify what those expectations should be. It is therefore very important that the mediator be explicit with regard to confidentiality provisions and provide these in written documents as well. The mediator must then be careful to abide by the specific confidentiality provisions.

In the area of general negligence, under current nebulous standards, an attorney would have difficulty in proving liability by a breach of duty. However, as previously pointed out,[58] there are a few standards which, for the most part, are consistent. These include duties to remain impartial and avoid conflicts of interest. Mediators should be knowledgeable about those standards, and adhere to them. Where there is doubt about what the standard of practice is, the mediator must rely on her own judgment in making a decision. When there is a fine line, implementing a policy embracing "better safe than sorry" is advisable. As time passes, research and practice should determine more specifically what the operable standard of practice is within any mediation organization or entity. Once determined, violations of these standards will possibly result in negligence.

2. DAMAGES

Even where a disputant is able to prove a breach of duty, thereby establishing liability against a mediator, in order to recover, damages must also be proven. In a truly consensual process such as mediation, there may be difficulty in establishing damages, particularly where the claim concerns the mediation process itself rather than a peripheral issue such as a slander claim. Admittedly in claims such as slander or tortious interference with a business relationship, the damages may involve events which occur outside of the mediation process. If liability under these theories is established, recovery against the mediator is probable. Likewise, in a case where the mediator provides professional advice, and the advice is incorrect, if the party shows that she relied upon such advice to her detriment, recovery against the mediator is likely. However, in claims against the mediator which turn on the elements of the process, establishing damages will be more difficult. Even if the mediator breached a duty with regard to performance in the mediation, the claimant must also establish that, but for those actions in the mediation, there would have been a better outcome to the case. What this better outcome would be will rely on speculation, and proving it may

Celeste King, attorney for Lloyds of London, January 26, 27, 2000.

57. See Chapter 11.

58. See § E this chapter.

be a difficult task.[59] To date, there has not been a reported case where a plaintiff has successfully prevailed on this issue.

G. IMMUNITY

1. POLICY CONSIDERATIONS

There are a number of situations where a mediator may be immune from liability. One of the older dispute resolution devices, arbitration, has historically provided immunity for the arbitrators. Immunity was initially premised on the fact that the arbitrator was an extension of the court or judge, and as such, should be given immunity.[60] Extension of this immunity to mediators has not been unequivocally established. In fact, some argue that the mediator's role is so dissimilar to that of the court, that a new common law immunity premised along the lines of judicial and arbitral immunity is unlikely.[61] Yet a few courts have begun to address this issue directly, and a number of states have enacted statutes providing immunity for the mediator.

If immunity is absolute, or sufficiently broad, the consumer of mediation services will have no recourse for any damage resulting from participation in mediation. Since mediation is such a new field, essentially without regulations, rules or standardized procedures, there must be a way to guard against abuse of the process and the parties by the mediator. Furthermore, mediators resemble service providers who have not traditionally been protected by immunity.[62] These include lawyers and therapists. Conversely, mediators, particularly those who volunteer, need to do so without fear of having to expend time and money in the defense of malpractice claims. A compromise between these two considerations has resulted in enactment of immunity statutes aimed primarily at protection of the pro bono or volunteer mediator.

2. STATUTORY PROVISIONS

A survey of statutes show that at least nineteen states provide some immunity for mediators. These include: Arizona, Colorado, Florida, Iowa, Maine, Minnesota, Oklahoma, Utah, Washington, Wisconsin, and Texas.

Most of these statutes provide for immunity in the volunteer or pro bono setting, often under specific programs or conditions. There has yet to be a statute which provides blanket immunity for all mediators in all actions. Nearly all of the statutes provide a qualified immunity and include an exception for wanton and willful misconduct.

---

59. See, for example, *Lange v. Marshall*, 622 S.W.2d 237 (Mo.App.1981), where a claim was made against a lawyer acting in a mediative role in a divorce action, and the plaintiff was unable to establish damages.

60. Judicial immunity was first established in Bradley v. Fisher, 80 U.S. (13 Wall.) 335, 20 L.Ed. 646 (1872), based upon the need for independence and freedom to act in the administration of justice. This was first extended to arbitrators in the United States in *Jones v. Brown,* 54 Iowa 74, 6 N.W. 140 (Iowa 1880), which noted the similarity between a judge and arbitrator.

61. Nancy H. Rogers & Craig A. McEwen, Mediation: Law, Policy & Practice, Chapter 11, § 11.03 (1994 and Supp. 1999).

62. *Id.*

For instance in Colorado, the Dispute Resolution Act limits the liability of mediators to willful or wanton misconduct.[63] In Iowa, statutory immunity covers both informal dispute resolution as well as the farm mediator. In Iowa all mediators, employees, and agents of a center as well as members of a dispute resolution center's board are protected from liability. The immunity does not extend if there is bad faith, malicious purpose, or wanton and willful disregard of human rights, safety or property.[64] In Iowa farmer-lender mediation, members of a farm mediation staff, including a mediator, employee or agent or member of the board of the service is not liable for civil damages for a statement or decision made in the process of mediation unless the member acts in bad faith, with malicious purpose, or in a manner exhibiting willful and wanton disregard of human rights, safety, or property.[65] In Washington, employees and volunteers of a dispute resolution center are immune from suit in any civil action based on any proceedings or other official acts performed in their capacity as employees or volunteers, except in cases of wilful or wanton misconduct.[66] The Supreme Court of Georgia did not wait for the legislature, and instead established by court order immunity for all neutrals in a court-annexed or court-referred program.[67]

3. CASE LAW

In a few instances, the courts have addressed this issue.

HOWARD v. DRAPKIN
Court of Appeal, Second District, 1990.
222 Cal.App.3d 843, 271 Cal.Rptr. 893.

* * *

Defendant Robin Drapkin ("defendant"), a psychologist, performed an evaluation of plaintiff and her family and plaintiff now claims that defendant acted improperly in carrying out that task.

In this appeal we are asked to determine whether the alleged wrongful actions of which plaintiff complains were performed in such a context that defendant can claim (1) common law immunity as a quasi-judicial officer participating in the judicial process or (2) statutory privilege under Civil Code section 47, subdivision (2) ("section 47(2)")[1] for a publication in a judicial proceeding. We conclude that defendant, acting in the capacity of a neutral third person engaged in efforts to effect a resolution of a family law dispute, is entitled to the protection of

---

63. Colo. Rev. Stat. Ann. § 13–22–305(6) (1997).

64. Iowa Code Ann. § 679.13 (1998).

65. Iowa Code Ann. § 13.16(1) (Supp. 1999).

66. West's Rev. Code Wash. Ann. § 7.75.100 (1992).

67. Uniform Rules for Dispute Resolution Programs, Supreme Court of Georgia, Rule 6.2 amended Dec. 30, 1993.

1. Civil Code section 47, subdivision 2 provides in relevant part that with certain exceptions for dissolution of marriage proceedings, "A privileged publication or broadcast is one made— ... [P] 2. In any ... (2) judicial proceeding...."

quasi-judicial immunity for the conduct of such dispute resolution services. We also find that the litigation privilege provided for in section 47(2) applies to the facts of this case. We therefore affirm the dismissal of plaintiff's complaint.

* * *

With respect to defendant's alleged non-disclosures, plaintiff asserts that defendant (1) failed to divulge her lack of expertise in the area of child and sexual abuse, (2) failed to disclose that she and Robert had a prior professional relationship in that they had spoken and participated together in professional seminars and (3) failed to disclose that she was a close personal friend of the wife of one of the partners in the law firm which represented Robert in the underlying action.

* * *

This appeal raises the issue of the availability of (1) quasi-judicial immunity by reason of defendant's involvement as a neutral dispute-resolving participant in the judicial process and (2) the absolute privilege under the provisions of section 47(2), as a complete bar to plaintiff's actions.

* * *

The concept of judicial immunity is longstanding and absolute, with its roots in English common law. It bars civil actions against judges for acts performed in the exercise of their judicial functions and it applies to all judicial determinations, including those rendered in excess of the judge's jurisdiction, no matter how erroneous or even malicious or corrupt they may be.

* * *

The rationale behind the doctrine is twofold. First, it "protect[s] the finality of judgments [and] discourag[es] inappropriate collateral attacks." (*Forrester v. White, supra,* 484 U.S. 219, 225, 108 S.Ct. 538, 543.) Second, it "protect[s] judicial independence by insulating judges from vexatious actions prosecuted by disgruntled litigants."

* * *

Under the concept of "quasi-judicial immunity," California courts have extended absolute judicial immunity to persons other than judges if those persons act in a judicial or quasi-judicial capacity. Thus, court commissioners "acting either as a temporary judge or performing subordinate judicial duties ordered by the appointing court" have been granted quasi-judicial immunity.

* * *

Plaintiff seeks to establish that California's version of common law judicial and quasi-judicial immunity is applied only to public officials (judges, grand jurors, prosecutors, commissioners, etc.). If that were so, then arbitrators would not be protected by common law quasi-judicial immunity. We believe that in California, it is not so much one's status as a public official which has generally been the litmus test for judicial immunity but rather the above-referenced analysis of "functions normally performed by judges." It just so happens, that with the exception of arbitrators, and sometimes referees (*Park Plaza Ltd. v. Pietz* (1987) 193 Cal.App.3d 1414, 1418–1419, 239 Cal.Rptr. 51), such functions have usually been performed by public officials.

* * *

We are persuaded that the approach of the federal courts is consistent with the relevant policy considerations of attracting to an overburdened judicial system the independent and impartial services and expertise upon which that system necessarily depends. Thus, we believe it appropriate that these "nonjudicial persons who fulfill quasi-judicial functions intimately related to the judicial process" (*Myers v. Morris*, *supra*, 810 F.2d at p.1466–1467) should be given absolute quasi-judicial immunity for damage claims arising from their performance of duties in connection with the judicial process. Without such immunity, such persons will be reluctant to accept court appointments or provide work product for the courts' use. Additionally, the threat of civil liability may affect the manner in which they perform their jobs. (*Moses v. Parwatikar* (8th Cir.1987) 813 F.2d 891, 892, cert. den. 484 U.S. 832, 108 S.Ct. 108, 98 L.Ed.2d 67.)

* * *

In arguing for extensions of immunity to the category of persons who function apart from the courts in an attempt to resolve disputes, defendant and amicus emphasize that in this day of excessively crowded courts and long delays in bringing civil cases to trial, more reliance is being placed by both parties and the courts on alternative methods of dispute resolution. Along traditional lines, the provisions of article VI, section 22 of the Constitution, which allow the Legislature to provide for the appointment by trial courts of officers such as commissioners, references and masters (*Tagliavia v. County of Los Angeles, supra*, 112 Cal.App.3d at 763, 169 Cal.Rptr. 467), are becoming ever more important. We have court commissioners (Code Civ. Proc., § 259) and voluntary and mandatory referees (Code Civ. Proc., § 638 et seq.). In addition, contracts for binding arbitration (Code Civ. Proc., § 1280 et seq.) and provisions for non-binding arbitration (Code Civ. Proc., § 1141.10 et seq.) help relieve court congestion. So also does Civil Code section 4607's provision for mandatory mediation of child custody and visitation disputes.

More recently, other aspects of alternative dispute resolution efforts are being used with greater frequency. There are voluntary settlement conferences which are conducted by volunteers working with the court through, for example, local bar associations. In addition, if it is necessary, the parties can choose a mediator or neutral fact-finder with the expertise to facilitate a resolution of their particular dispute. As amicus notes, mediation is traditionally a non-binding dispute resolution alternative. While most mediation is voluntary, some is compulsory, like that provided for in Civil code section 4607.

* * *

We therefore hold that absolute quasi-judicial immunity is properly extended to these neutral third-parties for their conduct in performing dispute resolution services which are connected to the judicial process and involve either (1) the making of binding decisions, (2) the making of findings or recommendations to the court or (3) the arbitration, mediation, conciliation, evaluation or other similar resolution of pending disputes. As the defendant was clearly engaged in this latter activity, she is entitled to the protection of such quasi-judicial immunity.

* * *

WAGSHAL v. FOSTER

United States District Court, District of Columbia, 1993.
1993 WL 86499.

This federal civil action against a state-court-appointed mediator and his law partners, brought by a litigant who believes himself to have been wronged by the mediator in the course of court-ordered "alternative dispute resolution" ("ADR") proceedings, is presently before the Court on defendants' motion, in advance of answer, to dismiss or for summary judgment on the ground of judicial immunity.

* * *

In June, 1990, Jerome Wagshal brought suit in the Superior Court of the District of Columbia against the manager of real property owned by Wagshal ("The Sheetz case"). In October, 1991, the Honorable Richard A. Levie, the Superior Court judge to whom the case had been assigned, ordered a stay of discovery pending efforts to bring the case to settlement through the Superior Court's ADR program, and referred the case, over Wagshal's objection, to a "case evaluator." In the Superior Court ADR is mandatory.[1]

* * *

Wagshal then objected to the first case evaluator appointed as having a "conflict of interest," and Judge Levie accordingly appointed

---

1. The alternative dispute resolution program of the Superior Court is a formal division of the court established by order of its Chief Judge, known as the "Multi–Door Dispute Resolution Division," and offers mediation, arbitration, and case evaluation processes to litigants in lieu of trial and judgment. "Case evaluators" for cases such as the Sheetz case are members of the District of Columbia Bar, with at least five years of relevant litigation experience, who volunteer to serve without compensation, undergo required training, and are approved as such by the court.

For purposes of this case the functions of mediators and evaluators are indistinguishable.

the defendant Mark W. Foster, Esquire, as a substitute on November 21, 1991.

* * *

Wagshal's counsel then interposed an objection to Mr. Foster as an evaluator, questioning Foster's neutrality once again on the basis of a perceived "conflict of interest," and, when Wagshal refused Foster's express request that Wagshal either waive the objection or make an issue of it before proceeding with evaluation, on February 19, 1992, Foster wrote to Judge Levie to recuse himself as an evaluator... In his opinion, however, Foster thought the Sheetz case could and should be settled. He suggested to the court ... implying that Wagshal's attitude represented the principal impediment to the success of the process.

* * *

In a telephone conference call hearing on February 20, 1992, Judge Levie agreed with Mr. Foster's observations that the alleged conflicts of interest were "attenuated"—indeed, would have been of no consequence to him had he been asked for a ruling—but he acceded to Mr. Foster's recusal and excused him from further participation in the conference. Judge Levie then reiterated his determination to maintain the stay of discovery in place and to try once more with case evaluation the court is advised that a third evaluator was appointed, and the Sheetz case eventually settled.

* * *

A review of the case law, however, reveals that court-appointed mediators and their like have not been around long enough to have generated much in the way of precedent with respect to the extent to which they enjoy the immunity of the court whom they serve when they venture into a private controversy represented by a pending case, and in the course thereof, antagonize one or more of the parties. Other, more traditional agents of the judicial process have, however, historically been held to possess such immunity when they act in their official capacities,[2] and this Court concludes that court-appointed arbitrators, mediators, case evaluators, and others who are directly involved in ADR programs with express authority from the court may properly invoke the same protection, for similar reasons.

In the instant case it appears that Mr. Foster was discharging his duty to the Superior Court of the District of Columbia, and acting with the knowledge and approval of the judge by whom he had been appoint-

---

2. Judges have absolute immunity from damage liability for actions taken in their judicial capacity. *Forrester v. White,* 484 U.S. 219 (1988). This absolute immunity may be extended to other officials when their activities are integrally related to the judicial process and when they perform a judicial function as an officer of the court. *Schinner v. Strathmann,* 711 F.Supp. 1143 (D.D.C.1989) (psychiatrist appointed to determine defendant's mental competency to stand trial). See, e.g., *Imbler v. Pachtman,* 424 U.S. 409, 430 (1976) (prosecutors);

Crosby–Bey v. Jansson, 586 F.Supp. 96, 98 (D.D.C.1984) (probation officer); *Simons v. Bellinger,* 643 F.2d 774 (D.C.Cir.1980) (court-appointed committee monitoring unauthorized practice of law); *Wolff v. Faris,* 1989 WL 84718, 1989 U.S. Dist. LEXIS 8520 (N.D.Ill. July 19, 1989) (conciliator in custody dispute); *Howard v. Drapkin,* 222 Cal.App.3d 843, 860 (1990) ("[A]bsolute immunity is properly extended to neutral third persons who are engaged in mediation, conciliation, evaluation or similar dispute resolution efforts."); *Austern v. Chica-*

ed, in all the respects with which plaintiff finds fault with his performance. He therefore possesses that court's judicial immunity, and this complaint, and each count thereof must be dismissed as to all defendants.

For the foregoing reasons, it is, this 5th day of February, 1993,

ORDERED, that defendants' motion to dismiss or for summary judgment is granted, and the complaint is dismissed with prejudice.

————

If this trend continues and immunity is established for all mediators, and courts continue in their use of the process, will the result be a process without rules, procedures, standards, or regulation? Some fear that will occur if immunity is extended without limits.

H.   QUALITY MEDIATION DOES NOT EXIST

There are some who would propose that it is impossible to establish quality in mediation. The only "quality" is no mediation. Although most mediators, participants and legal scholars support the use of mediation, some criticism of the process has been leveled. In general, these critics point out that the traditional legal system has more safeguards for the individual and for society than the mediation process. With the increased use of mediation, and other dispute resolution procedures, combined with a lack of protection for the consumers, a system may develop very unlike that which we currently know. While some may find this a favorable result, others have expressed grave concern. And even more concern has been raised because of the lack of criticism about ADR.[68]

One criticism is based on gender.[69] The primary focus of the critique is on mandatory mediation in custody disputes. The use of mediation is disapproved for these matters for a number of reasons. These include the fact that the woman will not have the opportunity to have blame assessed;[70] when the individuals are treated alike advantages are accorded to the husband;[71] there is an inability to express anger which is often necessary in custody cases;[72] the mediation process may contribute to prejudices;[73] lawyers who are protectors of rights are excluded;[74] and a direct confrontation with the soon to be former spouse may be intolerable.[75]

At first glance, these concerns as described appear to be valid. However, mediation is a flexible process, and each program, and in fact,

go *Board Options Exchange, Inc.,* 898 F.2d 882, 886 (2d Cir.) (arbitrators), cert. denied, 111 S.Ct. 141 (1990).

68.   See Eric K. Yanamoto, *ADR: Where Have the Critics Gone?,* 36 Santa Clara L. Rev. 1055 (1996).

69.   Trina Grillo, *The Mediation Alternative: Process Dangers for Women,* 100 Yale L. J. 1545 (1991).

70.   *Id.* at 1560.

71.   *Id.* at 1568.

72.   *Id.* at 1572.

73.   *Id.* at 1587.

74.   *Id.* at 1597.

75.   *Id.* at 1601.

each mediator, is different. Generalization to all mediation is misplaced.[76] For instance, where the parties agree to voluntarily participate in mediation, if the situation becomes uncomfortable, they can leave. Moreover, in the majority of programs, in direct contrast to the California model, the mediator is prohibited from making any report to the court, other than whether a settlement was achieved. Thus, the mediator makes no decisions, and maintains all of the information as confidential. Moreover, while lawyers are sometimes discouraged from attending mediation with their clients[77] rarely is their presence prohibited. In fact, an innovative area of law practice is developing known as mediation advocacy.[78]

Some have expressed fear that the informality of ADR fosters racial and ethnic prejudices.[79] Mediation is again compared with the courts, as courts are assumed to possess procedural safeguards which assist in preventing the demonstration of prejudice.[80] While pre-trial and trial procedures may, in theory, be structured to guard against explicit bias, in the real world these rules are manipulated. It has been demonstrated that in an informal setting such as mediation, individuals will more likely act on their prejudices than if they are placed in an environment where they must conform.[81] Consequently in the informal mediation environment, the chance of overt prejudice is increased.

Other related criticisms have also been leveled. While the mediation process provides safeguards for the private person, such as confidentiality, it may also be more intrusive. One example is in the request or expectation of shared information.[82] Although disclosure is encouraged in the mediation process, it is the rare situation where a mediator would *require* a party to reveal secret information. Most mediators can sense if a person is uncomfortable speaking about certain information, and will not pursue the subject. Moreover, the mediation process can actually assist in preserving confidential information, particularly when the process is conducted in a caucus format.

Probably the most common critique of the mediation process is that the public or social order is not served by its use. If cases settle, then issues will not be litigated. Consequently new public policies cannot be made. Some believe that this works specifically to the detriment of minorities.[83]

It is also argued that the courtroom is the preferred site for dispute resolution since imbalances between parties can be mitigated by judges.[84]

---

76. See Joshua D. Rosenberg, *In Defense of Mediation*, 33 Ariz. L. Rev. 467 (1991).

77. This is usually in divorce cases or pre-litigation matters. The rationale is cost savings.

78. See Eric R. Galton, Representing Clients in Mediation (1994).

79. Richard Delgado et. al., *Fairness and Formality: Minimizing the Risk of Prej-*

udice in Alternative Dispute Resolution, 1985 Wis. L. Rev. 1359 (1985).

80. *Id.* at 1367.

81. *Id.* at 1387.

82. *Id.* at 1397.

83. *Id.* at 1398.

84. Owen Fiss, *Against Settlement*, 93 Yale L. J. 1073, 1075 (1984).

In the mediation setting, if the mediator subscribes to complete neutrality and impartiality[85] and takes the parties as she finds them, the imbalance will not be corrected. In fact, it may carry over into the terms of settlement. The failure of ADR to live up to its promise to save time and money has also been noted.[86]

Some contend that a primary purpose of our legal system is to shape the world we live in; to determine societal standards. The job of the courts is not to make peace or determine rights for private parties, but rather enforce the Constitution and statutes, interpret values, and apply them to reality.[87] If all cases are settled in a private manner, then the purpose of the lawsuit has been rendered to that of resolving private matters.[88]

While some of these criticisms are valid, it is doubtful that in all cases our legal system is able to give force to values. Witness the non-compliance and disregard for courts that is prevalent. Even if it were to be assumed for the sake of argument only, that the poor, disadvantaged, and minority groups would fare better in adjudication, what are the realistic possibilities that members of those groups ever actually get to court? What should the balance be? For one percent of a group to find a resolution through adjudication or for ninety percent to conclude their disputing?

QUESTIONS FOR DISCUSSION

15–1. Florida Rule of Civil Procedure 10.240(e)(4) provides for the reinstatement of mediators. A key to being reinstated is a finding of "fit to mediate". What does this mean?

15–2. The procedure for the Florida disciplinary process is as follows:

Rule 10.230   Hearing Procedures

(a) **Assignment to Panel.** Upon referral of a complaint and formal charges from a complaint committee, the center shall assign the complaint and formal charges to a panel for hearing, with notice of assignment to the complainant and the mediator. No member of the complaint committee shall serve as a member of the panel.

(b) **Hearing.** The center shall schedule a hearing not more than 90 days nor less than 30 days from the date of notice of assignment of the matter to the panel.

(c) **Dismissal.** Upon the filing of a stipulation of dismissal signed by the complainant and the mediator, and with the concurrence of the panel, the action shall be dismissed.

---

85. See Chapter 7.

86. See James S. Kakalik, et. al., *An Evaluation of Mediation and Early Neutral Evaluation Under the Civil Justice Reform Act* (Rand, 1996).

87. Fiss, *supra* note 83, at 1085.

88. *Id.*

(d) Procedures for Hearing. The procedures for hearing shall be as follows:

(1) No hearing shall be conducted without 5 panel members being present.

(2) The hearing may be conducted informally but with decorum.

(3) The rules of evidence applicable to trial of civil actions apply but are to be liberally construed.

(4) Upon a showing of good cause to the panel, testimony of any party or witness may be presented over the telephone.

(e) Right of the Mediator to Defend. A mediator shall have the right to defend against all charges and shall have the right to be represented by an attorney, to examine and cross-examine witnesses, to compel the attendance of witnesses to testify, and to compel the production of documents and other evidentiary matter through the subpoena power of the panel.

(f) Mediator Discovery. The center shall, upon written demand of a party or counsel of record, promptly furnish the following: the names and addresses of all witnesses whose testimony is expected to be offered at the hearing, together with copies of all written statements and transcripts of the testimony of such witnesses in the possession of the counsel or the center which are relevant to the subject matter of the hearing and which have not previously been furnished.

(g) Panel Discovery. The mediator or the mediator's counsel shall, upon written demand of the counsel or the center, promptly furnish the following: the names and addresses of all witnesses whose testimony is expected to be offered at the hearing, together with copies of all written statements and transcripts of the testimony of such witnesses in the possession of the mediator or mediator's counsel which are relevant to the subject matter of the hearing and which have not previously been furnished.

(h) Failure to Appear. Absent a showing of good cause, if the complainant fails to appear at the hearing, the panel may dismiss the action for want of prosecution.

(i) Mediator's Absence. If the mediator fails to appear, absent a showing of good cause, the hearing shall proceed.

(j) Rehearing. If the matter is heard in the mediator's absence, the mediator may petition for rehearing, for good cause, within 10 days of the date of the hearing.

Interestingly, if not ironic, the Florida Bar has a Grievance Mediation Program (F.S.A. Bar Rule 3–8.1). Discuss these somewhat inconsistent approaches.

15–3. While the current case law appears to provide immunity to neutrals, it does so only when they are mediating a pending case. In order to protect herself, should a mediator require the parties to file a lawsuit before serving as a mediator in a matter? What are other viable options?

15–4. The State of Virginia has enacted Standard Guidelines for the Certification of Mediation Training Programs. Comment on this approach to "quality control."

15–5.[88] You are mediating the following divorce action. The parties have been married for over eighteen years. The husband, C. Vanderbilt Cabot–Lodge, has a combined J.D./MBA degree. He was in law practice for ten years, and thereafter went to work for a major corporation, where he now serves as CEO. Judy, his wife was only 19 when the couple married. The couple has three children, Jack and Jill who are in high school, and Joe who is three years old. The mediation is focused on the division of property.

The estate includes: a six bedroom homestead; a drug store, heavily indebted, that Vanderbilt spends 15 hours a week, managing; a record archives business, financed on debt, that he spends 10 hours a week managing; a six story office building he owns and manages, subject to first and second mortgages totalling more than the market value of the building; 38 different stocks, all bought on margin; tax free bonds pledged as security for other assets; a tract of land which used to be a chemical company dump site. The EPA is demanding $3,000,000 worth of environmental clean-up of that site; and inter vivos trust which Vanderbilt created to hold about a million dollars worth of assets immune from creditors. The couple appears before you without counsel, seeking a quiet, quick, confidential and inexpensive way to divide these properties. It is agreed that together the couple has only $3,000 readily accessible cash.

Vanderbilt brought the preceding list of properties to the mediation, and offers ideas as to valuation and how they should be divided. You assume from what he has said that these values are based largely on what he paid for the properties in the past, extending back 20 years.

Judy trusts his "business judgment", but you wonder whether he really knows the property values.

Whether he know the values or not, you believe that inherently, his figures must be biased, and that it is not in Judy's interest to rely on his valuation.

(a) What is the mediator's responsibility? For the process? For the agreement?

(b) Should you as the mediator urge both of them to get counsel?

(c) Should you recommend to either or both that appraised values of each property be obtained?

(d) Should you recess the mediation until further information is available?

88. Used with permission, from Tom Arnold, A Short Discussion of Ethics Issues in Mediation (1992).

(e) What if both of them really want the case concluded today and don't seem to care about fairness?

(f) Suppose Judy informs you privately that she has a rich, young lover she wants to marry next week. She will give up anything to get this over with today. Judy and Vanderbilt are nearly in agreement on accepting his values.

Is it proper for the mediator to intervene?

(g) Should the mediator consider the fairness of the potential agreement?

(h) Is a proposal to these parties that they employ counsel and experts to evaluate the property, a neutral act or an act favoring Judy? Does it destroy the integrity of the mediator's neutrality?

(i) Does proposing counsel and experts destroy the concept that the parties are free to make their own deal without mediator interference?

(j) Suppose you find Vanderbilt to be an engaging fellow, not really out of sorts with his wife, just too busy to give her the time and comfort she needs. And you find her to be a warm person, still much in love with her husband, but in need of a little attention.

Do you address this issue? To what degree? Do you suggest, recommend or urge that the parties seek a therapist?

Chapter Sixteen

SPECIALIZED APPLICATIONS OF MEDIATION

This text has examined mediation primarily as a process for resolving conflict. The recent ADR movement[1] has primarily focused on the use of mediation in community-based programs and as an adjunct to the courts. Consequently, the use of mediation has been in the context of assisting individuals to resolve legal or quasi-legal disputes. And within these areas, a number of specialized applications of mediation has developed. Moreover, as use and experimentation continued, mediation, along with its derivative and hybrid processes, has proven effective in resolving an expansive array of conflicts and problems.

It has been claimed that mediation can assist in the resolution of disputes from A to Z—from agricultural to zoning matters, and everything in between.[2] This chapter will highlight several of the diverse applications of mediation. Within many of these specialized areas, there are distinctive differences in the way the mediation process is conducted. As noted in a previous chapter, mediation styles differ.[3] This is often a product of the individual personality of the mediator. Variations also result from the type of dispute mediated. In some of these specialized applications, there may also be specific modifications of the process. Comparisons between traditional, classic mediation and that employed in the specialized applications of the process are helpful in describing some of the diversity of mediation use. Mediators are urged to receive additional training prior to mediating in some specialized areas. In some instances, specialized training is mandatory. Moreover, where the mediation process is statutorily indicated, specific rules may direct the mediator's actions.

The following description of the variety of areas where the mediation process is used is by no means exhaustive. Compiling a complete list of all of the specific applications of mediation is likely impossible, since

---

1. See Chronology, Chapter 2, § B.
2. E. Wendy Trachte, Broadening the Scope of ADR: Developments from A to Z, B-3, Alternative "Trial Notebook" South Texas College of Law and AA White Dispute Resolution Institute, November 1992.
3. Chapter 15, § E.

new uses are continually discovered. Many of these specialized areas have developed without direction, while others are mandated by statute. For example, statutes exist which advocate mediation use in barber disputes,[4] matters involving mobile homes,[5] disputes between dentists and patients,[6] and cases concerning human skeletal remains in burial grounds.[7] This small sample demonstrates the expansive application of the mediation process. In many of the areas described, specific projects, or practices have developed. That is not to say, however, that a general practice mediator might not encounter many of these disputes in practice.

A. AGRICULTURAL DISPUTES

A number of mediation programs have been created to focus on resolving disputes between farmers and lenders.[8] These programs developed in the mid-eighties when the farmers were caught in a financial squeeze between high costs and low profits. Foreclosures were numerous and many believed that mediation could provide protection from immediate home loss for the farmer.[9] Mediation use was mandated by the Agricultural Credit Act of 1987.[10] A federal agency, the farmers Home Administration, oversaw mediation programs in many states.[11] Some states enacted mandatory programs while other states offered voluntary mediation.[12] Farm mediation programs differ from more traditional mediation projects in one important respect: the statutes and rules surrounding these programs presume an inherent imbalance of power between a farmer and a lender. In these programs, the farmer must be provided legal information, financial advice and the like prior to the mediation.[13] Such information and counsel is not provided directly by the mediator, but by the organization which administers the program. Nevertheless, it is viewed as a form of the mediation process which attempts to balance the parties' power.[14] In these mediations, the mediator may also assume a more active role in equalizing the parties' positions.[15]

Mediation in the agricultural setting may also be observed in disputes between migrant farm workers and growers. These disputes involve parties with an ongoing relationship; it is in everyone's best

---

4. Kan.Stat.Ann. § 65–1824 (1992).

5. Colo. Rev. Stat. Ann. § 38–12–216 (1990); Nev. Rev. Stat. 118B.024 (1999).

6. 59 Okla. Stat. Ann. § 328.60 (West 1999).

7. Mont.Code Ann. 22–3–804 (1999).

8. For a detailed examination of farmer-lender mediation, see Leonard L. Riskin, *Two Concepts of Mediation in the FHMA's Farmer–Lender Mediation Program*, 45 Admin. L.Rev. 1 (1993) and Cheryl L. Cooper, *The Role of Mediation in Farm Credit Disputes,* 29 Tulsa L.J. 159 (1993).

9. This occurred prior to the enactment of Chapter 12 of the Bankruptcy Code.

10. See Agricultural Credit Act of 1987, 501–12 7 U.S.C.A. §§ 5101–5106 (1998).

11. Riskin, *supra* note 8 at 38.

12. Donna L. Malter, Comment, *Avoiding Farm Foreclosure through Mediation of Agricultural Loan Disputes: An Overview of State and Federal Legislation*, 1991 J. Disp. Resol. 335.

13. See Cooper, *supra* note 8, at 170.

14. See Chapter 7 for a more complete discussion of issues surrounding *power imbalances.*

15. Riskin, *supra* note 8.

interest to resolve them quickly. Disputes along the chain of commerce from the farmer to the grocer are also ripe for mediation. As time progresses additional use in this area will no doubt develop.

B. SCHOOLS AND UNIVERSITIES

The use of mediation in schools and universities is one of the fastest growing areas of practice. Mediation can be used in schools and universities in a number of ways. The first and most common application is peer mediation programs. Peer mediation employs student mediators to resolve disputes that occur between other students-peers. When a dispute or conflict arises, instead of resorting to traditional forms of discipline, teachers refer the disputing students to a peer mediator. This mediator is a student who has been trained in mediation or conflict management skills.

There has been some experimentation with peer mediation, also termed school based conflict management, in nearly every state. Peer mediation programs have been implemented from elementary level schools to high schools and colleges.[16] Some statutes require that school districts develop teaching outlines in the mediation and dispute resolution area. The National Association of Mediation in Education (NAME), now CREnet (Conflict Resolution Education Network) serves as a national clearinghouse for materials and information regarding peer mediation programs. At the university level, student mediation programs are often administered through offices of student affairs.[17]

Administrative concerns in schools and universities provide another area in which the mediation process can assist in resolving disputes. These may occur within the educational institution itself as in conflicts between departments. In other cases, mediation can resolve conflicts between an outsider, such as a parent or other interested party, and the administration. Mediation in truancy cases has been specifically provided for in some states.[18] Another area in the education field where mediation is appropriate and statutorily recommended consists of disputes involving special education issues.[19] In fact, over thirty states have mediation procedures in place.[20] In the mediation of these disputes, it has been found that difficulties arise due to imbalances of education and socioeconomic status between the school districts and the parents.[21] Nonetheless,

16. See, William S. Haft and Elaine R. Weiss, Note, *Peer Mediation in Schools: Expectations and Evaluations*, 3 Harv. Negotiation L. Rev. 213 (1998).

17. See Jeffrey C. Son, *University Officials as Administrators & Mediators: The Dual Role Conflict & Confidentiality Problems* 1999 B.Y.U. Educ. & L.J. 19, 25 (1999).

18. See Iowa Code Ann. § 299.5A (Supp. 1999).

19. N.Y. Educ.Law § 4404–a (Supp. 1999). For detail, see Peter J. Kuriloff and Stephen S. Goldberg, *Mediation: A Fair Way to Resolve Special Education Disputes? First Empirical Findings*, 2 Harv. Neg. L. Rev. 35 (1997) and Linda Singer & Eleanor Nace, *Mediation in Special Education: Two States' Experiences*, 1 Ohio St. J. on Disp. Resol. 55 (1985).

20. Kuriloff and Goldberg, *supra* note 19, at 65.

21. *Id.* at 61–62.

research demonstrated that a majority of the parents who participated in mediation would do so again.[22]

And within a school district, college or university, employment issues, which are encompassed under labor and employment is another area where mediation is prevalent.

A variety of third party claims against schools and universities have also been resolved through mediation. Alleged violations of the Americans with Disabilities Act filed by students against a university have been successfully resolved through mediation. Medical malpractice claims filed against university hospitals have been mediated. Additionally, mediation has been used to resolve sexual harassment claims against university professors and staff as well as age and sexual discrimination disputes. Finally, mediation has successfully resolved land dispute claims involving university owned properties.

C. RELIGIOUS INSTITUTIONS

Religious institutions, such as churches and synagogues, experience conflicts which may disrupt the feeling of community or impair the otherwise salient goals of the institution. Such conflicts may take a number of forms. A dispute may arise regarding whether the physical site of a synagogue should move, with half the congregation in favor of the move and half opposed to it. Or, a congregation may become split over the practices and philosophies of a priest. A church may become torn over the inclusion and recognition of gay members. And, disputes may arise over the content and efficacy of a religious school program.

Such disputes, if not dealt with effectively, may be devastating to a religious institution, resulting in destructive feuds between congregants or the splintering of the institution itself. Ironically, conciliation and the peaceful resolution of disputes is inherent as a philosophy of all major religions. Mediation or conciliation is clearly etched in both the Old and New Testament. Some early work in mediation was done by religions as the Mennonites.[23]

Additionally, religious institutions may be involved as either plaintiffs or defendants in civil litigation. Mediation has been used successfully to resolve sexual harassment or indecency with children claims against priests, ministers, and rabbis. Mediation has also been used effectively to resolve construction disputes involving church facilities. Also, mediation has proven effective in resolving medical malpractice claims involving church owned hospitals.

Because of the religious imperative regarding conciliation and forgiveness, several religious institutions are beginning the process of

---

22. *Id.* at 64.

23. The Mennonites were early leaders in this respect. See also Ronald S. Kraybill, *Reparing the Breach: Ministering in Community Conflict* (1981). The Christian Con-

ciliation Service was also a leader in this regard. Currently, the United Methodist Church is in the process of establishing a nationwide conflict resolution project, JUSTPEACE.

creating mediation systems to resolve disputes within the church or claims against the church. Such systems set out the religious basis for mediation and conciliation, train congregants and staff to serve as neutrals in certain disputes, and identify outside neutrals who are sensitive to the religious principles of the institution to resolve third party claims. Such religious institution conflict resolution systems are designed to prevent the escalation of conflict and through the mediation process apply principles of conciliation and forgiveness as a basis to resolve disputes.

D. DIVORCE AND FAMILY

Family and divorce mediation is one of the oldest "specialties" in the mediation profession. During the development of mediation and alternative dispute resolution in the seventies and early eighties, a primary focus was placed on cases involving divorce, and specifically child custody matters. Many of the pioneering state statutes and court programs were in the family and divorce area.

Divorce mediation differs from traditional or generic mediation in a number of ways.[24] "Generic" mediation, whether it be in a neighborhood conflict or in a pending lawsuit, is seen as a one time intervention. That intervention may last an hour or an entire day. But mediation is not considered an ongoing, continuous process. Furthermore, the mediation process is not normally segmented. However, because of the number of issues, and in particular the emotions involved in family law matters, the structure of the process in divorce mediation is extended over a period of weeks, and in complex cases, months. The actual sessions with the parties and the mediators are normally limited, generally to an hour, although some mediators extend the session to an hour and a half. The mediation typically takes from six to eight sessions, but it will continue until all property and custody issues are resolved.

In the divorce area, co-mediation is commonly used.[25] The mediation team usually consists of a therapist or other individual from the social and behavioral sciences and a lawyer. An accountant is sometimes included when the focus of the case is on asset division and financial matters. When the process was first used, divorce mediators met with the parties without their counsel present. Lawyers served primarily to review only the final agreement upon completion of the mediation. A number of issues were raised about the lack of representation during the process. Thereafter, it became general practice for the mediator to urge the parties to obtain legal and financial advice after each session. Currently in an increasing number of instances, lawyers attend each mediation session with their clients. In limited instances, an accountant

---

24. For more information on divorce mediation, see Jay Folberg & Ann Milne, Divorce Mediation: Theory and Practice (1988) and John M. Haynes, The Fundamentals of Family Mediation (1994).

25. Co-mediation means two mediators, usually from different backgrounds. See Chapter 15, § E.

or a therapist for a party may also attend. The children do not normally participate. It is important that the divorce mediator stress to the parties that he does not provide professional advice. Rather, the parties should be encouraged to obtain independent counsel.

Another aspect of mediation use in family matters concerns the termination of parental rights.[26] In at least one state, a statewide program in this area has been implemented. Mediation is used at an early stage—when the child is first removed from the home, to assist in determining the possibility of reuniting the family. Mediation is also used at the later stages in the process to finalize the conditions of termination of parental rights and establishment of adoption. No doubt additional applications for mediation will become apparent.

E. EMPLOYMENT AND LABOR

The labor and employment area is historically seen as the birthplace of the mediation process. Mediation was not, however, used in individual complaints, but rather in union or collective bargaining matters. In the traditional labor mediation model, the mediator meets with representatives of each group and then is very active in formulating solutions with each representative negotiator.

Recently there has been an increased use of the mediation process to resolve individual complaints about employment issues, as well as to resolve intra-organizational disputes. Major corporations have designed entire dispute resolution systems through which employees may resolve their grievances.[27] The largest public employer in the United States, the United States Postal Service, has designed and implemented a mediation program entitled REDRESS (Resolve Employment Disputes Reach Equitable Solutions Swiftly) to resolve employee grievances. Mediation can also be effective in resolving charges of discrimination in employment. For example, the Equal Employment Opportunity Commission (EEOC) conducted pilot mediation projects in an attempt to resolve charges of discrimination in the work place. The agency has now integrated mediation in its work on a national basis. In employment cases, the actual mediation process used may vary. In the EEOC pilot, both the employer and employee must first agree to mediate. If a voluntary agreement to mediate is not obtained, the mediation does not take place. On the other hand, in programs which are established within organizations, this is not the case. In some companies which have implemented a mediation program, such as the postal service, it is implicit in the program's design that the responding party, the employer or a supervisor, will attend the mediation. One unsettled issue encountered in intra-organizational pro-

---

26. The Texas Department of Protection and Regulation Services (also commonly known as Children's Protective Services or CPS), has instituted a statewide mediation program. It is funded by the Childrens Justice Act Project which is in the office of Child Abuse and Neglect in the U.S. Department of Health and Human Services.

27. For a description of Dispute Systems Design, a new field of practice in ADR, see Chapter 17, § D.

grams is with the choice of mediators; specifically, the use of an in-house or out-house mediator.

Mediation of private sector employment disputes has also become widespread and successful. Many employment agreements provide for the mediation of all disputes as a condition of employment. Additionally, the very emotional nature of employment disputes lends itself to mediation. Mediation provides the employee with an opportunity to be heard and express their feelings regarding perceived injustices and wrongdoings. Mediation also provides the employer with an opportunity to explain the basis of a termination. Because employment disputes involve a pre-existing relationship, mediation may provide resolutions which restore such relationships or which sever such relationships on a constructive, mutually satisfactory basis.

In this regard, mediation has successfully resolved wrongful termination claims, age and sexual discrimination claims, claims under the Americans with Disabilities Act, sexual harassment disputes, whistle-blower claims, and disputes involving retaliation for filing workers compensation claims.

In mediating labor and employment cases, one of the most important aspects of the process is an initial issue determination. A primary issue is employment. The mediator together with the parties, must first determine whether continuation of employment is a possibility. The answer to that threshold question will likely shape the remainder of the mediation. If continued employment is agreed to, the mediation will take one direction. In the case where the relationship has been terminated, a different set of options will be explored.

F. PUBLIC POLICY MATTERS

Dispute resolution in the public sector raises a number of concerns very different from those in general or generic mediation. Decisions made in public policy mediations can affect everyone in the community, and as such, may impose upon the mediator certain duties and obligations not otherwise established. The range of public policy mediation is quite expansive and includes general matters within government as well as specific environmental concerns.[28] Governmental entities have begun to experiment with the mediation process, not only in the federal sector, but also at the state and local government levels.

1. GENERALLY

Mediation of public policy matters differs from traditional mediation in a number of ways. One significant variation concerns confidentiality. Unlike traditional mediation which generally operates under the cloak of

---

28. While environmental ADR is often considered a specialized area, these cases possess most of the same variables and considerations as public policy cases, generally, and therefore are considered part of public policy. For additional details, see Charlene Stukenborg, Comment, *The Proper Role of Alternative Dispute Resolution (ADR) in Environmental Conflicts*, 19 U. Dayton. L. Rev. 1305 (1994).

confidentiality,[29] issues in public sector mediation are not private matters. Since most matters touch and concern a great number of individuals who cannot be present during the mediation process, it is imperative that discussions subsequent to the session take place. Many requirements are placed on public entities and organizations that represent "the people". These requirements may directly conflict with the tenets of mediation. Such potential conflicts can arise in the following instances: a duty to inform the public of decisions made during negotiations; the presence of the decision-maker when it is a body politic; and requirements for open meetings and public records. Other differences include the length of sessions or time it requires to reach resolution due in part to the number of parties involved, and the alternative options available should no agreement be forthcoming. In many other conflicts, the parties' options are self help or litigation. In the public policy context, lobbying and protesting are often seen as viable alternatives by various groups. And if an agreement is reached, it is usually contingent upon subsequent approval by the governmental entity.

In the context of public policy dispute resolution, many of these issues are now being addressed with greater frequency. When confronted with these issues, the neutral should openly acknowledge that the mediation process in the public policy arena is quite different from the traditional process. Hence, many of the safeguards and characteristics of mediation will differ when applied to public policy matters. It is important that the participants in the process are fully aware of the parameters and guidelines under which mediation will take place.

A number of organizations have formed which deal exclusively with public policy matters. The MIT–Harvard Public Disputes Program at the Harvard Negotiation Project has been a longstanding leader in this effort.[30] Several states have initiated efforts to increase the use of mediation in these cases, and have created statewide offices for public policy disputes. These states include California, New Hampshire, Texas, Maine and Vermont.[31] These statewide offices assist state and local governmental entities in the implementation of mediation and other dispute resolution devices as integral parts of public service. Specialized training for those mediating in public policy matters is strongly advised. It is anticipated that as the use of mediation increases, some of the issues surrounding public sector mediation will be clarified.

2. ENVIRONMENTAL ISSUES

Matters of the environment effect all individuals. Moreover, these matters are complex and based in large part upon scientific principles. Consequently, litigation surrounding environmental cases can take years, perhaps even decades to resolve. Environmental law is a relatively

---

29. For a complete review of confidentiality and the complexity of affiliated issues, see Chapter 11.

30. See Lawrence Susskind and Jeffrey Cruikshank, Breaking the Impasse (1987).

31. Peter S. Adler, *State Offices of Mediation: Thoughts on the Evolution of a National Network*, 81 Ky. L.J. 1013, 1019 (1992–93).

recent established speciality, and as such, remains in the process of development. Yet, early on it was recognized that ADR procedures could be effective in environmental concerns. The mediation process has been used successfully in a number of environmental cases.[32] It is important in environmental cases that the mediators have specific expertise and rely on the assistance of engineers and other experts to provide the necessary technical information. It should also be recognized that environmental concerns can be quite emotional for a number of people. To the extent it is feasible, all members of the public who are affected should be provided an opportunity to participate in the mediation of these cases. Therefore, environmental mediations do not take place in one day or one session— they take place over a comparatively lengthy period of time.

Mediation in environmental disputes often occurs after a complaint is made or a lawsuit has been filed. However, as mediation use increases and more state and local governments become aware of the benefits, there is another form of the mediation process also termed negotiated rulemaking, which can be utilized in enacting rules and regulations with regard to environmental matters. The mediation process derivative is regulatory negotiation or "reg-neg".[33] Through the reg-neg process, also termed negotiated rule-making, a rule-making authority negotiates the passage of the rule with the affected parties prior to enactment of the rule.

3. THE FEDERAL SECTOR

In 1990, the United States Congress embraced ADR by enacting several pieces of legislation that have encouraged and urged the implementation and use of ADR within and by the federal government. The first was the Civil Justice Reform Act of 1990,[34] which required each federal district court to design a cost and delay reduction plan. The legislation encouraged the use of ADR in such plan. The ninety-four federal courts submitted plans and a majority included ADR provisions. These provisions ranged from implementation of a complete and detailed court-annexed ADR program to a simple statement which encourages the litigants to consider the use of ADR. In 1998 Congress again sent a message to the federal courts by enacting the Alternative Dispute Resolution Act of 1998[35] which mandates that each federal district court establish an ADR program.

Also in 1990, Congress passed the Negotiated Rulemaking Procedure Act[36] and the Administrative Dispute Resolution Act.[37] The Administrative Dispute Resolution Act encourages each federal agency to establish a dispute resolution policy. It provides a broad grant of authority to the agencies to select a number of alternative dispute resolution methods.

32. Susskind and Cruikshank, *supra* note 30, at 162–175.

33. See next section and Chapter 17, § A, 3.

34. 28 U.S.C.A. §§ 471–482 (1993).

35. 28 U.S.C.A. §§ 651–658 (1998).

36. 5 U.S.C.A. §§ 561–570 (1996).

37. 5 U.S.C.A. § 571 et seq. (1996).

Over the last decade, a number of federal agencies have encountered alternative dispute resolution. However, their actual use of ADR process- es was very limited. There had not been a comprehensive, government- wide statement or emphasis on the use of these processes. In the early eighties, the Administrative Conference of the United States (ACUS) made recommendations for the use of ADR. One goal of the Administra- tive Dispute Resolution Act was to send a clear message to all federal agencies that the use of ADR processes is supported, recommended and urged by Congress.

The Act considers a variety of procedures to be used as alternatives to litigation including mediation, fact finding, mini-trial, arbitration, conciliation, or a combination thereof.[38] The Act also sets forth proce- dures for confidentiality,[39] as well as determining who is eligible to serve as neutrals for both inter and intra-agency disputes.[40]

By enacting the Negotiated Rule–Making Act of 1990, Congress essentially codified much of what has been developed over the past few years, in legislative circles, known as negotiated rule-making or "reg- neg". The Negotiated Rule-making Act of 1990 specifically urges federal agencies to utilize the reg-neg process in their rule-making. Negotiated rule-making is neutral conflict assessment consisting of a three-step process. These steps include a determination of: (a) affected parties; (b) feasibility of process use; and (c) notice and meeting.[41]

The Federal Aviation Administration was the first federal agency to try a negotiated rule-making process in 1983.[42] The Animal and Plant Inspection Service of the U.S. Department of Agriculture has utilized the reg-neg process in regulating treatment of a killer sheep disease.[43] Vice President Al Gore's recent National Performance Review contains strong recommendations for the increased use of the reg-neg process by federal agencies.[44]

4. STATE AND LOCAL GOVERNMENTS

Many of the same dispute resolution practices encouraged by Con- gress are now the subject of experimentation within state and local governments. For example, the Texas Water Commission implemented a mediation program. While mediation has not been so thoroughly inte- grated at local government level as to affect policy making, has been progress in that direction. The city of Austin, Texas, used a consensus building process to resolve a conflict regarding a revitalization project in

---

38. 5 U.S.C.A. § 571(3) (1996).

39. 5 U.S.C.A. § 574 (1996).

40. 5 U.S.C.A. § 573 (1996).

41. 5 U.S.C.A. § 563 (1996). See Chap- ter 17, § A infra for more detail on the process.

42. Lawrence E. Susskind, et al., When ADR Becomes the Law: A Review of Federal Practice, 9 Negotiation J. 59, 61 (1993).

43. 3 World Arb. & Mediation Rep. 336 (1992).

44. 4 World Arb. & Mediation Rep. 215 (1993).

the downtown area. Mediation or consensus building has also been used to resolve conflicts involving racial tensions.[45]

A number of states now have statewide offices of dispute resolution.[46] These efforts at dispute resolution on a larger scale were originally sponsored by NIDR (National Institute of Dispute Resolution) as a result of a need for coordinating the mediation of complex public policy disputes. Goals of these state offices include the statewide unification of services and a systematic approach to the mediation of governmental disputes.[47] Each state varied in its approach to sponsorship and implementation. Nevertheless, the goals of education of government administrators, establishment of case referral procedures, and identification of mediators were achieved. Moreover, the primary goal of cooperative inter-agency work was realized.[48]

G. GAY AND LESBIAN MATTERS

"There is no such thing as a gay divorce" declared one mediation brochure. Several issues surrounding the gay and lesbian community, legal as well as general conflict issues, cannot use traditional methods of dispute resolution. In particular, these include relationship dissolution and family restructuring. As a result, some individuals have developed mediation practices specifically for such conflicts. A primary focus is on issues surrounding the dissolution of relationships.[49] Obviously, sexual orientation is but one aspect of an individual and recognize that will likely be involved in all facets of mediation. However, there may be particular concerns,[50] and mediation training has been designed by the gay community.[51] Matters involving health care and claims of discrimination in the gay community can also be assisted by the mediation process.

Many disputes and issues facing individuals who are HIV positive are not of the nature to be determined by a judge or jury. In many instances, both time and monetary resources are limited. Because of the medical prognosis of patients, proceeding through a lengthy litigation process would be futile. A speedy resolution is important. In addition, these persons often need or desire confidentiality. In these matters, the mediation process can usually provide confidentiality, particularly in cases before a lawsuit is filed. Efforts to develop programs focusing on the use of mediation in disputes concerning HIV positive individuals is in progress.

---

45. See Wallace Warfield, Robert Ricigliano, Theodore Johnson and Andrea Chasen, *Problems without a Process: Using an Action Dialogue to Manage Racial Tensions*, 4 Harv. Negotiation L. Rev. 83 (1999) (describing a program which utilized a more derivative process).

46. These include Ohio, Florida, Oregon, Hawaii, Minnesota, New Jersey, California, New Hampshire and Texas.

47. Adler, *supra* note 31, at 1017.

48. *Id.* at 1018.

49. See Clark Freshman, *Privatizing Same–Sex Marriage Through Alternative Dispute Resolution: Community Enhancing versus Community. Enabling Mediation*, 44 UCLA L.Rev. 1687 (1997).

50. See Isabelle R. Gunning, *Stories From Home: Tales From the Intersection of Race, Gender and Sexual Orientation*, 5 S. Cal. Rev. L. & Womens Studies 143 (1995).

51. *Id.*

H. HEALTH CARE ISSUES

Health care affects everyone. During the time individuals receive treatment, a number of conflicts can arise. Mediation has been used in the health care industry in disputes over provision and type of treatment, cost and payment, and allegations of medical negligence or malpractice. And with the evolution of managed care and all the accompanying conflict surrounding such an approach to health care,[52] a greater need for mediation exists.

The mediation process can benefit parties during the treatment phase of the patient-health care provider relationship. Because health care is so important, the time during which individuals are involved in treatment can be a very difficult time, full of emotion and conflict. There are many opportunities for the use of mediation in these situations. Moreover, resolving disputes at an early stage in the patient-provider relationship can help maintain the relationship and prevent later conflict. Some states have recognized this and have provided statutory authority and mandate for mediation in these types of disputes.

Disputes over bills can be resolved to the benefit of all parties through mediation. Mediation saves time and money, which is important to the patient, the provider and third party payors such as health organizations. In at least one state, disputes regarding in-patient reimbursement are referred to mediation.[53]

In 1997, three national organizations, the American Arbitration Association, the American Bar Association, and the American Medical Association joined forces to form the Commission on Health Care Dispute Resolution. The commission considered the application of ADR to health care disputes.[54] The final product of the Commission, the Due Process Protocols, provides recommendations which include that ADR should be used to resolve disputes over health care and access issues arising out of the relationship between patients, private health plans and managed care organizations, that ADR should be used for disputes between health care providers and private plans, and that in the use of ADR due process protections be afforded to all participants.

Mediation has also been very effective in assisting the resolution of medical negligence or medical malpractice cases. While the initial response to the growing number of medical malpractice cases was the creation of screening panels and use of arbitration,[55] mediation has become a viable alternative. Many states have statutes which advocate or

---

52. See e.g., Mark O. Hiepler & Brian C. Dunn, *Irreconcilable Differences: Why the Doctor–Patient Relationship is Disintegrating at the Hands of Health Maintenance Organizations and Wall Street*, 25 Pepp. L.Rev. 597 (1998).

53. N.Y. Pub. Health Law § 2807–c (Supp. 1999).

54. Roderick B. Matthews, *The Role of ADR in Managed Health Care Disputes*, 54 Disp. Resol. J. (1998).

55. *Health Care Providers and Alternative Dispute Resolution: Needed Medicine to Combat Medical Malpractice Claims*, 4 J. Disp. Resol. 64, 66 (1988).

mandate the mediation of medical malpractice cases before they can be brought to trial or sometimes even to the court house.[56] Many malpractice cases are also mediated after a lawsuit is filed, particularly in those jurisdictions where pre-filing screening does not occur. Mediation has been effective in resolving a large number of these cases,[57] and provides additional benefits not available through courts, such as future error reduction.[58]

In other instances, those involved in the health care industry recognize that mediation can be helpful in resolving disputes within the work place, particularly hospitals. These institutions have implemented mediation procedures for dealing with intra-organizational disputes, which include issues ranging from general employment grievances to matters of physician privileges.

Another area within the hospital where mediation has been determined appropriate is to assist in life and death decision making. Most of the work in this area has focused on the elderly.[59] One state legislature has mandated a hospital mediation system for all disputes arising in the context of the issuance of orders not to resuscitate.[60] Now mediation is increasingly recognized as a process to assist bioethical committees, and its application is expanding to include treatment as well as life and death decision making in neonatal care.[61]

I. INTERNET AND CYBERSPACE

Use of the Internet to advertise mediation generally is common.[62] What is becoming even more common, however, is conducting the *actual* mediation in cyberspace.[63]

In this process, the mediator can gather the disputing parties in a "chat room" and conduct the process on-line. While advocates of Internet mediation claim time, speed and convenience are primary benefits, other considerations demonstrate drawbacks as well. For example, much of mediation is premised upon communication, nonverbal as well as verbal. These interpersonal dynamics often critical to resolving the dispute, are unavailable online. However, it is this "distancing" that others see as beneficial in resolving matters.[64] Issues of confidentiality are made more complex by the use of this technology. Nonetheless, the

---

56. Mont. Code Ann. 27–6–701 (1993). See also Woods v. Holy Cross Hospital, 591 F.2d 1164 (5th Cir.1979).

57. For a more detailed examination of particular factors involved in mediating these types of malpractice cases, please see Eric R. Galton, Representing Clients in Mediation (1994).

58. Edward A. Dauer and Leonard J. Marcus, *Adapting Mediation to Link Resolution of Medical Malpractice Disputes with Health Care Quality Improvement*, 60 Law Contemp. Probs. 185 (1997).

59. Diane Hoffman, *Mediating Life and Death Decisions*, 36 Ariz.L.Rev. 821 (1994); Robert Gatter, *Unnecessary Adversaries at*

the End of Life, Mediating End of Life Treatment Disputes to Prevent Erosion of Patient–Physician Relationships, 79 Bost. U.L.Rev. 1091 (1999).

60. N.Y.–McKinney's Pub. Health Law § 2972 (1993).

61. Kimberlee K. Kovach, *Neonatal Life and Death Decisions: Can Mediation Help?* Cap. U. L. Rev. __ (forthcoming 2000).

62. See <http://www.mediation.com.>

63. See Joel B. Eisen, *Are We Ready for Mediation in Cyberspace?*, 1998 B.Y.U. L. Rev. 1305 (1998).

64. *Id.* at 1329.

medium exists, and it is anticipated that innovative adaptations of mediation, such as the Internet will continue to evolve.

J. DISPUTES INVOLVING ATTORNEYS

The legal community has been very active in the promotion and implementation of mediation. If the profession is to practice what it preaches, then the mediation of lawyer-client disputes should increase. Many complaints filed against attorneys by their clients resulted simply from lack of communication. Once the parties are able to better communicate, such disputes are often resolved. The use of mediation in attorney-client matters is in its infancy. Many state and local bar associations are experimenting with pilot projects. Mediation between attorneys and clients can be used in disputes over skill in representation or negligence claims as well as in fee disputes. While mediation can assist in the resolution of legal malpractice claims as it does any professional negligence matter, more importantly, if resolution of an attorney-client dispute can be reached early, claims of malpractice may be prevented.

Many times dissatisfaction and claims of attorney malfeasance or malpractice arise out of a disagreement over attorney's fees. If fee disputes are handled expeditiously, the matter may be privately concluded. The use of ADR can be quite effective in resolving disputes over attorney's fees.[65]

Another distinct area in which disputes involving attorneys can be resolved is in the area of law firm dissolution. In fact, at least one bar association established a mediation project specifically for these cases.[66] The Pennsylvania Bar Association provides mediation, and if the matter is not settled, subsequent arbitration of disputes involving law firms. The matters mediated include dissolutions or lawyer departures, internal disputes within firms, and fee disputes between lawyers of different firms.

K. CRIMINAL ARENA

Many of the early mediation practices evolved, at least tangentially, from within the criminal justice system. Some of these mediation programs started within prosecutor or district attorney's offices.[67] These offices served as the referral source of cases for the programs. While in nearly all of the referred cases a formal criminal charge had not been filed, allegations of criminal activity had been made. Yet these cases were successfully mediated.[68] However, debate still surrounds the propriety of

---

65. For elaboration, see Alan Scott Rau, *Resolving Disputes Over Attorney's Fees: The Role of ADR*, 46 SMU L.Rev. 2005 (1993). For a discussion of attorney-client disputes and the use of ADR in general, see Kimberlee K. Kovach, *Resolving Disputes with Clients*, 18 Barrister 3, 54 (1991).

66. Penn. Bar Association–Lawyer Dispute Resolution Program Rules (1989).

67. For example, the Columbus, Ohio Night Prosecutor Program was located within the Columbus City Prosecutor's Office. The Houston Neighborhood Justice Center, now the Dispute Resolution Center, utilized the Harris County District Attorney's Office.

68. Research of these programs indicates an over eighty percent satisfaction rate. Royer F. Cook, et al., Neighborhood

mediation in criminal matters.[69] Even more controversial are cases involving domestic or co-habitant violence.[70] Yet, research has demonstrated, particularly when the parties know each other, that mediation can be beneficial. Some jurisdictions have trained police officers to mediate "on the spot" when called to a domestic or neighborhood disturbance. Mediation programs have utilized police officers to refer the parties to mediation while on the scene. Rather than arresting the parties, the officer issues a ticket which mandates the citizen's appearance at mediation.

The foregoing examples involve mediation prior to the filing of a formal complaint or charge. Mediation after a complaint is filed is also possible. This essentially consists of mediating a "plea bargain", and has not traditionally been an arena considered part of more traditional negotiation, or one in particular where mediators are necessary. Yet, in many instances, a neutral third party mediator could assist all parties in finding a creative resolution.

Participation in mediation can also occur after adjudication of the complaint as part of the offender's probation or restitution. These mediations are often called VORP (Victim–Offender Restitution Programs or Victim–Offender Reconciliation Programs).[71] Victim-offender mediation is focused on negotiating the terms of restitution to be provided to the victim by the offender. In many of these instances, where there is an ongoing relationship, other matters enter into the mediation as well. Studies have shown that both victims and offenders benefit from the process. Participants report not only satisfaction with the mediation process, but thereafter view the criminal justice system in a more favorable light.[72] VORP or VOM (Victim Offender Mediation) is continuing to expand as more of the criminal justice system focuses on restorative justice issues.[73]

VORP mediation differs from traditional mediation in a number of ways. One is that the focus is on restitution rather than a broad, open-ended discussion of issues. Another is the specific selection criteria for those participating. For instance, most VORP programs deal only with

Justice Centers Field Test, Executive Summary Final Evaluation Report (1980).

69. See Jennifer Gerarda Brown, *The Use of Mediation to Resolve Criminal Cases: A Procedure Critique*, 43 Emory L. J. 1247 (1994).

70. For an in-depth discussion of these policy considerations and issues, see Karla Fisher, et al., *The Culture of Battering and the Role of Mediation in Domestic Violence Cases*, 46 SMU L. Rev. 2117 (1993); Donna Coker, *Enhancing Autonomy for Battered Women: Lessons From Navajo Peacemaking*, 47 UCLA L. Rev. 1 (1999); Nancy H. Rogers and Richard A. Salem, A Student's Guide to Mediation and the Law § 9.02 (1987).

71. This name was first given to the process by a juvenile probation department in Elkhardt, Indiana, where a probation officer recognized the mutual benefit that offenders and victims might gain by sitting and discussing the event with each other. See Stephen Wodpert, Victim–Offender Reconciliation Programs in Community Mediation: A Handbook for Practitioners and Researchers (Karen Grover Duffy, et al., eds., 1991).

72. Mark S. Umbreit and Robert B. Coates, *Cross–Site Analysis of Victim–Offender Mediation in Four States*, 39 Crime and Delinquency 565 (1993).

73. See generally Howard Zehr, Changing Lenses (1990).

property offenses and require that the offender have no more than two prior convictions. Recently, however, work has begun to utilize mediation in more violent cases, and even cases involving rape and murder. Disputes occurring within the confines of a prison system have also been referred to mediation for resolution. In fact, some state prisons have created mediation programs to handle prisoner complaints.

L.   TRANSACTIONAL MATTERS

Mediation is generally considered a dispute resolution device. It is a process used to assist parties in resolving a dispute, and is often defined as such. Yet, it also has been defined as a process which assists parties in a negotiation. Many negotiations take place in a transactional context— in putting together a deal, a sale, a contract. Mediation can be quite effective in providing assistance to the negotiating parties in such transactions. For instance, in the negotiation of a complex contract or business arrangement, if the parties are unable to reach an accord on the specific terms, the assistance of a mediator may be beneficial. Additionally, in the negotiation of partnership documents or formation of a corporate entity, a neutral, third party mediator can provide structure to the negotiations. Unlike mediation in dispute resolution, in a transactional matter, the parties are clearly planning to work together, and the mediation process may have even greater long term benefit.

M.   SPORTS TEAMS

ERIC GALTON, MEDIATION PROGRAMS FOR COLLEGIATE SPORTS TEAMS
Dispute Resolution Journal, 1998.

Success in sports requires diverse members of a team to row with the same oar and focus on the "we," rather than the "me." While coaches attempt to teach leadership skills and teamsmanship along with technique, collegiate sports programs are not immune to conflict. Disputes arise between players and between players and coaches. Such disputes, if not dealt with effectively, may adversely affect team morale and performance on the field. The conventional approach to such conflicts has typically been authoritarian in nature. The coach lays down the law. Someone wins. Someone loses. But the dispute festers and impacts both the players and the team.

Dispute resolution techniques, especially those like mediation, which empower players to communicate and generate their own solutions, may be more effective than the authoritarian approach. Mediation creates "win-win" solutions, provides leadership training, and increases the attitude that we are all in this together. The premise is, that by training an entire team about mediation and specifically identifying seven or eight team members who will serve as team mediators, teams will be able to resolve disputes more efficiently and effectively. The hope is, that because disputes are minimized and resolved more creatively, the team is able to focus on team goals, and performance on the field will be enhanced.

The disputes which might affect a sports team are as myriad and diverse as the problems which affect any business or organization. Players competing for the same position or attempting to generate better statistics may become involved in a dispute. Off-field social disputes between players may translate into on-field disputes. Disputes may originate based on racial divisions or economic lines. A personality dispute may develop between a coach and a player without either communicating what the dispute is really about. Sometimes these disputes create obvious conflicts and sometimes the tension is more subtle. To be sure, the coach wishes to retain his status as the final arbiter or decision-maker. Certain disputes or violations may not be mediated. But the vast majority of disputes typically arise from poor communication and are susceptible to creative problem solving.

Interestingly, collegiate sports teams are perfect candidates for the mediation programs. Most players believe in the concept of team and very much wish to succeed. While team members wish to vanquish the opposition, most players desire stability and collegiality within their own team. Unfortunately, a player's competitive juices or matters and pressures outside the team may create conflict. The problem, not unique to collegiate sports, is whether there is a safe haven or process to deal with these issues. A visit to the coach's office may not appear to be an acceptable option. Fighting may not appear acceptable but may happen anyway. Harsh, careless words may be exchanged, and a player may harbor hurt feelings which affect performance. The internalization of these feelings creates a time bomb which could go off at any time.

In terms of format, the mediation training has two critical phases—the general training for the team and coaches which involves two, three-hour sessions; and the specialized training for the team mediators, which involves seven, three-hour sessions. The general training must be highly interactive in order to generate interest. The trainers must convince the team that the program will serve to better the team and provide the players with a valuable life skill. The coaching staff must support the program. Role plays are essential to involve the players in the process. The special training for the team mediators must be adequate to ensure they will properly administer the mediation process.

* * *

The coaches should select, applying principles of diversity, team mediators who truly represent the team. The coaches should also determine what disputes are or are not suitable for mediation.

Collegiate sports teams, and their individual members, serve as role models for America's youth. Players, under intense scrutiny both on and off the field, find themselves involved in conflicts. Many of these conflicts adversely impact both the players and the team. An effective conflict resolution program provides the players and the team with important life skills and a way to resolve disputes peaceably. A conflict-free team functions better, and represents its college or university more effectively.

Businesses suffer when internal discord or conflict adversely affects morale. Sports teams are no different. Coaches may retain ultimate authority and benefit from player mediators who effectively deal with disputes which might adversely affect team performance.

N. INTERNATIONAL AND CROSS–CULTURAL CONSIDERATIONS

Mediation in the international context can take a number of different forms. International disputes are usually thought of as those between people of different nations. These disputes may concern political or security issues, in which case the disputing parties are often groups. Disputes involving people from different nations also include economic and environmental matters. Here, the number of participants may be more limited. Mediation in security or political issues is usually conducted by an outside nation.[74] The process differs in that the neutral mediator is not completely neutral but has relations with each country. Nonetheless, he does not favor either side.[75] The mediator has three primary roles: communicator, formulator, and manipulator.[76] It is the last role which clearly distinguishes this type of mediation from the more traditional process.[77]

What has become known as cross-cultural mediation is the mediation between individuals from different cultures. The parties may be from the same nation or different nations. Cross-cultural considerations are necessary as mediation use grows within the United States, as persons in conflict may be from a number of different cultures. Often when disputes arise, people are unable to negotiate and reach agreements because of a lack of mutual understanding. Mediation of cross-cultural disputes is particularly problematic because of the threshold difficulties associated with a lack of understanding and knowledge about the parties, their interests and cultural directives. It is important that mediators intervening in cross-cultural disputes have a sense of these additional issues. As the mediator is attempting to facilitate communication and understanding, he must first realize these inherent, collateral issues. As in many types of specialized applications of the mediation process, specific training is necessary.

Different cultures have varying concepts of the role of an intermediary in negotiation. Some of the roles a mediator may assume include:

74. Saadia Touval and I. William Zartman, Mediation in International Conflicts, in Mediation Research: The Process and Effectiveness of Third–Party Intervention, 118 (Kenneth Kressel, et al. eds., 1989).

75. *Id.* at 126.

76. *Id.* at 127.

77. For additional information on International Mediation, see Mediation In International Relations: Multiple Approaches To Conflict Management (Jacob Bercovitch and Jeffrey Z. Rubin, eds., 1992).

providing assistance with the relationship, assisting in data collection or exchange, assistance with the process, and providing advice or decision-making. While the first three may be seen as traditional mediation, the last is seen primarily in other ADR processes. Therefore the mediator, before beginning the process, must be sure that he and the parties are clear about what his role is to be. As mediation use continues to expand throughout the world, additional opportunities for international and cross-cultural applications will, no doubt, increase.

Chapter Seventeen

PREVENTATIVE AND CREATIVE USES OF MEDIATION: DERIVATIVE, COMBINED AND HYBRID PROCESSES

In previous chapters the mediation process has been described and analyzed. The reader should now be able to clearly understand the process and be developing basic skills. Different types and styles of mediation have also been identified. As each mediator develops her skills, she is likely to adopt the style which best corresponds to her own personality and which is also likely to meet the needs and desires of the parties. As additional methodologies develop and process modifications made, no doubt additional styles of mediation will emerge.

Several other processes resemble mediation, particularly in their theoretical basis. Yet, while sharing philosophical roots, these other dispute resolution techniques are sufficiently distinct to warrant different names. These derivative processes include consensus building, conciliation and regulatory negotiation.

Traditional mediation can also be added to another process to form a "combined" process. Even when combined, however, mediation is a distinct stage that either precedes or follows another process. The most common example is med-arb, mediation followed by arbitration. The mediation process can also be blended into another ADR process to form a "hybrid" process. The mini-trial is one such product. Since all of these techniques utilize some form of mediation, it is appropriate to discuss them further.

A. DERIVATIVE PROCESSES

1. CONCILIATION

The term conciliation is often used interchangeably with mediation. In some countries, conciliation is used more often than mediation. Some contend that no marked differences exist and the two are satisfactory synonyms. This view fails to recognize distinct differences.

Some say that the primary difference between mediation and conciliation resides in the role of the neutral. In a conciliation, the neutral merely brings parties together to discuss matters, whereas in mediation, the mediator has a much more active role.[1]

"Conciliation" and "reconciliation" come from the same root word, and have similar meanings.[2] In the context of dispute resolution, conciliation often includes a reconciliation. The parties involved in a dispute or conflict not only come to a final resolution of a specific dispute, but they are also able to reconcile their views of the relationship. This is most effective in terms of individuals who have ongoing relationships. In fact, in the United States conciliation involves focus on the interpersonal aspect of the conflict, as compared to mediation's greater emphasis on substantive matters.[3] In conciliation, the neutral is seen to take a more passive role in the intervention.[4] In some situations, it is possible for the parties to reach conciliation without resolving the original dispute. Both parties' emphasis is on the maintenance of their relationship, and through conciliation they agree to continue negotiations rather than resolve the specific dispute. In fact, one element of the conciliation might involve walking away from the conflict.

In mediation, reconciliation between the parties is often an integral part of the process. However, reconciliation is not a necessary component. For example, in pending litigation cases such as personal injury matters, no previous relationship may have existed. The parties may not have a need or a desire for reconciliation. A resolution can be mediated without a conciliation. On the other hand, mediators who mediate at the community level in disputes such as those between neighbors, landlords and tenants, and others involving long-term relationships, find that they get better results by combining mediation and conciliation.

2. CONSENSUS BUILDING

The consensus building process is similar to mediation in its focus on assisting parties in a dispute in reaching a voluntary, mutual, and satisfying agreement. Consensus building, however, is different in a number of ways. In most traditional mediations, there are two sides and two distinct views of the situation in conflict. Even though many lawsuits and disputes involve multiple parties, the parties tend to split into two alignments on either side of a set of issues. In consensus building, there are often many different groups with a variety of interests. Coalitions frequently form. While each group may have representatives at the mediation table, much intra-group negotiation takes place away from the table.

Consensus building is traditionally used in large public policy disputes, such as disputes involving environmental issues. Therefore, the

---

1. Walter A. Maggiolo, Techniques of Mediation 13 (1985).

2. From Latin *conciliare*, to bring together, and *re-*, again (American Heritage Illustrated Encyclopedia Dictionary, 1987).

3. For a detailed discussion, see Dictionary of Conflict Resolution 102, 104 (Douglas Yarn, Ed. 1999).

4. *Id.* at 103, 104.

convener (as the neutral is often called in this process) attempts to find a few issues upon which a consensus can be built. While at first glance such a process appears more difficult than a classic mediation, in many ways it is easier. Often a number of interests overlap. Some of the parties may have shared goals. Consequently there is greater opportunity for integrative bargaining.

Unlike traditional mediation, consensus building is not a one-time intervention. As its name implies, it is a building process that takes place over a number of successive meetings, spread out through weeks and even months. The pre-mediation phase is also quite lengthy. In fact, it is often the longest phase of the process. As part of the pre-meeting stage of the process, the facilitator/convener may meet with the potential stakeholders in order to assess their positions and determine the logistical requirements. Further, the convener meets with these interested or affected parties to help them choose their representatives for the consensus building process. Protocol for the consensus building meetings can be determined based on past experience and the individual needs of a party. Protocol may include, for instance, agreements about dealing with the media. The convener may also wish to talk to each party about agenda setting.[5] Lastly, the convener may engage in joint fact finding, and determine whether there are any consultants or advisors who may assist consensus building.[6] The actual negotiation or mediation phase can then begin.

Since the issues have been identified in the pre-meeting stage, the consensus building starts with brainstorming possible solutions. Part of building a consensus includes a "packaging" stage, where the convener meets in private sessions with each of the groups to determine which partial solutions might be able to be bargained for and packaged up together.[7] If an agreement is reached, the mediator then writes up that agreement and assists in binding the entire group. Because everyone participating in the process is a representative of others, the penultimate step is ratification. During ratification the meeting participants go back to their constituencies and "sell" the agreement so that each group's sign-off can be obtained.[8] Lastly, consensus building often involves the neutral convener in an implementation or post-negotiation phase as well.[9] This is not true in generic mediation. However, because of the magnitude of most such disputes and the complexities of their agreements, the parties may need assistance from the neutral, particularly if there are elected or appointed officials who must be consulted, or if there is a need for a monitor. The neutral is also called upon if a need occurs for renegotiation of the agreement. Many of these processes are public, and if an agreement is reached, it is published.

5. This is unlike mediation where agenda setting is a step in the mediation.

6. Lawrence Susskind and Jeffrey Cruikshank, Breaking the Impasse 142 (1987).

7. *Id.*

8. *Id.* at 143.

9. *Id.*

Team mediation is sometimes used as part of a large, complex consensus building process. Team mediators can be an effective way to handle some of the intricacies the consensus building process. *Team mediation* generally means that there is more than one mediator. While two mediators are technically a team, most two mediator teams are referred to as *co-mediators* and act in tandem. The lead role is exchanged evenly between the two. Co-mediators never separate; in a caucus, both mediators meet together with one party at a time. It is necessary that the two mediators coordinate their actions and strategies. It is recommended that co-mediators know each other well and have an ongoing working relationship.

In contrast to the almost Siamese twin-like relationship of co-mediators, team mediation, usually involves more than two mediators, and they act more independently. As with most teams, there is a team leader, who is primarily responsible for the direction of the sessions. Each member of the team works with an individual constituency. The team members then exchange information. Particularly when the number of parties is large, team mediation can save a great deal of time.

3. REG–NEG

Regulatory negotiation or reg-neg, as it is known, originated within the Administrative Conference of the United States,[10] and now its use is encouraged by statute.[11] Reg-neg[12] can be viewed as a specific form of consensus building. Regulatory negotiation is an attempt to shorten the rulemaking process for federal (as well as state[13]) agencies. Rather than the traditional method of drafting and enacting a rule, and thereafter sending it out for comment, in the reg-neg process, all interested or affected parties are contacted and invited to take part in the initial design of the rule. Discussions continue until all reach consensus about the content of the rule or regulation. The third party neutral, who acts much like a mediator, is called the convener and is responsible for each step in the process.

The first step is to determine which groups would be affected by the proposed legislation. Secondly, the convener determines whether it would be feasible to use negotiation among all of those affected to resolve any disputes. If the convener decides to use negotiation, notices of the meetings are published in the Federal Register. At the meetings, interested parties help draft the new legislation, eliminating the normal wait for feedback and revision.

The negotiation of regulations is very similar to consensus building. The main difference is that reg-neg is more focused. In the consensus

---

10. Office of the Chairman, Administrative Conference of the United States, Negotiated Rulemaking Sourcebook, (hereinafter referred to as Sourcebook) (1990).

11. 5 U.S.C.A. § 561 (1996).

12. See Chapter 16 § F *supra* for a discussion of the application of reg-neg.

13. At least two states have enacted a negotiated rule-making statute. See 1993 Montana Negotiated Rule Making Act, Mont. Code Ann. § 2–5.–101, et seq. (1999) & Tex. Gov't Code Ann. § 2008.001 et seq. (West 1997).

building process, usually there is an issue that needs closure, but the specifics of resolution are left to the parties involved. In regulatory negotiation, however, the goal is specifically identified at the beginning of the session, i.e., a draft of a regulation. The entire process therefore, is more limited. Likewise, in general consensus building, anyone with an interest may participate. In regulatory negotiation, the convener may limit the number of parties to fewer than fifteen,[14] or she may allow as many as twenty-five,[15] but rarely more than that. Moreover, in reg-neg only those parties who are directly affected by the proposed rule may attend the session. Another distinction is that in regulatory negotiation the convener rarely does any follow-up. Once a consensus is reached, the rule is implemented.

4.   CONVENING CONFERENCES

A convening conference is a relatively new process created by dispute resolution systems designers.[16] Mediative in nature, convening conferences are built upon the principles of consensus and collaborative problem solving, and have as their purpose the selection of the ADR process which will best assist in resolving a given dispute.[17] In this process, the first step after a dispute is identified is a meeting with a neutral. Rather than focusing directly on the conflict, however, the disputing parties first confer about process options. The neutral may act as a technical consultant concerning ADR, and then use her collaborative problem solving skills to assist the disputing parties in the selection of an appropriate ADR process. Such conferences are the first step in resolution of the dispute. The inventors of this technique suggest that a clause calling for a convening conference should be an option to the more common automatic mediation or arbitration clause. Using this process provides maximum flexibility and allows the disputing parties to make early decisions about the process.

B.   COMBINED PROCESSES

The mediation process may be combined with a number of other dispute resolution techniques in order to achieve a settlement. The most common combined form is the med-arb process in which the parties first engage in the mediation process. If an agreement is not reached in a predetermined amount of time (or at the discretion of the mediator), the parties enter arbitration. A number of different forms of this process are now available.

In the original med-arb process, the neutral began the proceeding as a mediator, but with the understanding that any matter unresolved

14.   Philip J. Harter, *Negotiating Regulations: A Cure for Malaise*, 71 Geo. L. J. 46 (1982).

15.   Sourcebook, *supra* note 10, at 37.

16.   For an explanation of dispute systems design, see § D *infra*. The process of

convening was first suggested by Karl A. Slaikeu and Ralph H. Hasson, *Not Necessarily Mediation: The Use of Convening Clauses in Dispute Systems Design*, 8 Negotiation J. 331 (1992).

17.   *Id.* at 332.

would be arbitrated. Because the same individual served in both a facilitative and adjudicative function, the process was criticized. The criticism included the contention that since the mediator knew that a decision might have to be made, the mediator could not remain non-judgmental during the mediative phase and listen with an ear in an attempt to find overlapping interests. Instead, she would be focused on determining the facts. Moreover, the type of presentations which should be made by the parties or their advocates differs drastically in each process, and to be effective in one necessarily damages effectiveness in the other.

As a result, another form of med–arb evolved. In the newer form, the parties attempt to mediate, but if a resolution is not achieved during the session, the parties begin arbitration with a *different* individual serving as the arbitrator. The difficulty in this form of med–arb is that it is necessarily repetitious when mediation fails and consequently more time-consuming and costly. A third form labeled "co–med–arb" has thus been recently designed.[18] Because of the aforementioned criticisms of the med–arb process, this new version attempts to eliminate the defects of its predecessors, yet still provide the benefits of both mediation and arbitration to the disputants. Specifically, the co–med–arb process uses two neutrals simultaneously listening to the initial statements of the parties. The first neutral then acts as the mediator, leading a non-judgmental mediation session. Should that effort fail to completely resolve the matter, the second neutral presents the parties with a binding arbitration decision of those issues left undecided. However, as long as the two neutrals remain together, the parties, or their representatives are still faced with the dilemma of the type and extent of information that should be disclosed, as well as the manner of presentation.

Traditional forms of med-arb dictate that the mediation process be conducted prior to the arbitration. A few practitioners have experimented with arbitration first, followed by mediation. The neutral provides a non-binding suggested arbitration award and then assists the parties in mediating their dispute. This novel approach has been severely criticized because the mediator, having rendered an award, can no longer be impartial or neutral about the outcome of the case.

Just as mediation has been combined with arbitration, it can also be joined with the evaluative ADR processes. The order of the processes varies. In some cases, parties need certain information to assist them in the negotiation of a settlement. Evaluative processes, such as the moderated settlement conference, neutral case evaluation, or the summary jury trial, could take place prior to the mediation. Or the parties could try mediation first. If the mediation does not result in a settlement (primarily because of inaccurate or incomplete evaluation or assessment of the case), the mediator may recommend that the parties participate in an evaluative process. After the evaluative process, the parties may choose

18. For further elaboration of this concept, see 3 World Arb. and Mediation Rep. 21 (1992).

to mediate again or negotiate a resolution without the assistance of a neutral.

C. HYBRIDS

The word "hybrid" indicates the actual merger of two different processes, which results in a composite. Rather than merely combining the mediation process with another process, there is true integration. If mediation is integrated with an evaluative process, the result is a completely new process, e.g., the mini-trial.[19] The mini-trial uses mediation concepts in the facilitation of communication between the parties and the neutral expert advisor may actually mediate. The form of mediation, however, may likely be non-traditional. The neutral expert advisor first provides the parties with an opportunity for direct negotiations. She then shares her evaluation, after which facilitated discussions resembling mediation take place. As the use of mediation continues to grow, additional opportunities to integrate it with other processes will occur, and additional hybrid processes will no doubt result.

D. DESIGN ISSUES

While it may be impossible to prevent disputes, it is possible to plan for their occurrence. The idea is essentially "planning for disputing." Providing "dispute systems design" is a new specialty in the ADR field. Major organizations, corporations, and businesses try to design, in advance, efficient ways of handling disputes. Often mediation is included. The mediation process, or a form of it such as consensus building, may also be helpful in the design of a system to resolve disputes.

Dispute resolution systems design has at least six components: the assessment of the current system for dispute resolution; the determination of specific goals and objectives of a new system; the design for the new system; education of users about the new system; actual implementation of the new system; and evaluation.

In assessing the current system, a dispute resolution consultant works with the organization to determine how disputes are currently resolved. Factors such as the cost for each type of dispute, in terms of money as well as loss of employee time, are typically examined. Further, the current dispute resolution procedure is evaluated on the basis of its effect on public relations. A number of other issues can be examined in the assessment phase. For example, it is useful to appraise the skills of individuals involved in resolving disputes, to analyze the usual types of outcomes, and to gauge the frequency of disputes and their rate of recurrence.

In the next stage, the designer holds a meeting with a management team to determine exactly what the organization is hoping to achieve by designing a new dispute resolution system. In some instances, they may

---

19. See Chapter 1, for a more complete description of this process.

only wish to save money. Other organizations may seek to improve morale among the workers. Some companies will focus on an enhanced public image. Whatever the objective, it can usually be achieved by a combination of processes. In order to design a workable plan that will meet the goals of the organization, however, it is important for the organization to be very specific in defining those objectives. It is likely that the consultant will utilize the principles of collaborative problem solving and mediation in determining the objectives.

Once the goals are determined, the plan can be designed. This plan can be as complex or as simple as the participants deem appropriate. It may specify a one-step process: if a dispute occurs, the parties are immediately directed to one ADR process. Most plans, however, call for multiple steps. For instance, a first step after a dispute arises might be a convening conference including all parties in dispute.[20] A common alternative first step is to schedule a private meeting of a party with staff from the human resources department. Another option is an initial mediation. If the first step, whatever it may be, is not successful in resolving the dispute, then the disputants go to the second tier or step. Here, a mediation, an evaluation, or an arbitration may take place. If this second step is also unsuccessful, the third step may include processes such as case evaluation and ultimately, litigation. As is apparent, the design of the plan is open to the creativity of the organization as well as the consultant.

It is then important to educate the potential users of the new system about the mechanics of access, as well as benefits. For once a plan is implemented, it is vital that it is used.

Once the plan is complete, it is implemented. An important part of implementation is continued education. Clearly those directly involved in the day-to-day operation of the dispute resolution plan must be aware of in its use. Furthermore, all members of the organization should be aware of the new plan. In short, when integrating mediation into the culture of an organization, it is critical to make sure that everyone, from custodian to CEO, understands the process.

Lastly, the evaluation and "loop-back" phase occurs. Any time a new plan is put into place, it should be evaluated. As evaluations are completed and reviewed, retooling may be needed. A continuous evaluation and design loop results. Because of the novelty of dispute systems design, it is recommended that at least initially, evaluations be continual.

20. See § A, 5, *supra.*

E. CONCLUSION

"A mind, once stretched by a new idea, never regains its original shape."

—Oliver Wendell Holmes

Through the mediation process, it is hoped that the minds of mediators, lawyers, and disputants are stretched. If we, as dispute resolution professionals, "walk the talk," the principles of mediation will become integrated into our professional and personal lives. New applications for the process will develop and new ways of solving disputes will emerge.

The field of dispute resolution generally, and mediation specifically, is in a state of constant change. Although mediation may no longer be in the "embryonic" stage, it has not yet fully matured. Those involved in the mediation process have a unique opportunity to fashion its future. It is up to all of us to continue to shape and form the principles and practice of mediation.

QUESTIONS FOR DISCUSSION

17–1. Revenue Realty

Plaintiff is Pat Smith, d/b/a Revenue Realty. Revenue Realty employed the defendant and counterclaimant, Tommy Thompson, as a realtor about three years ago. As part of his employment, Thompson signed a covenant not to compete in the Denver area. The covenant was to be effective for three years from the date of termination. Revenue Realty has sued Thompson for violation of the covenant. The background of the case is as follows:

The covenant not to compete was part of a larger agreement which provided that Revenue Realty would provide the brokerage license, office space, multiple listing service, and advertising to Thompson, while Thompson would be employed as a real estate agent. It also included a generous commission split of 50–50 along with the non-compete clause.

Problems began between Smith and Thompson about five months ago. Thompson "sold" a house to Frank and Betty Grey for $374,500. The Greys, however, did not qualify for financing. Thompson was then "let go" by Smith.

Thompson claims that the firing was caused by his refusal to tell the Greys not to reveal an $80,000 personal loan from Betty Grey's uncle (Buck Booth). Disclosure of that loan would result in the Grey's "debt/income" ratio being too high. Since the uncle's loan was a family matter, it would not be discovered in a typical credit check.

Smith asserts that a downturn in the economy has impacted the real estate market and that Revenue, like many other agencies, had to pare down its staff. About four weeks ago, Thompson was terminated by Smith. Two weeks ago, Smith learned that Thompson was, in fact, competing.

Revenue then brought suit against Thompson to enforce the covenant not to compete, to collect monies owed on an expense account that Thompson charged, and for return of a two-year-old Lincoln Continental. Thompson has counter claimed for wrongful termination, for commissions allegedly owed him of $27,400, and for a declaratory judgment voiding the non-compete clause.

At the preliminary injunction hearing the court has referred the case to ADR.

Appendix A

MATERIALS FOR MEDIATION ROLE PLAYS

GENERAL INSTRUCTIONS FOR ROLE PLAY PARTICIPANTS

Active participation in mediation exercises and simulations is one of the most vital components in the development of mediation skills. This is true whether the participation is as a mediator, a party or a party's representative.

It is important when learning about mediation that you understand the process, not only from the mediator's role but also from that of the participants. Therefore, it is imperative that when playing the role of the disputing party or advocate for a party that you are "in role". To get yourself ready, first become familiar with the content of the dispute. Then think about how you would feel and act, if truly in that situation. The emotions and reactions that you demonstrate during the role play should be consistent with the instructions provided to you and your own personality. Some of you may have a tendency, when involved in conflict, to react strongly while others have a more subtle approach.

If you play the part of the participant realistically, it is much easier for you to feel that role and observe how the mediator's conduct, good or bad, affects you. Moreover, you are then able to provide more accurate feedback to the individual in the role of mediator.

MEDIATION PROCESS WORKSHEET

List highlights of the mediator's introduction.

Critique the opening statements:

    (a) Party A

    (b) Attorney A

    (c) Party B

    (d) Attorney B

    (e) Others

What types of communication took place during the mediation?

What were the identifiable issues?

What were the interests of the parties?

What type(s) and styles of negotiation did you observe?

Additional Comments:

MEDIATION ANALYSIS

	D1	D2
Issues:		
Interests:		
Initial Position:		
Alternatives:		
BATNA:		
WATNA:		

MEDIATION PROCESS FORM

Preliminary Arrangements

Mediator's Introduction

Opening Statements

Information Gathering

(Venting)

Issue Identification and Restatements

(Caucus)

Identified Interests

Agenda Setting

Generation of Options

Negotiation

Agreement

Closure

A SLIPPERY GRAPE

On a beautiful Sunday after attending services at the Goodwill Church of The Rock, Vi Wynette decided to go grocery shopping for a prayer meeting that evening. Vi was shopping for ingredients to make a famous ambrosia salad which consisted of numerous fresh fruits, coconut, small colored marshmallows, mayonnaise, and several bottles of Big Red soft drink.

Vi entered the local grocery store, the Big Bag–N–Save, and proceeded to the soft drink aisle. After getting the Big Red, Vi headed for the fresh fruit section of the supermarket. Vi spied the grapes, and decided that they would make a wonderful addition to the salad. After selecting the grapes, Vi went toward the pineapple.

Suddenly, Vi heard a familiar voice, Lula May Thompson, a fellow member in the choir. Vi decided to backtrack to have a chat. As Vi moved the shopping cart around, the heel of the left shoe slid on a grape peel causing Vi to fall. Only a tight grasp on the cart prevented a total collapse.

Vi felt severe pain in the left knee and lower back, as well as a shooting pain in the right shoulder. Vi screamed out loudly, causing several customers and store personnel to rush over. The produce manager, Bob Weedon, appeared and as he picked Vi up, he exclaimed, "I've been telling them boys to keep this aisle clean. I knew someone would get hurt."

Vi was then taken by the ambulance to the local hospital for X-rays and observation. Upon release the following morning, only Advil was prescribed. Vi felt continuous pain and two days later asked the advice of Lula May. Lula May referred Vi to her chiropractor, Dr. Nelson. Vi saw Dr. Nelson on several occasions throughout the month. Nelson's diagnosis was that with constant adjustments, Vi's injury would be manageable and would not prevent further activities nor participation in the local bowling league.

Vi has hired an attorney and is seeking compensation for the injuries, medical bills, lost wages and mental anguish. Vi, through the lawyer, has indicated that $100,000.00 for medicals and past wages, plus $50,000.00 in mental anguish would settle the case. Big Bag has offered $5,000.00 in cash and $250.00 in super saver coupons.

The parties have agreed to try mediation before filing suit.

RUNS–N–ROSES

Plaintiff is a corporation operating under the name Rammel Properties, Inc. It owns several prime commercial properties, along with some not so prime retail strip centers throughout the city. The Chief Financial Officer and President of Rammel is Mr. William Fold, who is a majority stockholder.

The Defendant, Lee Brachy, is an individual. Brachy was a computer programmer who decided to take early retirement and change careers. Brachy chose to open a drive-through flower shop. Brachy and Rammel negotiated a lease agreement. During the negotiations, Brachy also negotiated certain build-out provisions with a leasing agent, Sue Storm. These included specific plumbing and thermostatic requirements. However, inadvertently these special build-outs were not reduced to writing.

Brachy entered into a franchise agreement with Runs–N–Roses Internationale' after reading in a magazine about this new concept founded in California. After signing the lease agreement, Brachy left her company and moved to California where she attended a three-month training session for a new career as a mobile florist. However, two months into the training, and six weeks prior to the Grand Opening of Runs–N–Roses # 38, the franchisor Runs–N–Roses Internationale' filed for Chapter 7 Bankruptcy. All bouquets were quickly liquidated. Brachy took this event as a divine indication that all is not well in the drive-through floral business, and has decided to forego a life-long ambition of self-employment. Brachy immediately informed Rammel that the shop would not be opening, and has been working off and on as a programmer.

Fold, as well as the leasing agent (who receives a commission of all lease agreements) are upset; additional money (loosely estimated to be several thousand dollars) was spent to outfit what was to be the drive-through area of the lease space. Because Brachy was told that the flowers must be kept at precise temperatures, special watering systems and temperature checks had been ordered.

Rammel has brought suit against Brachy for all sums due under the lease. Brachy has counterclaimed alleging that Rammel was the first to breach by not having the premises ready in accordance with the lease agreement. The court has referred the case to mediation.

THE BANKRUPTCY OF BETTER THAN A BONNET
General Information

Mr. Sal Salem owns 55% of the stock in Better Than A Bonnet (BTAB), a hat manufacturer in the Richmond, Virginia area. Mr. Salem, as the majority stockholder, is also the president of the corporation. Over the last ten years a substantial profit had been realized. About eighteen months ago, Sal convinced the Board of Directors to expand the company throughout the nation. However, at about the same time, due to the faltering economy and the scientific breakthrough in hair transplants, the hat market went into a steep decline. Due to pressures from creditors and under stress of a threatened divorce, Sal sought help. BTAB filed for bankruptcy protection under Chapter 11 about four months ago.

The primary creditor, Tokyo Mortgages, has the first lien on all of the equipment. Tokyo also claims personal guarantees of three individuals: Salem; Mr. Rocky Rico another stockholder and the corporate vice-president; and Mrs. Salem, whose great-grandfather founded Richmond Savings over one hundred years ago.

The remaining stockholders in Better Than a Bonnet consist of twelve family friends, who led by Rico, have instituted an adversary proceeding against Mr. Salem personally for breaches of fiduciary duty. They argue that Mr. Salem has fraudulently squandered company funds under the guise of business travel and entertainment. Additionally, The Felt Company (TFC), a Hong Kong direct supplier of raw materials for hat manufacture, has filed a Motion to Lift Stay, attempting to foreclose on BTAB in order to force the return of a large felt delivery.

Sally Salem, not an understanding woman, has filed for divorce. She claims one-half of all of the stock owned by her husband. Nearly twenty years ago, BTAB began as a sole proprietorship based on a wedding gift from Sally's father. The company incorporated a year later, and the stock was then distributed. Mr. Salem's interest presently is valued at approximately 1.2 million dollars.

Due to the number of related matters at a recent status conference, the Bankruptcy Court suggested that the primary parties try mediation. Present at the mediation are Sal, Sally, Rocky, Jako Datsu from Tokyo, and Charles Smith, the U.S. sales representative for The Felt Company. Each individual is accompanied at the mediation by an attorney.

Appendix B

JOINT CODE *

STANDARDS OF CONDUCT
Introductory Note

The initiative for these standards came from three professional groups: the American Arbitration Association, the American Bar Association, and the Society of Professionals in Dispute Resolution.

The purpose of this initiative was to develop a set of standards to serve as a general framework for the practice of mediation. The effort is a step in the development of the field and a tool to assist practitioners in it—a beginning, not an end. The standards are intended to apply to all types of mediation. It is recognized, however, that in some cases the application of these standards may be affected by laws or contractual agreements.

Preface

The standards of conduct for mediators are intended to perform three major functions: to serve as a guide for the conduct of mediators; to inform the mediating parties; and to promote public confidence in mediation as a process for resolving disputes. The standards draw on existing codes of conduct for mediators and take into account issues and problems that have surfaced in mediation practice. They are offered in the hope that they will serve an educational function and provide assistance to individuals, organizations, and institutions involved in mediation.

Mediation is a process in which an impartial third party—a mediator—facilitates the resolution of a dispute by promoting voluntary agreement (or "self-determination") by the parties to the dispute. A mediator facilitates communications, promotes understanding, focuses the parties on their interests, and seeks creative problem solving to enable

* Drafting participants:

Chair John D. Feerick and David Botwinik for the American Arbitration Association; James J. Alfini and Nancy H. Rogers for the American Bar Association; Susan Dearborn and Lemoine Pierce for the Society of Professionals in Dispute Resolution; Bryant G. Garth and Kimberlee K. Kovach, Reporters; and Frederick E. Woods, Project Staff Director (1994).

the parties to reach their own agreement. These standards give meaning to this definition of mediation.

I.   Self–Determination: A Mediator Shall Recognize that Mediation is Based on the Principle of Self–Determination by the Parties.

Self-determination is the fundamental principle of mediation. It requires that the mediation process rely upon the ability of the parties to reach a voluntary, uncoerced agreement. Any party may withdraw from mediation at any time.

COMMENTS

- The mediator may provide information about the process, raise issues, and help parties explore options. The primary role of the mediator is to facilitate a voluntary resolution of a dispute. Parties shall be given the opportunity to consider all proposed options.

- A mediator cannot personally ensure that each party has made a fully informed choice to reach a particular agreement, but it is a good practice for the mediator to make the parties aware of the importance of consulting other professionals, where appropriate, to help them make informed decisions.

II.   Impartiality: A Mediator Shall Conduct the Mediation in an Impartial Manner.

The concept of mediator impartiality is central to the mediation process. A mediator shall mediate only those matters in which she or he can remain impartial and evenhanded. If at any time the mediator is unable to conduct the process in an impartial manner, the mediator is obligated to withdraw.

COMMENTS

- A mediator shall avoid conduct that gives the appearance of partiality toward one of the parties. The quality of the mediation process is enhanced when the parties have confidence in the impartiality of the mediator.

- When mediators are appointed by a court or institution, the appointing agency shall make reasonable efforts to ensure that mediators serve impartially.

- A mediator should guard against partiality or prejudice based on the parties' personal characteristics, background or performance at the mediation.

III.   Conflicts of Interest: A Mediator Shall Disclose All Actual and Potential Conflicts of Interest Reasonably Known to the Mediator. After Disclosure, the Mediator Shall Decline to Mediate Unless All Parties Choose to Retain the Mediator. The Need to Protect Against Conflicts of Interest Also Governs Conduct that Occurs During and After the Mediation.

A conflict of interest is a dealing or relationship that might create an impression of possible bias. The basic approach to questions of conflict of interest is consistent with the concept of self-determination. The mediator has a responsibility to disclose all actual and potential conflicts that are reasonably known to the mediator and could reasonably be seen as raising a question about impartiality. If all parties agree to mediate after being informed of conflicts, the mediator may proceed with the mediation. If, however, the conflict of interest casts serious doubt on the integrity of the process, the mediator shall decline to proceed.

A mediator must avoid the appearance of conflict of interest both during and after the mediation. Without the consent of all parties, a mediator shall not subsequently establish a professional relationship with one of the parties in a related matter, or in an unrelated matter under circumstances which would raise legitimate questions about the integrity of the mediation process.

COMMENTS

- A mediator shall avoid conflicts of interest in recommending the services of other professionals. A mediator may make reference to professional referral services or associations which maintain rosters of qualified professionals.

- Potential conflicts of interest may arise between administrators of mediation programs and mediators and there may be strong pressures on the mediator to settle a particular case or cases. The mediator's commitment must be to the parties and the process. Pressures from outside of the mediation process should never influence the mediator to coerce parties to settle.

IV. Competence: A Mediator Shall Mediate Only When the Mediator Has the Necessary Qualifications to Satisfy the Reasonable Expectations of the Parties.

Any person may be selected as a mediator, provided that the parties are satisfied with the mediator's qualifications. Training and experience in mediation, however, are often necessary for effective mediation. A person who offers herself or himself as available to serve as a mediator gives parties and the public the expectation that she or he has the competency to mediate effectively. In court-connected or other forms of mandated mediation, it is essential that mediators assigned to the parties have the requisite training and experience.

COMMENTS

- Mediators should have available for the parties information regarding their relevant training, education and experience.

- The requirements for appearing on a list of mediators must be made public and available to interested persons.

- When mediators are appointed by a court or institution, the appointing agency shall make reasonable efforts to ensure that each mediator is qualified for the particular mediation.

V. Confidentiality: A Mediator Shall Maintain the Reasonable Expectations of the Parties with Regard to Confidentiality.

The reasonable expectations of the parties with regard to confidentiality shall be met by the mediator. The parties' expectations of confidentiality depend on the circumstances of the mediation and any agreements they may make. A mediator shall not disclose any matter that any party expects to be confidential unless given permission by all parties or unless required by law or other public policy.

COMMENTS

- The parties may make their own rules with respect to confidentiality, or the accepted practice of an individual mediator or institution may dictate a particular set of expectations. Since the parties' expectations regarding confidentiality are important, the mediator should discuss these expectations with the parties.

- If the mediator holds private sessions with a party, the nature of these sessions with regard to confidentiality should be discussed prior to undertaking such sessions.

- In order to protect the integrity of the mediation, a mediator should avoid communicating information about how the parties acted in the mediation process, the merits of the case or settlement offers. The mediator may report, if required, whether parties appeared at a scheduled mediation.

- Where the parties have agreed that all or a portion of the information disclosed during a mediation is confidential, the parties' agreement should be respected by the mediator.

- Confidentiality should not be construed to limit or prohibit the effective monitoring, research or evaluation of mediation programs by responsible persons. Under appropriate circumstances, researchers may be permitted to obtain access to statistical data and, with permission of the parties, to individual case files, observations of live mediations and interviews with participants.

VI. Quality of the Process: A Mediator Shall Conduct the Mediation Fairly, Diligently and in a Manner Consistent with the Principle of Self–Determination by the Parties.

A mediator shall work to ensure a quality process and to encourage mutual respect among the parties. A quality process requires a commitment by the mediator to diligence and procedural fairness. There should be adequate opportunity for each party in the mediation to participate in the discussions. The parties decide when and under what conditions they will reach an agreement or terminate a mediation.

COMMENTS

- A mediator may agree to mediate only when he or she is prepared to commit the attention essential to an effective mediation.

- The mediator may only accept cases where they can satisfy the reasonable expectations of the parties concerning the timing of the process. A mediator should not allow a mediation to be unduly delayed by the parties or their representatives.

- The presence or absence of persons at a mediation depends on the agreement of the parties and mediator. The parties and mediator may agree that others may be excluded from particular sessions or from the entire mediation process.

- The primary purpose of a mediator is to facilitate the parties' voluntary agreement. This role differs substantially from other professional-client relationships. Mixing the role of a mediator and the role of a professional advising a client is problematic, and mediators must strive to distinguish between the roles. A mediator should therefore refrain from providing professional advice. Where appropriate, a mediator should recommend that parties seek outside professional advice, or consider resolving their dispute through arbitration, counselling, neutral evaluation, or other processes. A mediator who undertakes, at the request of the parties, an additional dispute resolution role in the same matter assumes increased responsibilities and obligations that may be governed by the standards of other professions.

- A mediator shall withdraw from a mediation when incapable of serving or when unable to remain impartial.

- A mediator shall withdraw from the mediation or postpone a session if the mediation is being used to further illegal conduct, or if a party is unable to participate due to drug, alcohol, or other physical or mental incapacity.

- Mediators should not permit their behavior in the mediation process to be guided by a desire for a high settlement rate.

VII. Advertising and Solicitation: A Mediator Shall Be Truthful in Advertising and Solicitation for Mediation.

Advertising or any other communication with the public concerning services offered or regarding the education, training, and expertise of the mediator shall be truthful. Mediators shall refrain from promises and guarantees of results.

COMMENTS

- It is imperative that communication with the public educate and instill confidence in the process.

- In an advertisement or other communication to the public, a mediator may make reference to meeting state, national, or private organization qualifications only if the entity referred to has a procedure for qualifying mediators and the mediator has been duly granted the requisite status.

VIII. Fees: A Mediator Shall Fully Disclose and Explain the Basis of Compensation, Fees and Charges to the Parties.

The parties should be provided sufficient information about fees at the outset of a mediation to determine if they wish to retain the services of a mediator. If a mediator charges fees, the fees shall be reasonable considering, among other things, the mediation service, the type and complexity of the matter, the expertise of the mediator, the time required, and the rates customary in the community. The better practice in reaching an understanding about fees is to set down the arrangements in a written agreement.

COMMENTS

- A mediator who withdraws from a mediation should return any unearned fee to the parties.

- A mediator should not enter into a fee agreement which is contingent upon the result of the mediation or amount of the settlement.

- Co-mediators who share a fee should hold to standards of reasonableness in determining the allocation of fees.

- A mediator should not accept a fee for referral of a matter to another mediator or to any other person.

IX. Obligations to the Mediation Process: Mediators have a duty to improve the practice of mediation.

COMMENTS

- Mediators are regarded as knowledgeable in the process of mediation. They have an obligation to use their knowledge to help educate the public about mediation; to make mediation accessible to those who would like to use it, to correct abuses; and to improve their professional skills and abilities.

Appendix C

PROPOSED RULES FOR GOOD FAITH PARTICIPATION IN MEDIATION

from Kimberlee K. Kovach, Good Faith in Mediation—
Requested, Recommended, or Required? A New
Ethic 38 S.Tex.L.Rev. 575, 622–623 (1997).

The following are mere suggestions which have not benefitted from the wisdom of deliberation and debate. They are set out herein for the sole purpose of initiating the discussion process.

Model Rule for Lawyers Requiring Good Faith Participation in the Mediation Process

Rule 1.7   Good Faith in Mediation

A lawyer representing a client in mediation shall participate in good faith.

(a) Prior to the mediation, the lawyer shall prepare by familiarizing herself with the matter, and discussing it with her client.

(b) At the mediation, the lawyer shall comply with all rules of court or statutes governing the mediation process, and counsel her client to do likewise.

(c) During the mediation, the lawyer shall not convey information that is intentionally misleading or false to the mediator or other participants.

Statutory Basis for Good Faith Requirement

MEDIATION CODE 001.   All parties and their counsel shall participate in mediation in good faith.

"Good Faith" includes the following:

a.   Compliance with the terms and provisions of [cite to state statute or other rule setting forth mediation; for example Texas Civil Practice and Remedies Code s 154.001];

b.   Compliance with any specific court order referring the matter to mediation;

c. Compliance with the terms and provisions of all standing orders of the court and any local rules of the court;

d. Personal attendance at the mediation by all parties who are fully authorized to settle the dispute, which shall not be construed to include anyone present by telephone;

e. Preparation for the mediation by the parties and their representatives, which includes the exchange of any documents requested or as set forth in a rule, order, or request of the mediator;

f. Participation in meaningful discussions with the mediator and all other participants during the mediation;

g. Compliance with all contractual terms regarding mediation which the parties may have previously agreed to;

h. Following the rules set out by the mediator during the introductory phase of the process;

i. Remaining at the mediation until the mediator determines that the process is at an end or excuses the parties;

j. Engaging in direct communication and discussion between the parties to the dispute, as facilitated by the mediator;

k. Making no affirmative misrepresentations or misleading statements to the other parties or the mediator during the mediation; and

l. In pending lawsuits, refraining from filing any new motions until the conclusion of the mediation;

002. "Good Faith" does not require the parties to settle the dispute. The proposals made at mediation, monetary or otherwise, in and of themselves do not constitute the presence or absence of good faith.

003. Determination of Good Faith

a. In court-annexed cases, the court shall make the final determination of whether good faith was present in the mediation.

b. Where a lawsuit has not been filed, the responsibility for finding a violation of the good faith duty rests upon the mediator, who shall use the elements of this statute and context of any contract between the parties as a basis for deliberation and decision-making.

004. Consequences for the Failure to Mediate in Good Faith

If it is determined that a party or a representative of a party has failed the mediate in good faith, the following actions can be instituted at the discretion of the court or mediator:

a. The individual shall pay all fees, costs, and reasonable expenses incurred by the other participants.

b. The individual will pay the costs of another mediation.

c. The individual will be fined in an amount no greater than $5,000.00.

d. The individual, at their own cost, will attend a seminar or other educational program on mediation, for a minimum or eight (8) hours.

Appendix D

NATIONAL STANDARDS
FOR COURT–CONNECTED
MEDIATION PROGRAMS*

EXECUTIVE SUMMARY

1.0 ACCESS TO MEDIATION

1.1 Mediation services should be available on the same basis as are other services of the court.

1.2 Each court should develop policies and procedures that take into consideration the language and cultural diversity of its community at all stages of development, operation and evaluation of court-connected mediation services and programs.

1.3 To ensure that parties have equal access to mediation, non-judicial screeners should have clearly stated written policies, procedures and criteria to guide their discretion in referring cases to mediation.

1.4 Courts should take steps to ensure that *pro se* litigants make informed choices about mediation.

1.5 Courts should ensure that information about the availability of mediation services is widely disseminated in the languages used by the consumers of court services.

1.6 a. Courts should provide orientation and training for attorneys, court personnel and others regarding the availability, nature and use of mediation services.

   b. Prior to and at the filing of a case, courts should provide to the parties and their attorneys information regarding the availability of mediation.

1.7 In choosing the location and hours of operation of mediation services, courts should consider the effect on the ability of parties to use mediation effectively and the safety of mediators and parties.

2.0 COURTS' RESPONSIBILITY FOR MEDIATION

* Center for Dispute Settlement and the Institute of Judicial Administration.

2.1   The degree of a court's responsibility for mediators or mediation programs depends on whether a mediator or program is employed or operated by the court, receives referrals from the court, or is chosen by the parties themselves.

    a.   The court is fully responsible for mediators it employs and programs it operates.

    b.   The court has the same responsibility for monitoring the quality of mediators and/or mediation programs outside the court to which it refers cases as it has for its own programs.

    c.   The court has no responsibility for the quality or operation of outside programs chosen by the parties without guidance from the court.

2.2   The court should specify its goals in establishing a mediation program or in referring cases to mediation programs or services outside the court and provide a means of evaluating whether or not these goals are being met.

2.3   Program Management

    a.   Information provided by the court to the mediator

       (1)   When parties choose to go to mediation outside the court, the court should have no responsibility to provide any information to the mediator.

       (2)   When a court makes a mandatory referral of parties to mediation, whether inside or outside the court, it should be responsible for providing the mediator or mediation program sufficient information to permit the mediator to deal with the case effectively.

    b.   Information provided by the mediator or the parties to the court

       (1)   If the program is court-operated, or if the case is referred to an outside program or mediator by the court, the program or individual mediator should have the responsibility to report information to the court, in order to permit monitoring and evaluation.

       (2)   If the mediator or program is chosen by the parties without guidance from the court, the provider should have no responsibility to report to the court.

2.4   Aggregate Information

Court-operated mediation programs and programs to which the court refers cases should be required to provide periodic information to the court. The information required should be related to:

    a.   The court's objectives in establishing the program; and

    b.   The court's responsibility for ensuring the quality of the services provided.

2.5   The court should designate a particular individual to be responsible for supervision, monitoring and administration of court-connected mediation programs.

2.6   Complaint Mechanism

Parties referred by the court to a mediation program, whether or not it is operated by the court, should have access to a complaint mechanism to address any grievances about the process.

3.0   INFORMATION FOR JUDGES, COURT PERSONNEL AND USERS

3.1   Courts, in collaboration with the bar and professional mediation organizations, are responsible for providing information to the public, the bar, judges and court personnel regarding the mediation process; the availability of programs; the differences between mediation, adjudication and other dispute resolution processes; the possibility of savings in cost and time; and the consequences of participation.

3.2   Courts should provide the following information:

     a.   To judges, court personnel and the bar:

         (1)   the goals and limitations of the jurisdiction's program(s)

         (2)   the basis for selecting cases

         (3)   the way in which the program operates

         (4)   the information to be provided to lawyers and litigants in individual cases

         (5)   the way in which the legal and mediation processes interact

         (6)   the enforcement of agreements

         (7)   applicable laws and rules concerning mediation

     b.   To users (parties and attorneys) in addition to the information in (a):

General information:

         (1)   issues appropriate for mediation

         (2)   the possible mediators and how they will be selected

         (3)   party choice, if any, of mediators

         (4)   any fees

         (5)   program operation, including location, times of operation, intake procedures, contact person

         (6)   the availability of special services for non-English speakers, and persons who have communication, mobility or other disabilities

         (7)   the possibility of savings or additional expenditures of money or time

Information on process:

         (1)   the nature and purpose of mediation

         (2)   confidentiality of process and records

         (3)   role of the parties and/or attorneys in mediation

         (4)   role of the mediator, including lack of authority to impose a solution

         (5)   voluntary acceptance of any resolution or agreement

> (6) the advantages and disadvantages of participating in determining solutions
>
> (7) enforcement of agreements
>
> (8) availability of formal adjudication if a formal resolution or agreement is not achieved and implemented
>
> (9) the way in which the legal and mediation processes interact, including permissible communications between mediators and the court
>
> (10) the advantages and disadvantages of a lack of formal record

3.3 The court should encourage attorneys to inform their clients of the availability of court connected mediation programs.

4.0 SELECTION OF CASES AND TIMING OF REFERRAL

4.1 When courts must choose between cases or categories of cases for which mediation is offered because of a shortage of resources, such choices should be made on the basis of clearly articulated criteria. Such criteria might include the following:

a. There is a high probability that mediation will be successful in the particular case or category of cases, in terms of both the number and quality of settlements.

b. Even if there is not a high probability that mediation will be successful in the particular cases or category of cases, continuing litigation would harm non-parties, the dispute involves important continuing relationships, or the case, if not mediated, is likely to require continuing involvement by the court.

4.2 The following considerations may militate against the suitability of referring cases to mediation:

a. when there is a need for public sanctioning of conduct;

b. when repetitive violations of statutes or regulations need to be dealt with collectively and uniformly; and

c. when a party or parties are not able to negotiate effectively themselves or with assistance of counsel.

4.3 Courts should make available or encourage the availability of mediation to disputants before they file their cases in court as well as after judgment to address problems that otherwise might require relitigation.

4.4 While the timing of a referral to mediation may vary depending upon the type of case involved and the needs of the particular case, referral should be made at the earliest possible time that the parties are able to make an informed choice about their participation in mediation.

4.5 Courts should provide the opportunity on a continuing basis for both the parties and the court to determine the timing of a referral to mediation.

4.6 If a referral to mediation is mandated, parties should have input on the question of when the case should be referred to mediation, but the court itself should determine timing.

4.7   Courts should establish presumptive deadlines for the mediation process, which may be extended by the court upon a showing by the parties that continuation of the process will assist in reaching resolution.

5.0   MANDATORY ATTENDANCE

5.1   Mandatory attendance at an initial mediation session may be appropriate, but only when a mandate is more likely to serve the interests of parties (including those not represented by counsel), the justice system and the public than would voluntary attendance.   Courts should impose mandatory attendance only when:

   a.   the cost of mediation is publicly funded, consistent with Standard 13.0 on Funding;

   b.   there is no inappropriate pressure to settle, in the form of reports to the trier of fact or financial disincentives to trial; and

   c.   mediators or mediation programs of high quality (i) are easily accessible; (ii) permit party participation; (iii) permit lawyer participation when the parties wish it; and (iv) provide clear and complete information about the precise process and procedures that are being required.

5.2   Courts may use a variety of mechanisms to select cases for mandatory referral to mediation.   Any mechanism chosen should provide for an assessment of each case to determine its appropriateness for mediation, which takes into account the parties relative knowledge, experience and resources.

5.3   Any system of mandatory referral to mediation should be evaluated on a periodic basis, through surveys of parties and through other mechanisms, in order to correct deficiencies in the particular implementation mechanism selected and to determine whether the mandate is more likely to serve the interests of parties, the justice system and the public than would voluntary referral.

6.0   QUALIFICATIONS OF MEDIATORS

6.1   Courts have a continuing responsibility to ensure the quality of the mediators to whom they refer cases.   Qualifications of mediators to whom the courts refer cases should be based on their skills.   Different categories of cases may require different types and levels of skills.   Skills can be acquired through training and/or experience.   No particular academic degree should be considered a prerequisite for service as a mediator in cases referred by the court.

6.2   Courts need not certify training programs but should ensure that the training received by the mediators to whom they refer cases includes role-playing with feedback.

6.3   Courts are responsible for determining that the mediators to whom they refer cases are qualified.   The level of screening needed to determine qualifications will vary depending upon the type of case involved.

6.4   Courts should orient qualified mediators to court procedures.

6.5   Courts should continue to monitor the performance of mediators to whom they refer cases and ensure that their performance is of consistently high quality.

6.6   Courts should adopt procedures for removing from their roster of mediators those mediators who do not meet their performance expectations and/or ensuring that they do not receive further court referrals.

7.0   SELECTION OF MEDIATORS

7.1   To enhance party satisfaction and investment in the process of mediation, courts should maximize parties' choice of mediator, unless there are reasons why party choice may not be appropriate. Such reasons might include:

     a.   there is significant inequality in the knowledge or experience of the parties.

     b.   the court has a particular public policy it is trying to achieve through mediation, which requires selection of a particular mediator or group of mediators.

     c.   party choice would cause significant and undesirable delay.

7.2   When a court determines that it should refer the parties to a private mediator who will receive a fee, the court should permit the parties to choose from among a number of providers.

8.0   ETHICAL STANDARDS FOR MEDIATORS

8.1   Courts should adopt a code of ethical standards for mediators, together with procedures to handle violations of the code.

Any set of standards should include provisions that address the following concerns:

     a.   Impartiality

     b.   Conflict of Interest

     c.   Advertising by Mediators

     d.   Disclosure of Fees

     e.   Confidentiality

     f.   Role of Mediators in Settlement

9.0   CONFIDENTIALITY

9.1   Courts should have clear written policies relating to the confidentiality of both written and oral communications in mediation consistent with the laws of the jurisdiction. Among the issues such a policy should address specifically are:

     a.   the mediators and cases protected by confidentiality;

     b.   the extent of the protection;

     c.   who may assert or waive the protection; and

     d.   exceptions to the protection.

9.2   Courts should ensure that their policies relating to confidentiality in mediation are communicated to and understood by the mediators to whom they refer cases.

9.3 Courts should develop clear written policies concerning the way in which confidentiality protections and limitations are communicated to parties they refer to mediation.

9.4 Mediators should not make recommendations regarding the substance or recommended outcome of a case to the court.

9.5 Policies relating to confidentiality should not be construed to prohibit or limit effective monitoring, research or program evaluation.

10.0 THE ROLE OF LAWYERS IN MEDIATION

10.1 Courts should encourage attorneys to advise their clients on the advantages, disadvantages, and strategies for using mediation.

10.2 Parties, in consultation with their attorneys, should have the right to decide whether their attorneys should be present at mediation sessions.

10.3 Courts and mediators should work with the bar to educate lawyers about:

   a. the difference in the lawyer's role in mediation as compared with traditional representation; and

   b. the advantages and disadvantages of active participation by the parties and lawyers in mediation sessions.

11.0 INAPPROPRIATE PRESSURE TO SETTLE

11.1 Courts should institute appropriate provisions to permit parties to opt out of mediation. Courts also should consider modifying mediation procedures in certain types of cases to accommodate special needs, such as cases involving domestic violence. Special protocols should be developed to deal with domestic violence cases.

11.2 Courts should provide parties who are required to participate in mediation with full and accurate information about the process to which they are being referred, including the fact that they are not required to make offers and concessions or to settle.

11.3 Courts should not systematically exclude anyone from the mediation process. Lawyers never should be excluded if the parties want them to be present.

11.4 Settlement rates should not be the sole criterion for mediation program funding, mediator advancement, or program evaluation.

11.5 There should be no adverse response by courts to nonsettlement by the parties in mediation.

12.0 COMMUNICATIONS BETWEEN MEDIATORS AND THE COURT

12.1 During a mediation the judge or other trier of fact should be informed only of the following:

   a. the failure of a party to comply with the order to attend mediation;

   b. any request by the parties for additional time to complete the mediation;

     c. if all parties agree, any procedural action by the court that would facilitate the mediation; and

     d. the mediator's assessment that the case is inappropriate for mediation.

12.2 When the mediation has been concluded, the court should be informed of the following:

     a. If the parties do not reach an agreement on any matter, the mediator should report the lack of an agreement to the court without comment or recommendation.

     b. If agreement is reached, any requirement that its terms be reported to the court should be consistent with the jurisdiction's policies governing settlements in general.

     c. With the consent of the parties, the mediators' report also may identify any pending motions or outstanding legal issues, discovery process, or other action by any party which, if resolved or completed, would facilitate the possibility of a settlement.

12.3 Whenever possible, all communications with the judge who will try the case should be made by the parties. Where the mediator must communicate with the trial judge, it is preferable for such communications to be made in writing or through administrative personnel.

13.0 FUNDING OF PROGRAMS AND COMPENSATION OF MEDIATORS

13.1 Courts should make mediation available to parties regardless of the parties' ability to pay.

     a. Where a court suggests (rather than orders) mediation, it should take steps to make mediation available to indigent litigants, through state funding or through encouraging mediators who receive referrals from the court to provide a portion of their services on a free or reduced fee basis.

     b. When parties are required to participate in mediation, the costs of mediation should be publicly funded unless the amount at stake or the nature of the parties makes participants' payments appropriate.

13.2 In allocating public funds to mediation, a court may give priority for funding to certain types of cases, such as family and minor criminal matters.

13.3 Where public funds are used, they may either: (a) support mediators employed by the court or (b) compensate private mediators. Where public funds are used to compensate private mediators, fee schedules should be set by the Court.

13.4 a. Where courts offer publicly funded mediation services, courts should permit parties to substitute a private mediator of their own choosing except in those circumstances under which the court has decided that party choice is inappropriate. Parties should have the widest possible latitude in selecting mediators, consistent with public policy.

b. Where parties elect to pay a private mediator, they should be permitted to agree with the mediator on the appropriate fee.

14.0 LIABILITY OF MEDIATORS

14.1 Courts should not develop rules for mediators to whom they refer cases that are designed to protect these mediators from liability. Legislatures and courts should provide the same indemnity or insurance for those mediators who volunteer their services or are employed by the court that they provide for nonjudicial court employees.

15.0 THE ENFORCEABILITY OF MEDIATED AGREEMENTS

15.1 Agreements that are reached through court-connected mediation should be enforceable to the same extent as agreements reached without a mediator.

16.0 EVALUATION

16.1 Courts should ensure that the mediation programs to which they refer cases are monitored adequately on an ongoing basis, evaluated on a periodic basis, and that sufficient resources are earmarked for these purposes.

16.2 Programs should be required to collect sufficient, accurate information to permit adequate monitoring on an ongoing basis and evaluation on a periodic basis.

16.3 Courts should ensure that program evaluation is widely distributed and linked to decision-making about the program's policies and procedures.

Topical Index

References are to Pages